THE RECRUITER

THE
RECRUITER

* * *

SPYING AND THE LOST ART OF
AMERICAN INTELLIGENCE

* * *

DOUGLAS LONDON

hachette
BOOKS

NEW YORK

Cover design by Terri Sirma
Cover photograph © Brooks Kraft/Getty Images
Cover copyright © 2021 by Hachette Book Group, Inc.

Hachette Books
Hachette Book Group
1290 Avenue of the Americas
New York, NY 10104
HachetteBooks.com
Twitter.com/HachetteBooks
Instagram.com/HachetteBooks

First Edition: September 2021

Published by Hachette Books, an imprint of Perseus Books, LLC, a subsidiary of Hachette Book Group, Inc. The Hachette Books name and logo is a trademark of the Hachette Book Group.

The Hachette Speakers Bureau provides a wide range of authors for speaking events. To find out more, go to www.hachettespeakersbureau.com or call (866) 376-6591.

The publisher is not responsible for websites (or their content) that are not owned by the publisher.

Print book interior design by Sean Ford.

Library of Congress Cataloging-in-Publication Data

Names: London, Douglas (Operations officer) author.
Title: The recruiter : spying and the lost art of American intelligence /
    Douglas London.
Description: First edition. | New York : Hachette Books, [2021] | Includes index.
Identifiers: LCCN 2021008054 | ISBN 9780306847301 (hardcover) | ISBN 9780306847325 (ebook)
Subjects: LCSH: United States. Central Intelligence Agency—History. |
    London, Douglas (Operations officer) | Intelligence officers—United
    States—Biography. | Intelligence service—United States. | Secret
    service—United States. | National security—United States.
Classification: LCC JK468.I6 L66 2021 | DDC 327.1273—dc23
LC record available at https://lccn.loc.gov/2021008054

ISBNs: 9780306847301 (hardcover), 9780306847325 (ebook)

Printed in the United States of America

LSC-C

Printing 1, 2021

Para mi Alma viva, and my five amazing children, Steve, Mike, Melissa, Jenny, and Emily, my true and proudest legacy. And to the foreign agents who risked all to protect a country most would never see, and a people who would not know of their sacrifices for our freedoms.

CONTENTS

THE RECRUITER

CIA REQUIRED DISCLAIMER

All statements of fact, opinion, or analysis expressed are those of the author and do not reflect the official positions or views of the Central Intelligence Agency (CIA) or any other US government agency. Nothing in the contents should be construed as asserting or implying US government authentication of information or CIA endorsement of the author's views.

FOREWORD

This nonfiction account of the changes the CIA underwent over the course of my thirty-four-plus years of service is based on actual experiences. The CIA required four months to review this manuscript during the spring and summer of 2020, over the course of which I was pressured against its publication in ways both subtle and not. In ultimately yielding, the CIA redacted significant portions, primarily where the anecdotes cast senior officials in a bad light. In the Trump age, image was everything at the

CIA, and the Agency was fearful of what might provoke the president's next outburst. At its own peril, and that of the country it is charged to protect, under both Mike Pompeo and Gina Haspel, the CIA's leadership agonized over controlling and shaping that image.

In maintaining my oath to the Constitution, legal obligation to the Agency, and moral commitment to the agents I recruited, ran, and managed as a senior spymaster, I changed all the names, aliases included, and distorted descriptions and details that might facilitate their identification. I extended this same protection to colleagues, regardless of their role as forces of good, or bad, in the Agency's history. It's important from the outset to understand that the term *agent* refers to a recruited foreign spy operating on the CIA's behalf. The American CIA staff who recruit and clandestinely handle these agents are case officers, not agents.

I chose "war stories" about agents and operations that best reflect my experiences and express the themes on which I was writing. So as to avoid endangering agents or compromising classified information, I necessarily had to dance around revealing details such as locations, nationalities, physical appearance and attributes (including gender), and time. There were cases and operations too sensitive for me to discuss in any fashion, and others the Agency censored in their entirety or in bits and pieces, most often to protect its image rather than the operations. The final product sufficiently obscures while still illuminating the rather extraordinary life I and other CIA case officers had the privilege to lead.

CIA requirements did, however, detract somewhat from the narrative, regrettably creating vagaries and gaps I am not at liberty to explain. For example, because I am precluded from providing explicit references to living undercover or even the mention of specific US government facilities, or American officials residing abroad, the task of narrating a spy's life was somewhat more complicated. It certainly frustrated my editors! In the end, these impediments, while challenging, do not detract from the story's fundamental message that the CIA is a critical institution to American national security, but one at a crossroads and in need of significant reform. Espionage is about people: their strengths, weaknesses, drives, eccentricities, and fears. More precisely, espionage is about the human soul, and the ability of those who can see therein. That goes for the agents we recruit to spy against their own, as well as the Agency officers who bear responsibility for discharging the mission.

While I apologize in advance for the occasional painfully vague and convoluted explanations that dance around the passages, and wording struck down by Agency censors, I ask the reader to focus on the people and their stories. See into the hearts and souls, as I did for almost four decades, of the spies, the agents, the bureaucrats, politicians, and intelligence careerists. Do that and you will find what it is that brings life to the world's second oldest profession. Spycraft, a trade deemed by many as distasteful as the world's second oldest profession, is charged with a noble mission and is guided by an ethical code; and it is practiced by an assortment of heroes and villains, flawed characters all, me included, on all sides.

PROLOGUE

The first time anyone referred to me as a spy was 1986. I was living in the Middle East and meeting a host government official whom I had been cultivating for several months. "Bilal" had invited me to his house late in the evening, as he liked to do, when the streets were quiet, the household staff gone, and his family busied themselves in their part of the large house. As was our custom, we sat on his veranda, sipping the Johnnie Walker Black I regularly gifted him, eating nuts, and looking at the stars.

Bilal liked to talk. And the first thing you noticed was his ear to ear smile while relating stories, telling jokes, or simply cracking wise at your expense. Playful and impish, Bilal loved to tease. He provoked and relished arguments as a pastime, studying how best to get a rise from someone and hit a nerve. But Bilal was quick to retreat when sensing offense. He was, as are most of the Arabs I have known over the years, a caring and generous host.

Some twenty years my senior, Bilal had slowly, cautiously, taken me into his confidence, testing me often along the way for discretion, all the while working to mask his true self. That's how Bilal operated. A successful career official despite hailing from a minority ethnic group and tribe, Bilal had early on managed to balance performing his job exceptionally well with playing the fool. He possessed a unique set of linguistic and cultural skills that his government prized, because these abilities allowed him to effectively engage with one of the country's principal rivals. But he downplayed his own ambitions and subordinated his tribal loyalties as his seniors scrutinized him as a potential threat. And by seniors I refer to those at the upper echelons of authority within his organization. Bilal managed to catch the eye of seniors to whom he proved both useful and loyal, showing them what he knew they wanted to see. My task was to peel back the layers he presented me, one by one.

I developed a pretext to meet Bilal early into my assignment. I was interested in him based on feedback I'd received from colleagues outside the Agency. Bilal was forthcoming, pro-American, and decidedly unpretentious, all rare traits among the local officials we normally encountered. Unlike his ethnically mainstream colleagues, Bilal appeared to seek greater validation from his official American contacts, a desire to be liked and respected. I hoped and suspected there was more to it. Was Bilal testing the waters?

Over the course of months, Bilal and I had gone from meeting at his office, to the occasional lunch at a discreet location, to quiet, weekly evening meetings on his veranda. That's not the school solution that aims to decreasingly conceal such relationships from public view, but which is at times a byproduct of relationships, local operating considerations, and practicalities. The goal of a case officer is to move relationships that might begin in the open to a genuinely clandestine footing as soon as practicable. Our conversations spanned history, religion, and politics, to families and personal experiences. Bilal was far more intellectual, well read, and complex than he liked to let on. From meeting to meeting, he shared increasingly revealing insights as to how things really worked in his country, and why. But it was several meetings before Bilal uttered even the least critical word about his fellow nationals, weeks before he acknowledged their ill treatment of his minority group, and still more time before he confessed deep resentment for their discrimination and repression.

Case officers have to be efficient with their time. The job is a lifestyle in that one must account for every minute of the day toward an operational purpose. The clandestine work of securely recruiting and handling agents requires expertise in, and manipulation of, the environment, as well as the people in it. It's a rather time-consuming trade with deliberate attention paid to shaping one's recognizable pattern of life so that you can disappear when, and as, necessary. There's little time to waste drilling dry holes. If you've invested pursuing a target who will never succumb, you've missed those who might. So a case officer's most prized gift, as a friend once so indelicately put it, was "smelling blood." That is, the sixth sense to sort through contacts and quickly penetrate veneers to size up who's willing to spy. I smelled blood with Bilal.

I was on my first overseas assignment and young even relative to typical junior officers. While Bilal was intrigued by my willingness to banter and my blue-collar background that was different from most of my diplomatic colleagues, I nevertheless treated him as a mentor. My professed interest was to learn, particularly what he could teach me about his group, and how his ethnic minority status helped or hindered him within his ministry, and while serving abroad. I teased and provoked as well, which he liked. But I knew when to be serious and, at the right moment, philosophical. There was great intellectual depth to Bilal that he kept bottled up inside, and with it, great loneliness. It's not easy to be "on" all the time, particularly when playing a role.

Bilal eased his way into more delicate and revealing subjects through stories and metaphors. Over time, he increasingly allowed me to probe and deconstruct those metaphors for the reality in which he lived, identifying the motivations I would manipulate to leverage his cooperation. Peeling back the layers on someone's soul and most inner space requires shifting gears to identify and in turn seamlessly leverage what you've found. The testing and probing confirms or refutes the needs, wants, and fears you have assessed, and an openness to your approach. But unlike a surgeon working off of X-rays, at times it's a surprise, so you go with your instincts and feel your way. Bilal tested me for discretion at every turn, just as I tested him. Sharing risk, even if feigned and perceived, is a key in moving through the locked doors of someone's soul. In the process, I foreshadowed who I really was, and my true agenda, but nothing from which I couldn't mount an expeditious if dubious retreat.

On this particular evening, I planned to *pitch* Bilal, that is to say, ask him to become a clandestine CIA agent. First comes the setup. I recapitulated all that he had taught me about his country's magnificent people and potential, as well as the unfortunate consequences of the manner in which it was ruled. Replaying Bilal's own pronouncements and declarations, I highlighted the personal slights and offenses to which Bilal had been subjected, an effort to increase the emotional temperature of the conversation. Because he was forced to restrain his true sentiments, I articulated Bilal's frustration in watching inferior men from the right families and cliques advance, and how that at times those promotions were based on the work he himself had done for them. But I praised Bilal for outsmarting them, for playing them to seize opportunities to better serve his country and still advance his career. "It was Allah's will that we met," I resolved, "inasmuch as I am sure he crossed our paths not only so that we might become friends, but so we can together accomplish something bigger than ourselves." An appeal to Bilal's genuine religious beliefs, and not a material reward.

"I was protecting you…I couldn't tell you earlier…I wasn't ready to burden you with maintaining my security," I told Bilal, "but I am in fact a CIA officer. My job is to collect information beyond the surface that the US can use to more effectively support your country's stability, prosperity, and protection. Information that your country deems secret out of concern for embarrassment." Bilal would undoubtly feel I had lied to him about my CIA identity, so I wanted to appeal to his interests, not my own.

"US aims here are benevolent," I continued, "but even friends need to see the realities, good and bad, to help one another. That's where you can help."

Bilal listened attentively, and despite his usually animated comportment, watched my eyes without expression, taking in and measuring my each and every word and corresponding emotion. I continued, "Your inside knowledge of the country's plans and capabilities with this particular rival, and broadly across the region and with the US, is underappreciated here, as you have said. But it would make an immense difference in America's understanding and capacity to act more effectively to support stability and mitigate the risks of miscalculations from which everyone suffers." I leaned closer to Bilal. "This is what you're doing already, and why. To make a difference. To contribute. You subject yourself to degradation and risks, keeping true feelings tightly locked away, playing your superiors so that you can make a difference."

He exhaled. I'd hit a nerve. "You attend meetings and read reports of a daily nature on subjects with which you are expert. That expertise could do more for your country if shared with us, given how your superiors neglect it. Partner with us, Bilal, and together we can achieve what you're working so hard, by yourself, to accomplish." The specificity of our expectations and the agent's risk is key.

My pace was steady, but not rapid. Not easy for a New Yorker like me. I wanted Bilal to hear precisely what it was he was being asked to do, and why, and to help him process the reality as opposed to what he might imagine. You'd be surprised, or perhaps you wouldn't be, at the crazy things people expect the CIA to ask them to do. Kill people, break into locked safes, sabotage equipment. In reality, the last thing we want agents to do is put themselves at risk by acting in any way out of pattern. "An added benefit for me," I explained, "would be the ability to contribute modestly to your family's well-being." I wanted to tie the money to a specific family need, not the cash itself; to help him rationalize his espionage toward a more noble purpose, as for his family, and to provide him the fig leaf that taking the money was doing *me* a favor. "It will make me feel like a better friend knowing you'll be able to use your monthly CIA consulting retainer [citing the precise figure the CIA censors will not allow me to reveal], to help pay for the kids' tuition…helping your country, and your family."

When I finished my pitch, I had laid out why I was making this request, the reason I had not told him earlier about my CIA affiliation, precisely what he was being asked to do, his compensation, and how we would do it. I paused for his response. You prepare for the questions, concerns, emotional reactions, or arguments that might be put forward. In the business, we call this sparring. At times the reactions are predictable, but on occasion they're unexpected. And for me, this was the first time.

"So, Douglas, you are a spy?" Bilal replied more rhetorically than inquisitively. "And your job is to steal my country's secrets. So how do I know you can be counted on? To protect me? My family? Have you any idea what they will do to me, my family, if I am caught? What would my father think of me?"

There it was. A spy. For the first time. And I rather liked it. To answer his question about how I could be counted on, I replied, "Because I'm not alone. It's not just me, but the CIA, an organization that prizes your security more than any information you might possibly provide. When you work with us, you're part of a team."

"What other spies do you have in my country?" Bilal asked. "How can I trust you if I do not know you are capable?"

"How could you trust me if I ever revealed their identities?" I responded. "I would sooner give up my life than reveal your identity, or that of any other who took such risks for their country, and mine."

Bilal smiled and said nothing for a moment.

Thankfully, Bilal said yes. Not immediately, mind you. Bilal walked me through all manner of scenarios he might experience, but principally, it seemed to me, he wanted to know whether or not it had been a setup from the start. Though it had been, and Bilal would always suspect as much, I told him it was serendipity. This offered him the face-saving pretext he so dearly hoped I would provide. You might say it was to ease my own guilty conscience, but I believed Bilal had been looking for this, for me, for someone. Bilal, like most agents, didn't want to see himself as a traitor, but rather, a victim. More philosophically for him, a victim of destiny, and a quiet hero. And that's what case officers do to help their agents live in the very complex world of espionage.

Corny? The emotion, the flowery words, the animation? The theater? Of course it is. But that doesn't render it untrue. Being dramatic doesn't make it insincere. I'm selling something, a product in which I believe, and to someone who secretly yearns for it. What I am asking, and the possible consequences, warrants drama and emotion. Yes, culturally, one could say that Arabs are often rather emotional, so my pitch was aligned as such. But who wouldn't be emotional if asked to commit their all?

To risk not only their lives, but to subject their family to whatever local consequences might result. Everyone needs validation, but even those at the end of their ropes can smell insincerity. Bilal knew I meant every word I said, because I did. When he agreed, I knew he was committed, body and soul. And that's why we owe our agents more than seeing them as mere employees, or worse, expendable.

WHERE HAVE YOU GONE, GEORGE SMILEY?

The CIA finds itself today at a crossroads. It's an organization that has sought to reinvent itself after the debacles of 9/11's intelligence failure and its subsequent ethical compromise in facilitating the Bush-Cheney fabrications that justified America's invasion of Iraq. Years of trying to be what it thought necessary to survive its greatest existential crisis since Watergate, the CIA fundamentally changed its core mission, values, and culture: a metamorphosis designed to earn White House approval and guard itself from the encroachments of the Department of Defense and the FBI, agencies seen as threats that might steal its turf and authorities, and perhaps swallow the CIA whole.

A slippery slope of compromises, facelifts, and revised narratives justifying a unique set of capabilities and authorities undertaken to preserve the Agency would instead leave it barely recognizable for the institution it was meant to be. Established in 1947 as a small, elite, independent, civilian, and nonpartisan foreign intelligence service, the CIA's charter was intelligence collection, analysis, and covert action. Freeing CIA from association with defense, law enforcement, and diplomacy theoretically protected it from grading its own homework as a policy maker, as was the case for the Pentagon, the Department of Justice, and the Department of State. Small, under the radar, and relatively chaste from the political pressures of its larger counterparts, the CIA was intended to speak truth to power.

After 9/11 and Iraq, however, the CIA's leaders anxiously bartered the organization's soul for its survival, and their own. In so doing, to save itself,

9

the CIA actually became more vulnerable to the risks it most feared. The CIA undermined its credibility and moral high ground by allowing for the political weaponization of the intelligence it gathered. By seeking to offer a replication of the military and FBI, albeit one more agile and efficient in overcoming those larger agencies' bureaucratic and legal constraints, the uniqueness of the CIA's capabilities, culture, and value was invalidated.

Not that the CIA was perfect before 9/11, nor was it free of compromising itself for the approval of whatever administration sat in the White House. The CIA's public history is replete with scandal and failure. Largely, though, such mistakes were acknowledged for what they were—transactional more than systematic—aberrations in which the CIA lost its way. They were not reflections of what we wanted to be. And as sensational as these failures were given the public exposure, they were dwarfed by the successes preserved in secret. The mistakes did not change the CIA's fundamental ethos, its risk calculus, or the standards to which we sought to live. The post-9/11 changes are more profound, and as such, more threatening to the CIA's ability to provide the mission for which it was intended. Fundamentally, this mission is to serve as the nation's premiere foreign intelligence service for collecting and analyzing secrets, and for conducting necessary and legally sanctioned covert action directed by the president and briefed to Congress. And the first warning sign that the CIA was beginning to slide down that slippery slope might have been something as silly as how we allowed for the perversion of the word, *spy*.

Have you ever seen the 1986 movie *Spies Like Us*, starring Chevy Chase and Dan Ackroyd? One of my personal favorites, it was a farcical take on espionage and the 1980s so-called Star Wars ballistic missile defense initiative. No, it's not required study material, but besides being entertaining, it offers two immediate learning points. The first is that Dan Ackroyd has aged far better than Chevy Chase, and the second is that the term *spy* has lost its luster.

Growing up, I recall the term *spy* defining a noble endeavor when associated with the "good guys." Granted, I have a special place in my heart for the film, having seen it during a break toward the end of my training with my fellow suffering trainees. There is absolutely nothing accurate in the movie, which is probably why it was so fun, but it says something to me about the change in our country's outlook on intelligence, and, most relevant to this book, the CIA's culture. Would it have been half as catchy if titled, *Intelligence Officers Like Us*? While a rose by any other name might smell as sweet, there's far more intrigue, drama, and, dare I say, romance associated with the term *Spies* than *Intelligence Officers*. Words matter.

So it came to me in the middle of what was an otherwise blissful sleep, that I had a story to tell about my thirty-four plus years in the world's second oldest profession. Actually, I'd argue espionage is the very oldest, since after all, it might help identify and locate a brothel in the first place. I must admit that the two professions are not entirely without certain practical similarities. Both tend to be a cash business, and like those other professionals I've spent an inordinate amount of time on a street corner somewhere, or picking someone up.

There've always been good spies and bad. The ultimate test of good or bad depends from which side you are looking. In the United States these days, in any case, the term *spy* has taken on a rather negative connotation, particularly in the aftermath of the damage done by a series of notorious traitors such as Aldrich Ames, Robert Hanssen, Edward Lee Howard, Harold Nicholson, and yes, Edward Snowden. While fancying himself a whistleblower and victim, with an unfortunate and unaware following, the truth about Snowden is hardly noble. But that's not my story to tell, at least not today.

Even the famous British traitor Kim Philby, following his discovery, was more commonly referred to as a mole rather than spy, inasmuch as spying for Queen and country as a case officer for the British Secret Intelligence Service, or MI6, was his "day job." In the early 1980s when I began my service, it was considered rather honorable to speak of ourselves as spies, since we were the good guys. We were the shadow warriors of espionage protecting the homeland, whether it was stealing our adversaries' most prized secrets or going where our uniformed service members could not to disrupt a threat. Influencing world events from underground, we operated from behind the scenes so as to prevent the need to actually go to war. Our leader at the time I entered duty, William Casey, then holding the portfolio as director of Central Intelligence (DCI), not merely director of the Central Intelligence Agency (DCIA), had himself been a member of the wartime Office of Strategic Services, or OSS, from which the CIA was born. Casey was not without his own sins, but certainly he infused the CIA with the traditions and mentality of a spy service.

At first blush I must agree that it seems a waste of energy to make much ado about how we currently use the word *spy*. It's not fundamentally what this book is about, but rather was the trigger for it. I thought as much myself, initially, suspecting that the cringe I felt for the use of this word was merely the consequence of aging and coming to the end of my active career. Was I now that curmudgeon rocking on his porch, observing the neighborhood and mumbling incoherently about those meddling kids, loud music, lost values, and disrespect for traditions? But upon reflection, introspection, and clinical consideration of how both espionage and American politics evolved over my lifetime, I came to believe that there was something more to my errant thought. Something worth exploring. Espionage had become more politicized, and in a way that profoundly altered the CIA and its service in protecting the homeland.

Now wasn't the first time nor would it be the last that our nation's leaders would seek to use the CIA as an instrument of political leverage. But this was different, profoundly dangerous, and quite possibly irreversible. The CIA was compromising its objectivity and integrity to tell its masters what they wanted to hear and divine solutions for their political interests. Proposals that stretched the CIA's unique legal authorities and profound capabilities, but which were at odds with the nation's interests. Actions that would undermine the organization's credibility with intelligence consumers, the workforce, its foreign partners, and ultimately, the American people.

One can debate whether the CIA was used in the right causes over its history. But those who led the CIA during its existential crisis after the events of 9/11 and Iraq fundamentally altered the Agency's very soul, undercutting its capability as an espionage service. While seeking to boost the organization's value to successive White Houses, CIA executives enabled politicians to undermine the Agency's core mission. And under Trump, its very credibility. A vicious cycle that rewarded patronage over merit and nurtured risk aversion. Running the CIA was now a vicious cycle that rewarded conformists, cronyism, and fealty. Unquestionably, CIA officers took heroic risks in conflict zones throughout the world, suffering casualties along the way. But operating in this covert action realm, with CIA leaders patting one another's backs for their expeditionary spirit, merely replicated a military capability owing to the Agency's innate agility and generous authorities. Regrettably, this slide came at the expense of foreign intelligence collection needed to avert such crises in the first place.

Agency officers have their own political views and opinions, but they do not operate in a partisan world. They might not agree with the politics of a particular policy, but they execute without hesitation at full throttle. They do not obstruct, slow roll, or operate in any sort of "deep state" cabal. Today's DCIAs, as did their DCI forebearers, however, inevitably do operate as partisans. Understandable, inasmuch as they are presidential appointees, regardless as to whether or not they were a service careerist, as was DCIA Gina Haspel and DCIA John Brennan. Upon moving into the CIA's seventh floor executive suite, their job is to support the president's policy, and those who wish to retain their positions for any significant period of time push back and rock the boat ever so cautiously. It's a mind-set that certainly skews their sense of what's best for America, or CIA.

I served under six Republican and five Democrat administrations. I witnessed changes, often cyclical, with history unsurprisingly repeating itself now and again. But post-9/11, the Agency became an increasingly toxic environment, today's political environment only adding to that dynamic. Politicians from across the aisles share responsibility, as does the media. The very nature of espionage practiced by a secret government agency operating in an open society makes defending itself and its work more problematic. CIA can't defend itself against those political leaders who spin, cherry-pick, or falsely depict its intelligence for partisan gain.

The Trump administration's disregard of congressional oversight's checks and balances and the integrity of the inspector general process further imperiled CIA's ability to speak truth to power.

The CIA is an organization that must practice an unethical art in the most moral, just, and ethical manner. But in truth, the CIA had already brought much of the damage upon itself long before the forty-fifth president of the United States moved into the White House.

Perhaps it's best for me to begin by framing my story and managing your expectations. I adored being a CIA case officer. A former chief for CIA's Near East and South Asia Division within the Directorate of Operations, for whom I once worked, had a wooden plaque in his front office that summed up the spirit succinctly. "Espionage is Good." As serious of a business as it is, with the high stakes of lives on the line, God forgive me, it is incredibly fun. This by no way means to suggest that I ever approached the work without treating it with all the intensity and seriousness it demanded. But it's not "a job," and it can't be executed best without relishing the excitement and satisfaction of doing it right. It's a career and given all the frustrations, sacrifices, risks, and demands the job entails, you have to enjoy the life in order to commit to it with the standards that the responsibilities require.

Every organization has to change with the times. It evolves as the world changes around us, and is influenced by successive generations. It's not about yearning for the good old days, presupposing that things were better, simply because they were different. The CIA no doubt should be different today than it was in 1984. And to be fair, what organization is perfect and without palace intrigue, climbers, failures, and injustice? Still, stepping back, there was something deeper. Not just wrong, or merely different, and more profound than a questionable policy at any given time. I realized it was rather like the fable concerning the frog in the pot. You know the one. Where the frog is tossed into a pot of tepid water, unable to sense the temperature's incremental increase until it came to a boil, by which time it was too late for the frog to leap to safety.

If the metaphor held, and the CIA was like the frog in the pot, then when had the temperature begun to change and why didn't anyone notice? Or did they notice but simply not care? Perhaps the CIA was mortgaging one existential threat for another, with payment due on another's watch. My tenure accounted for roughly half of the Agency's lifespan and unfolded quite symmetrically across seventeen years on either side of 9/11. Chronicling my time, a case officer's life over that span, brought me to the realization that the Agency's cultural change that began with 9/11 gained speed over the ensuing years. We were not merely doing things differently, but rather, we *were* different. And not entirely for the better.

CIA had been taken down this path by a leadership that in the years following 9/11 developed into a cult of personality. The senior ranks became an evermore homogenous collection cut from the same mold, focused more on ambition than the mission, the organization, or the workforce. While there were thankfully brilliant exceptions, the cadre had drunk their own Kool-Aid as to their own brilliance and worth.

Whether or not you'll find any of the stories I've included in making my points to be salacious might be a matter of perspective. The very idea of former CIA officers writing about the Agency is a contentious issue among my peers, and one about which I find myself likewise conflicted. Some colleagues argue that to "Honor the Oath" means to stay silent. I've come to believe that such silence equally requires the Agency's leaders to conduct themselves selflessly in the best interests of the country, in adherence with the Constitution and the Agency's legal authorities. Doing the right thing, for the right reason, regardless of political pressures or self-interest, can be a rather high bar for even the most ethical and righteous. But it goes with the territory given the scope of responsibility and price of failure.

When I think of a spy, an image arises of George Smiley's character in the John le Carré novels. Smiley would find himself variously behind enemy lines in the midst of a war, outfoxing the hunters on the wrong side of the Iron Curtain, or leveraging his powers of persuasion in signing up a new agent. But in all such cases, he did so with wit, cunning, innovation, and verve, not brute force. Yes, he carried and necessarily brandished a weapon in self-defense at times, but if he was a soldier of any sort, he was a silent warrior. For spying is not about the size of the dog in the fight, but the size of the fight in the dog. Chess matches are won by the ability to see through the fog of war and leverage human dynamics, and to look multiple steps ahead, anticipating future moves and their consequences. That was the mindset of the CIA Clandestine Service I joined in 1984. Today, I fear it's not even the model to which CIA still aspires.

JUST ANOTHER NIGHT...

The house was quiet, dark, and perfectly still. The kids were long asleep, tucked into their beds with songs and bedtime stories. I gave my wife a light peck on the cheek before quietly closing the bedroom door behind me. For them, and most people in this city, the day was done. Mine, however, was only just beginning. I paused at the top of the stairs, moving stealthily, and hoping to cast no shadows. A quick peek through the slightly drawn curtains of the upstairs landing window offered no evidence of the older model, four door sedan that routinely loitered at the end of the street, two or three shadowy silhouettes within. Descending downstairs to the study, it was time for my pregame. I checked my go bag for what I'd need this evening.

The compact backpack offered a number of useful pockets to organize my gear. A hat and light jacket to change into at just the right time to alter my profile were stuffed into the large, middle cavity. Some water for my journey fit snuggly in a side pocket. A few pens, a red penlight, and several three-by-five index cards were placed in a small front pocket. Some of the cards were blank, and others had keywords to remind me of the questions I needed to ask. Enough to trigger my recall without divulging the entirety of the question or topic, were the cards to fall into the wrong hands. A thin, zippered interior pocket contained two envelopes. One with US dollars, for the monthly salary I was to pay, the other in local currency, for expenses. Oh yes, there were also some small stones in my pocket that I could use to scare away the city's many rabid dogs I might encounter, and a can of pepper spray for still worse contingencies given the parts of town I'd be transiting.

My uniform was that of the odd, eccentric Western tourist who might be out and about in such a city, and at this time of night. Jeans, running shoes, a loose-fitting shirt with pockets, and an admittedly goofy looking baseball-style cap. I would exit the house from the back, keeping the rear patio dark, and slowly slide the door open and closed to minimize the noise and reduce the emitting ambient light. The heat and humidity immediately hit me as I opened the door and slipped out from the air-conditioned house, my glasses instantly fogging. While the host government security service's surveillance team that routinely kept an eye on me had not been visible through the window, there was no sense in taking any chances. And why did I have to be concerned in the first place?

Friends and foes alike play "spot the spook." Every country wants to protect its secrets, even from friends. Truth is often revealing in competitive international political and economic realms, and more important, compromising. And sometimes, the truth is simply embarrassing. But for rivals and adversaries, the interest in protecting secrets is more profound. This country was no friend of the US, and one that often sought to attribute its own internal economic and security problems to America's meddling. So my precautions here were anything but academic.

I'd exit through the back alley and trespass, ever so cautiously, through the yard of the adjoining home. Luckily, they had gotten rid of their pesky dog. This would lead me to the series of quiet residential streets I'd work through to make my way to a more heavily trafficked thoroughfare by which time I ought to be beyond whatever surveillance bubble covered my house, and from where I could catch my first taxi.

Some time, several taxis, a great deal of walking, and a few counter-measures later, I found myself *black*. It's an incredible sensation. You are off the grid and invisible to your enemies. Eerie silence perhaps to others, but not to me. The stillness and darkness is akin to moving through time and space as if the rest of the world is standing still. It's the time as a spy when you have disappeared into your clandestine dimension. You are now entirely immersed into the darkness of the night and the random-ness of the city you have so thoroughly cased. Each and every one of your senses is alive, like those of a predator. You register, filter, and identify every sound and movement for danger. Even the neighborhoods you traverse have different smells, feelings, chemistry that you understand and manipulate to keep the enemy at bay. No one knows who you are. You're just an obscured shadow on the street. You are unseen to your enemies, the hunters trying to catch you in the act of espionage, seeking to identify your agents and compromise your operations.

It's an exhilarating feeling of power and control. A sensation perhaps shared by military Special Forces operators and, conversely, criminals. But, whereas they normally operate in teams, the case officer works alone. In fact, not even other intelligence officers, those who do the targeting, analy-sis, operational support, and administrative work, can fully appreciate the experience. You are master of your domain. Not arrogance, but confidence, the certainty you must possess in order to shoulder the responsibility for your agents' lives and their secrets, which you must safely secure, vet, and transmit home. You're about to conduct a clandestine operational act to meet a penetration of the local government's most sensitive institution in order to steal their most highly guarded secrets. Information that very well can save lives or influence policy decisions to your country's advantage, and that enhances the safety of your fellow citizens.

I make my way to the initial contact point. There is little to no activity on the street and I'm deliberately a bit early. Timing is everything, and I need a safe spot from which to hunker and observe without heating up the site. After all, a clandestine act is intended to be hidden, not disguised. I have a story in mind should a suspicious casual approach, or worse, a cop. How many hours had I spent in my career waiting for someone in the darkness? Sitting in parked cars or standing in the shadows of some back alley, the weather seemingly always either unforgivingly hot or brutally cold. Or occasionally inside a more comfortable, climate-controlled safe house or hotel room, watching the door and waiting for the sound of footsteps, and a knock. Still, there's a certain feeling of security in a car or on the street, from which you can make your escape. There's nowhere to go if trouble finds you in a hotel room or safe house.

Precision is key to security, but agents' discipline varies, despite it being in their best interests to execute a plan as directed. Minimizing exposure means engineering contact that is ideally never witnessed, but if so, would appear plausible to the casual observer from afar, and able to withstand scrutiny if challenged. My agent was exceptionally sensitive this night. He was a senior official within his ministry who could at best safely steal an hour or so away from family, colleagues, and responsibilities no more than once a month to meet. Leaving him standing for more than a few minutes was a risk. And despite my sensation of invisibility, loitering too long myself would eventually heat up the spot where I stood. Someone might notice. Someone might call the police. So our window was deliberately short. If neither of us arrived within the margins, we would revert to another prescheduled time and place, thus negating the need to communicate via any electronic means. Phone and computer communications, after all, were forever. To me, they were the devil.

I caught his tall, lanky silhouette from a distance. At least, I certainly hoped it was him. A little late for my taste, but still within the window. As he drew closer, his familiar gait providing me a sense of reassurance that slowed my rapidly beating heart, I likewise began to move. I liked "Ilyes." He had a presence. Imposing, thoughtful, distinguished, and eloquent with a booming, albeit understated professorial delivery that concealed his deep passion for justice. Ilyes was a successful and now senior

government national security official. In fact, his career was very much
on the rise when we first crossed paths. Assigned outside of his country
at the time, parroting the party line with foreign counterparts while hob-
nobbing on the diplomatic circuit, Ilyes wanted for little. He enjoyed a
relatively good salary, housing, and the perks that came with being part
of the elite. But Ilyes had a deep sense of right and wrong, honor, and the
most romantic sense of chivalry. He often quoted to me, and those I had
followed, the line attributed to Edmund Burke, "The only thing necessary
for the triumph of evil is for good men to do nothing."

Ilyes, a productive reporter for many years, had been recruited long
before I even joined the service. He took his turnovers in stride, patiently
teaching new handlers some of the more useful and practical skills
their instructors omitted at the Farm, the CIA's training facility. An
ever-professional demeanor, never did I hear him utter a vulgar word.
Even his deep-seated hatred for an oppressive government was offered in
restrained tones, careful as he was not to undermine his reporting credibility with bias. Ilyes reported the facts, readouts of meetings he attended,
internal dynamics, and best of all, documents. His reporting provided insight on leadership security strategies, policies, and dynamics that served
US policy makers well, given the regional tensions and the poor state of
our own bilateral relationship. Not one to ever let down his guard, simply
getting Ilyes to smile at one of my attempts at wit, or rewarding me on
even rarer occasions with a joke of his own, was a victory.

Coming upon one another, we paused briefly, enough for me to ensure
all was well through a brief series of questions concerning safety and
matters of urgency we refer to as "the mad minute." I outlined what
would follow during our meeting and guided him along a walking route I
had previously cased. I'd be able to collect the documents he had brought
while debriefing him on their content and other matters of interest. We'd
need to find a place to stop, now and then, for me to pass his salary,
review his expense accounting, and take any notes I couldn't manage to
capture while we were on the move.

A brief word on money. It is often the grease on which case officers depend to make espionage work. But the CIA is a US government agency bound to the same processes and accountability as any other. Our management is flatter with more delegated authorities to the field so as to address the time-sensitive risks and opportunities inherent in the dynamic and often perilous nature of operational work. And its classified nature requires protecting details that might compromise sources and methods. Still, case officers require a formal, bureaucratic process of approval, audit, and certification to secure money for operational expenses and agent compensation that is memorialized in end-to-end documentation as it is in any taxpayer funded government institution. It's merely done with more protections, delegations of authority, and appropriate classifications.

Salary requests must be proposed, supported by a reasonable explanation concerning amount, and approved both in the field and then again by ranking officials at CIA Headquarters. The same goes for any obligations or commitments made to an agent for which the taxpayer bears the cost. And yes, receipts are required, per normal government standards, or a suitable personal certification when circumstances do not allow. Still, there's a uniquely profound level of trust that is not found in any other US agency.

An illustrative example is one in which I provided a cash payment to an agent in an amount sufficient to buy a plush New York City condo for contributions in thwarting a major terrorist operation. I delivered the heavy satchels of cash alone during a clandestine meeting, no witnesses, no body cam. I came away with the scrawled X my agent affixed to a handwritten receipt I had prepared, which I then submitted along with only my attestation as the official accounting. Trust like that, however, is earned and proven not only through deeds, but with the most exhausting and painful security reinvestigation process that makes passing a kidney stone a preferable experience. One undergoes such reviews multiple times throughout a career, and they can come randomly, at any time.

Clandestine agent meetings have to be conducted in a rather short period of time. The longer you and the agent are exposed together in public, the greater the risk, regardless of the tradecraft and precautions that endeavor to conceal the contact from view. Case officers have to prioritize the short time so as to address the most important intelligence questions, review security, make meeting arrangements, offer training when required, provide new tasking, and accomplish the necessary administrative requirements. All this must happen while possibly in a moving car during the hours of darkness or on a brief walking meeting, as was the case with Ilyes on this night.

One more thing, perhaps the most important, is that all of this business can never appear to the agent as *business*. It must be conducted while leveraging rapport, assessing the agent's state of mind, and while reinforcing and gauging the very motivations and considerations that leveraged the agent's cooperation in the first place. It's espionage, but it's also deeply personal. So, in the course of the exchange between Ilyes and myself, I share a generous amount of banter and conversation concerning family, sports, and personal subjects both mundane and dramatic. It seems casual on the surface, but such topics are employed and manipulated not only for atmosphere but likewise to answer specific questions, ease into sensitive issues, and address agenda items.

Espionage is about relationships. Agents are all human beings with hopes, dreams, fears, and communities. Even the ever-reserved and proper Ilyes. They don't want to be treated like prostitutes, nor even employees, and they deserve respect. You dehumanize them or otherwise take them for granted at your own peril. The bond is everything, inasmuch as it facilitates the trust that is absolutely necessary to make the entire enterprise work. It's a reality that's hard for anyone else in other occupations to fathom. The case officer has to make the agent feel like a friend, a valued member of the team, and trusted, whether or not that's actually the case.

At the end, Ilyes and I share a manly embrace, exchange warm, knowing smiles, and part ways in different directions. I look back for just a few brief moments for any signs of trouble as he fades out of sight. I still had to make it home while carrying stolen documents, so there was no opportunity to celebrate, and I couldn't afford to run into a random checkpoint or police patrol. But a few hours later, I'd be home. I'd have time to steal two or three hours of sleep before showering, shaving, and putting on my suit to arrive at the office at the opening of business to perform my official day job. I would again resume my public persona of Clark Kent, after my evening as Superman. Just another night for a CIA case officer.

Agents do place their lives in your hands. But to be fair, espionage is certainly not the only business where people entrust their lives to others. But with agents, it's not just their lives, but that of their families as well, given the consequences of exposure, ranging from shame and incarceration to brutal torture and death. And some of those consequences exceed even life and death. They extend to reputation, legacy, and the agents' very souls. Agents all have their reasons for spying. Some are noble, like Ilyes, others are more mercenary. The case officer identifies and leverages those motivations to secure and maintain an agent's cooperation. But in the end, it all comes down to trust. Do my case officers care? Will they keep me safe? What will they do for me, and my family, were I caught?

Don't believe the movies. We don't blackmail our agents. If it worked, we might. But it doesn't. We need agents to be honest with us, and for many, we are truly the only individual in the world with whom they can be totally transparent, more so even than their spouse or religious guide. That honesty allows us to protect them, which we do, not merely owing to our ethical responsibility, but selfishly to maintain the flow of intelligence they produce. The honesty enables us to accurately contextualize the veracity and authority of their reporting, without which, the intelligence is of no use.

The transparency between an agent and case officer, and the material benefits CIA has realized in their cooperation, provides a degree of control. That transparency provides the means to incentivize cooperation and likewise evaluate their access, motivations, the veracity of their information, and their freedom from bias or hostile control. You can't directly ask agents to do much, or evaluate their reliability and veracity, if they don't understand and accept your reasoning, the context for your interest, and how it impacts their security. An agent is aware of the risk, and likewise, the reward, whether it's their own ideological satisfaction, or a material, normally monetary, transaction.

Your buddy in the host nation's army might share some gossip over a few drinks, but drawing him or her out on the specifics of why a particular armor unit mobilized for the border, precisely how he or she came to know such information, and urging them to keep you current, requires a lot more than friendship. Intelligence is only as valuable as the context of its acquisition: How direct was the source's access? How much credibility does the source possess? How did the source acquire the information, and why did he or she provide it? Once again, it's trust. And in espionage, one must be able to depict trust in an almost mathematical means so that the consumer can assess the information's value. Reaching such milestones requires the agent to be a fully committed and willing partner. Victims of blackmail and coercion will do the minimum, and they have no reason to be any more transparent than they need to be.

It's true that you never "fall in love" with your agents, nor do you ever fully trust them. You can't. Things happen. Life changes over time. They're human. But case officers meet their agents in the dark backstreets of the most austere and dangerous locations. I depended on them for my own security, as much as they depended on me. All that considered, I preferred that an agent embraced a positive view of me rather than be someone I had to coerce. Real spies persuade, thugs coerce.

THE UNITED STATES INTELLIGENCE COMMUNITY, AND WHERE CIA FITS

T rust me, more war stories are forthcoming to illustrate the practical consequences and realities of espionage. But before we get into that we need a bit more context for our exploration of the CIA's post-9/11 changes. The Intelligence Reform and Terrorism Prevention Act of 2004 created the Office of the Director of National Intelligence (ODNI). The legislation had two principal purposes. The first was to establish an enduring framework facilitating greater collaboration and transparency among the eighteen organizations of the United States Intelligence Community (USIC). The second, perhaps more politically important perspective, was to provide accountability to the American people for 9/11's failure. If no individuals would bear the responsibility, then certainly it fell on organizations to shoulder the blame. The easiest to blame was the one that couldn't openly defend itself, CIA. And CIA did share the blame, though the failure was as much if not more a collapse of leadership, both political and across the USIC. While the 9/11 Commission envisioned the ODNI to be more than simply a means to punish the CIA, the reality memorialized in the 2004 legislation actually increased the roles and power of most all the other USIC organizations, at the CIA's expense, particularly the Department of Defense, which claims nine of the USIC's eighteen organizations.

By statute, "The Director of National Intelligence serves as the head of the Intelligence Community, overseeing and directing the implementation of the National Intelligence Program budget and serving as the principal advisor to the President, the National Security Council, and the Homeland Security Council for intelligence matters related to national security." But the DNI failed to receive the key authorities that the 9/11 Commission intended, nor even those that the 2004 legislation allowed.

The direction and management of the country's overall intelligence programs remain within the realm of the National Security Council (NSC), meaning that the ODNI operates largely as an administrative bridge rather than the brains controlling the USIC's central nervous system. Under the National Security Advisor, it's the NSC that captures and articulates the president's objectives and priorities. And unlike the directors of CIA, National Security Agency (NSA), Defense Intelligence Agency (DIA), or FBI, for example, the ODNI runs no operations nor does it oversee the intelligence community's individual agencies.

Although on paper the president's primary intelligence advisor, the DNI was never going to achieve the DCIA's depth of understanding and operational situational awareness. Geography alone assured as much. The DCIA interacts daily with the CIA's operational and analytical executives and experts, and is regularly briefed on the nuts and bolts of operations. Another reality was that the DNI was deprived both the budgetary purse strings and control in naming the individual USIC heads as the 9/11 Commission recommended. Although the 9/11 Commission hoped to empower the DNI to more effectively oversee and coordinate NSA, the National Reconnaissance Office (NRO), and the National Geospatial-Intelligence Agency (NGA), all remained well ensconced within the defense secretary's orbit and effectively beyond the DNI's reach.

Regarding the homeland, FBI made quick work of negating the 9/11 Commission's recommendation that the DNI likewise assume responsibility for domestic intelligence control. Led by then FBI Director Robert Mueller, the FBI likewise successfully resisted congressional interest in developing an independent domestic intelligence agency designed along the lines of Great Britain's MI5 or France's Direction Générale de la Sécurité Intérieure (DGSI—the General Directorate for Internal Security). Considering the contributions MI5 and the DGSI make internally against their primary focus of counterterrorism, counterespionage, and cyber, it might be worth revisiting the utility of standing up a similar organization in the US. Unlike law enforcement agencies, MI5 and the DGSI focus on intelligence collection, analysis, and preemption versus evidentiary pursuit and judicial prosecution. Such focus by a domestic intelligence agency under scrupulous oversight and operating in full accordance with the protection of civil liberties would be timely given the rise in domestic terrorism, cyber attacks and foreign interference, and counterintelligence efforts.

Further diluting the DNI's practical influence, the recommendation that the three deputy positions be concurrently occupied by the under secretary of defense for intelligence (USDI), DCIA, and FBI executive director was never realized. Rather, these positions are filled by three Senior Intelligence Service (SIS) grade officers who are permanently detailed from their home agencies. For CIA, at least, this detail often amounts to an external exile for a senior officer who has lost favor with the DCIA.

The DNI is hardly the nation's top spy, but that's not to say the office has neither an impact nor a role to play. His or her fief is restricted to analytical and advisory centers to facilitate the principal constructive role in integrating and coordinating information found by individual agencies. Within the cabinet, the DNI can help the president process and understand what intelligence professionals have concluded, whether the news is good or bad, providing a safe space in which the USIC can do its work, free from pressure, political or otherwise. The DNI shares appropriately sanitized conclusions with the public so as to demystify the process, and secure buy-in and confidence concerning the threats the nation faces.

Unfortunately, the ODNI has experienced bloat and politicization over its lifespan. Whereas the 9/11 Commission recommended but one independent center, the National Counterterrorism Center (NCTC), the ODNI would eventually expand by three more to address counterproliferation, counterintelligence, and cyber, in addition to a correspondingly growing number of supporting offices, national intelligence officers, and the more recent phenomenon of national intelligence managers. And rather than buffer the USIC from politics and bullying, following the departure of DNI Dan Coats, a former GOP senator, the subsequent DNIs under President Trump were either professionals too weak to push back, or they were unqualified political loyalists, like GOP political operative Richard Grenell and stalwart Trump supporter, GOP Congressman John Ratcliffe.

Appreciating the legislation's impact on CIA starts by understanding how its condemnation from 9/11 was truly an existential crisis. At least that was how Agency leaders saw it, and it certainly had a tremendous effect on their direction. And if 9/11 didn't take down the CIA, the subsequent body blow after America's 2003 invasion of Iraq over weapons of mass destruction that never materialized almost did. The Agency needed to offset its further loss of credibility. Redemption would only come through its ability to deliver in the covert action realm. Bear in mind that the CIA was created in 1947 to collect foreign intelligence, perform analysis, and conduct covert action. It's the latter part of that charter that is unique among the USIC agencies and branches of military service.

In the aftermath of 9/11 and Iraq, the biggest threat to CIA's place among USIC agencies in terms of its relevance and utility was the Department of Defense (DoD). Not just for CIA's failures, but perhaps more so because of its success. Whatever the verdict regarding the CIA's culpability in not averting 9/11, its response was nothing short of magnificent. Secretary of Defense Donald Rumsfeld felt outmaneuvered and rather thrown under the bus when the Agency was able to put boots on the ground in Afghanistan far quicker than his armed forces. CIA officers were on the ground in Afghanistan in days, versus weeks or months, collecting intelligence and linking up with friendly indigenous forces. While DoD was still trying to determine its authorities, develop a plan, and calculate the logistics, the CIA was paying off warlords to begin pushing back the Taliban, coordinating attacks, buying—well, perhaps renting—political support, and enabling the incoming DoD Special Forces elements who would coordinate massive US air support to our proxy forces.

Rumsfeld felt humiliated at the Agency's ability to so quickly and decisively accomplish what he insisted would take far longer. He thereafter moved to take those steps necessary for DoD to replicate, and ideally outperform, the special missions the CIA conducted. And at least as perceived by CIA, Rumsfeld took this all rather personally. Such attitudes were clear when meeting with our DoD counterparts.

The CIA's leaders believed that Rumsfeld and his successors would leverage the Agency's errors to marginalize it to the largest extent possible. There was even fear within the CIA that DoD might make a play to absorb the Agency outright, either invoking some type of wartime powers, or by virtue of public and political sentiment. It was no coincidence that the CIA would, by 2006, have a uniformed military officer as its director. And General Michael Hayden made a point of retaining his active military commission and wearing his uniform throughout his tenure as DCIA, rather than retire and serve as a civilian, as would later be the case with General David Petraeus when he served as DCIA.

Career CIA officers, and specifically, Directorate of Operations leaders, began refocusing and rebranding. Ironically, whereas the military was reforming to decrease hierarchy and flatten management among special operations elements to replicate the CIA's agility and creativity, the Agency moved in precisely the opposite direction. Moreover, CIA needed to win over DoD, or at minimum, appease it. CIA leaders increasingly aligned resources and mission to support military requirements, priorities, and preferences. Often, devoting efforts against tactical matters and low-hanging fruit at the expense of CIA's primary strategic mission.

At the risk of subjecting the reader to overwhelming legalese and technical jargon, it's important to understand the dynamic in the context of how the CIA and DoD each leveraged their authorities. CIA operates under Title 50 through which it derives the unique authorities concerning covert action. And DoD's application of its traditional, defense-related Title 10 authorities were, subsequent to 9/11, expanded by virtue of the 2001 Authorization for the Use of Military Force (AUMF). Moreover, Rumsfeld interpreted the AUMF as identifying the entire world as the battlefield in the Global War on Terror (GWOT).

Section 503(e) of the National Security Act defines covert action as "an activity or activities of the United States Government to influence political, economic, or military conditions abroad, where it is intended that the role of the United States Government *will not be apparent or acknowledged publicly*" (my italics). Although Section 3093 of Title 50, US Code requires congressional notification "in a written finding to be reported to the congressional intelligence committees as soon as possible after the approval of a finding, and before the covert action starts," it's the president's prerogative to decide when or where to use the covert action capability. The president may authorize the conduct of a covert action only if he or she determines such an action is "necessary to support identifiable foreign policy objectives of the United States, and is important to the national security of the United States."

The narrative distinguishing Title 10 from Title 50 goes on to explain that DoD activities, "on occasion, may appear similar to clandestine activities or covert action conducted by the intelligence community. However, they differ in that they are conducted under a military chain of command, generally in support of, or in anticipation of a military operation or campaign conducted under Title 10 authority."

All the above translates more simply to the fact that while DoD certainly conducts *clandestine* missions, and likewise collects intelligence, it is not permitted to undertake *covert* missions in which the US government can deny its involvement. In other words, as of today, only CIA is authorized to conduct covert missions for which its operations and activities can be denied by the United States. That's right, we can look the world in the eye, so to speak, and legally say, "Wasn't us." If DoD performs the mission, the US cannot. This was a deliberate choice that was made to preserve the integrity of the military and protect our service members under international conventions, while still providing a means for policy makers to exert force and influence without attribution. Spies have no such protections, as Nathan Hale's execution during the Revolutionary War and statue outside the CIA's main entrance is meant to signify.

It's not to suggest that CIA gave up on spying. But it was clear that DoD was moving into HUMINT (intelligence gathering from human sources) in a big way. Under the AUMF, DoD could operate anywhere in the world under the pretext of preparing the battlefield in the GWOT context or as an ancillary to combat operations. Citing the AUMF and its Title 10 authorities, DoD could, and on occasion did, conduct HUMINT activities without the coordination or even knowledge of not merely the local CIA station chief, but even the ambassador. And DoD dwarfs CIA in terms of size and resources, establishing a growing number of collection elements and its own independent HUMINT training programs.

Although no small number of these DoD activities ended in spectacular disaster, such operations were often focused on purely tactical missions or the low-hanging fruit that CIA did not pursue. Many were the result of commands seeking greater control and independence owing to a lack of trust in the CIA's fidelity and transparency. The danger is that whether operations are of low or high value, they bear the same risks. Operations were being run by less savvy or trained military intelligence commands on the same turf where CIA ran more sensitive and strategic efforts in partnership with or otherwise concealed from the host country foreign counterintelligence services and governments.

Whether an agent handler is running a taxi driver or a senior government official both require the same degree of clandestine tradecraft. If caught, both similarly go to jail, or worse, and CIA's cooperation with the local service, as well as broader US equities, subsequently suffer. Such compromises for this low-hanging fruit further increase the risk to other ongoing and more sensitive CIA collection activities.

Still, after 9/11, concerned it might not have the strength or influence to ward off DoD, the CIA's leadership therefore made a conscious choice. It reprioritized, taking a more a political rather than operational view to risk management, and focused on marketing its most seductive capability. Democratic and Republican White Houses have historically found the CIA's covert action capability irresistible. Although they should certainly know better from history, the CIA's leaders were likewise seduced by the rewards for leveraging these capabilities and authorities to curry White House favor. And from 2002 to 2004 it was all about self-preservation. While

Agency leaders at this time believed themselves saving the organization, these decision makers were in reality prioritizing their own futures.

The most damaging impact has been the CIA's cultural change from primarily identifying itself as America's premiere civilian spy service to behaving like a paramilitary organization. Whereas it previously prioritized stealth, nuance, and innovation, the CIA's culture increasingly reflected a more rigid, hierarchal, and unquestioning mentality focused on force. Despite the CIA's obvious hand in such kinetic activities, these operations were labeled as covert action and, with the exception of the Osama bin Laden raid, officially denied.

In prioritizing covert action capabilities as a politically preferable kinetic alternative to DoD or as an emotionally satisfying brand of justice that FBI could not deliver, the CIA found new life. It was able to provide successive White Houses solutions to sticky political issues that appeared to outmaneuver existing constraints with agility and efficiency beyond that which other agencies could offer. White Houses were further naively confident that such dirty business could be kept forever secret. Sadly, no small number of the CIA's leaders believed this as well, although a good spy knows that most secrets have a shelf life.

Undertaking questionable covert action missions was nothing new. After all, the CIA underwent a similar existential threat in the 1970s, owing to ill-considered adventures: The 1975 Church Committee's investigations took the CIA to task for abuses of its authorities in support of the Nixon White House. Subsequently, President Jimmy Carter's first director of Central Intelligence, Stansfield Turner, directed the infamous 1977 Halloween purge of 820 CIA personnel. Not long after 9/11, the CIA again compromised its integrity in two fateful episodes: the establishment of black sites, secret CIA controlled and operated overseas detention facilities where terrorist suspects were held and subjected to the Enhanced Interrogation Program (EIP), a euphemism for torture; and the CIA's support for the White House's rather jaundiced pretext for the 2003 invasion of Iraq. Only, unlike the 1970s, no accountability or consequences would be forthcoming.

The CIA's leaders who conceived and approved the concept of extra-judicially detaining terrorist suspects at secret facilities where they would endure EIP illustrates the tradeoffs made by these leaders in desperation to fend off perceived existential threats to the organization's survival—and their careers. These leaders should have known better but instead leveraged the CIA's alacrity and efficiency in solving what was then a pressing political problem, which was to garner White House appreciation. While directed and approved by the White House, the blame and resulting taint fell squarely upon the Agency, as it should have, but unfortunately not among the leaders who came up with the idea but rather the midlevel and junior officers executing the mission that their superiors had authorized.

Establishing black sites without giving thought to an endgame for the detainees, the facilities, and the host governments was folly enough. Where the Agency completely went off the rails was in applying enhanced interrogation, a euphemism for torture, a decision that remains beyond my ability to fathom. That the CIA should be involved in the debriefing of high-value detainees, I fully support. Detainees represent an excellent source of intelligence, and they can at times be persuaded to change allegiances, though great care needs to be taken with "jailhouse" recruits whose true loyalties require time and due diligence in vetting, an example of which we will address later in the book.

Case officers spend their lives developing the cooperation of others through rapport, trust, and leveraging motivations. I have spent my share of hours with detainees, and I approached them like I would any recruitment target, manipulating but not coercing. It doesn't always work, just as not all people are recruitable, but this approach offers the best road to success. That we outsourced this operational mission to interrogators and psychologists whose approach ran counter to our aversion to using coercion to recruit sources, is incongruous to the CIA's ethos and culture.

Likewise, there are exhaustive studies that reflect the willingness of Agency leaders to cherry-pick and spin the intelligence so as to align with the politically convenient White House narrative linking Saddam Hussein to al-Qa'ida and 9/11, and Iraq's possession of weapons of mass destruction. I was there, and we knew better. But when the vice president of the United States and his minions became regular participants at the CIA's internal meetings debating the merits of the argument, midlevel career CIA officers and experts were left without top cover from their leaders to push back, resulting in unsurprising outcomes such as acquiescence, group think, and the compromised integrity of their findings. The most senior CIA leaders backing the unsupported assertions and their camp followers all advanced professionally, never facing accountability for their misdeeds or failures. Those who resisted faced professional exile, in some cases, which was career ending.

The change the CIA began to undertake after 9/11 therefore reflected a more politically attuned risk calculus, one that would ultimately infect the very way it would do business. The new mindset would encourage sycophants among future leaders and reward conformity at the expense of merit and speaking truth to power. What was intended to save the CIA, and the unique mission for which it was created, would erode the standards for which it prided itself as an elite and principled civilian spy service. The CIA would reinvent itself as a bright shiny new toy hammer at the White House's disposal, but one far easier to use in securing political rewards. And as the adage goes, a hammer is always looking for a nail.

WHERE DOES OUR INTELLIGENCE COME FROM?

The *Central* in CIA infers that it would have the broader management duties of coordinating the various means of intelligence collection among the other agencies involved in the overall endeavor. Setting the standards and managing the coordination and execution of America's Human Intelligence operations among all US collection agencies was a unique mission, and one intended to leverage the CIA's political independence from the White House and its other executive agencies. Long before 9/11 and the creation of the Office of the Director of National Intelligence (ODNI), closer scrutiny of efficiencies incrementally resulted in the realignment of various intelligence collection responsibilities to other mission managers. In its earlier days, the CIA had an independent capacity to service all forms of collection, including technical. To some extent, it keeps a hand still in collection areas under the command of other agencies, if only limited to facilitation, innovation, and specialization. At a minimum, apart from leveraging its agility as a smaller, flatter organization, doing so enables its ongoing coordination and management responsibilities in the foreign field.

Intelligence comes in six basic forms:

SIGINT—Signals intelligence is essentially all that is transmitted electronically whether by radio waves, digital, telephonic, or instrumentational telemetry. That's a fancy way to describe eavesdropping, wiretaps, and cyber hacking. The National Security Agency (NSA) is responsible for collecting, processing, and reporting SIGINT, but other US intelligence agencies also conduct or otherwise enable such operations.

Talented as our scientists, engineers, and technical experts are, they often require an "in" to gain access to a system or device. Enabling this technical collection depends on an agent. It's the agent who can provide something as simple as a target's "selectors," such as a telephone number, email, or other internet account against which we can then direct our efforts. SIGINT cannot tell you what the target is thinking. And it's the target's motivations and intentions that are crucial in understanding the "why" and the "so what" concerning the matter's importance and its impact on US national security. As such, SIGINT runs the risk of the subjective or inaccurate interpretation of verbatim transcriptions, some of which depends as well on the quality, experience, and bias of the translator. It's all too common for different United States Intelligence Community (USIC) agencies to transcribe the exact same intercepts with dramatically different interpretations.

IMINT—Imagery Intelligence is what we collect from satellites, aircraft, and whatever other technical tools that offer visual photography, radar sensors, and electro-optics. The National Geospatial-Intelligence Agency (NGA) is the manager for all imagery intelligence activities, both classified and unclassified. IMINT is similarly often dependent on HUMINT, which I'll expand on momentarily. It frequently takes an agent to tell us where to employ our national technical means of collection, and then how to interpret what it is we're seeing.

MASINT—Measurement and Signature Intelligence is technically derived intelligence data other than imagery and signals. That's a complicated way of categorizing what we learn through environmental samples taken from dirt, water, air, vibrations, and even sounds. The data results in intelligence that locates, identifies, or describes distinctive characteristics of targets that might expose nefarious nuclear, chemical, or biological activities. Consider the seismic indicators when a nuclear device is tested, the heat and residue when a missile is launched, and the toxic dust or runoff from chemicals and biological substances. Environmental data might also pinpoint where a picture, video, or recording was taken when trying to recover a hostage or when trying to determine the location of a terrorist based simply on the surroundings.

MASINT employs a broad group of disciplines including nuclear, optical, radio frequency, acoustics, seismic, and materials sciences. The Directorate for MASINT and Technical Collection (DT), a component of the Defense Intelligence Agency (DIA), is the focus for all national and Department of Defense MASINT matters. MASINT also depends heavily on HUMINT. Those samples do not collect themselves. Collection requires a person to physically have access and know where to look. At some point or another, case officers, or their agents, will find themselves scooping up vials of dirt or water near suspicious facilities, or wiping the surfaces of objects therein with cloth, while trying to have a ready cover for what they're doing.

OSINT—Open-Source Intelligence is publicly available information appearing in print or electronic form including radio, television, newspapers, journals, the internet, commercial databases, and videos, graphics, and drawings. Open-source collection responsibilities are broadly distributed through the USIC. OSINT might indeed be the fastest developing and most intriguing of the INTs, given the advances in artificial intelligence (AI), but one around which we are still struggling to manage and exploit. Collection, retention, and storage of such vast amounts of overtly available data increasingly pose significant implications—though resource and technical issues might prove easier to address than privacy considerations and ethical questions, at least in democratic societies.

GEOINT—Geospatial Intelligence is the analysis and visual representation of security-related activities on the earth. This is the art of finding a wanted terrorist or a secret underground nuclear facility. It integrates technical collection from of a variety of tools and techniques, which are understandably closely guarded. What I can share is that it's distinct from IMINT, which relies almost exclusively on some sort of photography. By contrast, GEOINT includes images and signals alike, along with what we learn through sources. Drones, for example, and other ground or airborne sensors, contribute toward geolocation. Whether it's full motion video or other signal or visual collection, the technology is similarly HUMINT dependent. Apart from knowing where to look, you also need to have an idea of what you are looking for. In the absence of preexisting photos, only an agent can describe your target or what they might be wearing on any particular day, let alone their pattern of life, profile, traits, and activities that increase your level in confidence that you are indeed looking at who you are aiming to find. And don't forget that whatever photo you might already have probably came from a HUMINT operation.

HUMINT—Human Intelligence is derived from human sources. To the public, HUMINT remains synonymous with espionage and clandestine activities. If you pull up the ODNI website, however, the descriptive narrative defining HUMINT emphasizes that while it is the oldest method for collecting information, it is no longer the most important. I began my tale by acknowledging that HUMINT might very well be the world's second oldest profession, but is it really no longer the most important? Read on and be the judge.

HUMINT is the collection that comes from people. But most HUMINT actually comes from open sources and official government-to-government diplomatic, military, and economic engagements, to name but a few. My job, and the CIA's premiere responsibility, is clandestine collection. That is, spying. These are the sources who provide us secrets, the people who have access to intelligence by virtue of their jobs, colleagues, friends, and family members. They are America's eyes and ears, secret penetrations of our adversaries among their military officers, diplomats, security officials, economic planners, scientists, business people, and so on, and terrorists or other criminals, and their friends and relatives. These are people who cooperate secretly with the United States government, breaking their country's laws or their group's rules.

Agents provide us documents, military manuals, and readouts from high-level meetings and policy discussions in which they or their associates participated, and so forth, and can speak to plans, intentions, and capabilities. They offer context and reason behind actions and events that inform our understanding and decision-making. Agents, therefore, not only provide the "what" but, more importantly, the "so what" with the "why" a government, group, or individual has taken a decision, allowing us to anticipate what they might do next.

Context is key, and that is perhaps HUMINT's most significant attribute. Once an event has occurred, it's history, be it a meeting that deliberated a decision or an action that transpired, such as a nuclear test or military operation. Therefore it is the "so what" and "why" that tells us what consequence the event held and what it means for the future. Only an agent can speak to the state of mind of the decision makers, their motivations, and their underlying agendas so as to appreciate their true intentions, and consequently, the threat or implications.

Historically speaking, the case of the Cuban missile crisis in 1962 illustrates this process. Reconnaissance gathered from U2 aircraft provided the tangible forewarning that the Soviet Union had placed nuclear missiles on the island, but it was the agents who provided the United States with insights into their intended use and the Kremlin's political dynamics and personalities. That broader and rather profound mosaic was vital toward informing our ultimate negotiating strategy and identifying red lines.

The CIA and other USIC agencies initially collect what is referred to as the *raw reporting* obtained by Human Intelligence agents by virtue of their access to such information or technical means such as SIGINT and IMINT. This reporting is considered raw, not finished intelligence, until it has been studied, assessed, and interpreted by analysts. The finished intelligence products that go to policy makers and other consumers are drawn from raw reporting, data points that come variously from the six aforementioned sources of collection. Consumers with appropriate clearances receive both raw reporting and finished products. The raw reporting, however, provides the daily reports that come directly from the various field collection sources. These are generally short, single subject, individual accounts of events, plans, intentions, and capabilities. Finished intelligence reports are authored on matters as tasked, as serial products, compilations, or when a stream of raw reporting on an issue warrants the identification of a particular trend, opportunity, or risk requiring the attention of policy makers.

In order to be true to the context of the raw reporting's acquisition, sourcing, and access, the CIA's approach is to capture raw intelligence as a snapshot in time, true at the moment, and provide it clinically to the reader without point of view, interpretation, or further analytical assessment. Every raw CIA intelligence report is drafted in the past tense. A raw intelligence report cannot predict what will be, and a report does not distract the analyst or decision maker with any attempt to do so. Raw reporting has no point of view and is not intended to influence the reader toward any conclusion. All those responsibilities belong to the analysts who deliver the finished intelligence products, such as during the Presidential Daily Brief. Rather, the raw report addresses what actually occurred. No one can look into a crystal ball. In fact, all plans and decisions are subject to change. A report will reveal that on a certain date, in a particular location, a named group of individuals met to discuss and agree upon a plan perhaps guided by a particular motivation. The report might say that the group planned to conduct a certain attack on a given date at a specific location, but it will not confirm it as destined; rather, it will inform our degree of confidence in its likely occurrence.

One such example would be 9/11. Given what we learned after the attack, as reflected in the 9/11 Commission Report, Osama bin Laden had actually sought to execute the "planes operation," as it was known to al-Qa'ida, on May 12, 2001, eleven months after the attack in Yemen against the USS Cole. Subsequently, bin Laden wanted the attack to align with Israeli Prime Minister Ariel Sharon's anticipated June or July 2001 White House visit. Operational realities on the ground, however, delayed the attackers from carrying out their plan any earlier. Were the CIA to have had an agent in bin Laden's circles, or collected Signals intelligence on his conversations earlier in 2001, we could not have said al-Qa'ida *would* attack the World Trade Center and Pentagon in May or June/July, but rather, as of that time, they *planned* to do so. That is, a snapshot in time presented in the past tense to most accurately convey context. It's then the analysts' task to deliver a projection based on that report and all other raw intelligence streams contributing to the mosaic.

The agent, and our report, can only speak to what transpired at a moment in time. But the context of the "so what" and the "why" informs the understanding of the analyst or decision maker as to the likelihood and intent of the plan. It outlines how those quoted or paraphrased in the report were in a position to make such decisions and their interests in doing so. In turn, our sourcing reveals how authoritative and credible the information is based on the individual who provided it, and the circumstances under which it was collected. The source is not named, not even the codename is revealed to the consumer, but included is a statement concerning our assessment of the source's access and reliability and the context under which that specific information was obtained. Such insights are not available from pictures or even the intercepts of what people say or write.

As a brand, the CIA's field reporting retains the highest credibility among USIC agencies that produce HUMINT. Sure, there's the mystery and sexiness of CIA, but our reporting likewise tends to understate versus overstate. Our foreign intelligence reports meticulously separate the source's opinion from fact, and provide context and rather accurate insights on the source's access and circumstances of collection. It is, as advertised, void of analysis, and is simply the raw reporting as opposed to a finished product. Where some of the other agencies get in trouble is in overstating their reporting, attempting to be predictive more so than factual, and blurring the subjective opinion of the source or collector with the factual details.

Consumers are also more likely to find sensational information that is weak on substance and context in HUMINT from agencies other than the CIA. Whereas other agencies report HUMINT that is secured from collectors of various degrees of training, almost all the CIA's foreign intelligence reports are obtained and drafted by those with the highest level of core collector training and certification, allowing a more sophisticated understanding of the subject matter and its value. What the CIA collects must be foreign, of interest, new, clandestinely collected, and authoritative. Such standards apply both to the secrets we steal from a recruited clandestine source, or that which a foreign intelligence service partner shares officially, such as the reporting that contributed to the raid against the Idlib, Syria, safe house that killed the leader of the Islamic State of Iraq and Syria, Abu Bakr al-Baghdadi.

In the aftermath of 9/11, I doubt it's a coincidence that the ODNI website declares that HUMINT is no longer the most important collection source. Such a declaration lends itself to the deliberate effort to minimize the role and value of traditional espionage and the redefinition of spying in the American psyche, and likewise the CIA's reduced influence and place at the president's table. The ODNI's explanation of the various INTs and the lead agencies also conspicuously omits the CIA's mention. Most of the cited agencies, NSA, NGA, DIA, are in fact all part of the Department of Defense (DoD).

Multiple agencies could be assigned intelligence requirements depending on their collection capabilities. If the requirement were, say, money laundering, then State, Commerce, DoD, FBI, and Treasury, among others, could likely secure a great deal of the required information through routine and overt engagement with foreign partners. Among them, one might have primary responsibility, the others in support, along with additional agencies that might offer complementary use of classified and technical collection capabilities. The logic is, Why steal what you can get for free?

The most sensitive and critical requirements come with the greatest risk. Information about counterproliferation, counterterrorism, counterintelligence, and our adversaries' defense capabilities and strategies is not so readily available in the overt world. That sensitivity and importance warrants the risks the CIA and its agents undertake. It is for this reason that the CIA is known as the collector of last resort. Why waste the CIA collecting on topics that other agencies can better address, and with less risk? White House pressure that the CIA should realign finite resources on narcotics trafficking, human smuggling, immigration, or the price of goods in less accessible areas is therefore a sensitive topic among careerists.

HOURS AND HOURS OF ROUTINE, AND A FEW MOMENTS OF ADRENALINE

After a lifetime pretending to be somebody else, well, rather, many different somebodies, it's a surreal experience transitioning from living in the shadows to a place where my former CIA affiliation is splattered across all manner of public media. I never was required to explain what I really did for a living except to those who already understood, be they colleagues, USIC partners, senior US or foreign government officials, and my foreign agents. Rather, to those outside the Agency, I wore the mask of whatever official day job I happened to be living at the time. Retiring afforded me the opportunity to emerge as who I was, and discuss what I truly did. This seemed like a good idea at the time, given how doing so enables me to compete for opportunities referencing my skills and experiences. But then, given the appropriately scrupulous process of declassification and all, what I can really tell people is, in the words of prospective employers, "intriguing, but not entirely revealing."

My résumé, like those of the many colleagues who face similar requirements, is entirely superficial and general. There's no mention of the countries in which I lived, the official jobs in which I outwardly functioned, nor the positions I held save reference to being a chief of station, an executive manager, or a collector. I can claim languages, but not the places at which I used them. And I have no unclassified documentation to account for the various professional certifications, awards, citations, and training I've received. And of course, I cannot discuss the true nature of my work, except in the most generic fashion.

I signed up for that, so no regrets. But as you might now surmise, that does tend to complicate the ordinary job interview between me and a civilian lacking USIC exposure. Harder still when it's someone from entirely outside of the government. Fear not. I quickly determined that interviewing is mostly about translating to the more common vernacular.

If asked what I did, or perhaps more important, what distinguishes an Agency case officer from an FBI special agent or member of the country's elite Special Forces, I claim to have been a problem solver who managed risk. That's the bottom line. A case officer addresses America's need for intelligence, which can be acquired through none other than covert or clandestine means. We recruit agents possessing such information by solving their personal and professional problems. And unlike FBI special agents, diplomats, and military service members, CIA case officers have no definitive standard operating procedure to guide them through every situation with which they might be faced. Law enforcement has a manual for most everything and operates on its home turf with a badge and gun. Military members train for muscle memory on the battlefield, with manuals, checklists, and immediate action drills concerning all manner of weapons and tactics.

There is little that law enforcement and the armed forces have not already seen and for which they can't therefore prepare and practice. Spying, however, is almost always situational, and unforeseen circumstances often occur. Which is why the answer to almost any espionage question is, "it depends." There are no perfect clandestine sites in which to meet an agent, no canned response to a target's behavior, and no boilerplate routes to use when trying to determine if you're under surveillance. Everything is tailored to the people, place, and conditions, unique and often with a lifespan of one use only. There are parameters, ideals, tradecraft, and best practices, but there is no checklist or manual for each and every situation an officer might encounter. It's a concept our law enforcement and military colleagues often struggled with when operating in my shadowy world…but I called it home.

For the most part, CIA case officers operate alone. There's no partner, no cavalry, no close air support, no do-overs. They operate in the most gray of worlds, one replete with dynamic, ambiguous, and often unchartered circumstances. Rather than manuals for every flavor of operational circumstance, CIA case officers rely on judgment, instincts, experience, and the legal parameters and authorities under which they are required to operate.

Subtract the drama, and what remains is the consistent thread that case officers have to make decisions, sometimes life and death decisions, without the benefit of a lifeline. And when we come into the office the next day and tell our story, there's no "spy cam" or witness to validate our word. *Ideally* there's no video or witness. With so much responsibility, it comes down to integrity. Faith in what the case officer reports impacts decisions that determine variously whether or not we conduct a military strike, challenge an adversary's treachery in a diplomatic forum, attempt a hostage rescue mission, or commit billions to a new program.

Most of a case officer's career is actually spent planning and writing about what they're going to do, and then, what they've done. Since you're generally the only one who actually conducted the operational act, whether it's meeting with a target you're developing, an agent you debriefed, a signal you posted, or a drop you have collected, how you write defines what you have done, and how you are known. I spent two years teaching at our training facility, known as the Farm. While there, I developed a reputation as "one of the four horsemen of the apocalypse." Okay, so that's not exactly a compliment, but it's not as bad as it sounds. Or is it? I wasn't hard on my trainees for the fun of it, or just because I could be—not that there aren't instructors who choose to be difficult for those more selfish reasons. I was challenging and real, confronting students with what they would face in the foreign field, applying my Marine Corps–instilled philosophy of "the more you sweat in peace, the less you bleed in war."

I'll relate but one such story among those that earned my reputation; it was during an exercise with a student we'll call "Cassie." I was playing the role of the operational lead she was seeking to develop for recruitment. The exercise is about teaching the student to develop rapport and trust with the target. Students then leverage their ability to have the target confide in them so as to enable them to assess the target's access to intelligence and what it might take to persuade the target to cooperate clandestinely. Cassie was bright, young, and well educated. Like most of our students, Cassie came from a rather privileged suburban life. It's not like she wasn't a hard worker, but neither had she endured much hardship or taken too many risks, and her attitude reflected as much. She had not likely ever received much criticism, let alone failed at any endeavor.

In role, Cassie, as the CIA case officer working clandestinely at the fictional local office, had elected to invite me, an official working for the notional foreign government, to dinner. In our fictional land, working for the government in a sensitive position as I did, my character would not have been authorized to meet unofficially with a US official, and doing so was a risk. Key to the training experience is staying in role and embracing the live problem, using our assumed personas and speaking to the fictional foreign land in which we are operating. As a venue, she chose a Chinese restaurant that featured an all-you-can-eat buffet. It was a popular local establishment. The food wasn't necessarily of the highest quality, but the dishes were varied and plentiful. Signs throughout the restaurant warned against taking home leftovers. Take what you want, but eat what you take, or leave it on the table. Left unchecked, you could easily feed a large family for a week based on what you could toss into a bag from one meal.

We had a perfectly lovely dinner. Cassie was doing a good job establishing rapport, showing empathy, eliciting information, and leading the conversation to subjects of interest. She was now trying to secure another meeting. Cassie was struggling to come up with an innocent but compelling reason that would be worth my while to meet again. I decided to see if she'd be willing to get out of her comfort zone since it was unlikely that Cassie had ever done anything wrong, let alone illegal, in her entire life. So, in response to her invitation, I said, "Tell you what. You do one thing for me, to prove I can trust you, and we'll have another meeting."

Cassie regarded me with unease, wondering, I expect, where the conversation was going. I asked, "You know how I love the egg rolls here?" Cassie looked at me with a sense of impending dread. "Yes," she answered. "Well," I continued, "I can't get them anywhere else. You can't order them off the menu for takeout, and they don't allow you to take any home." Cassie nodded. "So, if you go to the buffet table, and toss, say, half a dozen in your bag, then pass them to me in the parking lot, I'll meet you again."

While not exactly a high crime or misdemeanor, my suggestion that she surreptitiously lift a half-dozen egg rolls from the main buffet line in plain view was reprehensible in her mind. It wasn't just about the implication of stealing, but rather, Cassie thought it decidedly unseemly.

No doubt the idea of smelling up her designer purse was also a consideration. "How about I pay for them?" she countered. "I'm sure I can just go to the maître d', pass him ten bucks, and he'll give them to me in a nice bag." I shook my head, "No," protesting that if I couldn't rely on her for something as trivial as this, why should I risk my job by meeting again? Cassie looked at me with revulsion. Although silent as our eyes locked, her internal monologue betrayed the thought bubble, "What an asshole." But to her credit, she agreed, nodding her head, and softly mouthing, "Okay."

Cassie took the check, allowing me to head for the door. She stood, contemplating how she would best execute the petty larceny, and then moved toward the buffet. I paused to watch her cautiously peruse the dishes. Coming across the stack of egg rolls, Cassie discreetly opened her purse, looked to either side, and swiftly, albeit somewhat clumsily, flipped in six with two quick grabs. We met in the parking lot by my car, where she reached into her purse and withdrew six of the greasy prizes in her bare hands, deliberately passing them to me one by one as she counted, with an appropriately warm, albeit feigned smile, hating every moment of the ordeal. Cassie went on to do well in the field, but she never forgave me.

It wasn't long ago that I met with a young CIA analyst who previously worked for me and was thinking of applying to the Directorate of Operations (DO) to become a case officer. Over a cup of coffee, he asked for my perspective, advice for the process, and feedback on whether or not he had the mettle. Having dished out the best advice I could offer and exhausting his set list of questions, I asked if there was anything else I could tell him. He smiled, then mentioned having heard of my reputation while an instructor and wondered if he might ask what I was looking for in the students. Integrity, I told him. The practice of espionage was life and death, and I'd rather a student fail in training, own up to the errors, and apply lessons learned so as to succeed during the real thing when there's no one watching.

A parent or member of the clergy might have told you as a kid that you should act as if someone, God perhaps, *was* always watching. It's like that, I suggested. What you do while on the streets can't generally be checked. We license our case officers with breaking the most important laws around the world where they're posted, to make and manipulate friendships, and to lie, steal, cheat, and, if necessary, defend America, themselves and their agents to the death in the process. In return, we ask for unquestionable integrity and loyalty. To act as if their country was always watching, even when they believed for sure we were not.

We expect our case officers (C/Os) to tell us what really happened, even if they could get away with not doing so, even when they failed—especially when they failed. Case officers have to do the hard work and always question their agents, themselves, and overlook nothing, even something that seems like a coincidental anomaly. Lives are at stake. So they can't take shortcuts and run a shorter cleansing route to be sure no one is following them when it's minus forty-five degrees Celsius outside—and yes, I did work in one such former Soviet state where the temperatures routinely dropped this low—and we can't use the same meeting sites more than once, though it's hard to keep finding new locations; and we must test the agent, always, and not succumb to the belief that the agent's veracity or productivity is a reflection on us. Doing all of this requires an enormous degree of trust, faith, and authority. Not all case officers are up to it.

As a young case officer, I had a meeting set with a sensitive agent with whom we had some doubts. I was in a Middle Eastern country that was suffering from a great deal of violence, mostly at the hands of an al-Qa'ida-affiliated terrorist group. The United States government was not, at the time, on the best of terms with the local government, a somewhat repressive police state whose security services saw us more as an adversary than ally, despite the common enemy we shared. Over the course of my assignment, I had met and developed a member of the local intelligence service who we'll call "Khalid."

Now Khalid found himself in a bad spot, somewhat trapped between two opposing and equally menacing forces. On the one hand, Khalid came from a family that included several members with Islamic extremist sympathies and some with actual ties to the terrorist group his government was now battling. On the other hand, Khalid was a member of the country's security service whose job it was to identify, root out, and neutralize any such threats against his government from this terrorist group. In fact, it was this very background that drew the local intelligence organization's interest to Khalid when he entered into military service. They saw an opportunity to prosper from his extremist contacts, just as those extremist contacts believed they might take advantage of Khalid's membership in the armed forces.

Khalid was neither a flag-waving government loyalist nor a budding terrorist. He felt ill-treated by his government masters, who pressured him to inform on family and friends, and likewise was pressured by his extremist associates who expected him to be their inside man. Khalid saw evils in both, and in the vicious cycle of cause and effect between the opposing sides. He believed the government had reaped some of what they had sown. But he likewise opposed the extremists' use of terrorist tactics, which he believed only served to justify further repression. That's what brought him to me, or so he said.

Stuck between a rock and a hard place, Khalid wanted a lifeboat, a way out. I persuaded him to believe that the CIA was his best hope, but that we could only assist him if we knew about both what the terrorists were planning and how the security service planned to respond. In truth, we wanted to know about threats and operations that would place our own interests and community at risk; those undertaken by the terrorists posing a physical threat to us, and what the security services did in response that might cause a counterintelligence risk for our operations. We also wanted to assess the government's stability and capacity to restore order and protect the American expatriate and official communities, which is the threshold on which the United States government often depends in deciding whether or not to evacuate its official presence and discourage American civilians from travel.

Meeting Khalid required high-threat protocols. After all, the terrorist threat in the country was high to begin with, and Khalid's familial ties raised the bar higher still. Moreover, we could not forget that Khalid likewise posed a significant counterintelligence concern given his day job with the intelligence service. Back at this time, we came up with our own protocols based on local staffing resources and what the environment allowed. This was before 9/11 and the identification of locations such as Afghanistan, Iraq, Syria, Libya, and Pakistan as conflict zone service that brought with it the many additional training, protocols, and specialty career occupations we have since adopted to meet today's high-threat environments. In that era, it was just another Near East Division operation in a typically dangerous Near East Division post.

But that wasn't all of it. For added excitement, in the course of our meetings, given the threat and the impact of his intelligence, Headquarters had requested that we administer Khalid a polygraph. I can go on ad nauseam with my personal and professional insights concerning the use of a polygraph on an agent or staff officer, and as a vetting tool, but will spare you. For now, whether or not the test results were correct, the agent had, as measured that day, appeared to be lying about one of the key questions we had. The good news was that he demonstrated no deception when asked if he had been directed against us by the local intelligence service as part of a double agent effort. The bad news was that Khalid unfortunately appeared to be lying when asked whether or not he was meeting on behalf of his terrorist associates with the intent of doing me harm.

It was a time in which the field was given the authority to decide whether or not to continue meeting the agent. Technically, Headquarters then, and now, could always direct an order, such as dropping a case, but it was accepted that the field was best positioned to make such calls. Communications were conducted by cable, which is an official, written document of record that's transmitted through encrypted channels. We used the most secure and reliable channel available at the time. The process was slow, however, not due to any technical issues, but because cables have to be drafted and officially coordinated, reviewed, and ultimately approved by a senior before transmission—and that goes on at both ends.

The process assures that the cable is the final, recorded copy of what transpired, including the decisions and approvals. But the time lag required greater delegation of authority and autonomy to the field. This era predated the vast availability of multiple modes of secure communications now connecting Headquarters with the field, not merely to the chief of station, but anyone and everyone within the station. Today's technology allows everyone to provide their informal opinions, or to question decisions, in real time—a gift that comes with a highly serrated double-edged sword.

The chief of station, colloquially known as the COS, is the field commander in charge of the CIA's operations in-country, and serves as the president's senior intelligence representative there. The Intelligence Reform Act of 2004 placed this authority under the auspices of the DNI representative, versus the COS, though for the time being they are one and the same. For the Agency, being a COS is akin to being the captain of a naval ship at sea, with the DCIA's delegated powers and authorities. As the speed and availability of all manner of instant communications have likewise done to US Navy captains, a COS no longer exercises the power of God on earth, but it's still pretty close.

My COS was one of the best officers with whom I ever served, and remains today a dear, trusted friend. His values and integrity were without question. His decisions were not about his own success or failure, what would make him look good, what might cost him professionally, but rather, what was right. The CIA speaks a great deal about leadership traits, inclusiveness, and empowering our people. This fellow was willing to risk his rather promising career when he accepted my opinion on the matter. Of course I insisted we should meet Khalid. In hindsight, my certainty perhaps had more to do with hubris than dispassionate analysis.

Spying happens at night. Or at least, it really should. Night is the spy's friend. Yes, even with satellites, night vision, facial recognition, and cameras galore saturating most every major international city, there is something about the night. It's the stillness, the scarcity of people, or on occasion, the kind of people more likely to be on the street at such ungodly hours that heightens a spy's senses to feel potent and invisible in darkness. It just feels right. The plan was for the agent to be awaiting me to pick him up in a car along a dark and remote stretch of roadway. There was heavy vegetation on either side of this rarely used path, which served as a back-way cut-through that connected two neighborhoods. I had cased it repeatedly, but only at night at the times I expected to use it. I had even showcased the location to the agent during a previous meeting so he would know precisely where to position himself. A rule of thumb is to case a site at the time of day and in the season during which you will be using it, which I had done.

Working with a team, we arranged for folks to look for any signs of trouble. A plan was in place with set times and signals for advising me if the coast was clear and to let me know when the agent was in place. I'd make my way to the general vicinity in a manner to determine if I was free of surveillance, that is, free from any bad guys associated either with the local counterintelligence service, or the terrorists, who might be hoping to catch me in the act or ambush me. I'd wait for the signal before committing myself to driving down that remote, quiet slip of road where I'd pick him up at the previously identified location. Before internet use became ubiquitous and every human on the planet had a cell phone, we relied on schedules and physical signals. I will tell you that, even with technology, there's nothing more reliable and secure than this still-employed espionage method. Then, and now, you are best to stay off the telephone or the internet, since you never know who is monitoring these communications. Moreover, what you do on a phone or over the internet is forever.

My team had passed through the site but practiced caution so as not to heat it up by loitering or appearing out of place. So far so good, no signs of trouble, in fact, no signs of anything. The road was dead and not a soul was in sight. But when the time came for the agent to arrive, nothing happened. The team signaled the no-show and we fell back on plan B.

The primary time missed, we expected that the agent, were he to have been delayed for reasons other than danger or compromise, would arrive at the variant, in this case, a prearranged time, one hour later. We all left the general vicinity so as not to offer a suspicious presence to residents concerned about crime or militants, prompting them to contact the authorities or confront us themselves. Returning to the area, we put the same plan in motion. Again, no signs of trouble, but likewise, no agent.

It's human nature to think the worst, and in espionage, it's a survival instinct. Because this was the first meeting with the agent after the bad polygraph, I began to worry that when news arrived at Headquarters, my leadership would take his no-show as evidence that the case had gone bad. Still, while undergoing a CIA polygraph is a painful experience for all involved, the innocent and guilty alike, the agent was not made privy to the fact he had failed. Or more accurately, that he had reacted so significantly when asked if he was meeting with me to cause harm.

Then there's the unfortunate self-doubt that begins to go through a case officer's head. Was it my fault? Do I have the wrong date? The wrong time? I replayed our discussion from the last meeting and wondered whether he might have confused the time. For one thing, I was conducting this conversation in a foreign language, foreign to me, in any event. And while essentially fluent, neither my vocabulary nor grammar were perfect, and my language instructors had suggested my accent was reminiscent of the grunts from a Spanish cow. They were not an encouraging lot, my instructors.

"He had the wrong time!" I thought to myself excitedly. "Yes, it was yet an hour later," I convinced myself. But I didn't act on these thoughts. Especially when working with a team, there are rules for a reason, and we follow them to keep everyone safe. The agent had failed to show for the primary and variant, and trying again with the various players on the street was not prudent. In any case, there was still a plan C, which called for the next meeting to occur at the same location, at the same time, precisely one week later, if one or both parties failed to appear. This plan was designed to remove any need for either of us to have to make direct contact by phone or other means so as to reschedule. For now, the plan called for everyone on the team to leave the area by separate routes, and call it a night. And depart they did. Well, except, for me.

On my own, I decided to return again to the pickup site an hour later. I was certain the agent was not blowing me off, just as I was convinced he posed no threat. I let the rest of the team exit the area, mentioning nothing of my plan. No need to involve them with this, and I was sure all would be forgiven tomorrow if he showed up. Not exactly my best exercise in judgment. But when I say that I wasn't afraid, it's not to suggest I'm a hero, or even particularly brave. This is what I did, and what I was good at. It was fun, exciting, and involved risk, but I never consciously thought I was in danger.

There were times, over my career, where the risk was far more clear, violence more present, and I can say without reservation, I was afraid. Even during those times, though, the fear existed before, or after, I was conducting an operation. Never during. Never when I was in my world, in control. I was far more afraid at other times, such as sitting at home in a high-threat environment or conflict zone, where my shelter was an unprotected "pod" within a walled off compound with a war raging about me and indirect fire landing with unwelcome regularity and randomness.

More frightening still was standing huddled with colleagues within a safe haven, awaiting the concussion made by a Vehicle-Borne Improvised Explosive Device (VBIED), better known as a car bomb, that had been detected outside. On those occasions I was petrified, mostly because I had no control. Rather than actively deciding my fate, it was being determined well beyond anything that I might influence. On the street, I was master of my fate, controlling my destiny through the exercise of my skills.

When I began to drive down that remote road, I had no sense of apprehension or dread. That is, until I saw lights from a station wagon emerging from the vegetation backward onto the road before me, and blocking my way. Headlights likewise appeared from behind. The Marine Corps had taught me how to fight, but the CIA taught me how "to get off the X." I was armed, but case officers carry weapons as a last resort since engaging in gunfights rather undermines the clandestine principle of spying—that is, you were never there.

Still, things go wrong, so the Agency had not only armed me but trained me to use that rather large machine I was steering as a weapon for escape. It was the classic scenario we had been taught, a vehicle blocking the path ahead, another from behind to prevent retreat. During my early years, this instruction was affectionately called the crash and bang, and it was designed to train CIA officers how to crash cars through obstacles and shoot their way out of danger. Okay, yeah, it was a fun course. But it's a lot less fun when real.

It's amazing how fast the brain works under such circumstances and there's something to be said for the muscle memory from having re-peated this drill time and again, and this is one of those circumstances in espionage for which we can train and prepare. I slowly depressed the accelerator to build up the sufficient kinetic force with which to push my way through the blocking vehicle's rear, where absent an engine, it was the lightest and most vulnerable. Hoping my car would remain operable after pushing the station wagon aside, my mind began flipping through various escape routes to avoid a chase car. I considered the nearest points of refuge I could get to in time before the bullets starting flying, which is what I expected to happen. Police stations, army bases, and the nearest government installations that might have armed sentries all came to mind. I'd never be able to make it back to the office.

In the nanoseconds that passed, my mind raced with plans. Suddenly, I saw light appear from inside the station wagon. The dome light began to shine as the door cracked open. Were they going to begin shooting? My heart raced. You know the feeling, when you can practically feel your heart's every beat throughout your body? Emerging from the driver's seat, however, was not the terrorist caricature I had expected. In fact, the small, hunched-over figure was barely ambulatory. My heart was still racing as I let off the gas pedal and slowed to watch a small, elderly man shuffle toward the unseen dirt driveway before him. He meandered toward a short, rusty, red gate that the darkness of night and generous vegetation had so effectively concealed. I'd failed to notice it. There would be neither crash nor bang tonight, merely embarrassment for the super spy who came within seconds of running down a little old man.

When I arrived in the office the next morning, I told my COS everything even though there were no witnesses to my near debacle. I received more teasing than reprimand for taking that third pass by myself. Lesson learned. When I wrote up my cable to Headquarters reporting on the agent no-show, I included making that third pass, but my COS spared me the need to document the crash and bang that never was.

WELCOME TO THE DIRECTORATE OF OPERATIONS

Now having hopefully whet your appetite with some flavor for a case officer's life in the field, and your having survived an explanation of where CIA fits into the community, it would help to step back again to understand how the Directorate of Operations fits into the CIA. The CIA's official website explains that "the Directorate of Operations (DO) strengthens national security and foreign policy objectives through the clandestine collection of Human Intelligence (HUMINT), and by conducting covert action as directed by the President." In an effort to mask its role, the DO was originally named the Directorate of *Plans*. While always known likewise as the Clandestine Service, it was actually renamed the National Clandestine Service (NCS) after 9/11. The intent was to suggest distinction from the broader CIA and its elite charter. Moreover, having the deputy director of the CIA for operations now become director of the National Clandestine Service was meant to suggest some parity with the director of the Central Intelligence Agency.

It was a nice try, and somewhat practical, but ultimately was a casualty to the modernization efforts by former DCIA John Brennan. Brennan's stated goal was to improve efficiency and align CIA's structure to that found among other USIC agencies. This would be accomplished by facilitating intracommunity engagement. Modernization's redeeming measure was merging stakeholders among different agencies and those from diverse CIA occupational specialities into fusion centers not unlike a task force. The CIA's Counterterrorism Center (CTC), which was stood up in 1986, since 2015 renamed the Counterterrorism Mission Center (CTMC), was the model for drawing from DO and Directorate of Analysis (DA) skill sets and likewise representatives detailed or assigned from other USIC agencies.

Brennan's real intent was to reshape the Agency's purpose and power structure, and his organizational fusion was primarily meant to strengthen his direct, day-to-day control over operations, weaken the DO, and empower the DA with greater influence. Modernization allowed Brennan to place analysts into the CIA centers' operational leadership positions. And whereas DO offices previously reported to the deputy director for operations (DDO), or known at the time of modernization as chief of the National Clandestine Service, CIA centers now all reported directly to the DCIA. The DO's overall influence and control over operational decision-making was significantly reduced. Moreover, culturally, the DO's air of elitism, if not lost, was at least temporarily closeted.

Modernization further culled the DO's cyber operational elements into an entirely new organization, the Directorate for Digital Innovation (DDI)—a component that had blended operational, analytic, and technical elements, but was previously within the DO orbit so as to align it with field activities and render it more influential. Making it an independent directorate hindered synchronization with operations, undermined its standing with the DO, and essentially rendered it another technical directorate like that of the Directorate of Science and Technology (DS&T).

Now often in the hands of analysts, operational decision-making began to reflect a more cerebral and lengthy deliberation process. This was consistent with their training and culture, but anathema to operations pace and risk management. Slowing the process had an intellectual appeal. Analysts seek an exhaustive review of data so as to make the most informed decision. In operations, you never have the complete picture. Perfect becomes the enemy to the good. You must act before perishable time lapses that close windows of opportunity and heighten risk. No decision, therefore, is actually a choice, and is one that can come at great cost. While perhaps counterintuitive intellectually, in espionage, risk aversion increases danger to our operations and people.

The CIA's website further states, "The DO is the front-line source of clandestine intelligence on critical international developments ranging from terrorism and weapons proliferation to military and political issues. To gather this important intelligence, CIA operations officers live and work overseas to establish and maintain networks and personal relationships with foreign 'assets' in the field."

Sources are the lifeblood of an intelligence service. The DO's emblem, borrowed from its Office of Strategic Services (OSS) ancestor, reflects the pointy end of the spear. And if sources are the service's core business enterprise, then the case officer charged to recruit and securely handle those responsibilities would seemingly be the one wielding that spear. As the CIA transitioned post-9/11, the wars in Afghanistan and Iraq marginalized the value placed in these operational skills, as well as the character of the collection mission.

One would expect changes in priorities and operating procedures to evolve with society, technology, and geopolitical realities. Moreover, successive generations put their own stamp on any organization's culture and personality, and likewise bring energy and new ideas. One of the Agency's virtues has been a spirit of innovation and inclination to go big or go home. But the single most critical fundamental to intelligence collection that can't be discarded is people. How we pursue and communicate with people necessarily changes with the environment and technology, but not the importance of this communication.

A senior military colleague once complained to me that "the problem with the CIA is that you're more concerned about the sources than the mission. We just care about getting things done." I paused a moment to consider the cultural disconnect that often characterized DoD's mistakes in the clandestine world and replied, "That's because the sources *are* the mission, without whom you can't attain your goals."

Human beings hold the ultimate key to intelligence. We have engineered all manner of technology and machines to steal what they write and say aloud, or even see what they do in their hidden lairs and on their computers. But until such time as we can develop a technology to read hearts and minds, we still need to learn the secrets that lay hidden in their souls. Only that defines the "what" and "why" of their plans and intentions. That makes spying a necessarily personal and intimate business among human beings that requires boots on the ground, to borrow from the military's own mantra.

The CIA I knew when I began was far from perfect. And for a people-oriented profession, I found the DO woefully behind the curve of inclusion and racial equality. The CIA case officer of the early 1980s was more than likely White, male, and Christian. At the time, there were cafeterias for DO officers operating clandestinely that were separate from the rest of the Agency. This certainly lent to a pecking order, and not unlike in high school, cliques that separated the cool kids from others. And it was about prestige and power since, in reality, case officers did not enjoy material benefits over their peers. In fact, case officers were generally promoted more slowly than their analytic and technical counterparts.

Nevertheless, case officers called the shots, were the elite, and swaggered around the building with oversized egos. And being a great agent recruiter didn't necessarily translate into being a smart and compassionate supervisor. As they reached higher levels of responsibility, case officers were notoriously brusque and imperious in their management of subordinates. Brennan's modernization was in part a product of the scars that resulted.

Case officers of the early 1980s and the generations that preceded them focused on mission and operations and avoided the limelight beyond their own circles. They saw themselves as licensed thieves rather than bureaucrats. They abhorred face time with seniors or worse still, giving briefings at the NSC or on Capitol Hill, preferring instead to remain anonymous in their covert world. Just getting these people to put on suits was a challenge. That's not how DO officers gained attention or promotion in that era. Less was more when it came to briefing outside the building. Get in, get out, be candid, tell them what they need to know, but protect sources and methods while bringing as little attention to yourself as possible.

Case officers had no envy for the hierarchy of other organizations, namely DoD. They measured themselves against one another by how they did on the street, their recruitments, and their COS assignments, were they lucky enough to earn a station. Rank was less at issue when it came to the merit of an operational idea. And the last place any red-blooded case officer wanted to be was Headquarters. The field was home, and being a field case officer anywhere in the world was better than being the most senior manager at Headquarters. Indeed, those successful in the field were promoted fastest and rewarded with the best onward assignments.

Since 9/11, the opposite has been true. Officers who work the patronage system at home advance the quickest. Working Headquarters' hallways became the way to be noticed and get ahead. Today, officers compete for opportunities to brief Congress and seniors from other agencies. They line up to participate in all manner of focus groups, forums, and organizational associations. All of this allows one to check boxes, be seen, and get a name for oneself among the people who make the personnel decisions.

The years 2002 to 2004 represented a transition point. Poor performers who briefed well received a second life. This new cadre spoke to what their audience wanted to hear rather than what they needed to know. Such officers secured patronage from CIA leaders who were agonizing over how to maintain relevance with their political masters who appreciated political aptitude and adherence to the party line, regardless how dubious.

Finding itself stretched among multiple war zones and expanded operational theaters while concurrently shouldering an exponential explosion of terrorism and combat support–related intelligence requirements, CIA was desperately short on personnel, particularly those with the requisite training, experience, and certifications for conflict zone duty. This required placing weaker performers in critical positions, at home as well as the field. Less capable officers then became charged with significant management duties and external engagement. Those who could command a room and please their superiors at Headquarters profited at the expense of those willing to speak truth to power or who focused purely on mission.

I remember sharing my concerns with a senior colleague in the run-up to the Iraq war only to be reassured: "This will pass," I was told. "They might earn a promotion or two they wouldn't have otherwise managed, but no one would ever trust them with significant operational responsibilities and authorities." Oh, how my old mentor was wrong. He failed to recall that regardless of our ethos and mission, the CIA was an executive agency led by a presidential appointee and surrounded by lieutenants whose own ambitions aligned first and foremost with whomever was in charge. CIA executives in this new era rewarded personal loyalty and, sadly, obsequiousness over merit and well-considered operational risk.

The CIA's mission shift, focus, and cultural changes also redefined the DO's division of labor and fundamental paradigm. Barely on life support prior to 9/11, the CIA's Special Activities Division, which was home to paramilitary operations, expanded dramatically in size and influence. CIA's website observes that "Paramilitary Operations Officers play a unique role and provide unique capabilities in support of conventional and unconventional operations overseas," and "are required to successfully complete specialized training to prepare for service in hazardous and austere environments overseas."

The CIA's paramilitary case officers, or PMOOs, are recruited almost exclusively from the ranks of the military, and are largely veterans from among the Marines and the special operations community. They undergo operational tradecraft training to be certified as case officers, but they mostly spend their careers assisting, advising, and training military and Special Forces units from other countries, much like the work of the US Army's Green Berets. A few PMOOs have opportunities to rotate into traditional foreign intelligence tours. Most are exposed to some agent recruitment and handling opportunities, even in conflict zones. The experience is not entirely the same, however, as the CIA practices a decidedly different tradecraft in traditional environments than it does in conflict zones.

The American footprint in conflict zones is hardly subtle or under the radar. Rather, like most official Americans, aside from military service members in combat, intelligence collectors are more likely to be operating from behind near impenetrable fortresses as opposed to meeting their agents clandestinely on the street. And when beyond the walls of their fortresses, their movements trade degrees of clandestinity and stealth for physical protection through armored transportation, convoys, and protective escorts.

PMOOs spend a great deal of their time in harm's way, account for most of the CIA's casualties, and represent a proud element that accomplishes the impossible in the worst imaginable locations. Smaller, more agile and flexible than our military's special operations forces, and endowed with covert action authorities under Title 50, they can often do more with less, and move faster than our uniformed comrades. PMOO ranks swelled after 9/11 owing to their need in conflict zones such as Afghanistan and Iraq, and later the Libyan and Syrian theaters. Given the CIA's significant allocation of resources and attention to counterterrorism and areas of active combat, their broader influence grew, impacting more of the Agency's overall strategic direction. Taking nothing away from the PMOOs, they miss the broader experience of conventional case officers. Largely, PMOOs operate against a more narrow, tactical target set in environments lacking the complex and expansive counterintelligence (CI) threats found in the likes of Moscow, Beijing, Cairo, or Caracas. Still, owing to their bravery on the battlefield, PMOOs advance quicker than conventional case officers. Problematically, they tend to benefit from a reluctance of those who have not been so long under fire to challenge them in operational matters, a recipe from which have been borne some significant counterintelligence flaps in agent handling.

Not coincidentally, perhaps, DCIA Brennan's choice to lead the DO as he implemented modernization was a career PMOO. Unquestionably a well-respected and inspiring leader who was a legitimate hero on the battlefield, he nevertheless lacked traditional case officer operational experience. A division chief of the Near East and South Asia Division (NE) once said of this officer, not long after 9/11, that "there was no one he would rather have covering his six in a tight spot, but could never seriously consider entrusting him with agent operations."

While I continue to hold this officer in this highest regard for his heroism, honor, and commitment to those who worked under him, he did the CIA and Directorate of Operations no favor. As deputy director for operations (DDO), this officer staunchly defended and executed Brennan's vision, helping to expunge the Clandestine Service of dissenters. At the same time, he likewise advanced the careers of many PMOOs into the Senior Intelligence Service ranks and COS positions, despite their limited conventional operational experience. I'm not suggesting that none of them were worthy simply by virtue of their specialization, but it was another example to the DO workforce of ambition and cronyism as opposed to merit and mission.

Collection management officers (CMOs), according to the CIA website, "drive the collection of foreign intelligence and actively manage the two-way dialogue between US intelligence consumers and the DO." CMOs are a fickle breed, often the Rodney Dangerfields of the DO in that they have at times been their own worst enemies in trying to gain a position of equal respect to the case officer. Still often referred to as reports officers, over the years CMOs have been required to possess the same basic tradecraft training as case officers so as to enable them to recruit and handle agents in the field. Unfortunately, the CMO careerists flip-flopped many times over the last thirty years, downgrading and subsequently reinstating its core requirements, creating various subgroups with different training and certifications.

Making matters worse, the DDO prior to the one who fell on his sword at Brennan's modernization decree rather openly disparaged the CMO profession. That he was jilted as a young man by a CMO to whom he had proposed marriage, *I'm sure* had nothing to do with it. CMOs were having a tough time as it was when that same DDO prioritized the new targeting officer career track. In truth, CMOs play an invaluable role that includes counterintelligence and targeting. Moreover, they remain the linchpin in assuring for the quality, integrity, and protection of DO intelligence products.

Of the staff operations officer (SOO), the CIA website explains that they "provide the seamless integration between CIA Headquarters and DO offices in the field necessary to drive clandestine operations to success....Staff Operations Officers apply advanced knowledge and expertise of clandestine operations, operational tradecraft, and intelligence priorities when providing strategic guidance and operational case management." Without any intended disrespect for this critically important function, I see it as no accident that of all the specialties, the website's SOO description is the most lengthy. The SOO profession, like the targeting officer (T/O), developed in its present form after 9/11. The SOO workforce has been an outspoken, new career element seeking its place at the table among the DO's subcultures, and suffers a bit at times from what could be called *case officer envy*.

In reality, the SOO evolved from those once known as the DO desk officer. Staffed in the past on occasion by case officers returning to Headquarters but too junior to assume management positions, desk officers, in their day, saw to the daily life support of the field stations for which they were responsible. The desk officer was not unlike an aircraft's crew chief who knows how to get things done and provides the pilot with the ammunition, fuel, safety checks, and targets so they can do their job. The desk officer then, like the SOO today, responded to the daily correspondence the field generated, as well as addressed their life support, administrative, and operational requirements. SOOs trace new contacts, open files, conduct research on operational leads, and perform due diligence on existing cases and operational activities in collaboration with other Headquarters stakeholders.

Before the desk officer career occupation became more regulated and professionalized, its demographic was highly diverse and its growth opportunities extremely limited. The typical billets rarely exceeded journeyman officer ranks, with many of the desks staffed by case officer trainees serving their interim assignments prior to going on to the Farm for tradecraft training and certification. Given the scarcity of case officers, desk officer opportunities were among the few means women and, to some extent, minorities, and those without college degrees, could get their foot in the DO's door during the 1970s, 1980s, and somewhat into the 1990s. This was an era during which women and minorities outside of the limited number coming into the case officer and CMO pipelines often found their gateway as administrative and clerical support.

Today, college degrees are required, as is a greater flexibility to travel, thus closing the door for many with family responsibilities or other considerations, and who might otherwise excel at these duties. A good many of the very best desk officers of old came up through the ranks after serving various administrative and support positions, many in the foreign field. Another source of personnel for these positions came from the DO's mainly male case officers' wives, seeking their own careers upon returning from years abroad. Such women brought tremendous understanding of living and working in the foreign field, and at their best were the station's umbilical cord of support. Today's SOOs have the same core duties, but they bring greater skill sets and function more like program managers. While perhaps better educated than the desk officers of the past, their academic prowess does not always result in greater operational acumen. Though the same can equally be said of case officers likewise recruited for their academic credentials and professional CVs.

Among DO occupations, the newest and most unique is the targeting officer (T/O). According to the CIA website, the targeting officer "will identify the people, relationships, and organizations having access to the information needed to address the most critical US foreign intelligence requirements and find opportunities to disrupt terrorist attacks, illegal arms trade, drug networks, cyber threats, and counterintelligence threats." Targeting is among the fundamentals of intelligence operations. But its definition and occupational build-out changed dramatically after 9/11. We used to speak of targeting as identifying a lead for recruitment. It meant pulling together background data along with insights that might facilitate an operational approach. Such duties were shared among the case officer, CMO, and SOO. While that responsibility remains a targeting function, the post-9/11 inclination is to use geolocation for action, principally kinetic, in the support of "find, fix, and finish" operations to remove terrorist threats from the battlefield.

As such, 9/11 turned targeting on its head. Now we were hunters. As analysts began to fill the DO's expanding ranks, particularly in the Counterterrorism Center, they brought with them analytic tools and processes. Excited at the thrill of the hunt—and the rather tangible, short-term satisfaction of having their work in the DO come to fruition versus writing papers informing policy decisions—many decided to make the DO their home. They joined a number of analysts who had earlier left the directorate for various reasons, some personal, some professional.

In a relatively short period, targeting officers at CIA Headquarters came to comprise a plurality of a CTC unit's personnel inasmuch as case officers were largely abroad or those few at home were serving as managers. CIA centers are organized by both function, such as counterterrorism and counterproliferation, or geography, such as Europe and the Near East. Desk officers and then SOOs were manning billets in the geographic area components in support of field stations, their personnel, infrastructure, and operations. There were fewer SOOs in the Counterterrorism Center, today's Counterterrorism Mission Center (CTMC), which technically had no stations to support, only issues, targets, and programs. The targeting officers' ensuing influence in the direction of counterterrorist operations, even its operational tradecraft, became disproportionately greater than their operational training and experience. Given their effectiveness at man-hunting, however, their tradecraft lapses were overlooked in CTMC. But such traits, having been enabled for "manhunting" intended to geolocate a person for possible kinetic activity, allowed few of them to success-fully transition to support traditional recruitment operations against hard targets such as the Russians, Chinese, Iranians, and North Koreans.

Recruitment operations requires targeting that identifies the names of people who might work in a particular office, on a certain issue, or within a specific field. It also offers indirect assessment to validate their merit as targets based on backgrounds and prospective motivations, and ideally to highlight avenues and means a case officer might use in the approach. Geolocating a target to be removed from the battlefield is an art form in itself, and it concerns patterns, associations, and the target's place in the hierarchy of an identified terrorist group. But it is rather different from the art employed to find, cultivate, and recruit a spy.

Not only is targeting for recruitment more time-consuming, there will be more swings and misses than hits. There's immediate gratification in seeing a target removed from the battlefield. Some such targeters develop a thirst for blood, I regret to say, that can't be quenched by recruiting spies. I tried to bring several counterterrorist targeters over to offices I managed where we focused on agent operations, but they would not trade the satisfaction of "putting a target on the X" for more traditional, kinetic-free work, even with the prospect of expanding their skill set.

What was meant to be a specialized but complementary career track would develop into an entirely different outlook for the Agency's mission, one more aligned with that of a military organization that prioritized brute force over insight—a measure CIA historically applied as a last resort and when no other US agency could deliver, not as a default first choice.

IN THE BEGINNING

Experience reinforced my belief that case officers are born, not made. And a good case officer can usually recognize the right traits in another. There are innate behaviors, characteristics, and personality traits—or perhaps quirks—that contribute to success. We do a pretty good job of screening for a variety of these traits against a set profile and, in theory, graduate the right people. The CIA can teach anyone espionage tradecraft, the mechanics of it, and refine the natural talents and abilities that our candidates bring. Some things, however, can't be taught. Behaviors can be mimicked but not endowed, or harder still, unlearned. Fundamentally, it's about character. Just as Lincoln said about deception: "You can fool all the people some of the time, and some of the people all the time, but you cannot fool all the people all the time."

Most everyone has the capacity to pretend and manipulate to some degree, and in my experience, there are elements of good and bad in most everyone. Some people are naturally inclined toward other people, even drawing their energy from human contact. There are introverts and extroverts, and within those categories likewise a variety of intervals on the spectrum. Take the Myers-Briggs Type Indicator (MBTI) test, for example. It's a pretty interesting tool that we and many other organizations have used historically to profile how people see and interact with the world. Based on your answers, it will categorize you as extroverted (E) or introverted (I), sensing (S) or intuiting (N), feeling (F) or thinking (T), judgmental (J) or perceptive (P). I always came out "ENTP," but interestingly, the level to which I was extroverted decreased over the years. These changes I believe are telling, and they concern the effects of "being on" for a lifetime.

If being a case officer means performing, assuming a role, or "being on," then stage fright and performance anxiety are real issues. This can be managed by many people, but some can't tolerate the spotlight at all. And pressure is a bitch, to put it plainly, when one has to think on the fly under dynamic circumstances without benefit of a playbook, a partner, a coach, or a lifeline, and the choices are life and death. It's not my point that case officers are "the best of the best." Many, including myself, are deeply flawed, in more ways than we wish to admit. We have neither moral nor intellectual superiority, and we are hardly role models when it comes to traditional values. But for better or worse, we are endowed with traits that work to our advantage in conducting espionage, the ability to manipulate people and our environments being key among them.

One of my favorite television dramas is *The Wire*. Created by David Simon, and set in Baltimore, it is by far and away more than a police drama. The program variously addresses social issues and politics against the backdrop of a story pitting the police against narcotics traffickers, police against police, narcotics traffickers against narcotics traffickers, and all manner of social action in between. *The Wire* is brilliantly told and acted, perhaps with the exception of the second season, if I'm allowed to say. Like dramas of its time, such as *The Sopranos*, there's not so much good guys and bad guys, happy endings or complete failures, but the many shades of gray in all people and circumstances.

Police work is a vocation, as is espionage. And like espionage, where one is either enforcing or breaking the rules with some degree of institutional authority, and dealing with corruption, power, and occasional ugliness, there are temptations. Some who begin their careers with wide-eyed innocence and enthusiasm tire over time. And their commitment, and their performance, begin to waiver.

In *The Wire*, there are cops who start phoning it in, looking the other way, preferring not to rock the boat. Some of this owes to frustrations over corruption, be it in the courts, or in the lack of meritocracy in the department's cliquish rewards system, and worse. There are once good cops so beaten down by the system who just give up entirely while others play the game to advance themselves, or dodge trouble. There are those at all ends of the spectrum who see themselves above the rules. A few fall victim to corruption themselves, excusing their behavior with the outlook that everyone else is doing it. And then there are the "real police." It's how the core characters refer to the smaller population possessing God-given natural talent as well as integrity.

Dramatized for television to be sure, there are parallels in many careers, particularly those of a vocational nature or those having to do with public service. I find comparing police and case officers somewhat compelling. There are similarly "real police" among the case officer cadre, as there are those who have lost their way, phone it in, prize ambition and self-promotion over mission, or in rarer cases, join the dark side. Such outcomes are avoidable, as leadership can mitigate risks arising over the frustrations and temptations that divert those from their original more righteous path. That is, unless the leadership itself has become populated by those whose priorities have changed, which was the evolution I saw in the CIA's leadership after 9/11.

Leadership tends to repopulate itself in its own image. Strong, secure, compassionate, inclusive, and talented leaders will promote those with similar traits, and will do so fundamentally upon merit. Lesser leaders will promote those more exclusively on personal loyalty and a spirit of the star chamber protecting itself, and its power, from perceived threats. Corrupt leaders preach buzzwords, but they protect allies from transgressions, punishing those who question the status quo. Far too many become drunk with power and stature and see themselves beyond question. Surrounded by sycophants, they become deaf to alternative points of view. Nowhere is this more dangerous than in an intelligence service whose mission is to provide the unvarnished truth. And once leadership goes astray, it takes time, and generations of successive regimes, for an organization to right itself, if at all.

One senior leader comes to mind. He remains perhaps the smartest operations officer I ever knew. Where he lost his way was not simply his acerbic tongue. You'd never know to look at "Ian" that he started out in management as a rather compassionate sort. Superficially, he appeared a classic misanthrope, decidedly unapproachable and completely disinterested in people. The true embodiment of cold and detached, Ian maintained a profound and sincere love of dogs; but for Ian, hell was in being forced to be around people aimlessly chatting, or worse still, their young children. How could Ian ever recruit anyone or command genuine respect among his subordinates?

Standing in a crowd with him at a ceremony, a young woman who once worked for Ian approached to pay her respects. She began catching him up on her family, having married and had a child since they last worked together. Ian smiled politely as she went on. When she begged his pardon to run and grab photos of the baby from her purse, Ian maintained his labored smile while mumbling to me, "Oh joy." Still, despite, or perhaps due to, a bitter divorce earlier in life, he truly loved his subsequent wife of many years. And while maintaining the most serious, businesslike comportment for the most part, Ian could be absolutely charming.

Cold and irascible at one moment, Ian could quickly switch gears while hosting important contacts with grace and pay attention to their every need. His deadpan quips reflected a quick and imaginative wit, and a somewhat dark sense of humor made it all the funnier coming from him. But he was convincingly and often genuinely empathetic. Ian grieved for comrades lost, believed in second chances for those whose professional problems resulted from family issues or substance abuse, and would come practically to tears reflecting on the passing of his beloved dog. Of course, he did love dogs a lot more than people, even my own with whom he would not tire of playing catch during one inspection visit to my location in the field.

Where Ian commanded my greatest respect for years, however, was in his unmatched ability to blend those traits with a chess master's skill to see several moves ahead and the consequences down the road of any actions taken. More impressive still, Ian could apply these skills both to developing an individual target and, likewise programmatically on a strategic level, choreographing and conducting a campaign.

Ian was also the hardest worker I ever met, a true workaholic who unfortunately demanded the same of his subordinates. "Row well and live," he often said, drawing on the scene from Ben Hur's service in the slave galley of a Roman man-of-war. He was the "Soup Nazi" of case officers, if I may be indulged a *Seinfeld* reference. But underneath, very, very far underneath, his many layers of apparent outward detachment and disdain for people was a well-concealed compassion and humanity. Those traits guided him well in his earlier years, when I first came into his orbit. I could joke around with Ian and offer alternative points of view, even argue. And in practice, though not obvious to the masses, I knew that Ian took care of people, helped those who had fallen on hard times, and was forgiving, even of human frailty. He was every bit as unpleasant and intimidating as depicted, mind you, but was, in reality, fair.

Over the years, though, Ian's dark side increasingly possessed him. He never had to raise his voice to inflict punishment or instill fear. Rather, his aura and sharp, pointed, profanity-laced jibes did the work. None of this, of course, made him particularly beloved among his workforce. Ian's management style grew ever more harsh, divisive, and punitive, worsening as his operational successes mounted.

Famous for having proclaimed that his "carrot was the absence of a stick," Ian relied on an ever smaller circle of sycophantic followers who scrupulously tacked with the wind to tell him only that which they knew he wanted to hear. As those camp followers reaped promotions and influence, those who failed to act in kind, myself included, were cast aside. Pariahs, dead to him, we no longer merited trust or time. More dangerously for the Agency, rarely would any of his chief lieutenants dare offer him bad news or alternative points of view. Senior managers self-censored owing to the toxic environment of public evisceration, his morning staff meeting best compared to the games of the Roman Colosseum, with no one wishing to be the day's Christian thrown to the lions.

Ian is the poster child for how power corrupted many of the Agency's senior leaders post-9/11. Someone for whom I had the greatest respect and admiration, Ian was a tremendous operations officer, truly brilliant when at his best, and his personal comportment aside, a role model. I liked him as a person, despite his characteristic shortcomings, because he was fundamentally fair, compassionate, and inclusive while coming up the ranks. I could even forgive much of his manner, his bark, because I knew in truth, he would do the right thing for both the mission and our people.

As he reveled in his own greatness, and embraced his own Captain Bligh aura, Ian closed himself off to data, recommendations, and options. This included input that might have saved lives, including officers under his command, such as those lost December 30, 2009, at Forward Operating Base Chapman where seven of my comrades were killed when the jihadist Jordanian doctor Humam Khalil Abu-Mulal al-Balawi, aka Abu Dujana, detonated a suicide vest. Abu Dujana was the case of an opportunity too good to be true—and indeed it was. Arrested by the Jordanians who subsequently believed they had turned him into a double agent against his al-Qa'ida associates, Abu Dujana traveled to Pakistan and Afghanistan from where he claimed access to a celebrity list of al-Qa'ida members and those from their associated local terrorist partner groups. The access, it turns out, was true, but his agenda was not.

The attack is a cautionary tale taught to every CIA officer of how not to handle a counterterrorism agent or any high-risk operation. The promise of Abu Dujana's access and association was so promising it blinded the ambitious CIA managers who were removed from the direct hazards of the effort. Ian and CIA field managers in Jordan and Afghanistan rationalized, or blatantly dismissed, a long list of signs that even the most junior case officers would have recognized as warnings. Indeed, some officers did give such warnings or otherwise expressed reservations, but their input was dismissed and their dissent muzzled, one of whom bore the ultimate price, others whose careers were derailed.

Making matters worse, operational management of the meeting with Abu Dujana at Forward Operating Base Chapman was delegated to an excellent targeting officer, but one without operational training or field experience, who likewise dismissed the input of veterans. This officer, too, would perish, along with some of the very officers who questioned the security arrangements. For Ian, who was ultimately responsible, there were no consequences, only continued professional advancement and personal insulation from the input of divergent voices. Our own falling out was fueled by a meeting some weeks after the event when I presumed he would be leaving his position for other duties, if not retirement.

Ian's choices were increasingly decided by what he believed best show-cased his own brilliance. His judgment compromised by what served his own best professional interests, Ian saw himself as infallible. Few would dare challenge him, certainly not those working for him, but increasingly as well those to whom he reported. Ian became like the obsessed James Jesus Angleton of his own time. Angleton, the CIA's one-time counter-intelligence master, saw enemies everywhere, mostly where they were not, undermining a slew of operational opportunities on which we failed to act.

Ian's legend is now so institutionalized across the greater USIC, and former DCIA Gina Haspel having been so far in his pocket, that Ian continues to influence our course ahead in an extremely combustible part of the world. Subordinates confide in one another at the damage they believe he brings, but out of self-preservation they will neither push back nor dare risk his wrath by usurping the chain of command. It wouldn't help anyway, as they know he remained among Gina Haspel's favorites. It was Ian who gave her the high visibility jobs that helped catapult the former DCIA from the somewhat limited professional obscurity in which she began. Whether or not Ian remains or is moved aside with the new administration and arrival of DCIA William Burns will be telling regarding the sincerity of the new leadership in turning a new leaf.

"TYPICAL" CASE OFFICERS

In full disclosure, while being a case officer is incredibly cool, I am not a cool guy. Not long after retirement, I shared with one of my daughters a photo taken with then DCIA Gina Haspel. No doubt regretting it now, the DCIA shook my hand and observed, "What are we going to do without you?" My daughter, being sweet, supportive, and perhaps inordinately enamored with my life's work, commented how both that comment and the picture were "cool." "Not really," I explained, noting how the DCIA took a photo with all retirees, if they so chose, and had to say something nice, even to me. "Take the victory," she responded, "it's pretty cool."

When most of the world thinks of spies, they romantically picture James Bond, assume we all spend inordinate amounts of time in casinos with beautiful women, and kill people with reckless abandon, a Walther PPK in one hand, a shaken, not stirred martini in the other. But being a beacon for attention runs counter to the clandestine requirements of operating in the shadows in which case officers must operate. Though for a short time in the field, a Walther PPK was available to us as a backup weapon kept in ankle holsters should we be disarmed from our larger Browning semiautomatics! Oh, and by the way, we are not agents, like the FBI's special agents. We are officers, and only a fraction are actually case officers. Our agents are those people we recruit, variously among foreign governments, militaries, and terrorist organizations, and from whom we obtain, acquire, or steal the secrets our country needs to keep it safe.

Nowadays analysts, CMOs, SOOs, targeters, and other specialists can and occasionally do meet with agents, when security conditions allow. But only case officers can recruit, and they are ultimately responsible for the operation's secure management. Of all the CIA's occupational tracks, only case officers are required to spend at least 50 percent of their careers in the foreign field. CIA is, after all, a foreign intelligence service.

Case officers, like everyday people, come in all sizes, shapes, genders, and so forth. Tuxedos, white dinner jackets, and silk evening gowns are sadly not standard issue upon graduation from the Farm. But if pressed, I'd dispel the notion of how a typical spy appears or behaves. They generally don't resemble the actors who portrayed James Bond, and the better ones, while perhaps slick, do not act like used car salesmen. In fact, the best case officers I knew were somewhat reserved at their core, but could be the life of the party if and when the need arose. As painful and uncomfortable it might be for a more introverted person to turn it up a few notches, it's often easier for them to turn it up than for a naturally extroverted person to reign it in. That is, the best case officers are more along the lines of Smiley than Bond.

A case officer's job is to earn trust and respect. That comes from listening, assessing, and manipulating. The extreme extrovert needs to remain the center of attention and can't abide being quiet. If you want to earn someone's favor, you must show sincere interest in them. You must make them feel heard and appreciated. People yearn for the validation of another's interest. A successful case officer is *interested* and *interesting*. The life of the party might be entertaining, but who would place their lives in the hands of a court jester?

It's the little things that make the difference, and it's often as simple as good manners and basic civilities. Thank you notes, texts, or calls after a meeting, waiting to eat if your food arrives first, are all basic actions that go a long way toward making a good impression. Asking after someone's family or simply how their day is going before getting down to business has impact. I know of many agents whose willingness to cross the line came because someone finally showed interest, appreciated them, and appeared to share their beliefs.

People need reasons to betray their country, their job, friends, and even their family. Contrary to popular opinion, people don't spy for money. Rather, money may be the means through which they realize their needs. The case officer identifies those needs. He or she leverages the target's motivations, values, and character traits in presenting a clandestine reporting relationship with the CIA as the way to achieve them.

A case officer needs to be human, and though some of my colleagues may disagree, sincerity is served best with a degree of vulnerability. It breeds familiarity, which in turn facilitates intimacy. Case officers need not divulge genuinely vulnerable aspects of their lives, but enough to allow for the appearance of humanity, which empowers credibility as well as relatability. People are not going to confide in narcissists with a Teflon appearance. They might initially gravitate to a case officer who is entertaining enough to amuse, but they will commit their souls to those case officers who take the time to know them, deliver on their promises, and prioritize keeping them alive.

If pressed for an image of the prototypical case officer, I might disappoint. In fact, I'd personally be more inclined to think about some cross between Peter Falk from the 1979 movie *The In-Laws* and Walter Matthau from the 1980 film *Hopscotch*, rather than Daniel Craig, Roger Moore, or Sean Connery as Bond. Younger generations might be somewhat familiar with Falk from his role in the television series *Columbo*, and Matthau for his famous depiction of Oscar Madison in *The Odd Couple* or Morris Buttermaker in *The Bad News Bears*.

I fondly recall a scene from *The In-Laws* in which Peter Falk is sitting in a diner having a cup of coffee with a New York City cabbie. They're waiting for Falk's future in-law, played by Alan Arkin, an unwitting, innocent, and law-abiding dentist who believes Falk to be nothing more sinister than a copy machine salesman. Falk has cajoled Arkin into retrieving something important from his office that his "business competition" is trying to get their hands on, and as such is presently staking out the workplace. Arkin eventually accepts the pretext and agrees, only to find not business competitors waiting, but mobsters who intend to collect on money Falk owes them for stealing something as part of his rogue, undercover CIA operation.

While waiting for Arkin to return, the cabbie asks Falk what he does for a living. Falk confesses matter-of-factly to the rather astonished cabbie that he works for the CIA. Incredulously looking at the somewhat diminutive and disheveled Falk up and down, the cabbie sarcastically observes, "I can't believe you work for the CIA." To which Falk replies deadpan, "Why not?" The cabbie explains with a cynical laugh as he regards the physically unimposing Falk, "I don't know, I thought like, James Bond?" "Oh no," Falk corrects him, "they all look like me. I'm the classic agency type: muscular, low to the ground, compact. Are you interested in joining?" Falk asks. "I tell you, the benefits are fantastic," Falk goes on. "The trick is not to get killed. That's really the key to the benefits program."

In *Hopscotch*, Matthau plays Miles Kendig, a wisecracking, nonconformist curmudgeon serving as chief of station in what was then West Germany, a large and significant CIA command. He quickly runs afoul of his newly arrived Headquarters boss, "Meyerson," played by Ned Beatty. Matthau angers Meyerson by choosing not to arrest a senior Russia spymaster caught in the act of stealing Western secrets. We are given to believe that Meyerson hails from the CIA's covert action side, depicted in the movie as "the office of dirty tricks, assassinations," and so forth. Matthau, having been recalled, sits in Meyerson's Headquarters office, the walls adorned with photos of Meyerson in the company of the likes of Richard Nixon and John Wayne. Shooting trophies and glamour shots of Meyerson abound as do images of the various game he has hunted. This movie was made, after all, in the 1970s, and it's how the Agency was viewed in Watergate's aftermath. When scolded for having let the Russian go, Matthau defends his decision. Having plugged the leaks, he explains his choice to leave the Russian spymaster in place rather than waste months laboring to identify and understand the workings of whomever would succeed him.

Meyerson flies off in a rage, relieves Matthau of his command, and reassigns him to a lowly job until he is retirement eligible. Meyerson's punishment is designed to emasculate Matthau and put him in his place. But Matthau has other ideas and goes on the lam. Pursuing his own revenge, Matthau begins writing a book exposing the sinister and diabolical plots Meyerson has hatched, mailing it one chapter at a time not only to the CIA, but to every major intelligence service around the globe, friend and foe alike. Not merely a revelation of past and future operations, Meyerson sees the book as a personal attack. Taking the bait, Meyerson sets out in chase aiming to "terminate" Matthau, who lures his blood-thirsty adversary and a few dim-witted henchmen into one fiasco after another, always staying several steps ahead. Matthau's character never carries a gun or throws a punch. Rather, he is armed with intelligence, wit, self-deprecating humor, and charm, which, despite lacking the requisite James Bond physique, likewise wins him the girl.

Falk and Matthau play characters who would have made Sun Tzu and Machiavelli proud of how they leveraged their own strengths, and their adversaries' weaknesses. Both are depicted as rather human, preoccupied with a family or love interest, while balancing life with their undercover world. Though calculated and ruthless to a degree, they both evince vulnerability, communicate with sincerity, and find common values to which they relate with their accomplices, adversaries, and targets alike. Moreover, they're each decidedly unpretentious and exceedingly polite. Their focus is on collecting intelligence and disrupting threats through capers that require ingenuity, intelligence, and guile—having fun while at it.

In fact, the manner in which a case officer thinks and acts is better depicted by Peter Dinklage's portrayal of Tyrion Lannister in the HBO television series *Game of Thrones* than it is in films featuring James Bond or Jason Bourne. While Tyrion would certainly be limited on the street in clandestine operations, he thinks quickly on his feet, makes sound choices under the most stressful of circumstances, and knows how to manipulate people and leverage their motivations, hopes, and fears. Tyrion is a risk-taker who under it all has the best intentions and lives in a world of threats in which all of his foes command superior physical might. Whether trying to "get off the X" in self-preservation or direct a strategic campaign, he depends on wits and instinct, schemes, and plots. He shows no fear even at the point of death, relying on brain over brawn to defeat his enemies, and assist the more worthy. Like case officers, he has material resources at hand to incentivize, tempt, and control; is a pragmatist; and never breaks a promise. Also like case officers, "a Lannister always pays their debts."

Still, perhaps the greatest catch-22 in examining "typical case officers" is that those most successful in the operational trenches tend to be non-conformists. A good case officer needs to be an adherent of the policies and legal rules, but the most successful eschew convention. Often to their professional detriment, passion can drive them to place mission above pleasing those with influence over their advancement.

Balance can be hard to find in espionage's murky world of values and ethics. I've seen those who get it right. Good case officers are those who likewise lead with integrity. They are those who understand where compromise is required, not for themselves, but for the greater mission equities. But their numbers are small, as the CIA's leadership values conformists and team players over operational success. It rewards, or punishes, accordingly.

INTELLIGENCE WARS

S un Tzu wrote more than two millennia ago, roughly translated, that if you know your enemy, and know yourself, you should never be afraid to fight. However interpreted, the premise suggests that successful campaigns rely heavily on intelligence, deception, and choosing the time and place of battle. In fact, since 9/11, much has been said about the fight against terrorism being an Intelligence War. Words have meaning, whether to influence, inform, educate, or, as commonly practiced in espionage, manipulate. Just thinking about how Americans now think of the term *spy* is what led me to reflect on what that change meant in the first place. And extending that thinking to how the Intelligence War is being defined became equally intriguing.

While perhaps an occupational hazard after a career in the CIA's Clandestine Service, I interpret the spirit of an Intelligence War as a covert, low-intensity conflict. Practically speaking, all wars are intelligence wars of a sort. So, more precisely, the layman operative's definition of an Intelligence War is one in which our strategy is founded upon understanding, manipulating, and deceiving the enemy to leverage our strengths and exploit their weakness. It's a premise that I suspect Sun Tzu would enthusiastically support. But you don't have to be Sun Tzu to recognize that such fundamentals are key to any campaign's success, be it a hot war, cold, or in this case, something rather in between.

Napoleonic military tactics to identify and exploit the gaps in a foe's defenses, even one of superior strength, was similarly a watershed in the way a war fighter uses intelligence versus overwhelming force and firepower. Militaries since at least those Napoleonic days have employed cavalry to probe enemy defenses. Testing enemy defenses as they did provided intelligence as well as trip wires to warn of attacks, and offered a mobile, quick reaction element. And Frederick the Great's caution, to defend everything means to defend nothing, was a further homage to the vital role of intelligence: to focus on the strategic and to align resources to mission. Of course Frederick, a Prussian king in the mid-1700s, didn't have to worry about social media and constant opinion polls. This worry accounts perhaps for why, when it comes to fighting terrorism, our leaders choose to defend everything, albeit at significant costs, both materially and to our American way of life.

And what of Machiavelli? You really can't talk about espionage and all of its plotting and manipulation without pondering some of what he preached. Among other things, he wrote of keeping friends close, but enemies closer. We also attribute to him, whether or not he actually meant it, the quote about the ends justifying the means. What Machiavelli actually said, found in Chapter XVIII of *The Prince*, was that "men judge generally more by the eye than by the hand, because it belongs to everybody to see you, to few to come in touch with you."

While Machiavelli was addressing ethics and morality in leaders acquiring and maintaining power by any means, framed again in the case officer's optic, there are teaching points. In espionage, this has to do with control, leverage, and manipulation, three of the trade's cornerstones. All three call for nuance, stealth, insight, and deception. Regardless, from the optic of a spy, even one in the service of a noble and worthy cause, I'd necessarily disagree that the ends always justify the means. Were the means so ghastly as to actually create a different and unintended long-term end, then your victory might be short term. Such an argument is made concerning our military assistance to Islamic extremists battling the Soviet Union during their 1979–1989 invasion of Afghanistan. A worthy end, perhaps, but the means brought consequences that changed the world as we knew it. But as a spy, I accept

that the ends could call for drastic measures. The United States' use of
nuclear weapons against Japan to spare many millions of American and
Japanese lives in ending World War II to my mind merited the means
employed, at least at the time.

The world's second oldest profession began with spies and informants
whose placement in, or recruitment among, adversaries revealed the
opponent's plans, intentions, and capabilities. Fundamentally, if information is power, then intelligence is a unique variety of knowledge that is
critical to any competition. Defined as such, intelligence is the collection
and secure application of secrets concerning your adversary that your
adversary is unaware you command. For intelligence to be uniquely valuable to one competitor or another, the key is secrecy in its collection as
well as the protection of your own. Simplified, it's running a con where
the marks never know they were had.

Reflecting on whether or not America was truly fighting terrorism as an
Intelligence War requires an appreciation of what that should mean, and
a greater understanding of the tools, options, and decision points. Like so
much of life, the truth rests less on what we say, more on what we do, and
in the end, how it is perceived. Former President Trump's October 2018
rollout of the National Strategy for Counterterrorism is, on paper, consistent with the stated policies of his post-9/11 predecessors. It suggests a
holistic approach that maintains the imperative for preemptive action to
address both near- and long-term threats. The reality in prosecuting any
war depends, however, on the risk tolerance of the policy makers, and the
resiliency and risk indulgence of the governed. The equation is somewhat
more complex and nuanced when it comes to terrorism.

Some thoughtful writers argue that terrorism does not warrant the
blood and treasure we invest today. Others contend more bluntly that
the threat does not merit "forever wars." And it is often the emotional
factor that fuels political sentiments, which drives policy and action. The
weakness to some of these arguments is the suggestion of a zero-sum gain
considered within a rather black-and-white perspective. Greater acceptance of balance and the long game would achieve far greater results.

Terrorism does not go away when you choose to ignore it. As we are sadly cursed to realize from Afghanistan, there are no peace deals to be made or withdrawals to be negotiated with terrorists. I'm not referring to the Taliban, which I consider an insurgency rather than a terrorist organization, but the terrorist organizations to which they provide support and safe harbor, such as al-Qa'ida. Burying our heads in the sand will not insulate us from the threat from al-Qa'ida, the Islamic State, and those organizations whose charter is the violent destruction of all the apostate enemies of their interpretation of Islam.

But we must see all threats in the bigger picture and with appropriate balance when it comes to blood and treasure. Whereas Russia, China, and perhaps now even North Korea and Iran are potential threats to our country's existence, terrorism is not. But while incapable of physically destroying America, terrorism touches each of us daily and emotionally. One need only visit a federal facility or go to an airport for this reality to be driven home, or see the fear in children and their parents when practicing school lockdown drills.

We must address terrorism appropriately given its impact on our way of life, and the reality of the world our children and grandchildren inherit compared to that of past generations. But I can't debate the fact our response to terrorism was so overwhelming in focus and resource alignment as to have possibly done more harm than good. Might we have actually compromised some of the very freedoms and civil liberties that terrorists sought to undermine? And was a strategy that defaulted to hard power and death making us safer, or was it creating more enemies by ignoring and often fueling the very conditions that inculcated new terrorists?

While the pressure we applied abroad through America's preemptive strategy certainly disrupted a great many evolving threats, it also caused a decentralization of groups like al-Qa'ida that increasingly delegated management and responsibility to preserve operational security. Moreover, it led to the birth of new organizations such as al-Qa'ida's numerous partner groups and regional affiliates across the Middle East, South Asia, and Africa, as well as the likes of the Islamic State. In turn, we found ourselves often in the dark contending with lone wolves in the homeland inspired by foreign terrorist organizations that, owing to our pressure, were now operating from deeper underground.

Still, just as quickly abandoning all such efforts would be even worse. Rather, a more thoughtful balance of hard and soft power, and likewise a holistic use of American tools of power, is better than either in the extreme. Counterterrorism is won in the long game, in phases, and incrementally, with a continued willingness to accept some degree of sacrifice, and likewise, enduring some amount of risk. Just as we've dedicated perpetual efforts in safeguarding the Korean Peninsula, NATO, and nuclear deterrence, so too must we maintain the appropriately necessary investment of blood and treasure in counterterrorism.

That's where the concept of an Intelligence War has merit, when applied appropriately. Necessity being the mother of invention, after 9/11, as I've mentioned, the CIA was able to move faster than the US military in placing a rather small band of Agency officers on the ground in Afghanistan. CIA teams leveraged proxy forces, good intelligence, existing personal relationships, audacity, and bags and bags of money. They used local forces to drive the Taliban from power and chase al-Qa'ida largely across the border into Pakistan's Northwest Frontier Province and Federally Administered Tribal Areas.

Beyond our reach otherwise, or even that of the Pakistan government, the CIA's innovation, agility, and special authorities enabled the CIA as the pointy end of America's spear to continue pursuit of al-Qa'ida deep into Pakistan where the US military could not operate. In the first few years after 9/11, CIA acquired intelligence that enabled a then cooperative Pakistani liaison partner, the Inter-Services Intelligence Directorate (ISI), to capture al-Qa'ida operatives in the settled areas of Karachi, Peshawar, Lahore, Rawalpindi, and elsewhere. Those al-Qa'ida operatives beyond ISI's reach in the settled areas, or those they increasingly became unwilling to pursue, were targeted through other special capabilities and covert action authorities in which US involvement was denied.

The Taliban and Haqqani Taliban Network (HQN) were untouchables from the get-go with Pakistan's ISI. The HQN operates under the Taliban's umbrella. Its current leader, Sirajuddin Haqqani, is likewise one of the Taliban's two overall deputies. HQN's leadership operates from the sanctuary of Pakistani territory, according to United States sanctions and United Nations Security Council assessments. The HQN is a distinct Sunni Islamist militant organization with its own particular interests, largely criminal, and it historically operates on both sides of Afghanistan's eastern border with Pakistan. The HQN was founded by Sirajuddin's now deceased father, Jalaluddin Haqqani, who was known for his prominent role in resisting the Soviet Union's 1979–1989 occupation of Afghanistan during which he worked closely with the US. Meanwhile, he likewise developed lasting relationships and bonds of obligation with those who would later form al-Qa'ida's core.

It should therefore have come as no surprise when al-Qa'ida operatives collocated or in close contact with Taliban and HQN notables within Pakistan often mysteriously went to ground shortly after we shared our locational information with ISI. Al-Qa'ida was a common adversary, but US and Pakistani interests in Afghanistan became increasingly divergent within the first year following the Taliban's fall. So, in turn, given ISI's inability in some cases and unwillingness in others to address threats to US interests, we developed an incredibly effective hammer. A capability that was both a blessing, and a curse.

Espionage at its core is a cerebral exercise. Being smarter and agile is more unique than just being another agency with soldiers, guns, and bombs. The spirit was to serve as a balance and complement to the military, which exists to create hammers and deal with nails. If an Intelligence War is about being surgical, that capability is designed for use in proper balance. But its use is seductive. The CIA's capabilities offered tangible, immediate gratification to presidential administrations that were throwing vast resources at counterterrorism, were hungry for success, and were desperate they not bear responsibility for another 9/11 type event. Overlooked were the second- and third-order consequences that a broader, more strategic vision informed by intelligence should have provided.

FINDING AND MAKING CASE OFFICERS

O ne doesn't get people to share state secrets without first tunneling through the heart and soul. There are pure mercenaries among the ranks of agents, but even they require thorough understanding in order for a case officer to securely manage and effectively evaluate their information. The case officer's tool is manipulation. A foul sounding word, perhaps, but more revealing, reliable, and humane than any alternative. When done right, and dare I say even ethically, our agents become far more than a mark, a codename, or a paycheck. We case officers become invested in them, prioritize their needs and security, and know them like no one else. We defend them when called for, but are likewise the first to highlight their transgressions.

A case officer has a responsibility to the agent that is not entirely reciprocal. Like a military troop leader, while committed to doing all that can be done for their agent's safety, the case officer must still be prepared to put them in harm's way to serve a vital mission. Unlike a military troop leader, however, case officers can never fully trust their agents, the obligation not entirely working both ways. Whatever secrecy agreement agents sign to work with CIA, and despite how legitimate their bond might be with the case officer, there is no overarching tie of faith, country, or family that binds them to us. Although some agents truly see themselves as "members of the team" and act accordingly, for most the motivations to cooperate and risk their lives are situational. All of which is why deft exercise of manipulation is key, and why so few particularly excel in the art.

If we have vetted the trainees right, those we hire are already well acquainted with manipulation. Our trick is finding those who do it for the right reasons, with a conscience, and who can walk that fine line between right and wrong. And given the varieties of people with whom we deal, the case officer must remain above temptation themselves, as well as possess inherently sound judgment and freedom from cultural bias. These character traits and behaviors are unlikely to be learned. Some of our agents are ideologically motivated heroes, others are self-indulgent opportunists, and the rest span a wide cross section of killers, thieves, smugglers, poets, romantics, and traitors with a questionable moral compass, at least from our American optic. Regardless, the case officer works to develop trust so as to understand and leverage their agents' motivations. It can appear to make the line between right and wrong at times thin and blurry.

Case officers don't make extra money, compared to other CIA staff and US government counterparts, are generally promoted slower than analytic, technical, and administrative peers, and have the Agency's highest rates of divorce and substance abuse. While there are medals, it is not at all like the military. Case officers are rarely decorated and many DO managers believe that, short of being wounded in the line of duty, case officers need no medals for just *doing their jobs*. Ironically, leadership tends to pin most of the issued medals on other senior officers, versus those in the trenches.

Military officers, FBI special agents, and law enforcement officials have grand graduation ceremonies at which family members pin on bars or present credentials. Case officers graduating from the Farm have a private ceremony attended by senior CIA and USIC officials only, receive a handshake, and are presented a certificate that they just as quickly return to be held in their personnel file owing to clandestine operational considerations. When I retired in 2019, I finally saw the various commendations and awards I had earned over the years. We wear no uniforms, display no symbols of rank, and have no ribbons. Case officers only have their names and reputations.

Today's case officer candidates share with those of my day all manner of extraordinary credentials and remarkable backgrounds. In fact, we prize such highly elite résumés even more today. Many trainees enthusiastically leave far higher paying jobs in the private sector or successful careers in the armed forces and other parts of the United States government. They are by and large highly motivated patriots who wish to serve—selfless, mission-oriented, and willing to endure hardship to do the right thing. Not all of them will stay that way. And unlike when I began, reflecting the generational trend, new officers do not necessarily come with the expectation of serving in the CIA for a career. When I entered on duty, my type were referred to as career trainees. Today, in the DO, they're Clandestine Service trainees.

While the Agency most genuinely aspires for diversity among those we bring on board, our means of evaluating the candidates is self-limiting. The CIA pursues minorities and gender balance, which is good business, not just the right thing to do. The more it draws from different cultures, ethnic backgrounds, and languages, the stronger the CIA is as a foreign intelligence service. What it could do better, I'd argue, is to be less preoc-cupied with what schools the candidates attended, their grades, privileged suburban upbringings that enabled world travels, and family names, and focus more on character. In full disclosure, this is somewhat self-serving as I was very much the exception to the rule. Sure, everyone likes to say it, but in fact, I can assert without embellishment that there is no way the CIA would have ever looked at me twice today as they did so many years ago. And it is not just on account of my lack of marketable skills.

I was not, what you might call, an overachieving student, and my college, Manhattanville, a perfectly wonderful institution, was not pre-cisely among the Ivy League. I was an inner city Jewish kid from the South Bronx whose own parents never graduated high school. I was someone who, one might say if generous, played the angles simply to graduate both high school and college. More of what one used to refer to euphemistically as a second story man versus a budding Rhodes scholar. My GPA left something to be desired, I was merely and perhaps barely fluent in English, and my only experience outside of New York City was the one airplane trip that took me to Parris Island for twelve weeks to become a Marine.

Lest you think the USMC was my ticket to the CIA, any comparisons to Forrest Gump have everything to do with me being in the right place at the right time, versus heroics like saving my platoon mates in 'Nam. As a Marine Reservist who was trained as a field radio operator, I almost electrocuted myself the first time carrying a PRC 77 radio with the grunts. Something about rain, electricity, and bare skin. Who knew? That same summer, I almost overturned a deuce and a half truck carrying a squad of poor souls from my platoon during a training exercise at Camp Lejeune. A budding James Bond, or The Rock, I certainly was not. But I could spin a yarn and pull a caper with the best of them, and growing up I often had to in order to survive.

There were no CIA websites where you could explore careers, let alone apply for a job. In fact, there was no internet, no cell phones, and no social media. Not that the world was necessarily a simpler place. But in 1984, while one could send the CIA a letter or attend a job fair, it was ironically the CIA that came to me. My hero and college mentor was an extraordinary man who took an interest in me. A former Marine who had fought on Iwo Jima, Professor "Manfred," we'll call him, joined the Foreign Service after World War II and enjoyed a tremendous career, reaching the rank of ambassador. Upon retiring, living not far from Manhattanville and friends with our Political Science department chair, Professor Manfred elected to teach classes on international affairs as an adjunct, something I do myself today at Georgetown University as an ode to his service and mentorship.

He was a tall, imposing, bald, and bespeckled Dutch American man with a booming voice and tremendous presence. A refined, polished gentleman of the old world, sophistication oozed out of his every near-translucent white pore. Each turn of phrase sounded as if it came from a speech he might have given at the United Nations. Honestly, I would have paid money just to listen to this man speak, if I had had any money at the time. He was, I thought then, what I wanted to grow up to be.

Eureka! I thought at last. This barely literate Jewish kid from the South Bronx, somewhat a danger to himself and others as a Marine, would instead become a diplomat! Yes, I told my hero, mentor, and spiritual guide Professor Manfred, I was setting out to take and pass the onerous Foreign Service exam.

Obviously, things didn't quite turn out the way I had planned. To be fair and give Professor Manfred the benefit of the doubt, I sincerely believe he had my best interests at heart in steering me another way. One could argue he was trying to protect the Foreign Service from the likes of me, but I rather embrace the idea that he simply realized the Central Intelligence Agency and I were, as they like to say in today's human resources speak, "a better fit." What I had no way of knowing at the time was that Professor Manfred was in touch with the CIA. He would not share that with me, nor his role in "spotting me," until I had completed my first overseas tour.

Having at least gained the Agency's notice, there still would have been no possibility of getting through their screening had it not been for a veteran case officer who went by the alias "Joe." That he actually saw something in me not otherwise indexed among the many boxes candidates generally must check is in and of itself a credit to his ability to assess people. His willingness to go the extra mile and advocate, however, was a reflection of his code and sense of honor. At the time, under President Reagan and Director Casey, the Agency had far more qualified candidates than positions, though there was indeed a hiring boom. This was all quite clear to me when I made my first of two interviewing trips to Washington, DC. Two, inasmuch as the CIA only brought me up for half of the regular process on the first occasion, since I was clearly a long shot. And my fellow candidates were by and large far better educated, from big name schools, and enjoyed more affluent backgrounds.

"Joe" was a crusty, Africa Division veteran. I say this affectionately, mind you, as he did not exactly exude warmth, compassion, or fellowship at first glance, nor did he look like anything resembling James Bond. In fact, he was medium everything. Neither tall nor short, large nor slim, graying, medium-length blond hair, glasses, and clean-shaven. Peter Falk, right? Not someone who would stand out. Yet Joe would be the first and most important case officer I'd meet. And much about him, from his temperament to his look, but even more importantly his passion and compassion, would rather accurately model for me how I'd seek to comport myself over the ensuing four decades. Joe's job in the recruitment center was to interview and evaluate applicants. His was the first gate through which one had to pass to secure additional interviews, as well as to move on to the medical and security screening.

As I sat in the reception area awaiting my turn, one could not miss the oft sarcastic witticism audible through the closed door as he interviewed other candidates. This did nothing to help my already raised anxiety, but as I heard him call for me, loudly and somewhat cynically annunciating my name, with particular emphasis on my middle initial—Douglas *H.* London—I suddenly felt the freedom of knowing I had nothing to lose. The CIA had not thought enough of me to schedule the full battery of candidate screening, and this guy, I believed, was planning to roast me. Why not make the most of it? After all, this was a paid trip to our nation's capital, my first vacation ever, and I was already planning my sightseeing. My stress dissipated and it was like the curtain going up for a performer.

As it would turn out, Joe's initially acerbic, outward demeanor was, like his alias, a cover. During the ensuing interview, he engaged me deeply not only on my background, but my character. The banter was energizing as I regaled him with stories from my somewhat misspent youth. Having but the vaguest clue of what a CIA case officer really did, but for the few recommended books available in the early 1980s, only a few of which I actually, and only partially, read, I just told him my own story. And as it was, those books offered a rather shallow pool of work by either the disgruntled with axes to grind or journalists whose insights were indirect and often biased. Today, former Agency officers like me have penned more works than can be read in a lifetime, providing candidates the opportunity to be far better prepared than I was.

Joe walked me through a series of international issues to gauge my knowledge, and he contrived operational scenarios to test my critical thinking. He made fun of my "diverse" work experience, which spanned cab driving and the custodial arts to selling shoes and night shifts as a security guard. But he was equally self-deprecating, volunteering tales of his time spent in the African bush and his own comical miscues. Joe was deceptively warm, quick to tease, and likewise receptive to well-intentioned barbs. Oh yes, and then there was his candor. As we approached the end of our time together, Joe's eyes lowered to my paperwork. He looked up and observed, "Generally, I ask candidates interviewing for the Directorate of Operations if they'd be interested in pursuing the analytic track should they not make the cut." In fact, through the door, I indeed had heard him ask as much of the previous candidate.

Joe paused as I raised hopefully in my chair, since at this point I still really had no clue what a case officer did anyway and I badly needed a job. Looking me straight in the eye, Joe continued, "But you're just not smart enough." He let the statement just hang out there for a moment, perhaps gauging my reaction, or just thinking to himself. Shaking his head, Joe continued, "But you're clever, if not out of the mold, and quick on your feet. I bet you'd be willing to serve on the moon even, if we offered?" I nodded enthusiastically, "I'd go today." When I received a call some weeks later to return yet again to Washington to complete the interview process, I knew two things: first, Joe must have gone the extra mile for me, and second, I was getting the job.

I began my Agency career in September 1984. My class of career trainees, or CTs as we were called in the 1980s, were a mix of prospective DO officers, and likewise a select assortment of promising future stars from other Agency directorates. This differs from the way we do things today. Our Clandestine Service trainees, or CSTs, do not mix much with the new officers entering on duty from among other directorates except in specific classes. The CT process offered an opportunity to network and bond with other new hires from across the Agency, facilitating relationships that could span the life of one's career.

Even so, only the case officers and some of the collection management officers (CMOs), then called reports officers, would go through the Field Tradecraft Course, or FTC, after which they would be operationally certified as core collectors. Those variously from the administrative, analytical, and science and technology directorates, would experience the same initial ten-week Agency overview. Perhaps more useful to bonding, they would likewise now join the case officers for SOTC, the Special Operations Training Course.

SOTC was kind of like the Outward Bound program. DO trainees were required to take it before FTC at the time, since experience revealed that once trainees received their operational certification, the motivation for them to run around in the woods and obey orders dropped precipitously. The CIA had long included paramilitary training for its case officers. Though most would never need such skills in those days, the training offered some degree of exposure across generations, since new candidates, unlike their predecessors, largely came with no prior military service. Besides tying us to our Office of Strategic Services (OSS) roots, the CIA believed the value it added came in providing the case officers with experiences that might make them more effective in relating to military targets. More broadly, the new hires from across the directorates had the opportunity to bond under trying conditions.

I had spent just under a year serving various interim training assignments rotating among Headquarters' desks in different geographic area divisions in order to get some "seasoning." Some of the interim assignments were more interesting than others, and I learned a great deal about operations and the Agency's culture. After reading the exploits of those already in the field, I was anxious to move on with training to join them. So it was in the worst of the summer's heat and humidity that a gaggle of us trainees descended on the Farm. Most of us had never served in uniform. Just as many had never even been camping or should have been allowed use of anything sharper than a paper clip. Ahead of us were twelve weeks of military training. We would function as a military platoon, wear camouflage utilities, albeit it with our choice of head gear, and become close friends with the ticks, chiggers, snakes, and various other critters of the US South.

Given the mixed professional backgrounds of our class, and different training cycles, I knew few of my platoon mates. My first mistake came that very first day as we moved through different stations to collect uniforms and gear. Lined up outside a warehouse, our "deuce" gear on the ground at our feet, I noticed a fellow struggling with hooking canteen pouches to his cartridge belt. He was older than me, but that was a low bar, since I was by now twenty-three. He had a receding hairline and was mustached and fit, and I took him for an analyst. Having been a Marine, albeit a weekend warrior, I walked over to lend a hand. "Bill" didn't say a word at first, but glared at me with restrained anger. "Uh, no thanks, I think I can do this myself," Bill replied with no small hint of disdain. My new classmate felt no need to continue speaking or explaining. Chatting instead with a few other familiar comrades, he turned away from me.

Turns out Bill had been a member of the Army's Special Forces, including Delta Force, and was coming on board as a PMOO. My well-intentioned mistake would merit Bill's hostility throughout the course, and thereafter, even after I apologized. But then, Bill's own ego far outsized his talent, and my classmate would not last long at CIA, separating after only a few years. He went into business for himself in the mercenary trade.

Our instructors, on the other hand, were a colorful lot, mostly grizzled old paramilitary veterans from the CIA's Vietnam era. Keep in mind, the last American helicopter took off from the US embassy's roof in Saigon a mere ten years earlier, and as such the conflict and attitudes were still fresh in our instructors' minds. Although this was long before political correctness came into fashion, or the prevalence of Equal Employment Opportunity (EEO) grievances or #MeToo, our instructors were still required to behave with some degree of decorum among the young, suburban, and largely White collective of innocents. For the most part, they were encouraging, compassionate, and at times, hilarious. But they were salty, with their share of slips, or conscious habits, that would not die. The women in the platoon were referred to as Honey, or Darling, and those they did not like, or who were otherwise poor performers, earned affectionate nicknames such as Shit for Brains.

We largely indulged their oft colorful conduct, particularly among one or two instructors whom we feared would kill us in our sleep at the onset of a PTSD flashback, or just for the pure joy. We even made a song about one, "Dale," substituting his name in the ditty "The Freaks Come Out at Night," since he was forever overnighting in the woods hunting. Dale spent most nights that he wasn't working with us in the woods killing, skinning, and then consuming some forest creature or another. Dale was a Native American who had absolutely no sense of humor. Huge, bald, a protruding beer belly, and a menacing face incapable of smiling except perhaps when tasting blood, Dale communicated through scowling. I do believe we counted at least two dozen distinct scowls reflecting various flavors of his discontent. The few words Dale chose, most of which can't be found in the *Merriam-Webster Dictionary*, rather efficiently expressed his utter contempt for each and every one of us.

We all noticed that while Dale and the other instructors would work together, less evident was any sign of their mutual friendship. Dale kept to himself, animated only when leading a class on marksmanship or those skills that had anything to do with killing. Other instructors warned us to keep a bit of distance from Dale. They weren't concerned he might inflict violence upon us, but rather the likelihood that we would come into contact with the ticks and chiggers that covered the army field jacket he always wore while lying in the dirt or sitting in a deer stand.

Our weekly training modules exposed us to small unit land tactics as well as maritime and air operations. There was carryover from the CIA's OSS roots as we practiced insertions into "enemy territory." Be it overland from various aircraft or via small boats from the sea, we learned how to support "partisans." They let us operate the boats, but they were smart enough to keep our hands off the controls of anything in flight. Dangerous enough were our lessons preparing parachutes and dropping "supplies" to our freedom fighters from small planes at low altitude in both daylight and at night. Not every chute would open, regrettably, inasmuch as we were amateur riggers. I can but sadly imagine the number of poor, unsuspecting critters below that certainly paid the ultimate price from some of the cargo we dropped when the parachutes failed to deploy. Those like me who would later go on to airborne training were thankfully not allowed to pack our own chutes.

Medics taught field trauma, employing both classroom and Hollywood-esque, blood-soaked field exercises, at times during "surprise attacks" to instill realism. We were familiarized with the weapons we might encounter from around the world, which allowed us the opportunity to fire grenade launchers, anti-tank weapons, and practically every assault rifle, machine gun, and pistol in existence. A full week was dedicated to explosives and explosive ordnance disposal. While working with those who disarm, or alternatively fabricate, explosive devices, we learned explosive effects and how to recognize booby traps. Our precocious explosive ordnance disposal (EOD) instructors livened up the class with their brand of practical jokes that created some awkward moments for the victimized. More than one of us fell victim to trip wires in our quarters, and getting on the bus or relieving ourselves in the field could set off an explosion of firecrackers. I must confess, I have enough trouble trying to use a urinal when there's a line of folks standing behind me waiting, but that's nothing compared to having explosions going off all about.

Land navigation, among my least favorite modules, included practical tests administered both day and night. And I admit here and now, with apologies to classmates and instructors, that I might have, to put it gently, improvised during our final orienteering exam. We were required, you see, to take a practical exam that required guiding ourselves by map and compass over a course of several waypoints at night through the woods, swamps, and brambles. It was a journey that would take several hours. The goal was to find the correct end point, which for each of us meant locating a particular numbered stake along a trail, and to do so without the aid of flashlight.

We were timed, and given the egos and levels of testosterone, this im-mediately became a competition, particularly among the former military guys in the platoon, especially Bill. The instructors were likewise out in the woods with us, ostensibly to come to our aid should we fall into trouble, but likewise to assure that we didn't cheat. Dale would be out there. Would tonight be when he struck? "Falling into trouble" was more than a metaphor. The greatest risk was indeed tripping and tumbling among the rocks, streams, ditches, and occasional unmarked wells out in those woods. One of my classmates broke a leg falling into one such well that evening, and several others were otherwise banged up. And yes, one classmate had a terrifying encounter with a very territorial wild turkey, the emotional scars from which have yet to heal.

In my case, there was a good reason, several really, that I had not made a career out of the Marine Corps. Far more an inner city kid than the outdoors type, trekking through the pitch-black woods was an activity to be done as fast as possible, not to be enjoyed. Competing to produce a fast time was not my aim. Rather, my goal was survival. Still, my own competitive nature obliged me to chase at least a reasonable time.

I recall faithfully executing my training over the course of the first several waypoints and hours, shooting azimuths, counting paces, and negotiating obstacles. It wasn't pretty. I tripped, rolled down hills, plodded through marshes, and wrestled with the thick, thorny bramble branches. Now at the final leg, I plotted my path and set off. Almost done, I thought, and while clearly not near the front of the pack, I felt safe at being somewhere comfortably in the middle. But there it was before me: a water obstacle. As bodies of water go, it wasn't much more than a pea soup of marsh and muck. But there was no telling how deep it was, or what vast number of poisonous snakes might call it home. I half expected Dale to emerge from the water with a piercing shriek like that from the *Predator* movies. My map showed what should have been a small, easily traversable stream. So much for maps.

I was tired, beat up, bruised, and covered with scratches and God knows what variety of creepy-crawlies. But the spy gods were with me. The map showed a small, unpaved road no more than a hundred meters to my left. It seemed to roughly parallel the last leg of the route all the way to my final stake. Math was also not among my strongest, innate skills, but I tried to calculate the distance from where this road would intersect with the trail along which all of our stakes were placed. Not aiming for perfection, if I could just come within two or three meters of the right stake, and they were each about twenty-five meters apart, I could flank the hazard and still pass the orienteering test. I just had to be sure that none of the prowling instructors, Lord knows certainly not Dale, might discover me.

I found the road and walked it forward, and at a far more carefree and accelerated pace than what I might have negotiated through the swamp and brambles. Pausing on occasion, I scanned the area around me, taking cover to avoid instructors, but ultimately I spotted the trail. I turned back into the woods, so as not to be caught coming down the trail from the road, but close enough to see it. Counting the stakes back until arriving at that which I thought might at least be reasonably close to my target, I emerged from the woods. A waiting instructor checked me in. Ironically, it was the right stake, and by using the road, my time was among the fastest. Bill was astonished, but he maintained his pride by having finished first.

One of the touchstone modules was escape, evasion, survival, and counterinterrogation. It was the week we all knew was coming from the beginning, and we dreaded it. Neither previous graduates nor our instructors would tell us much about what lay in store, nor how or when it would happen. And to be sure, they changed the sequence from class to class. Surprise was key to gauging how we would fare under such simulated stress. But we all knew that, at some point, we were going to be captured and subjected to interrogation.

Our preparation was to develop cover stories for why we, Americans, might be found in a fictional enemy country where we were support-ing partisans fighting against the local government. Now, because this occurred before our actual operational training, during which the use of cover was taught, to say the stories we came up with were weak is generous. But that was the point: to see how we'd fare against professional interrogators without benefit of operational tradecraft instruction.

The exercise began during an impromptu medical exercise. We were rushed to the scene of an attack, finding the ground littered with role players sporting all manner of trauma and injury in blood-soaked clothes. Some of the role players were allowed to be sufficiently lucid to describe their injuries and test our medical knowledge. Others lay unconscious with prosthetics that simulated various wounds ranging from compound fractures, gunshot wounds, and shrapnel with the ensuing types of blood loss we had been taught how to triage in the event of a mass casualty event. We moved about the casualties, triaging, applying combat dressings, and moving the more serious toward casevac stations by use of litters and fireman carries.

Suddenly there was a burst of gunfire. In the distance, armored vehicles raced toward us. We fled, relying on those instructors playing the role of partisans to guide us from the oncoming threat. These partisans led us through the woods and into vehicles that ultimately took us to a part of the reservation none of us had seen. Then again, since we couldn't see where we were going, and the woods all looked the same to me, I could have well been back to the same spot.

As my platoon mates straggled in from different directions, we rallied in the same area and pitched two-man tents. Here we would spend the ensuing days learning survival skills. Dale, along with the other instructors, taught us to set traps for small animals, as well as how to skin and cook our woodland victims. Besides learning how to live off the land, we built shelters and manipulated land features to support survival in various weather conditions. It was actually among the most enjoyable periods of the training. The weather was cooperative and even Dale was laid back—perhaps content with the opportunity to kill, skin, and cook the critters. It was as if we were all on a large family camping trip, developing lasting friendships that many of us would enjoy.

Another night had fallen and everything seemed to be going just fine. At the moment we all began to get comfortable and forget who and where we were, we were awoken in the middle of the night. Our partisan guides ushered us into vans, presumably leading us to the next stop along our rat line to freedom. Not a good sign. We piled in. There wasn't a lot of personal space, something I was used to from where I grew up and having been an enlisted Marine. The windows were blacked out so we couldn't see where we were going. The ride was probably less than thirty minutes. For all we knew, we had driven in circles.

Hurried out of the vans, we were at a cabin in the middle of the woods. Hustled inside, the partisan guides introduced our hosts, ostensibly prostitutes running a local brothel. They would hide us until documents could be provided to facilitate the border crossings we would necessarily undertake to get back home. Another bad sign. Okay, it was inevitable, this is where it was going to happen. Although intellectually we all realized what was going on, and that this was a training exercise, it seemed amazingly real. The next phase was more real still.

Screams, blaring lights, and gunfire rang out from the still night. Heavily armed troops in combat uniforms bust into the cabin, their faces concealed behind balaclavas. Our captors shouted commands, forced us to the ground, and went person to person, placing a hood over each, banding our hands with plastic zip ties. We were dragged into vehicles and brought to the prison.

Now I'm not sure if the Farm's prison was converted from something else or not, but it later became a small museum. Serving at the Farm as I did many years later, seeing that building still gave me chills. It certainly seemed a lot bigger on the inside at the time of my detention than it would from the road all those years later. What was coming accounted for all the many waivers we had been required to sign for the physical contact and limited degree of deprivation to which we'd be subjected over the coming days.

We were separated and processed, told to strip naked, and given sets of khaki shirts and trousers, no underwear. Not coincidentally, the clothes were multiple sizes too large so that the pants would drop to our ankles if not held up. Hoods were placed again over our heads, and we were taken to our individual cells.

The aim was to simulate solitary confinement. Our guards blasted Indian sati music and recordings of babies crying, kept us standing in closet-sized, unlit cells, and rattled the doors and shoved us if we began to drift asleep. We never saw our guards' faces, either being hooded ourselves, or unable to see past their balaclavas when we snuck looks as opportunities arose. But we knew who they were. Our guards came from the local security force that secured the Farm. They were playing roles, and some of them could not conceal their compassion. Others, however, enjoyed the roles way too much and appeared to take great pleasure at the opportunity to torment us and push us around.

Over the course of what was honestly somewhere only between forty-eight and seventy-two hours, we were subjected to various forms of detention, treatment, and interrogation. Our occasional water was served in a small tin cup, the same instrument in which we received the few spoons of cold rice provided to each of us over the duration. That tin cup remains a souvenir I've kept until this very day.

I began in solitary, but would in time be placed in a small common room packed with my fellow inmates. The loudspeakers alternatively blasted propaganda recordings with piercing music. All of us were still hooded and required to stand, and we'd be punished when we tried to communicate with one another. If we misbehaved, or even just for good measure, we might wind up as I did for a spell, in a small cage, about the size of a kennel for a large-breed dog, the bottom lined with gravel.

All of this was an attempt to parallel some of the conditions American POWs experienced in Vietnam, which makes sense given that's what our Vietnam-era instructors knew best. The sleep deprivation was real. It was an education concerning its physical and mental consequences over the course of, at most, seventy-two hours. I vividly recall my hallucinations, at one point seeing things crawling down the walls when I snuck a peek from under my hood. But there were some revealing insights concerning human ingenuity and perseverance. Among almost all of us, we realized how to keep our pants from falling by tying the tails of our long shirts to the belt loops of our trousers. Okay, this seems like a small thing perhaps, but at the time it was an engineering marvel that provided necessary relief! Fortunately, the guards let us get away with it.

Our interrogators were professionals, all active duty US Special Forces interrogators. This was designed to add realism and they were given license to make it so. People act differently under stress. That's why our training, even that in the operational FTC, is designed to push the envelope. This exercise sought to apply physical and psychological pressures, the results from which, despite the limited time, were revealing. Our mission, after all, was protecting secrets, exposure of which could lead to lost lives, in this case, our fictional partisans.

Under no circumstances were we to reveal our true CIA affiliation. Not now, not ever, let alone on this training mission, nor compromise the identities of our colleagues, agents, or allies. Whether you are a CIA case officer or one of its foreign agents, revealing true affiliation when in custody always makes things worse. Always. That was the first lesson, one I saw validated time and again over the course of the ensuing thirty-four-plus years.

Still, we were told that the United States government ultimately wanted us to live. Moreover, we were told to have hope. Always hope. The CIA was never going to give up on us, nor our agents who might succumb to a similar fate. But there was a reality: the expectation that we would all, in time, under torture, reveal what we knew, or at least parts. Our goal was to survive. And in so doing, in the best case, we would force the enemy to peel away at our cover layer by layer before getting to the most sensitive information. The practical goal was to keep us alive, but also to stretch out the time to protect the secrets. This would allow our colleagues to affect damage control while they could, and ultimately secure our release through rescue or deal.

I took all of this very much to heart, as did most of us. Many of the trainees had never been treated roughly or yelled at, let alone physically manhandled and pushed around. Some, like Bill, couldn't help themselves but to appear cool and tough. To the later amusement of some of us, Bill resisted, tried to act the hero, and ultimately, was fictionally executed. Oh Bill.

Another colleague, "Robert," now a political writer of some notoriety who long ago left the Agency, elected to just make himself comfortable. Robert was above it all, and he felt no reason to tolerate the discomfort. He almost immediately made a deal to tell his captors everything he knew in exchange for a piece of bread. Yes, a piece of bread. Robert's taped confessions were played for the rest of us as inducement to cooperate, since he named and identified us all, along with our mission details. Afterward, Robert patted himself on the back for his ingenuity. Not one of us would ever trust Robert again. He lasted but two tours before resigning.

For me, the interrogations were a reprieve, the only somewhat entertaining part of the exercise, and most practically, a mental distraction. It's not that I'm particularly tough or brave. But I grew up in the South Bronx. I had endured enough beatings so as not to be afraid of a little rough treatment. And twelve weeks at Parris Island will accustom anyone to being screamed at and placed under physical and emotional stress by the world's foremost experts in intimidation, a Marine Corps drill instructor.

I was focused on the goal. My goal was not to appear tough and cool to my captors, but rather to create the appearance of being the least important person they should spend their time on. Playing dumb, perhaps not a particular stretch for me, was my aim. My cover story sucked, frankly, but I stuck with it, and I created a persona of a simple driver who was at the wrong place at the wrong time.

What helped was that in comparison to my fellow inmates, my real origin story was far more humble and therefore sincere. That seemed to confuse and frustrate my interrogators. I truly had worked as a cab driver, janitor, and department store clerk, among other less glamorous positions. So I welcomed my turns with the interrogators, since it was at least mentally stimulating, and gave me a sense of purpose.

My interrogators appeared in various roles. I had a Marine, actually a pair of them, who played the tough guys. One pushed me around, made threats, and with his partner, exercised the good cop, bad cop drill. Being Marines, of course, this quickly deteriorated into the bad cop, bad cop drill and I was tossed against the wall for the duration of their time. They were followed by Army Special Forces interrogators, all of whom were ethnically foreign and naturalized, adding to the realism. They alternatively took more sophisticated approaches, trying to disarm me, working at the weakest details of my story. Still, they took the "all is lost anyway so why not talk" approach. That I never divulged any secrets was fine, but I lost marks for not rolling to the next layer of cover, that is, the stories within the stories, within the stories. "Okay, I wasn't *really* doing this, I was actually doing *that*." Frankly, I just never felt I had to go that deep during the brief period of the training exercise, but I understood the learning point.

At the end, we were dramatically rescued in the middle of the night. A commando team played by our instructors stormed the prison. They led us through the halls and grounds, littered with dead role players on the ground, including our interrogators and guards, some of whom I seem to recall being accidentally kicked as we fled, and took us to waiting flatbed trucks. We were all piled in, squeezed next to one another like sardines, asshole to belly button as my Marine drill instructors would have commanded.

Besides the bliss of freedom, thinking back now, my clearest recollection was not of the rescue, but of sitting in the back of that truck. There was the prevailing body odor of this mass of long-unshowered, unfed, and unwatered humanity. Incongruously, a lovely, young female trainee within earshot whispered to a woman beside her, "Fuck, three days without a bra...my tits are killing me!"

The pièce de résistance of SOTC was airborne training. An homage to the CIA's OSS legacy, those of us who volunteered and could pass the required physical fitness test were welcomed to learn how to jump out of airplanes. As opposed to the military's three-week course, we'd do ours in two, but likewise would be able to earn our wings with five successful jumps. Cliché as it sounds, the prospect of jumping out of a perfectly good airplane, and let alone doing so five times, terrified me. But there was no way I would pass up the opportunity.

Not everyone signed up, but most did, including case officers and likewise those from the other directorates. The former military guys, almost all of whom were already airborne qualified, did it purely for fun. We were all in pretty good shape, so the physical fitness test was not a problem. I enjoyed the morning "platoon runs" to cadences that reminded me of my time as a Marine recruit—absent the drill instructor's constant yelling!

Ground week was fun. We scaled and descended from thirty-four-foot towers, practiced unleashing our harnesses when being dragged upon landings, and perfected our parachute landing falls, or PLFs. It was bonding for us as a group. It was also helped me appreciate the particular esprit de corps among airborne troops, a shared mentality regardless of the flag one saluted. Over the years, just having had that experience greatly enhanced my ability to connect with people in uniform, and particularly those from the Special Forces community. It facilitated relationships with allies and counterparts, and more importantly, military targets I pursued from other countries. I never embellished my exploits to suggest I was anything more than a "cherry jumper," as a classmate and former US 82nd Airborne member used to label me. But even those basic wings gave me credibility to sit at the table, and a means with which to connect with those who did such things for a living.

My experience was anything but perfect. We all took nicknames and wrote them out on tape affixed to our helmets. Mine was *Doug Danger*. A few of my old classmates still refer to me as such. Yes, *Doug Danger* was taking to the skies. There was plenty of laughter, but the training was intense and serious.

We went up in "sticks" of four into small, fixed-wing aircraft I am not permitted to identify. These are great planes that in the hands of a capable pilot, and the CIA's pilots are simply exceptional, can handle all manner of weather and accommodate the shortest of runways. Our class already had experience with this particular plane from the training module during which we packed chutes and pushed resupply drops to "partisans" from the aircraft's open hatch. For airborne training, we'd pile into the small plane for our static line jumps.

We'd go through the preparations and commands learned in ground week under our jump master's careful watch. Two at a time would jump, seating ourselves on the lip of the plane's open door, our legs hanging outside the aircraft. Our chutes were standard US military issue, not the neat, commercial type that sport jumpers use. Ours was a bit clumsy to steer, but responsive just the same, and descended rapidly in keeping with military needs.

The week was full of memorable images. I recall watching two oddly matched classmates launch from the plane above as I waited my turn on the ground. My buddy from the 82nd Airborne, a huge tree of a man, was paired with a petite female partner, about half his size, maybe less. They came out one immediately after the other, but my hulkier army friend sped far faster to the ground. He shot out like a missile, his lighter partner floating downward like a feather. So much for physics. Another classmate made the mistake of turning with the wind, as opposed to steering into it. The idea of turning against the wind is to slow oneself down. This helps steering to the precise drop zone target. We watched her accelerate as if fired from a cannon, clear across the landing zone, and directly into the nearby river. Fortunately, she was unharmed.

All in all, we accumulated a 30 percent casualty rate. This included a variety of broken legs, arms, various sprains, and contusions. Not everyone earned their wings. While I left the Farm with wings pinned on my chest, it was, to say the least, an eventful experience.

It was our last day of a fairly windy week that limited our jump windows. We only had this final morning. If the weather didn't improve, they'd call it off, and with it, a chance to earn our wings. We all sat on the runway apron. The wind gushed around us, turning a cold day more bitter still. The wind vibrated rhythmically against the aluminum hanger behind us. The weather was at minimum safety conditions. The instructors, thankfully, decided to chance it so that we'd have our final opportunity.

Now, turns out, I absolutely loved floating to the ground in my parachute. It was everything my 82nd Airborne friend had said it would be.

Beautiful, peaceful, with a certain tingle of pride and bravado that you're doing something God did not intend for humans to do. The experience was enthralling and blissful. Unfortunately, I was less thrilled about the anxiety of waiting my turn. The worst and most unnerving time was being on the plane and waiting to get into the seated position of the open door, and then launching oneself into the air. The long delay on the ground didn't help. I wanted to get into the air. Not from courage, but rather, fear. Once out the plane's door, one might say you're committed!

I had made four successful jumps by this point. Frightened and anxious, this would be it, my fifth jump. My 82nd Airborne buddy, ever prolific with folksy sayings, observed that all I had to do was fall out of the plane just one more time. Little did he know how much I'd take his guidance to heart.

It was time to go. I lined up with my stick and got into the aircraft. As with most fears in my life, my approach has been to confront them as soon as possible rather than delay and agonize. I volunteered to go early, and I absolutely could not wait to jump and just get this all over. My pairing was first up.

I was seated to my partner's right, another petite female trainee from the analytical side of the house. We moved clumsily toward the open door. The jump master checked our equipment and then directed the two of us into our seated positions. I could barely hear his loud commands over the noise of the open door, not to mention my heartbeat, so I carefully watched the hand signals. The cold wind blasted against us from the open door. My hands gripped the end of the deck, waiting to propel myself outward. The jump master kneeled behind us, his slap on our backs would be our signal to jump.

I vaguely made out the landing zone below us, red smoke rising from the spot. The pilot labored to keep the plane from crabbing sideways, owing to the wind, and I looked down as if to reassure myself that there was nothing to fear. My eyes caught my partner bailing out. My slap was nanoseconds away. Readying myself, leaning forward, there it was. I remember yelling out something deemed manly at the time but forget precisely what it was, now so many years later. Though a friend there at the time insists I was screaming all the way down to the ground, and in a less manly fashion than I recall. But out I went. I remember feeling the wind blast my face and the chute snapping me back as it opened.

The leap came with such violence; because of my zeal to get out, I dove clear into the wind and downward before my chute could deploy. My tether snapped and out came my chute. The gratifying sensation of being wrenched backward vibrated through my body. Only something wasn't right. I felt my body snap, but it wasn't the usual sensation of being pulled upright.

I wasn't able to look up at my chute. Rather, I was facing the ground, still inverted. Upside down. As the chute deployed, one of the two risers, the straps you grip that connect your upper body to the chute, had wrapped around my right leg. Several of the thinner, connecting parachute chords were likewise wrapped around my leg. It was rather like being an animal caught in a trap from a tree branch. I was descending to the ground upside down, and head first.

My best guess was being somewhere around 1,000 feet from the ground at this point. There wasn't a great deal of time to sort out this mess. Honestly, the first thing I can remember thinking in this moment was whether or not I had mailed my latest life insurance premium. I reached for the riser, but my own weight was working against me, leaving me no slack with which to slip the thick straps over my boot. Landing head first was not going to end well. As it was, the tangling of the riser and chords prevented the chute from reaching 100 percent inflation, so I was descending at a high rate of speed.

There was only one thing to do: try to get as upright as possible. I reached up for the riser tied around my ankle and began to literally climb my way up it as if it was a rope. Once again, physics was my nemesis; in the course of climbing the riser, it served to further collapse the chute. As the opening compressed, my rapid descent increasingly accelerated.

Doubled over, I worked to pry my leg free. I turned myself right side up while moving the riser slowly past my ankle and over the heel. A quick glance revealed the treetops approaching. Time was running short. I struggled but somehow managed to free myself from the riser, which was the widest of the tangling bands about me. There were simply too many of the more narrow parachute chords to pull over my boot. Still, I pulled myself upright, somewhat at an angle as limited by the tension of the chords in which my leg was wrapped.

All I could now do was go with what I had. Closing the distance to the ground gave me the sense of speeding up. I braced and curled into my PLF position, caught the red lights of an ambulance in the corner of my eye, and then, touchdown.

The impact was severe. I felt myself bounce and then hit the ground again before rolling over and coming to a stop. The sensation was like a gut punch. The wind was knocked out of me, but I never lost consciousness. I have images of people running toward me from the distance, and the ambulance. But I felt fine! In fact, I felt absolutely amazing! Nothing hurt. I released the snaps to free myself from the parachute, came to an immediate stand, and even jumped up and down once or twice to show everyone I was fine! That would prove to have been a mistake.

I wasn't completely fine. Adrenaline is an amazing thing. It would turn out that I suffered a compression fracture to my spine. Within a few minutes, as the adrenaline wore off, I would barely be able to stand, let alone walk. In fact, one of my classmates would have to drive me home the following night, with me laying in the back seat of her car. At the graduation ceremony the following day, held at the hanger, my instructors commemorated my dramatic conclusion in appropriate fashion. Called blood wings, the medallion's bare pins were hammered home into my chest with the heel of the chief instructor's hand. But in my case, the wings were slammed into my chest, upside down!

My 82nd Airborne friend did have one more comforting thought that he shared at our celebration. As my classmates watched my inverted, rapid descent in horror, and I hurtled headfirst toward the ground before them, they decided immediately how they would mark my fateful leap. They would chip in for a memorial of two boots protruding upside down from the point on the ground at which they expected me to impale myself.

It's with sincere regret that I say that we no longer do this sort of training: incarceration, interrogation, and hardship, let alone jumping from a plane. I understand, for one thing, it was expensive, and for another, the Agency worried that a more litigious generation of trainees would include those not inclined to abide the rough treatment and all the potential hazards associated with them. With the government, costs and fear of lawsuits have outsized influence over decisions, and too often at the expense of mission.

Short as it was, many of these experiences paid dividends manyfold over the expense. The counterinterrogation training became a useful tool in my operational quiver, offensively and defensively alike, over the course of my career. Believe me, it's better to first experience having weapons drawn on you in training rather than by a fourteen-year-old Afghan, Yemeni, Somali, or Syrian militant. As for airborne training, in addition to the experience and credentials earned that facilitated my later targeting efforts, I can't imagine anything other than Marine boot camp having instilled in me such self-confidence.

With SOTC behind me, I moved on to the Field Tradecraft Course (FTC). I won't share much detail here from my FTC experience as a student, or years later as an instructor, to preserve the tradecraft we learn and how and where it's taught. As has been well documented elsewhere, we train in a world meant to simulate an overseas posting with fictional countries and issues that parallel reality and align with current events. It's done at a crawl, walk, run pace, with deliberate degrees of pressure and surprises to force trainees to react as they might under real conditions. Trainees need to demonstrate composure amid crisis and develop critical skills such as time management, multitasking, and decision-making based on limited data. Most important of all, trainees prove their integrity by reporting faithfully and avoiding shortcuts for their own convenience.

Although we provide students the theory and mechanical tradecraft skills of running operations, the reality is that success comes from aligning the right basic personality and character traits with experiential learning over time. The graybeards in my day would often look down at us hungry young junior officers, suggesting that we remained trainees until we had at least two tours under our belts. Certification was merely a license to truly learn how to be a case officer. So much of one's success is dependent on instinct, which is indeed experience reinforced, as certainly I found to be the case in espionage.

Humans are fascinating. And a case officer's mission is Human Intelligence. In other words, divining the dearest secrets of our adversaries, and those of the agents we recruit to steal them. Among the many truths I've learned about people over the years of suborning them to espionage is this: if you've done your job right, you're inside their heads. You see the world through their eyes. There's no other way to understand their needs, wants, and values from which you can make a fairly informed analysis of how they will react to given circumstances.

The case officer's goal is to identify a need so important that targets are willing to spy for you and the United States government. They do so because only you and CIA can address their problem. That is what they must believe. But while some like to think that developing a prospective agent is a lot like dating, I'd caution that it's more like trying to have an affair with a person whose spouse is a mentally unbalanced, irrationally jealous, and violent partner who is capable of killing your date and you both.

Cultivating a willingness for someone to incur that sort of risk has to be founded upon a compelling motivation, but, more importantly, accompanied by trust in your discretion, reliability, and professional acumen. They must believe you will keep them safe and also make their risk worth the possible costs. You simply can't teach all of that, since there is never, ever, a 100 percent, surefire solution that fits every individual and their unique emotional, spiritual, and practical drivers.

CASE OFFICERS WHO GO BUMP IN THE NIGHT, AND THE NOT-SO-GOOD DOCTOR

After validating your courage in training from jumping out of planes and surviving interrogation, you'd think just running into someone and starting a conversation would be easy. But for many, including friends I have who have survived death-defying circumstances on the battlefield, making polite conversation that earns a stranger's interest is nothing short of terrifying. You might have found my suggestion counterintuitive that the best case officers aren't necessarily the most outgoing people. This idea is even more of a surprise since case officers must develop capers in which they thrust themselves into character and into the paths of their targets. But being reserved is not the same as being shy. Pressing forth requires great energy for the more reticent, but it's not a talent mutually exclusive to being extroverted. What's required is no small amount of courage, creativity, confidence, and, if you'll forgive the New Yorker in me, chutzpah.

The challenge to recruiting sources is not necessarily finding those with access. Yes, the greater the sensitivity of that which you are trying to steal, the more limited are those with the access. Still, identifying those with access is not the biggest challenge. The real trick is figuring out those who are most likely to cooperate and then finding a clandestine means with which to establish contact in such a way that they are even willing to talk to you before realizing your true intentions. In espionage, it's what we call the bump.

The idea is to engineer the appearance of serendipitous contact during which your elevator pitch must sufficiently engender their interest, create a willingness for them to see you again, and not raise any suspicions concerning your nefarious intent. You can't recruit them if you can't first securely meet them. And you can't always just pick up the phone to arrange contact without compromising operational security before you have even begun.

At the risk of describing it coldly, ultimately, case officers are predators. They hunt in pursuit of their operational game. Their task is to stalk prey from the high grass like a lion, and swoop in unexpected, disarming their target through wit, intellect, and emotional manipulation, rather than force. Unlike the lion, of course, our end is not the target's destruction but rather their cooperation. The bump is the manner in which we hope to bait and switch the target: from what they originally believed was our intent to the ultimate, even better, goal to address their personal, professional, or ideological yearnings.

Hollywood provides any number of examples. But they are most often found in movies concerning criminal con artists who are trying to get in front of their marks. While there are parallels between case officers and con artists, I confess, our cause is more honorable and our intentions more noble. After all, our commitment is to protect, rather than fleece, our targets. But we need a secure means to get our foot in the door and secure their attention to pitch our product, one they'll ultimately be free to buy or not, albeit with a fair degree of manipulation to see it our way.

I honestly can't recall with any certainty just how many times I've done this, nor can I calculate with any accuracy how many agents I have recruited. I say that more to suggest how the process became so instinctive over time, much like breathing, rather than to boast. But it never became any less exciting or satisfying over the years. And as many times as I had done it, I always had anxiety before the curtain would rise, whether venturing out in pursuit of a new agent or clandestinely going out to meet an existing one.

When feasible, it starts with assessing the lead indirectly so as to conceive of an approach that was both sufficiently compelling and outwardly innocent. We call this stage target analysis. Then identifying the right time and place that you might "run across" the target in such a way that minimizes the exposure so as to ultimately facilitate a clandestine relationship with a minimal public trail. The case officer gets one shot. If you can't make a connection in the time it takes to deliver an elevator pitch, or if you come across too creepy and stalkerish, you're done. Bumps don't always work. It's far easier to develop a relationship through introductions or by finding official reasons to have someone receive you. This gives you room to try again. But the nature of the game is clandestinity. Many of our targets lack interest in meeting an American official, and still more realize the risk if they are seen doing so.

Not long after 9/11, I was the chief of base in a highly volatile South Asian city. Al-Qa'ida had long owned this town, given its somewhat sympathetic populace, its central location for travel to and from their sanctuaries, and the availability of commercial and logistical resources. Anyone who was anyone in al-Qa'ida had at one time or another passed through, or operated from, this town, which boasted a deeply capable operational support network that included safe houses, financiers, and logisticians.

Terrorism is a family business. Whether it's the trigger pullers and bomb makers or operational support facilitators, the level of trust necessary for exposure to the inner sanctum is high. Getting in requires credentials and vetting. More often than not, such trust is derived through familial ties. Such was the case with the "Muhammadis," a rather prominent local family. The Muhammadis enjoyed money, which in turn, secured them power and political connections in a tale common among developing countries. At this time, anyone who had wealth invested in real estate. In this regard they were no different from other wealthy real estate owners and business-people. The Muhammadi family elders were, however, extreme Salafists who had long financed political causes and radical madrassas that taught a more activist and ultimately violent brand of Islam.

The Muhammadis were overtly connected to a fiercely Islamist political party that had been gaining increasing prominence locally and nationally, its influence extending into a growing accumulation of municipal and parliamentary seats. Such linkage placed any government efforts to look into the family as political, and thus risky. There would be no cooperation or support from our local foreign government partners, as the Muhammadis were placed off limits.

It's ideal when the US can secure the information or cooperation it needs from foreign partners through official channels. That's where our diplomatic, law enforcement, and military colleagues develop a great deal of the critical information and support that's needed to protect US interests. After all, most Human Intelligence is acquired without the need for espionage and clandestine operations. But when that is no longer an option, as the collector of last resort, in enters the CIA. What our diplomatic, military, and law enforcement colleagues are unable to secure through official channels and overt collection, and what our foreign intelligence partners are likewise unwilling to share, the CIA steals. And in this time period, still fresh after 9/11, the CIA officers in the field enjoyed a great deal of latitude in how to pursue targets and prosecute operations. We had likewise only recently invaded Iraq to search for the weapons of mass destruction that American leaders assured the world were there. It was, after all, the presence of these weapons that had necessitated our intervention, we claimed. As long as our actions were legal and coordinated with stakeholders, local CIA commanders such as myself were entrusted to assess the risk versus gain to conduct our business. We only had to come home for a "mother-may-I" when the calculus reflected a danger that warranted senior Headquarters endorsement.

My base was in a city swimming in al-Qa'ida operatives, as well internecine ethnic and political violence, and significant crime. Together with our local, foreign partners, we had already disrupted a dizzying number of threats and had captured a veritable who's who of senior terrorist operatives and facilitators. And along the way, we ourselves had been the subject of multiple al-Qa'ida attacks that ranged from car bombs and shootings to knife wielding assailants trying to storm our facilities. There was clearly a sense of urgency to disrupt al-Qa'ida's forthcoming homeland threats that were being planned, directed, and facilitated from this area of operations. This sense of urgency was shared by al-Qa'ida, which well understood the threat we posed to them. This is to say, al-Qa'ida was directing complex operations to eliminate their hunters, my base.

The Muhammadis were an interesting family. The patriarch, we'll call him "Saad," was a technical professional by vocation, and he had built a vast enterprise of companies developed with seed money from old family wealth. European educated and rather the playboy in his youth, Saad returned to his native country where he became increasingly pious, politically vocal, and ultimately more radical in his views. Despite having experienced Western life and reveling in it, or perhaps because of it, Saad increasingly set aside more than the required tithe of his growing fortune to militant Islamist causes. In 1979, the jihad to purge the Russian plague from Afghanistan was a natural cause for which he could devote his imagination and his fortune.

Too old to fight, Saad nevertheless immersed himself in the cause, as he would that of Muslims in the Balkans a decade later. Over the course of visits to the front lines, as well as those to the teeming refugee camps in the rear, Saad came to the life-changing realization that only over-whelming violence could shake the stranglehold with which European powers and America gripped the throats of the Muslim umma. More important for this story, he befriended a foreign Arab, whom the CIA will not allow me to name, but who would inspire and guide him over the years to come.

That foreign Arab, whom we'll refer to as the "shaykh," and who would assume a position at the top of al-Qa'ida's leadership, believed Saad's family could do more to support the cause with money and vocational skills than they could as fighters. Saad therefore directed his sons, we'll call them "Mazrour and Tamir," to devote themselves to medicine. As the shaykh had told him, the mujahideen had precious need for skilled physicians among their warriors and families. Saad's sons could do more to support the cause with scalpels than they could with swords.

The Muhammadi boys grew up having been nurtured with their father's fiercely radical philosophy. They learned to hate the West and dehumanize the Christians, Jews, and Muslim apostates among the European-American axis of evil. That said, they appreciated the education and resources such countries offered. Like their father, Mazrour and Tamir attended universities and medical school in Europe. But it was only the younger, Tamir, who dabbled in the more bohemian, scandalous, and philandering lifestyle their father had once sampled.

Given their age difference, the two boys experienced Europe at different times. Mazrour's scornful views of Westerners and their decadent lifestyle was reinforced, whereas Tamir seemed nonplussed. Attending undergraduate studies while his older brother Mazrour completed medical school, Tamir was able to chart an independent approach, or at least, one he could conceal from his more pious older brother. Mazrour returned first from Europe and quickly found himself in Afghanistan working with the shaykh, along with the Egyptian, Saudi, and North African fighters who formed al-Qa'ida's core. Toward the latter part of the war with Russia, Mazrour developed a formidable network and earned the trust of many among those who would advance to al-Qa'ida's key leadership positions.

Finally finished with his education, Tamir came home. His father bankrolled a comfortable private practice for him, arranged his marriage into another prominent, conservative local family, and used his connections to secure Tamir a place at the city's most prominent hospital. Saad was content to allow Tamir this life inasmuch as Mazrour became rather the al-Qa'ida camp follower, variously supporting their efforts in Afghanistan, the Sudan, and the Balkans, before returning to South Asia after 9/11.

Fast forward to post-9/11. CIA reporting regularly placed Mazrour in an ungoverned space within South Asia. A mosaic of uncorroborated intelligence suggested that the Muhammadis continued to facilitate travel, housing, and medical support locally for transiting al-Qa'ida VIPs and their families. Saad was rather old, still lending his support, but unlikely to be doing much on his own. We decided that Tamir might be the weak link. He was our best door for accessing the inner workings of this volatile operational theater.

Vectoring collection on Tamir, the picture that emerged was one of a rather self-indulgent and arrogant narcissist. Credible reflections of the assistance he provided his father in the family's support to al-Qa'ida were evident, but there was little to suggest he was likewise a true believer. At a minimum, regardless of the extent of his own personal role, he was well informed as an estate executor. And Tamir had indeed become a success-ful physician. Rather than devote his remaining energies to the jihadist cause, however, he was chasing money and women. And the women he chased were generally not only married, but his colleagues' wives. Bingo! Tamir appreciated a sense of risk and excitement. Not for a cause, but for ego. Our picture of Tamir was coming into focus.

Tamir liked expensive cars, tailored European suits, and women who would indulge a variety of fetishes. And he spent considerable money on jewelry for his various sexual conquests. As best we could tell, he played the role of pious conservative Muslim husband to his burka-covered wife, but was constantly scheming to satisfy his rather extensive and somewhat kinky sexual urges with new prey. The more conservative the women appeared superficially, the greater his satisfaction from his debauchery. No, cable TV has nothing on espionage.

It seemed his colleagues' wives were not merely convenient targets, given the energy and logistic he oft required to consummate his exploits. He craved the risk, but he also relished the sense of conquest over colleagues he believed to be beneath him. Tamir had sharp elbows and did not work and play well with his fellow surgeons. Not all hardened terrorists are likewise religious zealots. Many crave the power, belonging, or violence. Others come from criminal pasts. I knew of many who abused various substances. But just how committed to the cause might a guy like this be?

The city was a dangerous one and our team relatively small. Our limited footprint in an environment where we were outnumbered by targets and surrounded by threats was the best defense. CIA officers here did not venture away from our operational office or homes with convoys of armored cars and heavily armed escorts as they did in areas of active combat. Instead, we had to conduct our movements in a rather discreet manner, and we had to be mindful of any patterns that might allow our own hunters to identify opportunities to attack us. Our security came not in firepower, but from stealth.

We needed to approach Tamir in a manner where he felt neither threatened nor obligated by the exposure to report the contact to his family or his al-Qa'ida associates. That ruled out paying a cold call—just showing up, that is, at either the hospital or the private practice where he worked. Similarly, calling him or sending him an email was risky. Both required a compelling story and some degree of backstopping, that is, publicly available, verifiable information that would support my adopted persona, neither of which was plentiful. Worse still, it left an electronic trail that could ultimately be discovered.

Inviting Tamir to a US facility, even were we to have a compelling pretext that he'd accept, was a nonstarter. His visit to our well-monitored fortress would not go unnoticed even if he were to keep it to himself, something he'd have no reason to do anyway. We kept an eye on him for a while, building our understanding of his access and what made him tick. Finally we caught a break.

Tamir was going to be a guest speaker at a medical convention sponsored by a local pharmaceutical company at a downtown luxury hotel and conference center. We learned that the company was paying Tamir a generous honorarium for speaking, and no doubt for plugging their product, which he was more than happy to do. Tamir could never have enough cash, especially his own cash, that was distinct from the family's.

There were several upsides to bumping him at the conference. It was a secure location with extensive physical protection: everyone was required to go through metal detectors and submit their bags to X-ray examination. This mitigated against the possibility that anyone, apart from the hotel security, would be armed. Of course, that would likewise extend to me, since absent the ability to show my local diplomatic credentials, I'd be required to pass through security and would need to leave my pistol behind. At least the odds would be even.

It was also unlikely Tamir would be accompanied by any al-Qa'ida associates or thugs. They would stand out in the glare of public exposure, something they wouldn't want. And while we aim to operate in the shadows, I would probably not be the only Westerner in attendance. So my presence, particularly for a medical-related event, might not draw a great deal of suspicion, even if I were to approach Tamir in front of others. I merely had to be "somebody else."

Operating in alias and contrived personas is, after all, a lot of what we do. Still, when we gamed this out as a team, we could not precisely arrive at a consensus on the wisdom of doing it. In fact, I wound up being the one who would make the bump because, as chief, I didn't want my folks assuming a risk that I wouldn't accept myself. They all had rather full plates in our effort to pull off this complex operation, and in my position as chief I was more of a player-coach anyway. Plus the odds were long.

We determined there was limited risk at the bump location itself, the hotel. It's not like Tamir would immediately direct a team at his disposal to do me harm. He might, at worst, let people know, and they would come looking for me later. But that would take time. Regardless if things went well, or poorly, I had escape routes planned after breaking contact, which included associates who would be providing me overwatch and support. I'd be on my way to the safety of the office before the bad guys could react, according to plan, with the overwatch serving as a quick reaction force if things went off the rails. What the team couldn't do was protect me inside the hotel. But we incorporated a system by which if I didn't check in regularly by text with a coded sign of life, we'd throw anonymity to the wind and they'd come into the hotel looking for me.

The greater security threat came if things went well. Arranging a secure follow-on contact would be a great deal dicier. Tamir would know the time and place, and would have had the opportunity to alert his al-Qa'ida associates if he wanted to do me harm. Thinking ahead, we had chosen a few venues with physical features and inherent security strengths to manipulate that could mitigate against a threat, details I am not at liberty to expand so as not to expose operational methodology. Of course, Tamir would have to accept one of our options rather than demand control of the venue to allow us a means to offset the risk he and his terrorist associates posed. Whether or not to execute an operation ultimately comes down to managing risk, and balancing such risks against potential gains.

Tamir was slated to speak for an hour during an afternoon time slot. After the overwatch team provided me with the all-clear sign, I made my way to the area, staging my car outside the hotel's security perimeter but sufficiently close in a secured commercial parking area of a nearby bank. Although the car wasn't registered to me, it was better not to place it where Tamir or his associates could identify the make, model, and tag. This way we could use the same car at a future date.

The hotel was luxurious and huge. It had been developed as a conference center well before the events of 9/11 significantly reduced the flow of outside money and travelers, particularly among Westerners. It was owned by a powerful local family, rather than an international chain, and overcompensated in amenities and service for the lack of a brand name.

With my Caucasian face and tailored navy blue suit, hotel security barely gave me a second look. Although not armed, I somehow managed to set off the metal detector. Alas, I had forgotten to take the pens out of my pocket. The local guard supervisor smiled politely and waved a wand over me. Concerned so as not to offend me, he conducted the check with deference. He held the wand so far away that I could have been concealing a satchel of pipe bombs and he would have missed them. I could have probably even managed to get through with my pistol had I tried. A note to self for later.

The atrium was a bit run-down, but one could feel the Raj-era colonial aura they hoped to emulate. There was beautiful, highly polished teak and rosewood furniture in the reception area and lounge. Rather than paintings, the walls were adorned with lovely, understated symbols like those found on antique Islamic pottery. Highly polished brass ornaments were strategically placed to accent the lovely local fauna that decorated the area.

An army of servers in bow ties and gold vests, smiles painted on their faces, patrolled the floor offering fruit drinks, chai, and snacks to the high-end guests. I had barely taken two steps into the lobby before being descended upon by local staff who offered to be of service. I asked for the location of the conference, and despite declining further assistance I was subsequently escorted to the grand hall.

The concierge reached for the polished brass bars of the two massive white doors, each adorned with gold inlay. As the doors opened, a wave of noise hit me over a background sound of many various conversations going on among the crowd. Rows of variously occupied and empty folding chairs were encircled by stands representing the various hospitals, medical practices, insurance providers, pharmaceutical companies, research labs, and schools that were either sponsors or attendees. The room was busy and noisy. Waves of participants were engaged with the sponsor tables, the men primarily in Western suits, the women in local attire. I had arrived early enough to catch the conference during an interlude just prior to Tamir's presentation. The stage at the center of the room offered a podium with large speakers on either side, and a colorful banner depicted the conference name, dates, and sponsors.

There he was. Tamir was easily recognizable from photos we had found in open source materials of him speaking at events such as this, or those from his family's various charitable organizations. Even from a distance, there was something clearly recognizable about him. Perhaps it was his shiny, Italian suit. Rather compact, but fit, Tamir had a large coif of straight, perfectly combed, jet-black hair held in place by the generous amount of gel that reflected the fluorescent room light. Like many of the local well-to-do, a finely trimmed mustache and beard aged his otherwise rather young-looking face. He was not a bad looking chap, and an impish smile liberally flashed when he made a point. He was talking to a lovely young woman. No surprise. A quick announcement encouraged attendees to return to their seats, as the next speaker would soon begin.

Tamir mounted the three small steps to the stage with a youthful gallop. Sporting a broad grin, but not quite a toothy smile, he greeted his audience. He was an animated speaker, and despite not understanding the language, I easily registered the emotion in his tempo and delivery. Despite that he was addressing some medical procedure and the efficacy of the medications he chose to prescribe to accelerate patient recovery, which not coincidentally were produced by the event's primary sponsor, his presentation was well received. His talk contained premeditated pauses that were greeted with laughs, sighs, and other targeted reactions. I studied him intensely over the hour, occasionally asking those seated next to me what they thought. They described him as an entirely satisfying and charismatic whiz kid of medicine, and undoubtedly a useful salesman for their products.

As Tamir finished his closing remarks and expressed thanks to the audience, I began making my way through the crowd toward the front of the hall where he stood. Moving against traffic as the rest of the audience was headed for the doors or toward the stands that encircled the seats, I scanned the room for threats. Was there anyone who might recognize me? Who were watching me? Was Tamir?

Tamir was engrossed in conversation, and he didn't notice me at first. Speaking with dramatic flair animated by wild hand gestures and laughter, Tamir was shaking hands with some of the organizers and well-wishers. I maneuvered among them to break into his circle. I said nothing at first, just smiling and nodding as the small group chatted. As I was the only White guy in the house, it's not like they didn't notice me. I waited for Tamir to look my way. When he trained his eyes toward me after saying his final thoughts, I took the opportunity the pause afforded to interject:

"Good afternoon; brilliant speech," I offered as Tamir took my extended hand in a rather limp-wristed shake. "My name's David Langdon." Or let's just say that's what I chose to call myself. In this case, I'd selected a name with the same first and last initials of my real name. Given the CIA's concerns, I'm also precluded from sharing other details concerning my persona and its backstopping in these pages. So let's just say that I told him I was with the office with which I was officially associated and from which I worked clandestinely. Painful syntax, I regret, but it's the Agency's requirement.

"Thanks so much for allowing us to be included at this event," I said, as if he had something to do with permitting my presence. He didn't, of course. Rather it was a sentiment designed to flatter, to suggest my obligation to him, and establish familiarity.

Tamir didn't flinch, despite having no inkling of me, since, after all, I was crashing the event. "Oh it was my great pleasure," he said with a smile. "So you speak our language?"

"I'm embarrassed to say I don't," the rest of the small circle was now drifting to other distractions as Tamir and I began to angle ourselves away from departing straphangers, turning directly toward one another. "But some of the people with whom I was sitting were generous enough to translate."

"Why embarrassed, Mr. Langdon?" He asked.

"David, please," I insisted, "and as I'm a guest in your country, I should be equipped to speak the language, but that's just something Americans are unfortunately not particularly good at. Your own English, I must say, is more sophisticated than mine," I smiled.

"You're a superpower after all, David," he chuckled. "You get to speak whatever bloody language you choose!"

We both laughed at his quip as I feigned a degree of embarrassment.

"The chap translating for me said you were a real up and comer in your specialty."

"Yes, that's what they say." Tamir casually mentioned his role at the prestigious hospital with which he was affiliated. Humility was not his strong suit.

"Forgive me for presuming you're as young as you look, but I'm sure as it is in the US, that's quite an achievement." Tamir relished the flattery.

"Who am I to criticize your astute observations," Tamir quipped. "It's rather the feat here as well; I'm quite ahead of my batchmates."

"Did you go to school here?" I asked, already knowing the answer.

"European study [I can't name the city], baccalaureate, medical school and residency. Quite a ride. Fabulous teachers but disappointing facilities. We've some better equipment right here. Perhaps not as efficiently maintained, I'll grant you."

"Given all the brain drain, I applaud your returning here to bring your skills home." I added. "I'm sure the European medical establishment worked hard to lure you to stay."

"Not quite like the States, David," Tamir replied. "European doctors are comfortable, but not swimming in it like their American counterparts." Interestingly, I thought, Tamir passed right over the opportunity to claim social consciousness and went straight to money.

"And what brings a US official to a pharmaceutical conference, might I ask?" Tamir looked me over and grinned. "Because do forgive me if I say that you don't strike me as a physician."

I laughed politely and nodded. "No Tamir, not at all. I handle a lot of the office's admin issues, like outreach for services. In this case, medical support. We don't have our own medical staff, so we rely on the host country. I'm trying to make connections and develop options should any of our people have needs."

Tamir nodded his head, buying my cover story. "Do you make public speaking engagements often?" I asked. "Can't imagine you have a great deal of time given your responsibilities."

"Yes, David, a frightful schedule at that, but at the end of the day, medicine is a business, isn't it?" Tamir qualified while nodding his head, and again flashed his perfect white teeth. "One mustn't settle for vocational proficiency but rather make the most with the opportunities at his disposal."

And with that I was delivered my *conversational gate*, the opportunity to explore what Tamir had volunteered as open for discussion, and a topic I might steer toward my own agenda. "So you're both expert physician and successful entrepreneur, whereas I'm struggling just to do one job right."

Tamir again relished the flattery and rewarded me with another chuckle.

"It seems my great good fortune to have stumbled on to you," I offered.

"Why is that?" Tamir responded curiously.

"Among the needs I'm hoping to meet are local medical specialists. Having a European-trained specialist at our disposal would be quite the coup." I let the thought register as Tamir turned it over in his head. "Knowing how busy you are to do so yourself, though, I'd be grateful just to steal some time to solicit your thoughts on options."

"Happy to help, David."

"Perhaps we can get together for some tea in a few days and discuss it?" I offered, trying to lock in a next meeting.

"As luck would have it, David, I'm going to be ghastly busy the next couple of weeks." I nodded in understanding. "But I've some time now if your American government can spare you?" He smiled. "Come meet my family and we can have tea in my room."

I looked at my watch and realized the team would be getting anxious. I sent a quick text to assure them all was well, and that I was engaged with the target. I accompanied Tamir up the elevator to a room that the pharmaceutical sponsor had provided as part of his fee. It was a suite, and as a treat, Tamir had brought his wife and small children. They took advantage of the pool, facilities, and room service, all bills picked up by the sponsor.

Tamir had no apparent problem being with an American, an official at that. Neither was there any appearance that he sensed me for what I really was. CIA. Neither did he make pretenses about his greed, it simply exuded from him. On the elevator ride, Tamir regaled me with his practice's volume and lucrative fees. Almost as if describing a production line, he sounded more businessman than healer. Tamir laid out the math as a ratio of time, patient numbers, and procedure types with their various costs and resulting earnings. Tamir was rather proud of himself.

Pausing just outside the room door, Tamir asked me to wait outside for a moment. An innocent request, of course, given what I knew independently to be his family's conservative attitudes. Nevertheless, I was equally prepared for any other contingency, such as someone else coming through the door or his placing a call to the wrong people while keeping me there. Barely a minute passed before the door opened and Tamir's toddler son charged me at full speed, grabbing my legs in a hug.

"Take it easy Anwar and be gentle with Uncle," he playfully shouted to his son. Trailing Tamir was his wife, clad from head to toe in burka, not even her eyes visible, a baby in arms, and another boy younger than Anwar.

I knew better than to extend my hand to the wife, and so I bid her polite greeting in the local language, placing my hand to my heart, and giving each of the children a paternal kiss on the forehead. "I'm honored to meet your family, Tamir, that's so very kind of you."

Tamir walked me into the suite, offered a seat around the sitting area's coffee table, and told his wife to order room service to bring up tea and biscuits. We spoke for roughly an hour. I used my cover story to draw Tamir out on his own background, and that of his family. Tamir tensed up at times when my questions exceeded his comfort level, particularly those concerning his older brother.

In this trade, we teach young case officers to recognize reactions as green, yellow, and red lights from their interlocutors. Green is when people are most comfortable. Yellow is when they demonstrate some degree of sensitivity. Red is when you might have burned your bridges. At worst, Tamir was showing yellows, which was fine. It was merely feedback I could use to tinker with in an effort to overcome a closed door he might present. If a case officer isn't getting yellow signals now and again, they're not pushing hard enough.

"Oh, so your brother is also a doctor!" I exclaimed. "Smart family," I smiled, "but so competitive a field, did you try to outdo one another?"

Tamir chuckled. "Yes, he's likewise a doctor, but chose instead to do 'adventure medicine,'" he said in a smug and patronizing manner. Thank God for sibling rivalry, I thought to myself.

"Mazrour is almost always on the road, so he doesn't have the same opportunities as me."

"Making you a better doctor?" I asked teasingly. Tamir smiled, trying to find a humble way to concur.

"And your father's 'philanthropic efforts' must likewise impose a burden on your limited time," I suggested, luring him to address his degree of association with that aspect of his life. This overcame Tamir's initial sensitivity, since it framed the issue around him, clearly his favorite topic.

Tamir spoke obliquely about his father's support during the jihad against the Soviets as he likewise accounted for his brother's charitable medical service to the same cause. He made no mention of al-Qa'ida connections, but he could not help but share further insightful reflections concerning what he knew.

"Dad's a mark too often," Tamir observed, "these bloody chaps coming around time and again looking for handouts. Bloody nuisance."

"But it must make you feel good to help out your countrymen in need?" I asked gently, looking for clarification.

"They're not always our own people, and for every hour I have to spend on such rubbish, I'm losing solid billable patient time."

"Healing you mean?" I flattered.

"Billable healing at that!" Tamir chuckled. "Don't want to be dependent on Dad's money all my life, not that he'll have much left by the time those parasites are done." Some internal alarm bells in him began to ring, telling him that he might have gone too far. Tamir changed the subject. I switched back into innocent chitchat, having made the headway necessary toward establishing rapport, selling my pretext, and securing his interest in future contact.

My problem was his schedule. It precluded locking in a time and place. Still, you want to strike while the iron is hot and steer a future contact toward more discreet venues before your target has time to question the logic of your ruse. As our meeting concluded, Tamir and I exchanged phone numbers and email addresses. Both of mine, of course, were valid but throwaway numbers and internet accounts that were registered in alias and not associated with either me or the local office.

I wish this story ended with me telling you how I ultimately won Tamir over from the dark side and turned him into a productive, clandestine CIA reporter. But one fails more than succeeds in the business of recruiting assets, especially hard targets. Regrettable, too, inasmuch as Tamir's personality, character flaws, and motivations gave me a great deal with which to work. I needed time on target to secure his interest and overcome his suspicions, and soon, before there was more opportunity for him to think and analyze.

After waiting two weeks, I reached out to Tamir via phone, text, and ultimately email. He neither took my calls nor responded to my messages. A few days later, I received a call on the throwaway number I had provided him. My excitement quickly turned to disappointment when the speaker at the other end was, or pretended to be, a senior, older medical staffer from Tamir's hospital. He read me the riot act for illegally trying to privately secure the hospital's medical services through one of its lead specialists and complained how Americans always believed they're entitled to special treatment.

Clearly, I had lost Tamir. But the caller sounded legit, rather than an al-Qa'ida associate. In reality, al-Qa'ida's method would have been to set me up for a meeting at which they would try to kidnap or kill me. At a minimum, al-Qa'ida would have wanted to string things out long enough to gain counterintelligence information on our identities, modus operandi, and possibly other agent identifications. This chap merely chastised me in the Queen's English for poor form.

Roughly a month later, a brief but interesting article appeared in the main local daily newspaper. Attributing the scoop to its inside connections, the article highlighted an al-Qa'ida fatwa calling for the death of a CIA spy working out of a US office named David Langdon. It wasn't my first death threat, and it wouldn't be the last, but at least they didn't properly identify me. David Langdon would simply cease to exist. Tamir must have begun to realize the scam and told someone besides his hospital colleague. My money was on his older brother.

In the end, things did not work out too well for the Muhammadi family. Mazrour met his end in an explosion while collocated with a senior al-Qa'ida official in an ungoverned South Asian sanctuary. Another highly placed al-Qa'ida operative who was caught by a foreign partner further caused the Muhammadis some blowback. During his debriefings, the detainee detailed the support the family had provided him and other

al-Qa'ida members, including safe houses at which he and other operatives had stayed. More important to the locals, the detainee implicated the
Muhammadis in supporting attacks against the local Shi'a community.

This was a boon for the local foreign government intelligence service
that arrested Tamir and his father both. The embarrassing and rather incriminating information did not come from the CIA or FBI, but another
international partner. This provided the political room for the locals to
take advantage of the circumstances. Supporting the country's already
tense ethnic strife and facilitating the destabilizing and costly cycle of
violence often witnessed in this particularly volatile city compromised
Saad's political protection.

Both Saad and Tamir were held and questioned, but neither for long,
the two being treated relatively gently by local standards. The price for
their release was Saad's political cooperation, essentially refraining from
criticizing the army, which in fact ruled the country, and accommodating
their demands. Whatever Saad or Tamir shared on al-Qa'ida with the
locals, the CIA never received. Our local foreign government intelligence
partners claimed they provided nothing of value.

Tamir did not fare quite so well. Trying to recover from the consequences of his arrest, which likewise exposed his bad personal behavior
that our local foreign partner was less averse to leveraging than we had
been, he tried to relocate to another Middle Eastern country. Getting a
tip alerting us to his travel, we advised our local foreign partners in this
country, providing them a full dossier on Tamir and the family's al-Qa'ida
connections. Tamir was arrested upon landing. As you might imagine,
Tamir was not cut out for difficult conditions and did not do well in jail.
Detained for several years, over the course of which he was exhaustively
debriefed on his knowledge of al-Qa'ida personnel and activities, Tamir
gave away the details we sought.

By the time we had this information, it mostly provided historical value
as the Muhammadis had by then suspended their active cooperation with
al-Qa'ida following Saad's arrest, which was among the concessions the
patriarch was forced to make in order to secure his release and keep the

family fortune. Information that comes from a defector is useful, but the goal is to keep an agent in place, playing an active role in that organization so we can learn about their future plans, intentions, and capabilities. Al-Qa'ida lost a valuable source of support, but better for us to have kept the spigot open but under our control, with the CIA monitoring it for opportunities to effect more strategic and serious damage.

I'll grant you that this was a somewhat ironic outcome. I've often thought that had Tamir accepted my approach, things would have worked out so much better for him. Avoiding me did not spare Tamir the fate that ultimately ended his life as he knew it. Had I enough time to have convinced Tamir, and I might have, he could have very well kept his lavish and decadent lifestyle, providing no more information to me than he ultimately shared under far less comfortable circumstances with our local foreign partners. Instead, when finally released many years later, he was a broken man. I wonder, sometimes, if that thought ever crossed his mind as he shuffled in shackles under his guards' watchful control into the interrogation room time and again, a fate I would have gladly prevented for him.

OF MICE AND MEN, AND RACE AND RELIGION

The Agency of my day was not a diverse organization. Today's CIA still has a way to go in terms of diversity, but a stop at the Agency's Starbucks, the de facto organizational watering hole these days, will reveal an ethnic, racial, and cultural mix that likewise includes all sexual orientations. The collage is a more fitting reflection of the country. Still,

CIA needs to more aggressively court minorities and likewise overcome the challenges of an understandably rigorous security screening process to take advantage of the skills, backgrounds, and languages of the naturalized citizens and first generation Americans from the various parts of the world in which we need to operate.

CIA today is also a far cry from the days when the polygraph test included questions concerning your sexual orientation, a time during which the LGBTQ community was excluded. The justification being that inasmuch as society's prejudices forced many to conceal their orientation, closeted homosexuality left such officers vulnerable to blackmail. A backward logic, but consistent with the era. And not that it was 100 percent effective, as CIA still had a number of LGBTQ officers. They were forced to remain in the closet, and somehow overcome their periodic security reinvestigations.

When I joined in 1984, the CIA's halls were a sea of White males. It was a White man's world, moreover, a rather Catholic White man's world where racially intolerant and misogynist officers disparagingly quipped, "The DO, where the men are men, and so are the women." There were women at the Agency, but few were case officers. Looking at my own class, there was less than one woman for every ten men, two Latinx, two Jews, and not a single Black, Asian, or South Asian American. In comparison, there were disproportionately more women and minorities in the analytical and administrative directorates. The DO and Directorate of Science and Technology (DS&T), on the other hand, remained old boys' clubs. My DS&T colleagues complained that their office was even worse, and that it remains the last bastion of that old boys' club mentality, even today.

The CIA's demographic at the time more fittingly reflected an alternative variant of its acronym for which it was widely known: Catholics In Action. CIA's history speaks volumes to its East Coast, Ivy League, WASP, and Catholic roots. Photos show that Director of Central Intelligence Casey, who was a rather devout Catholic, kept a huge crucifix on his CIA office wall.

Having grown up as a New York City Jewish American, I had my share of experiences dealing with racism, but the Bronx's ethnic strife of the 1970s mostly pitted Italians and Irish against Puerto Ricans and Blacks. Jews were not universally popular, but they were still rather ubiquitous in New York. In any event, my family was largely secular. I felt prejudice, but not necessarily discrimination.

Marine Corps Recruit Depot Parris Island, South Carolina, in 1981 did not see a great many Jews. At the time of my training, I was the only one on the island. You might wonder how I know that. That knowledge was facilitated by my drill instructors (DIs). They were of course aware of my ethnicity and religion, because it's literally imprinted on one's dog tags. But at the outset of training, the DIs announced that "all Marines were Christians" and that we were required to attend Sunday church service. This was just fine by me. I never complained. Church was the only respite from the otherwise grueling week, since there was no liberty or days off at Parris Island. At church, I could hang out with my platoon mates insulated from the DIs' taunts, sing songs, and eat cookies.

There was no synagogue on Parris Island, or anywhere nearby. It was church and cookies or scrubbing toilets. Tough decision. Thank you, Jesus! At some point, however, a horrified officer learned that I had been "directed" to attend Christian church services. It was a somewhat unfortunate encounter, despite the officer's best intentions.

Regardless of the fact that I had nothing to do with it, my DIs endured an ass chewing. They then exorcised their angst by having me do "incentive physical training." To those not familiar, this is when the DIs merely bark out, "Begin!," and you perform whatever endless combination of push-ups, sit-ups, and mountain climbs that suits them. But what then to do about the island's only Jewish recruit?

The Marines addressed the issue by importing a rabbi. The poor man had to shlep, pardon the Yiddish, all the way from far away Charleston, South Carolina, just to come see me. Inadvertently, the officer's action had also served to highlight my "difference" for some of my less progressive or racially tolerant platoon mates from the Deep South, many who had never seen a Jew, and who referred to me variously as *heretic*, *Satan*, and the ever popular, *Ponchos Pilot*.

These were not the most educated or worldly fellows, I reasoned, so I did my best to get along while managing my expectations concerning their behavior. As an eighteen-year-old among other similarly aged kids who had never met anyone from New York City, let alone a Jew, I chalked it up to lack of exposure. And over twelve weeks of shared hell, even the worst among them came around to accept me as a fellow Marine. Not that they'd want me marrying their sister, but they would trust me next to them in a two-man fighting hole. From the CIA, however, I expected more.

My first exposure to CIA's anti-Semitism occurred while serving a relatively long training interim on one of the areas desks in the CIA's Near East and South Asia Division, known simply to us all as NE. As a later NE division chief would coin appropriately, the division's turf spanned from "Marrakesh to Bangladesh." Blending Arab, South Asian, Israeli, and Iranian operations, the "NE mafia" in reality belonged to the Middle East hands. More specifically, the Arabists who ran the division and defined its identity. These were officers fluent in the Arabic language, many of whom grew up in the region with missionary parents. Their outlook was founded on Christianity and American exceptionalism. They moved and spoke with an uninhibited and quite shameless swagger that was often accompanied by a cowboy-like recklessness and disdain for the rules.

The NE mafia had neither the time or interest in other parts of the world, nor much regard for colleagues from other CIA geographic divisions. To them, the Middle East was the center of the universe, and very much America's turf. That the 1979 Iranian Revolution and the emergence of Lebanese Hizballah turned much of the region for the US into a war zone of sorts made it that more interesting and fueled their sense of self-importance. The ensuing loss of colleagues in terrorist bombings and kidnappings only added to their swagger and the massive chips on their shoulders. Rather than being repulsed, I must confess, I was utterly drawn to it. They were the cool kids in the lunchroom and the bad boys whose club I wanted to join.

I arrived in NE as a young career trainee (CT) who was being provided extra *seasoning* by spending a longer duration in interim Headquarters assignments. Today, CIA brings in such prospects as professional trainees (PTs). In my day, though, we were simply referred to as extended interim CTs. Then, as now, the younger folks, or those without much life experience, spent a year or so of additional time doing short stints among the various CIA desks. We'd get experience, learn a bit more about the trade, and the DO could grow and evaluate the trainees' ability to secure certification at the Farm.

In many ways, PTs have significant advantages in their ability to compete and graduate, and likewise for what they offer the Agency. Most are too young to have done much of anything wrong to complicate their security processing. They are malleable and open to learning. Often more so than their older, worldly, and experienced Clandestine Service trainees (CST) classmates. Those coming to the CIA later in life arrive with their own baggage, attitudes, and in a few cases, a chip on their shoulders. And the additional time at Headquarters better equips PTs for the Farm's rigors. For one thing, they tend to be better writers at the Farm, since the CIA correspondence has a unique and unforgiving style they learn during the extended desk rotations.

I had a terrific experience on an NE desk working Arabian Gulf accounts. It was an exciting place. The operations were sexy. There was danger, excitement, real espionage, and tremendous esprit de corps. More than any other division, NE had suffered the blight of terrorist attacks for which Lebanese Hizballah, under Iranian support and direction, was mostly responsible at the time. The April 18, 1983, bombing of the American embassy in Beirut killed 17 Americans, including the CIA NE division legend Robert Ames. On October 23, 1983, Hizballah suicide attacks killed 241 US service members, mostly Marines, some with whom I had trained, as well as 58 French peacekeepers. For context:

- On December 12, 1983, Hizballah attacked the American and French embassies in Kuwait, along with several local infrastructure targets.
- On March 16, 1984, Hizballah kidnapped CIA's Beirut COS William Buckley, who later died in captivity owing to torture. He was one of several Americans seized in Lebanon over a roughly two-year period, an episode contributing to the Iran-Contra debacle. Buckley was a popular character in the NE Division family who volunteered to succeed his predecessor, who was killed in the April 1983 bombing. I routinely observed colleagues in tears as updates arrived concerning his treatment, and, ultimately, his fate. These colleagues were similarly close to Robert Ames and the other NE Division officers who perished in the April 1983 attack.
- Eighteen US service members were killed in an April 12, 1984, Hizballah attack on a restaurant near a US Air Force base in Torrejon, Spain.
- Hizballah tortured and subsequently executed two US Agency for International Development (USAID) employees during their December 4–9, 1984, hijacking of a Kuwait Airways flight.
- Hizballah executed a US Navy diver among the passengers of a TWA flight it hijacked June 14, 1985, en route to Rome from Athens.

Among all these attacks, though, apart from my desire to contribute to the pursuit of justice for the deaths of my Marine and CIA colleagues, the most personally impactful event was the December 1984 Kuwait Airways hijacking. Serving as a trainee with NE at the time, I volunteered to support the 24/7 watch center that was stood up over the duration. I was on the late shift along with two other young NE trainees reading the reporting and routine updates. We imagined ourselves in the circumstances of the two USAID employees who the captors believed to be CIA officers and subsequently tortured before summarily executing them. It wasn't the diplomatic passports that did them in, but one, a trained accountant, had the initials C.I.A. on his business card. The hijackers took this as confirmation of his affiliation with the spy service. In reality, it stood for certified internal auditor.

The three of us, young men and future case officers, all agreed that if we were to find ourselves in similar circumstances, we wouldn't go out that way. Rather than being tortured, knowing death was inevitable, we'd go down taking as many terrorists with us as possible. It certainly sounded macho enough in that small Northern Virginia cubicle. As it turned out, I was the only one of the three who would return to NE Division.

CIA was fighting the Soviets in Afghanistan, mediating conflicts between the Palestinian Liberation Organization (PLO) and Israel, and trying hard to keep India and Pakistan from pushing the nuclear button due to multiple escalations of hostility over Kashmir. NE was quite literally at war, a whirlwind of excitement and a lightning rod of attention. And the case officers were legendary...well, some were. Aggressive, daring, and polished, I thought, many had an almost spiritual connection with the people of the region. I sat eagerly at their knees, learning the history and cultures. I knew unquestionably that this was where I wanted to be, and what I wanted to do.

I was, and remain today, a rather secular Jew. And across a span of nearly forty years, much of it in the foreign field, I not only lived under various forms of cover as a CIA case officer, but religious cover to conceal my Jewish ethnicity from targets, and therefore necessarily, the broader official US communities in which I mostly lived. Still, I never sought to conceal my religion from CIA colleagues. But I soon came to realize, particularly in my era, that keeping my religion in the closet eased my ability to establish friendships among many colleagues, and superiors, who tended to hold anti-Semitic, or at least negative perceptions, of American Jews.

None of my children even realized I was Jewish until they were old enough to keep it secret while living abroad. And while concealing my Jewish ethnicity still didn't shelter me from being targeted by terrorist groups over the course of my career, including a specific al-Qa'ida fatwa of which I'm rather proud, it certainly couldn't help. Personally, and professionally, I was first and foremost an American, which is how I was raised by a Korean War–era Marine father. Neither my ethnicity nor religion ever had bearing on my conduct. Like my father, who was the only one among his tank crew to survive when a faulty shell exploded, I was excited and proud to serve my country.

In the early to mid-1980s, however, NE Division in particular reflected much of the Agency's Catholics In Action and East Coast Ivy League character. The character of that era is depicted exceedingly well in Kai Bird's biography of the legendary NE case officer Bob Ames, who I noted earlier was sadly among the April 1983 Beirut embassy bombing victims. He, like the other Arabists who ran the division, was generally quite religious and decidedly pro-Palestinian. This included the group chief and his deputy for whom I was now working. Both were among the most talented Agency officers I would ever know. As it so happened, they shared the same first name, so let's call them "Randy One," the group chief, and "Randy Two," his deputy.

Randy One was raised by a Protestant missionary family in the Middle East where he learned fluent Arabic. Randy Two studied at East Coast Catholic Jesuit schools where he too learned Arabic, which he later perfected while working in the Middle East before coming on board with the Agency. The Randys were kind men, good to me, and acted as interested mentors. But their opinions and bias reflected the times.

Randy One and Randy Two were both NE men to the core, excellent officers, and gifted Arabists, but that's largely where the similarities ended. They respected one another, but they weren't friends. The two could not have outwardly been more different. Randy One was polished on the surface, tall, fit, with a well-groomed mustache and perfectly combed, medium-length hair. His bearing reflected an air of sophistication that some thought suggested arrogance and elitism, a manner that rubbed some colleagues the wrong way. Randy One would make quips that only he found amusing, but he understood Arabs and the Middle East better than any CIA expert I would ever meet. In fact, his farsighted resistance in 2002 to the politically biased analysis that Iraqis would embrace the invading American military forces as liberators cost him his job.

Randy Two was also tall and thin, but a chain-smoking, hard-drinking Irishman, whose slight proportions were a result of his diet of cigarettes and coffee. A gentleman in mixed company, among men Randy Two's remarks were colorfully laced with profanity and misogynist quips. He sported a stern expression but possessed a soft heart. In fact, while always at the top of his game, Randy Two could nevertheless appear to have had a rough prior evening. He could come across as reserved and soft-spoken, and indeed he kept his own counsel, though he had an opinion on most things that was only shared with trust.

Randy Two was Randy One's blue collar counterpart and unlike Randy One, who was pretty consistent in personality and comportment, could instantly flip the switch and transition from aloof and introspective to a gadfly. He was the first case officer I ever saw with this capacity, and I found it intriguing. Randy Two could mimic his audience, role-playing alternatively as intellectual, warrior, or life of the party, as the situation required, and do so convincingly.

Randy Two the case officer was an entirely different person than Randy Two my manager. Glib, fun loving, a drink in one hand, a burning cigarette in the other, Randy Two particularly had a way with Arabs, connecting with them on a very personal level. In fact, I met my first agent in his company, though he wasn't supposed to bring me to the meeting as a trainee, and he told no one. Randy Two, you see, was a nonconformist, applying right and wrong over statutory and often outdated rules, and taking risks on behalf of the officers he led and the agents he handled. These are admirable leadership traits I witnessed far more often pre-9/11, and of which today's Agency pays great lip service but inconsistently supports.

Questions concerning my race came about rather organically. I was coming to the end of my long interim assignment with NE and Randy Two just happened to ask where I was going for my next training rotation, inquiring likewise to which division I was hoping to go at "the draft."

Then, as now, trainees could list their top two or three preferences, but like in sports, the area divisions then proceeded to draft their picks in rounds. Career trainees actually referred to the process as the meat market. When I told him what I thought to be both the natural and appropriate response of my interest in returning to NE, Randy Two paused. As was his way, Randy Two evinced little emotion of any sort, and he simply asked if I had mentioned my interest to Randy One. Replying that I had not, Randy Two invited me into his office for a private chat.

Rather than suggest his own particular point of view, Randy Two enlightened me as to how "many NE officers think." He cautioned that I might not be particularly well received by the NE mafia, a reference to the Arabic-speaking case officer cadre that held sway in the division which, in principle, included Randy Two himself. I was stunned, and at the moment was unaware this had anything to do with me being Jewish. Instead, I thought there was something off about me, or that I had done a poor job over the course of my training interim. When I began down that road, Randy Two stopped me. He observed I was a very strong candidate with the right traits, had a good attitude, and seemed to get along well with everyone. When I remained too dense to get it, he finally added, "Well, you're Jewish, aren't you?" I nodded affirmatively. Randy Two then explained how "the NE mafia would not likely take to the idea of having a Jewish case officer in their fold."

It was a bit odd coming from Randy Two, who while technically a member of the ruling NE mafia, wasn't quite pals with them, as reflected by his tensions with Randy One. In fact, when I did see Randy Two letting his hair down with colleagues, they were generally much like him, on the fringe, loners in fact, good case officers but not part of the in-crowd. Trying to maintain that I still didn't quite follow his meaning without appearing antagonistic, Randy Two explained further that NE Division officers were largely pro-Palestinian. The Israelis had been adversarial and had assassinated some of our better contacts.

Randy Two described the Israelis as hardly bastions of democracy and human rights when it came to Arabs living in Israel and the occupied territories, and were responsible for enabling the September 1982 Sabra and Shatila massacre in Lebanon. Randy Two suggested my NE colleagues would assume that, being Jewish, I'd have a pro-Israeli bias. Not to mention, he added, how difficult it would be for me to ever gain the trust of an Arab. Still, Randy encouraged me to speak to Randy One, offering, whether genuine or not, his own opinion that I'd figure out how to make it work in the field, but that convincing my own colleagues might pose a greater obstacle. I suspect Randy Two was perhaps most interested in hearing how Randy One would approach it.

My meeting with Randy One went largely as Randy Two envisioned. Randy One certainly liked me, had been a considerate boss and mentor, but was rather matter of fact in that it was a foregone conclusion: Jews would struggle in NE Division, with both their targets and colleagues alike. Randy One thought himself doing me a favor by guiding me to where I'd have greater opportunity. He was more resolute than Randy Two who, in truth, was not necessarily owning the same bias, but warning me about it. For Randy One, it was black and white. "Given the realities," he said, "you are best served by considering other DO divisions where being Jewish is less of a *handicap*."

In fact, there were not a great many Jewish case officers in the DO at the time. There were plenty of Jewish analysts, but spies? Well, those few of whom I was aware were generally serving either in our Soviet and East European or East Asia Divisions. In fact, both Randys encouraged me to give greater consideration to East Asia, where my ethnicity was likely to have the least negative impact, they thought. It made me reflect more about what this said about the Agency than whether or not I believed my ethnicity would color my outlook or distract me from doing what was in America's best interest.

Being a case officer is a lot like being an actor. One has to be all things to all people and role-play in order to earn trust and secure friendships. That many of those against whom I'd be working blamed Jews for their problems didn't faze me. That my own colleagues shared some of these sentiments, did. After a few of these well-intended conversations, I convinced the Randys that I remained interested in coming to NE, if they would have me. Randy One didn't argue, and Randy Two was privately encouraging. In turn, I was sent to NE Division's chief of DO personnel and assignments, referred to then, and now, as the PEMS officer, short for Personnel and Evaluation Management. NE's PEMS chief, a man who we'll call "Riley," was another Irish Catholic American, and a very experienced Arabist.

Like the Randys, Riley was not mean-spirited. Generally available, receptive, affable, and well intentioned with me, as well as the other young officers, Riley heard me out as I explained my interest and recapped the Randys' cautions and advice. I asked him directly whether or not my religion would inhibit NE from selecting me upon graduation. Riley sat thoughtfully, a quiet man on the surface, his alabaster skin contrasting handsomely with medium-length, raven-black hair. He was outwardly warm, soft spoken and serious, yet animated in conversation. Pausing reflectively for a moment, Riley agreed that I might find it hard in a division where the workforce was generally anti-Israeli and favored a settlement creating a Palestinian state. I responded, without copping too much of a smart-ass disposition, that I was American, not Israeli, and as a matter of fact, shared the same perspective. Being Jewish, I explained, did not make me pro-Israeli, and I too thought Tel Aviv should be reined in far more aggressively when it transgressed.

Riley sat back thoughtfully in his black leather executive chair, processing my response before responding. "Aren't you required to support Israel?" He asked incredulously. "You know, when you go to synagogue, by the rabbi, isn't it a religious requirement?"

I shook my head negatively. "To be honest, I haven't been to temple since my bar mitzvah, when I was thirteen, so I couldn't really say."

"But do you wear it on your sleeve?" Riley asked.

I was confused. "Wear what?" In my mind, I envisioned a Star of David chain or mezuzah that a Jew might hang around their neck, as Christians do with crucifixes. "No," I said, again shaking my head in the negative, "I don't wear any jewelry, just my watch."

Riley smiled, before softly correcting, "No, I mean rather, do you *act* Jewish?"

Once again, I was confused. Intellectually, I appreciated what he meant, and I envisioned caricatures and stereotypes. Perhaps he was picturing Tevye from *Fiddler on the Roof*? I replied straight-faced and truthfully, "As a matter of fact, most people presume I'm Irish." Riley took this in appreciatively, gesturing a thumbs-up with his hand and smiling. "Yes," he concurred, "you could certainly pass for Irish." Riley agreed to take up my matter with the NE front office.

Shortly after my meeting with Riley, I was summoned to the office of "Tom T." Tom was NE's overall deputy division chief. Among one of the greatest recruiters I ever met, Tom's nickname was Mister Rogers, owing to his warm, paternal demeanor, thoughtful, blue eyes, distinguished white hair, and outwardly mild manner. The mere sound of Tom's voice was soothing, and his words brimmed with sincerity. He was a bona fide Middle East and South Asia expert of the highest order, a brilliant spy who could calm a whirling dervish, so truly endowed with persuasive skills that he could literally sell water to a drowning man.

Despite his outward appearance, Tom was a ruthlessly effective spy with brilliant operational acumen. He had sufficient detachment to focus on the mission at hand. That is to say, if it was in America's interest, Tom would not think twice about convincing that drowning man to buy his water. I have also seen Tom angry, the outwardly kind demeanor replaced at a snap with a bitter temper.

Over the years, Tom was always kind to me, and he remained a respected mentor until his retirement. Tom was always available, and I'd sometimes stop to see him when passing through Washington or the major overseas commands he later held. If ever asked who I aspired to be like when I grew up, it was Tom. Even among my peers, when questioned as to who they'd choose to be *their* case officer, the answer, uniformly without pause for reflection, was consistently Tom T. His wisdom benefited CIA and our country for decades, which included his rising to the rank of deputy director for operations (DDO), the overall chief of CIA's Clandestine Service.

This would be the first individual encounter with my soon-to-become mentor, having only participated with him in group meetings or having heard him speak at functions. I rushed to the NE deputy division chief's office, my heart racing. As a young trainee, my appearance in the front office area was, on the few occasions I had been there, only to drop off or retrieve paperwork. I passed through, occasionally delivering cables and reports for senior management's review. It was 1984, after all, and there were no computers, only hard copy memoranda. Assuming correctly this had something to do with my meeting with Riley, I waited nervously to hear my fate, the two front office assistants eyeing me with little evidence of warmth, or interest. Luckily, the wait was short. Tom, whom I could never bring myself to refer to any way other than his last name, called me in by my first and introduced himself the same.

In truth, the DO was far smaller and more intimate at the time, perhaps under 2,000 in strength, no more than half of which were case officers. Today, there are CIA centers larger than that. Most senior officers referred to themselves in the presence of juniors by their first name and acted with more familiarity. Even the most senior case officer of the day all but recoiled at being referred to as Sir. CIA was designed to be decidedly different than the military in terms of protocol and ranks, since we were a spy service. Unlike intelligence services in many other countries, that's one of the reasons we never had uniforms. The intent was to create an environment where even the most junior case officers could spitball operational ideas with seniors, who were nonetheless treated with respect.

Today, seniors in the DO expect to be called Sir and be treated with greater deference. Even at its most familiar, the common expression is to refer to a senior as Chief. I honestly don't know when this began, as I must have been in the field at the time, but it was certainly after 9/11, and must have begun at Headquarters. Personally, the only time I'd indulge folks to call me Chief was when I was actively serving as a chief of station or base, or department chief. Otherwise, I insisted they call me by my first name.

Tom T was gracious and set me at ease. Though we had not previously met directly, another reflection of Tom's professionalism was preparation. A case officer always aims to *appear* to be the smartest person in the room, or at least sufficiently expert and substantive to earn the respect of the assembled, even when they are surely not. It's all about doing your homework and flashing when needed the well-rehearsed tidbits at the right time to reflect as much. He knew all about me, and he could work into his initial pleasantries even the rather low-level, unimportant, and oft trivial work that trainees were permitted to do. Tom shared his love of New York City, my home, and made an immediate connection with me, as he did with all, finding areas of commonalities and excuses to pay me compliments. It could all have been fabricated for effect, but nevertheless it was effective. Had Tom T told me at that moment to go directly from his office to that of East Asia Division, bypassing "Go" and the collection of $200, I would have done so without second thought.

Instead, Tom T, NE's deputy division chief, apologized profusely for the manner in which I had been treated and urged me to "consider" NE Division as my future home, adding how he would be honored and lucky to have someone of my talent on his team. I walked out of his office dumb and happy, though for all I knew, Tom might have at the very same moment picked up the phone to advise CIA's legal counsel that they had dodged a bullet by giving me the job. But it was 1984 at the CIA, and he really didn't have to do all that, so I'm pretty confident Tom's intentions to right a wrong were genuine.

Whether or not Tom truly believed NE would be lucky to have me on their team, well, I'll just give him the benefit of the doubt, and a little slack, since after all, he was a case officer. And so it was, in the meat market draft that was, romantically, the final day of training at the Farm after crossing the stage to receive my certificate—which, again, I promptly handed back owing to cover considerations—I was informed that NE Division had selected me first among their graduating candidates.

Only two of the graduating officers from that entire class would go to NE, the larger area divisions getting greater numbers. Ironically, both NE selections were the only Jews. The other was, again ironically, Robert, the colleague who collaborated with our captors during SOTC's interrogation training. Robert came to CIA as a rather distinguished scholar, with excellent Arabic and Farsi language skills. But would not last long with CIA. In fact, NE would not place him in the division's own turf, sending him instead as the NE referent to two consecutive assignments in Europe.

Unfortunately, what the Randys had foreshadowed and cautioned, with some degree of good intention, came to be realized on my initial overseas assignment. "Timothy" was my first chief of station (COS). A short, mustached man with thinning, reddish hair and a pale complexion, Timothy was White, Catholic, foul mouthed, and had little personal regard for those with different skin colors, religions, and ethnicities. Odd, I thought, for someone in the service of working with and befriending those with just such differences.

Timothy could turn it on when needed, and he spoke good Arabic. Yet he referred to Arabs and South Asians derisively as "rag heads," and me, as "my Jew." Unlike some of the other Catholic officers I had met in the Agency who had preceded their careers as missionaries and appreciated the cultures and histories of the region, albeit in the course of proselytizing, Timothy had no such interest and little if any intellectual curiosity. What Timothy had was a skill, Arabic, and familial connections to senior officers who had preceded him into the CIA.

Timothy objected to my assignment. Moreover, he did so openly. This was at a time when the COS had such right of refusal. Unimpeded by concerns over Equal Employment Opportunity (EEO) complaints or litigation, he was in fact quite forthcoming in articulating his views, albeit presented in the guise of practicality. Timothy argued that being Jewish, my religion would be a detriment in working against the targets for which I'd be responsible. CIA likewise made no effort to conceal Timothy's objection from me, nor even the particulars of his anti-Semitic argument. But Tom T remained NE's deputy and would have none of it. He overruled his COS and off I went. Of course, while I appreciate Tom's support, let's say that the episode did not further endear me to Timothy.

For added fun, Timothy was an alcoholic, and not even a closeted one. Drinking was an occupational hazard, often borne by some degree of necessity. We were not required to get drunk with those we recruited, ran, or even officially liaised. What would be the point of losing the judgment that alcohol impairs? But demonstrating a willingness to drink can be valuable in reflecting a nonjudgmental attitude against those who do. Many a glass I've raised with Russians, Arabs, Chinese, Iranians, and North Koreans, and so on, but "a" glass, to overcome their own predispositions, not more.

I needed to drink just enough to gain their trust and to eliminate from the outset any concern they might have of me being among the morals police. I've known some agents who wouldn't ever trust a case officer who was unwilling to imbibe, at least at the outset. But I never made the foolish mistake, as some case officers did, to keep up with others in an effort to demonstrate manhood. Many of those with whom I've raised a glass could drink us all under the table and remain amazingly lucid and functioning—until they died by age fifty, of course, from liver or heart disease.

The case officer lifestyle contributes greatly to substance abuse and we had, and have still, our share of those who fall victim. What I will say for the Agency is that it genuinely has a nonjudgmental and proactive approach to helping. There's no professional disgrace or punishment for acknowledging a drinking problem now, nor was there throughout the entirety of my career. The Agency, in fact, is willing to help, and it provides treatment and a pass for your first offense. Among those with whom I'm personally familiar who came clean and sought help, the Agency not only allowed for the time, but paid for treatment. Moreover, to their credit, I do not recall a case in which the CIA held it against the officers professionally, so long as they maintained their sobriety.

Rehabilitated, such officers went on to enjoy outstanding careers, returned to the foreign field, and those who merited it (appropriately or otherwise), rose to the highest positions of Agency leadership. Officers who tried to conceal their disease, or abused the pass they were offered, were not always discharged from service, but might be reassigned to positions of less sensitivity and denied further overseas assignments.

Mental health is another issue. Although the Agency has made great strides in recent years encouraging officers to reach out to mental health professionals who are increasingly available to those both at Headquarters and in the field, there's still somewhat of a stigma. There remains an unspoken concern among senior CIA officers that those with mental health issues are a greater security risk in safeguarding the life and death secrets they possess. And while America remains at war, with so many Agency officers routinely trained and issued weapons, workplace violence is yet another concern.

The sad reality is that, like the armed forces, the CIA has lost officers due to suicide, including an officer with whom I once worked who took her life in the field with an Agency-issued weapon. Recognizing the issue, over at least the last two years of my service, I witnessed Agency leadership directing managers to encourage officers to seek out assistance if and when needed, increasing resources to do so, and handling their cases with the utmost of confidentiality. Ideally this trend will continue.

Timothy, of course, neither sought out nor received such assistance, inasmuch as he believed that he drank, to quote him, "like any healthy, normal Irishman." Timothy arrived at the station late every morning, head down, often clutching a brown paper bag, shuffling across the reception area, making his way to his office. There were no hellos. He was acerbic and condescending when sober, and particularly mean spirited and foul mouthed when not. Summoned into his office, on the rare occasion we who worked for him actually earned an audience, it was more often than not to be subjected to an alcohol-induced rant.

Timothy was not about constructive mentoring. I learned many a valuable leadership lesson from observing Timothy, and all were about what not to do. The shame is, there is little more important to a young, impressionable, first-tour officer than the experience with their first COS, or in a larger station, their immediate supervisor. That experience shapes their opinion about the organization, the work, as well as makes or breaks their own confidence and belief in the sanctity of the mission.

After surviving Timothy and being rewarded with solid, fair, and inspiring leaders over the next few years, fast-forwarding, I ran again into another Timothy disciple, "Ted." Unlike Timothy, Ted was more proactive, lucid, and vindictive. By this point in my career, though, I had become more seasoned and salty myself. To be honest, I was far more arrogant than I should have been, owing to rather successful initial over-seas tours, earning a reputation for the sensitive agents I had recruited. I was less reluctant to confront small-minded officers, even those in my chain of command.

My attitude didn't help when it came to colleagues like Timothy and Ted, who were predisposed against me. In hindsight, I was naive to believe the Agency would take care of me based only on the merit of what I had produced, and immature to feel the need to retaliate against those who I perceived to have done me wrong. But ego goes along with being a case officer, and pride goeth before a fall. I would pass far more years and endure quite a few more blows before growing up enough to find the right balance, and by then, it was a bit too late to offset the damage.

Ted was a Headquarters-based senior officer in my NE chain of command who took an instant disliking to me. To be fair, I don't think Ted and I would have meshed well together regardless of our backgrounds and ethnicities. We butted heads early into this particular assignment, he being the office director for the region that included the field station in which I served. Ted was a bit of a bully to junior officers, and when he learned I was Jewish, our relationship deteriorated at an accelerated pace.

It all became rather clear to me during one of our less convivial engage-ments. I swung by Headquarters while back from the field on a break, on what we referred to as a rest and recuperation trip. Having promised my COS before leaving that I would try to make peace, I finally asked Ted what I had done to earn his disfavor, since at the time, I could not recall what had started the feud. "*You New Yorkers from the Lower East Side just* get under my skin," Ted answered, adding, "One of you people could never have recruited so many Arabs, I just don't believe it."

You people, from New York. Okay, I had heard that euphemism for being Jewish enough times over the years to recognize it for what it was. I won't deny that I invested limited energy in making amends prior to this statement, but less so after. My COS was a good man, and a rock star in the division, providing me protection and a bit of a buffer. But that did not prevent Ted from initiating his own, personal, counterintelligence investigation of my cases in an effort to challenge their operational success—or even existence. Ted wanted to prove that at least some of the cases were made up, which he found rather challenging since I had turned most over to my successors.

Ted was not exactly an operational superstar and neither was he considered one of NE Division's brighter minds. In fact, he owed his position to NE Division's old guard that had a soft spot for Ted due to compelling circumstances. Ted was one of the few Agency officers who survived the catastrophic April 1983 attack against our embassy in Beirut. For no other reason than luck, Ted had been out of the building buying a carpet when a Lebanese Hizballah operative drove his bomb-laden vehicle into the chancery, killing most of Ted's colleagues as they took lunch in the embassy cafeteria.

April 18, 1983, was a hard day for the CIA, as the Khost bombing was for us December 30, 2009. Sympathetic for the years of guilt and torment Ted suffered from not dying with his friends, NE leadership tolerated poor performance and excused his behavior toward me, as well as others. When Ted's investigation produced nothing, and his unsanctioned efforts came to their attention, the NE front office reprimanded him, and then apologized to me. Their apology was the first I had ever heard of Ted's holy effort to discredit my work, but it would not be the last.

THE CIA ON ITS DOWNWARD JOURNEY

Whereas Ted was not terribly shrewd, and Timothy not particularly vindictive, being a Jewish officer in Near East and South Asia Division would ultimately bring me to the attention of a senior officer we'll refer to as "Lex." In truth, Lex was an excellent street case officer with whom I shared mutual friends and common previous assignments. I thought we'd naturally be friends.

It all seemed to start out fine. I had great respect for Lex as a case officer long before ever having met him. Like me, Lex began as an NE Division case officer and was a former military officer. But he took to heart the class division and elitist mindset in that he had been an officer and I was enlisted. Lex would precede or follow me over the course of several of the same tours. Although he was not an Arabist, Lex rose quickly through the ranks, spending most of his career working South Asian and Iranian issues. Lex struck an imposing figure and embraced the intimidating posture he would assume when taking subordinates to task.

Unbeknownst to me, I began with two strikes in Lex's book, which were being Jewish and having been an enlisted Marine. Lex was religious and not merely Catholic but from the particularly ultraconservative Opus Dei. An equal opportunity bigot, however, Lex would prove to be likewise contemptuous of Blacks, Hispanics, and other minorities. His values and political views were decidedly conservative, defined by his religious faith, as well as his sense of class, station, and hierarchy. Lex was likewise homophobic and misogynist. I recall a cable he sent to all the CIA field stations and bases upon his assumption of a significant Headquarters executive position. The very first line began by identifying himself to those who did not know him as a Catholic, former military officer, and of the state from which he hailed, in that order. Who does that?

It wasn't a perfect operational record that propelled him up the ranks. When Lex was in his first senior manager position abroad, as a deputy chief of station, he oversaw the conduct of tradecraft concerning Iranian operations. Lex would leave a trail of bodies—specifically, dead Iranian agents. It was a major flap owing to Iranian counterintelligence perseverance and Lex's poor management of the tradecraft. But he did not bear this responsibility alone. Lex was deputy to a COS who similarly managed to evade accountability. Moreover, the COS ultimately became chief of NE at a crucial time in Lex's ascent. They shared the same buried skeletons, protecting one another, and he saw to Lex's upward rise. Not coincidentally, that NE chief, with whom I had the temerity to disagree at times, was likewise not among my fans. Can I pick my enemies, or what?

Lex was a master manipulator, and he used his professional skills not merely on agents but within the Agency's hallways. I witnessed the DO's culture change under Lex's leadership, and it took on a more militaristic, rank-conscious atmosphere that was otherwise absent pre-9/11. Lex valued an officer's rank, color, race, and sexual orientation over talent, and he assigned, advocated, or undermined their careers, accordingly. Moreover, Lex managed to create a false image of himself as being some sort of DO savior, given the political circumstances at the time of his ascension to power.

Part of Lex's skill was in managing the media and his image. He shrewdly used his high CIA office to propagate the fiction of his nobility and highlight his good relationship with the Republican White House. The press, delighted at the access, took on his messaging campaign without question. Meanwhile, Lex aligned himself with senior political figures, such as Vice President Cheney, who took advantage of his compliance and loyalty to their causes.

Lex even tested the political waters concerning a run for senate. While I'd like to think Lex thankfully chose not to run because there were enough of us who knew of the skeletons in his closet, the more likely truth is that he knew he didn't have the ability to compete in what was then a soundly blue state. At the time, he would have faced a blue wave that subsequently brought a Democrat to the White House. Lex, after all, was a shrewd man.

Lex was one of the most influential forces helping Vice President Cheney, a regular visitor to CIA in the run up to the second Gulf War. Lex was actively part of the effort to cherry-pick from intelligence, of which the White House based its justification to invade Iraq. Moreover, Lex relieved dissenting voices of their duties, such as Randy One, who by then had become chief of NE Division. Randy One had offered alternative realities to the CIA's analytic line concerning Iraq. He argued that the clandestine reporting the White House favored was flawed, as it was drawn from a small sampling of mostly questionable sources. Randy One supported his assessment with a larger body of reporting from proven sources that consistently argued the absence of WMD and the true anti-American sentiments of Iraq's Shi'a community.

Randy One cautioned that unlike what Lex, select CIA analysts, and the White House believed, the Iraqi people would not welcome US military forces as liberators and would oppose invading American forces, if not at the outset, then once they were in a position to do so. Despite the repression suffered under Saddam, Randy One was certain the Shi'a had not forgotten the scars from the early 1990s after the first Gulf War. Iraqi Shi'a, with America's encouragement, rose up against Saddam, only to be abandoned and slaughtered. As to the Sunni, while the Iraqi Army would crumble, dedicated Baathists, if not given a new purpose and empowered, would threaten the US presence. Indeed, many Baathists would later be among the professional ISIS counterintelligence vanguard and field commanders who raised havoc with our intelligence operations and led the group's brutal campaign to establish a caliphate.

Nonetheless, Lex was the White House's man, and he would see to their wishes. He replaced Randy One with "Bill," a more compliant, smart, and highly ambitious successor. Together, they told the White House what it so desperately wanted to hear, and they drove the "slam shut case" Colin Powell would make at the United Nations, which the former secretary of state has expressed regretting to this day.

Lex was likewise among the greatest proponents of the Agency's post-9/11 use of so-called black sites and enhanced interrogation measures, but he escaped the public accountability that befell CTC director and later DDO, Jose Rodriguez. Like our terrorist enemies, Lex had dehumanized our adversaries, and likewise as our enemies had done, he justified brutality based on his religious beliefs, his own version of the Crusades. An approach that did not lack sympathy in the building. Although directly responsible for the authorizations to secretly imprison and apply enhanced interrogation measures on specific detainees, Lex managed to avoid the repercussions. Such consequences instead fell largely on midlevel and more junior officers who Lex had directed.

Ironically, and indeed brilliantly, Lex jumped in to support the cacophony of voices that later blamed the DO for the "intelligence failures" concerning both 9/11 and the justification for America's invasion of Iraq. He could deflect blame for the transgressions of the past to become the champion of its future. Lex's moves weakened the DO relative to other CIA directorates, but more important, secured for him greater direct command and involvement with day-to-day operational control. It was a time for mother-may-I, and Lex was dear old mom. At the expense of foreign intelligence collection, Lex emphasized growing the power and autonomy of CIA's covert action capabilities, its paramilitary forces. With it, Lex instituted an increasingly hierarchal, militaristic approach to Agency command. For Lex, this was discipline, and to him, discipline equated to unquestioned obedience.

The greatest damage the Agency incurred due to Lex, and the DO in particular, resulted from his control over senior DO assignments over an extended period of time. He sought to remake the CIA in his own image, so to speak, having it function more like a regimented rifle company than an agile, inventive, and elite spy service. And like the generational consequences of Supreme Court choices, the cultural changes Lex effected were solidified by the commands he assigned to his camp followers and the promotions he approved. Those he advanced secured their positions through shared backgrounds, beliefs, and obsequiousness rather than merit, and disproportionately their gender, color, and faith.

According to a 2015 internal study commissioned in 2014 by then DCIA Brennan and overseen by famed civil rights attorney Vernon Jordan, "the CIA has consistently failed to promote minorities into its leadership ranks and progress in building diversity at the top of the spy agency has largely stalled in the last decade," a time frame that largely coincided with Lex's control. In fact, the study showed that while the representation of Black officers and other minorities among overall Agency ranks had risen slightly, to 23.9 percent, their inclusion in the Senior Intelligence Service ranks had decreased over this same time, such that minorities only accounted for 10.8 percent. The representation of Black officers in the workforce climbed only from 10.55 percent in 2004 to 10.88 percent in 2014, but had actually decreased over the same period as part of the senior ranks. Minority women and those with disabilities fared even worse, with minorities decreasingly represented as the grades ascended.

Lex evaluated others from the prism of shared political views, religion, and personal fealty to him. I recall sitting in Lex's Headquarters office when he was interrupted to take a secure call from a COS who was closeted but widely known to be gay. After the call, Lex muttered a disparaging reference to the officer's lifestyle to secure a chuckle from the attendees. Lex delayed that officer's promotion despite his success in one of the CIA's largest and most important stations, during which he ably executed a position well above his grade. Lex's senior personal selections created a lasting and reoccurring cycle of questionable DO leadership assignments, rejection of diversity, and to increasing levels of politically calculated operational risk aversion in the DO.

How did I manage to run afoul of Lex? Well, that was the question. One mutual friend asked me if I had perhaps slept with his wife? Ordinarily, a CIA officer is denied consideration for promotion, commendation, or command, usually by way of citing a memorandum of reprimand for a particular offense. I had no such reprimands, and I continued to receive substantive and challenging, often high-profile assignments, receiving strong ratings along the way. But all roads to promotion ran through Lex and he had made it clear to those Senior Intelligence Service officers willing to confide in me that I was not to be considered. Many of them likewise were unable to fathom why, inasmuch as Lex saw no need to explain his directive.

Those less fearful of Lex and particularly close to me acknowledged it was anti-Semitism concerning me, a Jew, one of the DO's few such case officers, in his NE Division. Lex viewed me much like his friend Ted, as one of those arrogant *Lower East Side New Yorkers who got under his skin*, and he perceived everything I did, or said, through that prism. It certainly wasn't because I was sleeping with his wife!

In two different, and particularly sensitive, high-profile operations I ran, Lex intervened. To be fair, Lex didn't micromanage only my operations, he had bigger fish to fry, and he cast his net wide throughout the service. In the first case, Lex questioned my reporting on what was indeed a sensational overture from a hostile adversary to cut a deal over a sensitive matter. Apologies for being so vague, but some details remain closely held while others are very publicly documented, first and foremost by Lex himself as well as former DCI George Tenant.

Prior to Lex moving back into my chain of command, I was chosen for a highly compartmented initiative. At the time, then senior Department of State official Ambassador William Burns (later nominated in January 2021 to be President-elect Joe Biden's Central Intelligence Agency director) was involved in back-channel negotiations facilitated by an Arab partner with representatives from a country with which we had long since suspended diplomatic relations due to their state sponsorship of terrorism. CIA had first included a CIA analyst in the diplomatic delegation to provide intelligence support. When the other party offered private breakout sessions between their country's intelligence service chief and DCI Tenant, or his delegate, we decided to see where it might lead.

DCI Tenant did not want his representative to be too senior. He hoped to avoid any appearance of reward for this adversary nation, which had American blood on its hands. The White House was likewise closely monitoring the engagement and allowed both State and the CIA a rather short leash given the political consequences of how damaging the exposure of dealing with this adversary would be. Moreover, while the ongoing diplomatic negotiations were secret, the subject matter lent itself to the projection of eventual disclosure in the form of a legal, international agreement. Still, the idea of a senior CIA officer in the room with the likes of that nation's intelligence chief, "Isa," and quite likely the architect of the very operations that had killed Americans, was worth some risk.

I was then the group chief who oversaw operations against that country, as well as throughout the region, equivalent in terms of protocol, rank, and authority with a military O-6, a full colonel, or Navy captain. I was assigned to the delegation's next session, and I was authorized to accept the one-on-one meeting with Isa as offered, as Tenant's representative, should Isa be in attendance. Ambassador Burns could not have been more gracious or inclusive. He choreographed with me the means to provide the best chances and top cover for discreetly breaking off with Isa on the margins of these early meetings. In turn, I was fully transparent with the ambassador throughout the effort, meeting him before and after my meetings with Isa during the diplomatic phase of our contact. We shared notes and integrated our strategies inasmuch as Isa had a great deal more influence with his country's leader than the diplomatic representatives among the delegation. As an aside, I am cautiously optimistic regarding Burns's tenure at CIA.

My instructions were to keep all documentation on the matter in hard copy and strictly for the DCI's secretariat. That meant no electronic records. Primarily, my function was to support the diplomatic channel that pursued reparations for the country's past acts of state supported terrorism, and suss out what Isa might be willing to entertain in an intelligence back channel to support that goal. Instructed to tell it like it is, I was to provide Isa with the realities as to why his country should comply with the diplomatic terms being discussed.

Isa was one of the most intriguing people with whom I ever interacted. He cut a rather dashing figure. Tall, handsome, and American educated, Isa's full head of silver hair was immaculately groomed. He wore only custom-made suits from Switzerland and Italy. And although it had been decades since his studies in America, Isa still spoke passable English. Charming, witty, and profoundly intelligent, it was all rather incongruous with his well-earned reputation for brutality. Rather than seek to intimidate his younger and far more junior American counterpart, Isa was gracious, polite, even warm, with self-deprecating humor about his English language skills and old school manners.

Isa and I worked well together during breakout sessions on the margins of these diplomatic engagements. He was frank, and even willing to offer less than flattering stories of his leader, most likely a means to earn my confidence in hammering out commitments as we worked through the roadblocks our diplomatic colleagues could not overcome. Though neither I nor that old fox would make the mistake of letting down our guard, on the surface, it was all friendship and collaboration.

We would take our dinners together, one-on-one, telling stories, making jokes, and discussing what a different future could look like between our two countries. Each of us was messaging the other and seeding ideas, circumstances, and possibilities to which our mutual masters might be receptive. Isa claimed to remember his time in America fondly, particularly the average people with whom he interacted. As we grew to know more of one another personally, Isa suggested we now had to refer to one another as "Brother." The devil he might be, and certainly was, we could work together, and my job was seeing to America's interests. It was profoundly entertaining matching wits with him, and knowing the large stakes for any slip or misstep.

When Isa claimed to have successfully lobbied his leader to accept the terms of the diplomatic agreement, I rewarded him with a hat and sweatshirt from his American college alma mater. Isa rewarded me with an offer: he proposed that we continue meeting in secret, not concealed from our governments, but from the public, in order to cooperate on counterterrorism.

Many of Isa's own dissidents and religious extremists had left to join al-Qa'ida, several of whom were among its top leadership. Still seen as threats to his government, Isa professed willingness to help the United States find these men in South Asia. He didn't care what we did with them, though he wouldn't mind eventually having some returned. It was no altruistic goal. These men represented significant threats to his own country as well as America, and they were out of reach for him—but not for us.

Isa claimed to believe he could trust me and CIA enough to conduct such exchanges secretly given our successful experience to date with the diplomatic back channel, which had by now been publicly acknowledged, allowing likewise a thaw in relations between the two governments. Tenant approved, as did Secretary of State Colin Powell, Defense Secretary Rumsfeld, and Vice President Cheney, so likewise did President Bush. Over the ensuing months, the exchange grew such that we each had to bring along a second officer to help with the volume of materials. Isa provided complete dossiers of the dissidents and extremists, including photos and, when available, phone numbers and email accounts. The details and continued monitoring that Isa's service maintained of their families at home provided us with an intelligence windfall. Long after my exit from the scene, many would be removed from the battlefield, and some would indeed find their way to Isa's prisons.

By now tensions were mounting in Iraq. America's response to terrorism had already deposed the Taliban in Afghanistan, part of the reason Isa's country had become more malleable in reaching the diplomatic agreement that had been struck. We were preparing to invade Iraq. Our adversaries understood that Washington was messaging to friends and foes alike, much like with Pakistan after 9/11, that they were either with us or against us. Coming not terribly long after 9/11, the US still enjoyed vast international support. To be fair, I was part of this, and I was directed to convey that very message to Isa in advance of the Iraq invasion. And it worked. Isa pledged that his government would not oppose the invasion in any form and would continue the counterterrorism (CT) cooperation from which both countries had profited.

I developed a constructive relationship with Isa and enjoyed our meetings, but I never lost sight that before me was a charming, albeit sociopathic brute of a man with a considerable amount of blood on his hands—the blood of his own people, and the blood of mine. I would hardly say we were friends, and though he referred to me as Brother, he would no doubt have just as easily ordered my assassination without hesitation or remorse, if so directed, or if more likely to advance his agenda. Rather, the relationship worked for him and his government; there had been confidence-building actions, and we both had delivered on our promises, developing a degree of trust. It was around this time that Lex moved from a senior position outside of my chain of command to one among DCI Tenant's chief lieutenants, from which he fired Randy One as NE chief, replacing him with Bill, and took ownership of my program with Isa.

Not long after our meeting to discuss Iraq, Isa surprisingly proffered a radical proposal that would seriously reduce bilateral tensions and in turn make Lex a virtual hero and national celebrity. The offer would facilitate the reestablishment of full diplomatic relations, normalization to enable US investment, and come with the willingness of Isa's nation to give up a destabilizing set of lethal capabilities. Ironically, it almost never came to be because Lex accused me of fabricating the reporting concerning the offer.

Lex clung to the accusations years earlier made by his friend Ted, that my successes were illegitimate and impossible. Despite the strong relationship I had developed with Isa and the volumes of corroborated CT intelligence reporting he had provided, Lex wasn't buying it. Notwithstanding the fact my meetings were now routinely attended by a second officer from my service as well as his, Lex insisted I had made the offer up.

Bill, the new NE chief, was in Lex's pocket, but was nevertheless a friend of mine who supported me as best he could. Given that I was acting as the DCI's representative, however, and that my reporting likewise went directly to him, Lex was obliged to follow up. As such, Lex engaged me in a series of strangely one-on-one meetings. This was then, and remains today, highly unusual given the protocol. At his level, Lex would have someone else in these meetings, either one of his executive assistants to take notes or a more immediate member of my NE chain of command, most appropriately Bill, if not both.

Initially, Lex had conveyed his accusations indirectly through Bill or his deputy "Sterling," who likewise supported me. Still, like Bill, Sterling's ambition would preclude him from ever going out on a limb to defend or otherwise protect me against Lex. When I finally went to see Lex in person, and in private, he surprised me by acknowledging his disdain for me. Lex did not like me, he admitted, nor did he think much of me as a case officer. I asked him why. He said nothing directly of my being Jewish as being a factor, of course, but accused me of making up the reporting about Isa so as to appear as if I was recruiting him, our adversary, as an agent.

I pressed for the context. What was it that had set him and me on this path in the first place? By now, a little older, a bit wiser, and far less arrogant or confrontational, I decided to adopt a more restrained and conciliatory tone. I hoped that doing so would give me a better chance to fix our dynamic. I certainly was no threat to Lex. Besides, how petty and vindictive did one need to be at his level? At a minimum, I wanted him to hear me on what was a rather historic intelligence opportunity. Whatever his issues with me, be they race, class, or my "obnoxious New York ways," I could not have overestimated Lex's interest in our status quo. Lex smiled malevolently, and said he would leave "that story" for another day. With that, he returned to the matter at hand, Isa.

I respectfully offered that I was not in any way suggesting Isa was either volunteering or susceptible to recruitment. While I had developed personal rapport with him and some degree of trust, I was not suggesting he could be recruited. Rather, based on our mutual ability to have kept our word to date concerning agreements and promises, he knew I was a reliable channel, and that he could trust what I told him in return to be true and in good faith.

This was no one-sided deal for America, I explained. Isa and his country would likewise be winners. He was proffering an arrangement that was in his country's best interests at the time, and serendipitously, advanced America's security as well. I acknowledged that my thuggish interlocutor was unquestionably loyal to his despotic master. But for one thing, he and his leader were frightened by what we had done in Afghanistan, and more recently in Iraq. They feared the climate would allow us to continue marching against our enemies, with little in terms of domestic or international opposition to get in our way. Facilitating our ability to locate terrorists, this likewise played directly to their interests as we were using our resources to neutralize enemies that were theirs, as well as ours.

Lex thought I was full of shit, grandstanding for attention and advancement. He had me slow roll Isa, and continue talking, at most, about my making a visit, but with a team, and only after a number of preconditions had been met. I didn't shut the door with Isa, but without the authorization to discuss the deal being offered, he was disappointed, and more reticent. At the next scheduled meeting, Isa didn't show, but rather sent one of his henchmen to conduct the CT exchange. And henchmen is no embellishment. This guy was huge, looking like a massive cannonball with legs, and appeared rather uncomfortable in his ill-fitting suit. We conversed in a bad mix of English and another language. Sending him was a maneuver, and a message, for which I had no answer. I again lobbied Lex to reply with a more encouraging response. But Lex would not budge.

Isa and I had a dedicated communications system in place, one that CIA will not let me further describe. We had it for emergencies or to reschedule meetings, but we had likewise recently used it to avoid a misunderstanding when the US had to send Marines to secure an embassy in an unstable African country undergoing internal strife and protests, and where his nation's own troops were present. Isa gave direction to his country's force not to interfere with the Marine deployment, and to facilitate its Noncombatant Evacuation Operations, known as a NEO, of civilian and nonessential US personnel, the Marines leaving a residual force to protect the embassy. This turned out to be a success for both countries.

We called one another from time to time, Isa pressing if I had an answer to his offer. Time and again, I had to say we were working on it. Isa was getting frustrated. Failing to produce results from the Americans, however, and clearly anxious over the prospect of becoming next on our hit list, Isa ultimately approached one of our European allies with the exact same proposal. Our European ally saw the initiative as credible, demanded no preconditions to talk, and offered us a seat at the table. Instantly, Lex bumped me from the entire process.

Aside from having me compile briefing books and coach him on engaging Isa, Lex replaced me from thereon out in the communications and ensuing meetings. He delegated to me the logistics of supporting the teams that would ultimately participate in the upcoming travel to Isa's country. Prior to his first trip to meet Isa in my stead, Lex sat me down alone and offered a revisionist take on the events that led to the historic coming engagement. "It was just a probe," he affirmed, "Isa's initial gambit to you, was just a probe, right?" Lex was not asking my opinion, but telling me as if he was setting the record straight. After all, how could Lex have been wrong?

It was no probe, I realized, and so did Lex. Isa made an offer. We dithered, and he took his chips and went elsewhere. It was lucky that he did. And regardless of the semantics, Lex chose not to pursue the offer. The engagement became a trilateral affair, and Lex would gain significant notoriety for the success, which is documented in books concerning the times.

As for me, I received a casual mention in my annual evaluation for having contributed to an "important, sensitive security initiative," which could not be further detailed given secrecy, and I was cited with a $3,000 exceptional performance award. On top of that, I was promptly shipped off to a small command in a high-risk conflict zone post. To be honest, Lex didn't order me there, but he allowed me no other options, vetoing the NE Division COS assignment for which I had previously been selected.

The other notable incident that I can likewise only discuss in vague terms occurred during this very posting—my exile, if you will. I was running a sensitive terrorist agent who had developed access to some of al-Qa'ida's senior personalities. Ever the reluctant agent, while certainly a Salafist, "Sulayman" was no terrorist. Though he personally abhorred violence, Sulayman's religious views and world outlook were still sufficient for him to willingly become a key al-Qa'ida foreign facilitator.

Sulayman funneled money and recruits to the group from abroad, increasingly garnering their appreciation and interest. Having assessed Sulayman, albeit indirectly from reporting we collected on him, he was practical and venal, rather than a "shooter" or true believer. Those traits, plus his promising access, led the CIA to mount an operation to turn him. We built up our knowledge of him through various other operational means. Afterward, while working with the local foreign partner on the ground, Sulayman was arrested in an effort to try a jailhouse recruitment. This tactic is always iffy, as addressed elsewhere in this book.

Station was given broad autonomy by the local foreign partner service chief, and the nation's chief of state. So long as we funded the unit, focused on counterterrorism, and did nothing to embarrass the government or hassle its cronies, regardless of their vices, we could operate largely independently. Expecting the worst, Sulayman responded positively when he was treated well and was befriended by the local foreign partner's officers, and ultimately ours.

Over a period of time, Sulayman was offered the opportunity to make things right, get his life back, avoid having to be chased worldwide by the CIA, and be given the chance to earn a great deal of money for his family. Rather than find himself languishing in prison, his bills were paid, his family fed, his criminal record exonerated, and his medical ailments treated. Of course there was a price if he wanted more, and people almost always do. Sulayman had to agree to go back into the lion's den and work his way up into al-Qa'ida's leadership.

Intelligent and soft-spoken, Sulayman indeed moved up the ranks. He was a religious scholar and quietly strong. Sulayman had a way of garnering respect and influence without threatening others or robbing them of their own importance. He didn't overstate his value, neither to us nor al-Qa'ida, but he consistently delivered on the incrementally important tasks the group assigned. Unlike those who tend to climb upon the bodies of those whom they bested, usurped, or used in their advancement, Sulayman was particularly skilled at leaving all with a good impression. Al-Qa'ida lower level and middle managers took satisfaction when they introduced him upward, as if his quiet, modest, and successful ways reflected well on them, versus threatening their positions. As such, Sulayman increased his communications and network with targets of interest. In so doing, his intelligence production was consistent, solid, and increasingly corroborated. Working his way up, Sulayman provided reliable building-block information on al-Qa'ida organizational dynamics and personalities.

Over time, Sulayman's interpersonal skills and reliability expanded his contacts, which facilitated further upstream movement within the network. He moved steadily into contact with increasingly well-placed al-Qa'ida facilitators and leaders, affording greater insights that contributed to disrupting or detaining midlevel terrorist targets. As he moved up the ladder in stages, we could arrange operations to remove targets in a manner that concealed his role, thus minimizing suspicion.

Sulayman's success exceeded expectations: ours, his, and even al-Qa'ida's. The better he performed for al-Qa'ida, the more they trusted him with information that was used to remove others in their network. In turn, as others were removed due to his clandestine work for the CIA, the more al-Qa'ida assigned him greater responsibility to offset the losses. This led to Sulayman's invitation to meet even more senior leaders I am not at liberty to identify, in still deeper and more dangerous ungoverned spaces.

Sulayman was hardly a warrior, though, and he did not hunger with such ambition. Content to remain in the shadows, and work the group's middle management, he was not suited nor prepared to manage the greater risks that came with moving too far up the food chain. Not even the financial rewards available for doing so could balance the fear for his personal security.

Sulayman was already traveling into the badlands—ungoverned territory where even if we had been collaborating with the local foreign partner, neither they nor we could have done anything to rescue him. He was routinely strip searched, interrogated, and accused of spying for the CIA. Mind you, this is all customary basic due diligence for al-Qa'ida and most terrorist organizations for an unknown who is to be introduced to senior leaders. Sulayman was compliant, respectful, and never revealed his CIA mission. Had he done so, Sulayman would have never returned.

Although he would come back each time with extraordinarily good intelligence, and was rewarded handsomely for it, this was all becoming too much for him. The greater his success, the more risk he would find himself facing, and the speed was increasing exponentially. Sulayman had provided us with initial awareness of what his al-Qa'ida associates suggested was a major US homeland plot. Taking care not to arouse the suspicion of his associates, Sulayman came away with intriguing nuggets over the course of time. The plot appeared significant, the threat credible, but the details were lacking. Sulayman's insights were limited to the rather small facilitation role that al-Qa'ida required him to play. Headquarters was falling over itself to send us our additional requirements, and they briefed the initial reporting, limited that it was, to a concerned White House.

Sulayman finally broke down, pleading with me that he was too scared to go further. The prospect of being found out and tortured was beyond his capacity to endure. Sulayman was certain he could not hold out if al-Qa'ida's questioning became more intensive. And he had experienced how al-Qa'ida's security scrutiny increased as he moved further up their corporate ladder. As it was, Sulayman always felt suspect when going through their security procedures. His knowledge of his guilt filled him with fear that he would eventually make a mistake and break.

Sulayman begged my approval to draw a line. He suggested inventing a story for his terrorist masters, how family obligations prevented his future travel into the ungoverned sanctuaries in which they hid. Case officers are always assessing their agents, whether they are performing well or poorly. That process is never-ending because life happens, circumstances change, and with it, so do needs, hopes, and fears. One didn't have to be a Freud to realize that Sulayman's nerves were frayed. Each trip in appeared to age him by years. Even if he acquiesced to my pressure, the stress was more than he could bear. I didn't doubt he would break easily were al-Qa'ida's due diligence to grow in severity or brutality, as it certainly would. The fact that he was being drawn into a circle of those supporting an al-Qa'ida homeland plot assured the reality that he would be placed under greater scrutiny.

Despite the enormous importance of the information he was providing on the plot, I endorsed his request to CIA Headquarters. Sulayman had been an excellent agent who had contributed to significant CT achievements. It was debatable how much more detail his current access would ever allow concerning the plot. But regardless, he was not suited to pursue it given the increasing challenges and risks that lay ahead. I cautioned Headquarters that we were asking too much of him, and that he had already done more than we imagined he could. It was time to take our winnings and move on. Sulayman had provided the first evidence of the plot, enabling us to align resources against the right targets to increase our knowledge and facilitate their disruption.

Sulayman was not asking to quit, but rather, to ease back on the throttle. While his potential increased access was compelling, the risks offset the gains. I suggested an alternative approach to keep Sulayman working at his previous levels. It would allow him to rather truthfully tell his terrorist masters that while he believed in their cause and remained their servant, his family obligations made further increased risks a selfish luxury. As well, his indirect role might still position him to contribute to our knowledge of the plot.

Sulayman could add the necessary theater, of which he was fully capable, that while he himself was honored to die for the cause, too many people counted on him. Sulayman thought it would work, as did I. He would maintain more distant and sporadic contact with our targets, which would still allow him to provide service to them, and value to us. At a minimum, we retained the flexibility to depress the accelerator again at some future point were Sulayman so inclined.

Lex, on the other hand, observing the high-profile operation from his senior perch, issued countermanding orders. I was advised that Sulayman's role providing reports on the plot offset other operational concerns. Moreover, Lex's direction suggested that Sulayman's desire to walk away was either a reflection of his haggling for more money or of my poor agent-handling skills. Lex's commands were delivered in an encrypted conversation over the station's secure phone system by my Headquarters-based chain of command. To emphasize the source of my direction, my Headquarters boss assured me that "Lex was prepared to step on us both with his size fourteen boots if we don't comply." The guidance was sent as well as by official cable, but curiously enough, or perhaps unsurprisingly as was his style, did not include Lex as a signee. Lex was nothing if not smart about paper trails. Succinctly, I was ordered to "force" Sulayman back. Over the phone I was simply told, "Make it work."

I argued my position over the secure phone and in official correspondence. Doing so did not further help me with Lex, nor did it assist my agent. Lex was unmoved, going as far as to direct the choreography with which to meet the agent, so as to reduce the agent's profile, albeit at the risk to my own safety and that of the team. We used increased security to meet Sulayman. Because he was coming directly out of the badlands, as with any agent under such circumstances, we could not be sure he had not been confronted and turned or compromised. The precautions were to guard against the possibility he had deliberately, or even unwittingly, brought terrorist associates to our meeting.

Lex's changes ran counter to our meeting security protocols. Not an isolated occurrence, but one for which Lex had established a precedent. The very same discard for such protocols facilitated Abu Dujana's

December 30, 2009, suicide attack at Forward Operating Base Chapman in Afghanistan, earlier described. CIA always balances security with efficiency, and risk against gain. There are tradeoffs, but we err to the safety of our people. That's why we developed protocols in the first place, to establish minimum force protection requirements. Even US military special operations forces operate in this same manner when assessing "threat to force" before approving high risk missions.

As with Abu Dujana's potential, the prospect that Sulayman might lead us to Ayman Zawahiri or Osama bin Laden was prioritized by CIA leadership at Headquarters and the field over the safety of our personnel on the ground. And with Sulayman, as would likewise be the case with Abu Dujana, pushback from the handling case officer was muted and ignored amid threats of professional consequences. The senior field and Headquarters managers who circled the wagons with Ian to deflect and conceal blame from the Khost tragedy, continued to be promoted and advanced to positions of even greater authority. Similarly, I was directed to go along with Lex's mandate.

After my arguments advocating for Sulayman fell on deaf ears, I complied. I used every bit of equity with Sulayman, the agent, to press him into accepting deployment once again into the bowels of the beast. He cried, I cried, but I told him that too many people depended on him, and as a man of God, he owed it to humanity to continue meeting these evil people so as to disrupt their sinister plots.

Such conversations might appear cliché and cheesy, a scene from a B movie in every sense, but it nevertheless was true, genuine, and convincing. This poor man agreed to go into what he feared would be near-certain death, and not a particularly pleasant one at that. It was not one of the shining moments of my career. I believed this was wrong and that it put Sulayman, whose life was in my hands, in unnecessary jeopardy. But I was not prepared to fall on my sword, end my career, and with it my livelihood. So I did it, and Sulayman agreed, or so he claimed.

It's not clear just when the wheels began to go off the rails. Time passed and I had long since turned Sulayman over to other handlers, having concluded my assignment and returned to Headquarters. When I arrived in Washington, my division chief, Bill, advised that all was now forgiven with Lex. I had served well, Bill explained, and demonstrated to Lex's satisfaction that I could be trusted. Still, no one, not even Bill, could articulate for just what I had been forgiven.

Bill, very much a like-minded Lex crony, had been installed over Randy One, who had voiced a dissenting opinion concerning the March 2003 Iraq invasion. Still, in most respects, Bill was a good leader. One of the quickest studies I have ever met in absorbing new material, he was inclusive and generally supportive of his subordinates, myself included. Bill exhibited none of Lex's racist or misogynist traits, my Jewish ethnicity being no handicap or flaw, in his mind. He communicated his intentions and expectations well, provided his lieutenants visibility into direction coming down from above, and was one of the hardest working officers I had ever met.

Still, Bill was ambitious, took care of his favorites, and envisioned himself one day climbing to where Lex now sat; and he came pretty close. As much as Bill was generally an honorable man with a code, he could be ruthlessly vindictive with perceived enemies and threats. All of that is to say, ideally, I accepted Bill's message as credible. I decided to take the win, happy to be professionally back on track, my exile now in the rearview mirror. Validating this, in fact, Lex endorsed my assignment to a senior Headquarters position, a Senior Intelligence Service (SIS) position that would, or rather should, facilitate promotion.

I would be working under another Lex crony, "Kelly," who had been installed as the chief of a functional, rather than a geographic, center. Here, I would be overseeing all of that center's HUMINT operations, and with a staffing complement larger than all of the CIA's Africa or Latin America Divisions. Apparently, even I had a price. Of course it wouldn't last. Kelly was an old NE Division officer as well, and we had collaborated together well in the past. But after a year of working for Kelly, I found he had fully drank Lex's Kool-Aid, as well as his own.

I had grown miserable trying to execute missions with which I didn't agree. Faced with a CIA inspector general's report highlighting the center's shortcomings and dysfunction, Kelly directed me and the other senior managers to ignore the recommendations and continue business as usual. Believing it hypocritical to remain in my position, which required me to endorse Kelly's philosophy with the large workforce I managed, I requested reassignment.

While not the ideal career move, I would opt out of the Senior Intelligence Service feeder position in which I served to volunteer for a critical-fill hardship assignment as COS in a former Soviet state. By doing so, I gave up the expeditious SIS pipeline, and at a time when I was in good stead with my masters. Instead, I chose a hardship assignment in a hostile operational environment. No one would ever accuse me of being smart when it came to managing my career. But being old school, I likewise subscribed to the notion that the worst job in the field is better than the best job at Headquarters.

Kelly would have his day of accountability, but for an operation that had already occurred while he was a senior field commander. He had pushed and directed for a careless operation against a terrorist target of Middle East descent. Neither CIA's Counterterrorism Center nor Near East Division would validate the target, but Lex had personally validated him by spoken dictate over the objection of substantive CIA experts. The reckless and poorly executed operation blew up in Kelly's face, and led to criminal charges levied by a foreign country against him and those who participated, CIA officers and foreign nationals alike. A standing Interpol warrant precludes Kelly's ability to travel internationally, as doing so would lead to his arrest. It also prompted Kelly's premature retirement, when the FBI refused to work with him on the eve of a senior domestic assignment. It didn't turn out all bad for Kelly, who managed to secure a cushy and high-paying private sector job thanks to his CIA contacts. And Lex once again managed to evade blame, facilitated as he was by the absent paper trail.

I didn't give Sulayman much thought for quite some time. In fact, it wasn't until some years, and a few assignments, later that a CTC targeting analyst approached me. Knowing that I had previously handled the case, the analyst sought out my thoughts on the merit of trying to reactivate Sulayman, based on a targeting study that suggested access that might address a key intelligence gap.

Reactivation would suggest that Sulayman had been terminated at some point (that terminology is fired in our lexicon, and it does not mean he had been killed). Given the passage of time, it came as no surprise to me that Sulayman's efforts had ridden their course. In fact, I was relieved merely to know he was still alive. I happily agreed to hear the officer out and hosted the eager analyst in my office. As the analyst outlined the circumstances, however, I was surprised to learn that Sulayman had in fact been terminated for intelligence fabrication.

The analyst explained, as I would subsequently see for myself from reviewing the file, that at some point after I turned him over to the next handler, Sulayman's reporting on the homeland plot became increasingly sensational and detailed. He had already been reporting tidbits on the plot from his limited, indirect support role at the time I had turned him over. There was little granular detail in Sulayman's early reporting such as dates, names, and specific targets, though it contained broad outlines on modalities, the operatives defining characteristics, and a few intriguing suggestions on the mechanics. But Sulayman's own interlocutors were too far removed to reasonably have known more.

Lex wanted Sulayman to meet the next higher echelon among the group's leaders to get more details. Doing so required Sulayman to travel farther into the country's ungoverned areas, where he would be entirely on his own to face his greatest fears. Still, under orders to do so, when I pressed him, Sulayman had agreed. After I exited the scene, Sulayman began to serendipitously provide more details for the plot, attributing them to the higher level officials he now claimed to be meeting. Again, when things are too good to be true in espionage, they usually are. Sudden, unexplained growth in an agent's access always warrants a closer look.

The reporting was gaining a greater audience, as a concerned White House directed FBI and other agencies to pursue the homeland end of the plot. The CIA would continue working to secure more actionable details and likewise target its external leaders. But despite more detail, the reporting became harder to corroborate. A decision was made to polygraph Sulayman as a means to validate the worrisome information.

The polygraph session did not go well. Confronted with accusations of deception, Sulayman confessed that he had fabricated the recent details. In fact, he never even made it to the next level of terrorist leaders. Sulayman justified his deception by insisting he had been pushed well beyond his risk tolerance, thus negating the moral contract in his mind to which the Agency would place his security above the value of the intelligence to which he had access. In fact, that genuinely is our default position, but Lex had seen things differently given the White House interest.

Although he thought he was prevented from breaking off the relationship, he saw himself free from the reciprocal obligation to report faithfully. And with me out of the picture, Sulayman made up his meetings with this particular senior terrorist figure. Forced by his CIA handlers to persevere, Sulayman invented a narrative to satisfy the new team. He insisted, however, that the initial threat reports were bona fide, as was all the reporting he had shared with me prior to my departure. The CIA severed its relationship with Sulayman, despite his strong, previous history, corroborated accomplishments, and significant ongoing al-Qa'ida contacts.

To be fair, there was not much choice. Once an agent has shown a proclivity to lie, the task of vetting the operation and standing behind the reporting becomes problematic. Unfortunately, CIA withdrew all the reporting concerning the plot—including that which he still insisted was true. A decision taken out of expediency, given the gravity of the threat Sulayman was reporting and initial evidence of corroboration, perhaps a more thorough deconstruction of when his reporting went bad might have been the wiser choice.

Ironically, another allied foreign intelligence service saw things differently. Not long after the CIA terminated Sulayman, the other service sought our concurrence to run him themselves. We outlined our concerns, but acquiesced. Our foreign partner was content with Sulayman's existing access, and with their ability to corroborate his ensuing reporting. To add insult to injury, they likewise believed his initial threat reporting to have been accurate. Sulayman continued with them for some time until his terrorist contacts from whom he collected intelligence had all been captured or killed, leading to his retirement. Ironically, the CIA continued to disseminate Sulayman's reporting as bona fide while he was run by our foreign partner, despite having withdrawn all of his intelligence while under our unilateral control.

The eager targeting analyst thought Sulayman could again be of value, suggesting he could reestablish contact with some of the lower-level facilitators in the organization who remained alive and by now had moved up. Ideally, Sulayman could repeat his previous success. The analyst came to the same conclusion as the foreign partner, that the initial threads of the threat that resulted in his termination were valid, a plot that was later disrupted through the removal of its key planners and operatives who Sulayman had accurately claimed to have been managing it.

I heard the analyst out, agreeing that to my mind Sulayman had been a reliable and effective asset. He wasn't wrong. Sulayman could indeed find a way to reconnect with old contacts who had since risen up. The reality, I observed, was that the waters were now muddied beyond recovery. The analyst would never convince Headquarters seniors to admit a mistake and reinstate Sulayman. Sure, it was one thing for them to turn the other way in disseminating the intelligence he provided for our foreign partner, but it was another to admit they had blown the call and were responsible for the subsequent mess they made. And even if they did, who was going to look this man in the eye and try to bring him back? The analyst smiled shyly, "Well you, of course." I expressed thanks for the flattery, but passed.

The analyst's proposal to recontact and reactivate Sulayman was, not surprisingly, rejected. The short answer from the counterintelligence seniors was that having been a self-confessed intelligence fabricator, we could never fully validate him. It was not entirely the wrong call, but it lacked the background and context as to what brought this man to the point of fabrication to begin with, and our own complicity.

Relieved as I was that Sulayman survived, and that he managed to enjoy a fairly happy and prosperous life thanks to the money earned from us and our foreign partner, I've always harbored guilt and questioned my choice. The right and honorable choice would have been to refuse pushing him rather than ultimately acquiescing to Lex's ill-considered dictate. Instead, I indulged myself in excuses that it was a lawful order, although not the right one, and that if I walked away they'd find someone else to do it and simply relieve me. And being right and honorable wouldn't feed my family if I lost my job. Moreover, I recognized that I too profited from abiding that direction, it having led to the subsequently more senior assignment Lex had allowed, despite my having failed to exploit the opportunity.

Even today I don't know whether or not I made the right choice. Politicians speak of compromising in order to ascend to positions where they can make real change. But do they? Do my colleagues at the CIA who likewise embrace that same shield to deflect criticism ever really cash in that equity to do the right thing? If I compromised my values in this case for the sake of career advancement, it makes me perhaps no better than Lex, Kelly, or Ian, and the rather foggy glass ceiling against which I ultimately bumped suggests it didn't make much of a difference.

WORKING AND PLAYING WELL
WITH OTHER US AGENCIES

Much of the CIA's change post-9/11 was designed to protect itself from larger agencies that were thought to be in the hunt to absorb the CIA's mission, authorities, and turf, perhaps eliminating it altogether. Relationships with other US government agencies was an important factor long before 9/11, but after, it would become a priority that offset operational considerations and, in some cases, right and wrong.

Such relationships can make or break a station's success, and that of its officers. Without such support, in some cases, stations can neither function nor have a facilitated means with which to exist. Particularly in the face of adversity, these relationships are critical. The responsibility doesn't just fall on the COS, but every officer and, when relevant, their family members. All CIA officers and their family members are the CIA's walking ambassadors by example among other members of the official US community. Of course, even the best intentions and actions can't guarantee success. Sometimes, you are judged not merely by what you do, but by those who came before.

My own interactions were a mixed bag. For ambassadors who come from the career Foreign Service ranks, their disposition toward the CIA often depended on their past experiences interacting with Agency counterparts abroad while still a junior officer. For political appointees, it hinged on their ideology and the mystique, good or bad, with which they associated the Agency. If positive, ambassadors would go the extra mile and take a metaphoric bullet for the station. If otherwise, well, you can imagine. While CIA officers might rely on their maturity and experience to realize the critical value of befriending their colleagues among other agencies from the outset, some unfortunately allow their egos to interfere.

When CIA officers patronize their interagency colleagues and deem them inferior, their future colleagues will reap the damage later. And regrettably, some case officers can act as if they were the cool kids at school, and live up to the worst stereotypes. It's thankfully more the exception than the rule, but perception is everything. As such, CIA officers need to go the extra mile to disabuse diplomatic colleagues of any myths to suggest their job includes reporting on other Americans, official or otherwise, that CIA officers receive unique perks, or that CIA can operate according to a separate set of rules.

I remember coming to a new post where I was living rather deeply in the ostensible persona for which I was officially known. I had to legitimately operate as an expert in a particular, esoteric field. Seeing to that, the CIA enrolled me in a series of academic courses before deploying me to provide those skills. I could walk the walk and talk the talk. Among other American officials, only my supervisor from the office of the other agency for which I was supposed to be working, where I had my day job, the ambassador, and the deputy chief of mission were aware of my CIA affiliation. In order to protect this illusion, I would have limited, almost clandestine contact with my own local CIA station, having to sneak into the CIA spaces to write up my intelligence work. I otherwise would sit in my day job's office and depend on it and that agency for all of my administrative support ranging from payroll to housing, finance, and transportation.

"Sal," my non-CIA, day job office boss, a small, nervous, and somewhat geeky-looking fellow, kindly greeted me at the airport on arrival. A veteran with his career service and this office, and a confirmed bachelor, Sal was intelligent, educated, articulate, but not very comfortable around people. He was the antithesis of the CIA personalities with whom I had become accustomed and my strong sense was that as a kid, Sal had been tossed in a gym locker a few times. I was worried this would not go well. Yet, he saw me to temporary lodgings, assured me there was a meal in the fridge, and told me not to bother showing up to work until after sleeping in the next morning. Excellent start, I thought. You can't judge a book by its cover.

When I came in the next morning, Sal welcomed me at the front gate, where the sentry on duty stood watch and cleared those for entry into the building. Sal made a show of walking me around the grounds in front of all the locally engaged employees, many of whom were informants for the local counterintelligence service. Having not yet met my station colleagues, since I had to downplay any overt evidence of knowing them, my office boss was truly taking care of me. I was relieved that Sal was going to be supportive. He took me to get lunch but didn't join me, since he brought a sandwich made at home, preferring to eat alone at his desk, as he apparently did every day. When I came back to the office, Sal offered that we'd discuss my duties and his expectations. On track, I thought.

I showed up at Sal's office happy as could be. This was going to be a great tour, I thought. Sal was welcoming, took me inside his office, and closed the door. He took a legal pad from his desk on which there were already several pages of written notes and pulled up a chair next to mine. I was ready. That he was somewhat anal-retentive in writing out in longhand his expectations was fine, I thought. Sal flipped the first page, looked down at the legal pad, and said, without any further eye contact, "Now let me review all the transgressions committed against me over the years by the Agency and what I expect from you."

Seriously, that was precisely how he put it. Sal took the better part of an hour, and dozens of pages, walking me through each and every slight, offense, and misdeed rendered upon him by CIA officers from his past. Though he never lost his composure, it took me every ounce of strength not to lose mine. He narrated each tale rather clinically, unemotionally, his eyes never rising from the page to meet my own.

There were the practical jokes, the absence of invites to Agency officer hosted social functions, and contacts CIA case officers had stolen from him. He offered example after example concerning the unreliability of Agency officers who were officially mandated to provide support to his own office and duties. Fundamentally, Sal felt CIA officers had treated him with disrespect, disdain, and indifference.

Sadly, I expect he was right. But now Sal was in a more senior position, with the ability to facilitate, or undermine, my operational success. His responsibility alone in knowing my true affiliation could have life and death impact on my agents, as well as myself. What could I say to him? Certainly nothing that would negate all the pain he had endured. My apologies were not going to change the past, but Sal had already demonstrated interest in the future.

My best move was just listening. I never interrupted, questioned, or defended the Agency as he methodically moved from story to story. I just listened, acknowledging by head nods and the like that I was paying attention. When done, Sal did not even have a question for me, and he smiled, albeit awkwardly, a sense of cathartic satisfaction apparent in his demeanor and expression. Sal was prepared to move directly into discussing my duties and his expectations. At the pause, I merely expressed understanding for the way he perceived the Agency based on his experiences, and I assured him that I would distinguish myself.

Sal was quirky, but knowledgeable, and I learned quite a bit from him, which helped me not only in the work I did for him but in my real job as well. He never quite dropped his guard with me, and he never thought much of my official work for his office, my papers awash in red from his corrections and rewrites. But Sal seemed to genuinely appreciate my effort, and I did not add to his yellow legal pad of stories. At least, nothing quite so dramatic as what he had shared.

Fortuitously, there was a coup. With it came the breakdown of law and order, and daily attacks against local government and foreign targets such as us. This included a bombing of the local US embassy, infrastructure, and locations that foreigners frequented. Perverse as my satisfaction of such conditions might sound, these circumstances relieved me of the need to fully live my fictional persona. I felt set free. With the chaos, all of the US mission's dependents were evacuated, as was its nonessential American staff, including Sal, and even the locally engaged (foreign) staff was sharply reduced. The fact I was deemed essential and remained in-country when my official supervisor was sent home more or less eroded what fictional depiction of my true organizational affiliation I had set out to depict. But the office building in which I worked now having but a skeleton crew simplified my access to the CIA station spaces.

Liberated as well from the demands of my day job for another agency, and another boss, left me free to roam the local streets to spy. The US ambassador was a pioneering female career Foreign Service officer for whom I had great respect, and who provided unflinching support. She would often observe with a playful sigh at how I seemed to revel at the chaos and in suborning ever more new foreign agents. "In chaos, Madame Ambassador," I mischievously replied, "there is opportunity."

Sal would in fact later become an ambassador, and you can only imagine what torture it must have been for that COS. I survived my interactions with Sal at the time, but there was less anxiety that he would raise a stink about me than there would be today. I had the backing of my management and had not, in truth, done anything to break our contract or to deliberately offend. CIA would not think twice about pull-ing an officer today who ran afoul of another agency, whether or not the accusations were founded. The post-9/11 CIA had to be liked by all, and was not able to afford more detractors.

THE AGENT'S WIFE

Those expecting me to recount my suave seduction of a target's wife that started with a death-defying hang glider chase will be sadly disappointed. This narrative is rather about the complexity of people, which requires case officers to see the world through the reality of another's eyes. I emphasized to younger officers that the art of espionage is in being able to anticipate several steps ahead. The reliability of your prognosis is driven by the likely results from any set of circumstances and variables. The more data you have concerning the target's background, character, motivations, and needs, the more accurate your assessment. But there is no 100 percent certainty in predicting human behavior.

To make the point, I offer a story from an early overseas tour. My deputy chief of station at the time, who years later would become NE's division chief, referred to me as "Hungry Doug," a backhanded compliment regarding my aggressive pursuit of recruitments. I was by this time perhaps midway through my assignment, had secured a few recruitments, and roughly a year of practical experience. I had come across a young man in the course of my official work, my day job. "Bobby" worked within one of the local government ministries we were hoping to penetrate. Having met Bobby in an official capacity, the trick was providing some innocent and relatable reason why I, this American official, would be interested in him personally.

Bobby was a technical expert, cleared through a vetting process, and hired into a sensitive position to support a requirement for which the ministry could not yet field proficient locals. Although well paid and relied upon for a critical function, Bobby was not a citizen, but rather, the hired technical help. Such outside experts are not always treated particularly well or shown respect in such circumstances. The poor treatment, lack of intrinsic loyalty, and financial motivation suggested that there was some operational potential.

Bobby's case seemed to differ from my earlier recruitments, each of which had been more complex and problematic. Certainly there was risk for Bobby in getting caught, the best case was being fired and expelled, the worst being imprisoned, tortured, and possibly executed. Still, Bobby was rather innocent to all these matters, seeing himself simply as a foreign technical expert working in a country that was willing to pay him far more than he would receive at home. He had decent quarters and was even able to bring his family to live with him. Bobby felt comfortable enough early into our contact to share a sense of his duties as well as his views on the locals, who he found arrogant and patronizing. They treated him like a servant, he thought. All of this permitted me to understand his access and motivations, and thereby helped me assess the risk versus gain of pursuing his cooperation. Textbook development.

Bear in mind, people can and do say, "No," when pitched to commit espionage, regardless of the approach, the justification, or the possible rewards. Not everyone is recruitable, or so I've come to believe after four largely successful decades. Life's changing circumstances can similarly alter one's receptiveness depending on where they find themselves. Life happens, after all. And I'll never forget all those many years back on my first day as a student at the Farm, the chief's opening remarks that "anyone can be recruited, but only when the circumstances so allow." Blackmail, insurmountable debt, a sick child, an unsanctioned romance, or other such scandal, and the variously desperate, unforeseen circumstances in which people sometimes find themselves. Such times, he warned, that lead human beings to do that which they believe they never would, or could; the unthinkable. As it turned out, this wasn't about our targets, nor was this encouragement to his new batch of predator trainees. No, he was talking about us. "Start each day asking yourself," he commanded, "what are my own vulnerabilities?" A sobering reminder of the human frailty in us all.

When targets do reject a pitch, however, it often goes along with reporting the case officer to the local authorities. At best, this results in the ambassador and/or COS being summoned, officially démarched, and told the offending officer is expelled, or as is known in the language of international diplomacy, "PNG'd," which is short for "persona non grata." Depending on the nature of the bilateral relationship between the host government and the United States, and the local politics, the episode could be handled quietly so as to prevent embarrassment to both parties. An autocratic leadership might be embarrassed that it failed to deter or catch a foreign spy sooner. A government seeking improved relations with the US, or the West in general, might similarly ill afford the bad press cast as betrayal from the American partnership being sought. Alternatively, the matter could be turned into a public spectacle that validates the local government's suspicions and animosity toward the US and its meddling.

That speaks again to why, as a case officer, winning over your ambassador is critical, since operations can and do go wrong, and it's often our diplomatic equities that are damaged. There're yet worse consequences, however, that can arise when a pitch goes bad and the local intelligence service runs the target back at you. That is, the target pretends to accept your pitch in an effort to allow the local counterintelligence service to further identify your operations and agents, and create a channel for them to feed disinformation to you.

Ultimately, "double agent" operations are designed to set you, the case officer, up for a pitch. Once the failure is revealed to you, that your agent was doubled all along, the hostile service will then "offer" you, the case officer, a one-time chance to avoid professional disgrace and humiliation by spying for them in exchange for protection, money, and better feed information to advance one's career. Believe me, we do it too, only we're a bit less heavy-handed than most. And in more places other than just Moscow and Beijing, such double agent ops usually end with a very rough arrest of the case officer in an ambush. Not pleasant, but fortunately something I never personally experienced. Well, not as the victim, in any event.

Obviously, all of this is part of the calculus in assessing the risk versus gain. A bad pitch can shut down a station's operations and, if nothing else, poison the chief of station's relationship with the ambassador. As chief of mission and thus the president's personal representative, by statute, the ambassador is kept *generally* aware of significant operational activity— just not the nitty-gritty details so as to protect sources and methods. A COS is almost never successful without the ambassador's support, or at least overall buy-in. Establishing a positive working relationship with the diverse array of career Foreign Service officers and political appointees serving as ambassadors can be more challenging with some than others, owing to political or professional biases and all manner of accumulated baggage they accrue over the years.

But everything with Bobby was going perfectly, and there was really nothing untoward I seemed to have missed. Over a rather short period of time, Bobby shared his frustrations at work and his personal and professional desires. He was quite good at his job but felt unappreciated. "Idiots" were promoted over him based on nepotism and cliques. Bobby's growing family was straining his limited financial resources as more children were added to his short- and long-term expenses. Despite the rather good pay relative to what he might have earned in his home country, Bobby and his wife were struggling financially because they were also expected to send remittances to their extended families. It's just how things worked. Undervalued, underpaid, and given to believe, with my encouragement, that he was financially strapped, Bobby had motivations that could be leveraged. A classic recruitment scenario. Ideal, no?

If you think about it practically, however, how many people do you know who fit those categories? Gazillions, right? In some countries, the average income for a professional holding a sensitive government or military position could be under $500 a month. Look at your own circumstances and of those around you and then count how many of your colleagues feel disrespected, unappreciated, and underpaid. And yet how many are willing to embezzle, or even falsify time and attendance, let alone commit espionage, business or otherwise? How many would take such risks to "get back" at their unappreciative masters or become corrupt to supplement their legitimate salaries? In truth, even in the commercial workplace, only a fraction.

Plenty of people have access, motivations, and vulnerabilities, but only a precious few can be converted into agents. That's where the case officer's skills come into play: assessing and manipulating targets to exploit those conditions and persuade the individual to go that final mile. It's more art than science, and that's why it's practiced best by but a precious small demographic even within the case officer cadre itself. Over the course of my career, I observed that roughly 20 percent of the DO's case officers recruited some 80 percent of its agents.

In fairness, most case officers spend less time on agent recruiting and handling as they assume positions of increasing responsibility, but they do so as a matter of choice. Even a COS can pursue targets among their official interlocutors and chase senior officials on the local diplomatic circuit. I always did, but admittedly, I relished it. Many are happy to leave such chores to their subordinates and the ascending generations, and play instead the role of big man on campus. I always thought, what's the fun in that?

In time, I was able to develop a conspiratorial relationship with Bobby. As a government worker holding a sensitive position, for example, he was required to advise his ministry's security office when he had contact with a foreign official. Such activity would have been disallowed except for sanctioned official contact, were my ostensible office duties to require his legitimate and continuing engagement. Bobby had permission for his initial visit to our building as part of his official duties. Disarming him from seeing me as a security threat, he chose early not to report our subsequent social contact. This allowed me to take advantage of his initial official visit to maneuver him into nonbusiness-related contact at the outset. I helped Bobby see it all as entirely coincidental and innocuous, negating the need for the *hassle* of reporting.

Once there was momentum and Bobby was enjoying the contact, at an appropriate decision point I reminded him of the prohibition against unsanctioned contact. It was an opportunity to innocently probe Bobby's willingness to transition to a more discreet and conspiratorial relationship. Clandestine cooperation means removing the contact from view. So I leveraged Bobby's circumstances and desire to continue meeting to make him appear to be the decision maker to further remove our contact from the public eye. Bobby had to believe that he was in control in crossing the Rubicon. Doing so required convincing Bobby that he was doing nothing wrong, that the rules were unjust, and that, given how they treated him, it was "his right" to do as he pleased. Rather than have him believe he was breaking the rules, my idea was to blur the lines for him until he was committed.

Over time, to protect him and conceal the contact from exposure, this evolved into a fully clandestine communications plan. We employed tradecraft to meet without detection, and we had practiced cover stories to withstand questioning in the worst-case possibility that our contact might be exposed. This was to guard against the risks of chance, of being seen by a nosy neighbor, friend, family member, or coworker who just happened to be in the wrong place at the wrong time. This was also to guard against the possibility that one of us had already come under suspicion and failed to detect people, or technology, that would have captured the fact of our contact.

The practice of "cover" sometimes confuses trainees. But like most things in espionage, it's not really rocket science but a matter of imagination and execution. Case officers are trained with the fundamentals, but cover is an intimate garment that must be tailored to fit each user and occasion. It's not what makes sense in your own head, but how it appears to others. That's the tricky part for trainees and agents who presume people see the world the way they do.

Cover in espionage means fading into the background so as not to trigger the curiosity of the nearby casual observer from "seeing something and saying something." Likewise, it means managing the more granular details to withstand later scrutiny. The former is known as far cover. An example of far cover might be sporting a tracksuit, headphones, and running shoes to account for being on a jogging path. But a typical error would be in presuming that, because you like to jog in the middle of the night, your jogging costume and activity would seem to be perfectly reasonable to any passerby at any time. Let me tell you, just because *you're* an early riser and think it's reasonable for someone to go for a run in the small hours, there are few places in the world where people actually go running at 4 a.m. And if your observer already knows that much about you to realize you like to jog at 4 a.m., believe me, you have bigger problems.

The latter is known as near cover. It's the story to which the agent and case officer are both committed if challenged, not only at the time of their contact but in the event of questioning days, weeks, months, or even years later. Near cover has to account for why the agent and case officer were meeting, must withstand time, and likely has to normalize whatever odd behavior or unfortunate coincidence brought you to the attention of the local security service. Say you missed the camera overlooking the stairwell on which you and your agent conducted a "brush pass," a nanosecond in which one of the two ships passing in the night handed a USB to the other. Even if ideally the camera failed to discern the USB being passed, it likely captured a pause and handshake. So you both need a story to explain the encounter, given that the two of you are precluded from having any nonofficial contact.

Near cover would have to account for the oddity of why these two people, one a foreign official, one an employee of the local government, happened to be in the same place at the same time in the middle of the night and merely slowed down, if at all, for some type of greeting. Believe it or not, it's doable. The story might only have to be sufficient enough to account for the oddity, and it could be based on just the right amount of simple details to align the backgrounds and patterns of both the agent and case officer. Such a tale should contain a cover for status (the bona fide of who you are) and a cover for action (why you're doing what you're doing at that moment). It can't be so convoluted as to require a glossary, annex, and footnotes to remember. And most important, both agent and case officer must tell precisely the same story, and every time. If the case officer and agent are already under deep suspicion for other reasons, however, especially operating in an autocratic state, you're probably past the point when even the most clever tale will suffice. Still, don't try this at home!

To help illustrate the point, I'd often refer trainees to the classic 1960s Dr. Seuss cartoon *How the Grinch Stole Christmas!* Bear with me now, since it might seem silly. Many of us will remember when the Grinch, outfitted as Santa Claus, was discovered by little Cindy Lou Who while he was pilfering the family tree and all of their gifts. In the midst of the Grinch's larceny, Cindy Lou stirs from her slumber and suddenly appears. Distraught by the scene before her, Cindy Lou challenges the thief and imposter regarding his actions. The Grinch launches instantly and effortlessly into employing his cover for status, layered with his cover for action.

Dressed appropriately, the costume serving as his official backstopping, the Grinch's cover for status was that of Santa Claus. It being Christmas Eve, Santa was obviously licensed to be in her house doing his job. And therefore, being that he was Santa Claus, his presence was logical and explainable. His status, that is. But why was he removing the tree and the presents rather than delivering them? The Grinch explained in soft, docile, and reassuring words how there was a light out in the tree. "Santa" would therefore take it back to his workshop for repairs and promptly return it before the sun rose on Christmas morning. This was his cover for action. That is, his cover story explained away logically that which appeared on the surface to be a criminal act. Thank you, Dr. Seuss.

Meeting Bobby as I did in the dark of night on a secluded street, much like the Grinch appearing to be Santa Claus, my official status was that of being a US government official, not CIA. That explained what I was doing in the country, and what enabled me to frequent venues at which I would interact, or at least meet, host government officials such as Bobby. Now, as for why I was driving around at night with one such official? I can't say what cover for action we actually used. Perhaps I was discreetly seeking his help in securing a work visa for a member of my household staff? Maybe I was contracting Bobby for his technical skills but understood such moonlighting was not permitted by his employer? Or, if the circumstances necessitated, the cover for action could be something even more nefarious to account for why I needed to meet him alone at night to transact this business versus sitting in his office. Whatever the reason, it needed to be below the threshold for espionage. Possibly, I was exploiting my local official benefits by quietly selling Bobby tax-free booze. It would be at a discounted price for him, but still earn a disproportionate profit for me.

Using these scenarios, Bobby, if caught, might face some disciplinary action. He might even receive a light criminal fine for buying black market alcohol, and at worst, I might get kicked out of the country, or the US might get a démarche for abusing its Vienna Convention privileges. At the end of the day, however, the story we used, akin to the Grinch's cover for action, at least offered hope that Bobby wouldn't be put up against a wall and shot.

As our relationship progressed, I began providing Bobby small gifts. Initially, this was under the guise of offering something innocent but useful for his family. A toy for the kids, a camera his wife could use for sending memories to the grandparents, all small but thoughtful gestures. This evolved into occasional cash to "buy his wife and kids something nice." As I blurred the lines of propriety, it elevated to, "Say, please use this cash to cover your kid's private school tuition or medical bills."

As choreographed, Bobby would gradually come to believe that it was really I who had been appreciative, not merely of our friendship but for the insights he was providing from his job. I began to deliberately highlight how his "advice and guidance" had gone a long way in contributing toward my political reporting. That his "insights" helped the US to better understand and, in fact, aid this country, and strengthen the countries' mutual security posture. Moving the chains further, I began to rhetorically question, while in Bobby's company, just why it was the local government officials could not bring themselves to share the same critical, innocent insights themselves, through our official channels.

Particularly for a guy like Bobby, who was at heart a decent, law-abiding fellow, the fig leaf remained important. In reality, and I believe why a CIA case officer is effective, there is a degree of sincerity in saying how a well-informed Washington is positioned to better shape events for the good. Okay, this may come across as naive, and it assumes the best intentions of our leadership, which as recent times have shown, is not always valid. Examining history, however, had a better-informed Washington, DC, realized that Hanoi viewed China as an enemy, would things have been different in the 1960s? Former Secretary of Defense Robert McNamara acknowledged as much in his memoirs.

By this time, Bobby was already acting as an informant. There was no formal agreement, but he was breaking the law, sharing state secrets, and accepting money. But in his mind, Bobby was conspiring with "his trusted friend," and doing nothing wrong. Not that any court in the world would see it that way. But to the CIA, an informant is not an agent, one of the fundamental distinctions between CIA collection and that of other USIC or even foreign intelligence agencies. It's not semantics. CIA goes through the exhaustive process to bring a source to recruitment in order to establish the degree of control and insights required to authoritatively allow for establishing the agent's credibility and reliability.

Control allows you to task your source, rather than elicit, and to test for veracity and access. In establishing increasing degrees of control, with an agent, the case officer strives for a conspiratorial relationship in which the agent is ceding to you that leverage in exchange for the incentivizing, positive forces being manipulated. It comes then with an intimacy and trust to enable the case officer to understand, and leverage, the agent's motivations for cooperating. HUMINT is about context. Without the ability to measure confidence in the agent's access and reliability, the intelligence is meaningless. Formally recruited agents are also tied to the organization, not the case officer, permitting the introduction of others into the operation over time.

The time had come for me to "pitch" Bobby. When making a pitch, the case officer must accomplish certain fundamental requirements. The case officer must make explicit to the agent what is being asked of him or her as a source, declare who is doing the asking, require confidentiality, and give the agent the freedom to stop at any time acting as a clandestine source. The agent is assured that we prioritize their security over their information in this secret relationship to which no other parties can be privy. And we put the benefits up front—that is, what's in it for them. Why they should undertake such an endeavor is predicated on their motivations and needs—material, ideological, and otherwise.

I had never once uttered to Bobby those three frightening letters, *C*, *I*, or *A*. But how much of an issue could it be? He was providing secrets for cash in clandestine meetings with a United States government official posted outside the United States. He was no dummy. For what other organization could I truly be working? And I had dropped a number of hints, foreshadowing my "special responsibilities." It wasn't going to be that hard to pitch Bobby, I believed confidently.

I met Bobby that evening as I had so many times before. Driving, I picked him up at a prescheduled time and place along a remote stretch of road in the city's suburbs. While a bit unlike how it's done in the movies, suffice to say we exchanged the necessary physical and verbal signals so that both Bobby and I could recognize one another and be assured all was well. Bobby entered the car, closing the door behind him. I quickly guided us back on the road, greeting Bobby while navigating through the "mad minute"—the opening mechanics in any operational meeting during which the case officer addresses security, meeting time, communications, and the need to address other matters of particular urgency.

Everything was perfect. We had our usual cheery conversation and moved into an intelligence debrief with me taking notes. I engineered a discussion that facilitated a transition into the pitch. I thanked Bobby for our friendship, and I recapitulated his motivations, reaffirming his "public pronouncements"; that is, thoughts Bobby had shared concerning his feelings for having been underappreciated, underpaid, and victimized by his employers. I brought up his family's material needs, introduced subtly in the context of how grateful I had been for the opportunity to lend a hand. Bobby had likewise helped me, I added, which in turn had been so valuable to the United States government.

Bobby listened attentively as we sat parked on the side of a quiet stretch of road. We were surrounded by only the night's stillness in the darkened car. I had not yet introduced the three scary letters, since sometimes hearing "CIA" is too much of a cold slap even for those among the willing. Rather, I confessed to working for a special, secret organization that collected critically valuable information used to inform my government's most important decisions.

I could see Bobby growing more anxious. Sweat was beading on his face. His hands trembling, Bobby began frantically tapping his foot. But I continued, and I explained how my job empowered me to bring Bobby "onto the team." Highlighting the benefits of joining a secret society, I continued, my confidential work gave me the resources and authority to help Bobby and his family by his doing exactly what he had been doing over these recent months. Contributing to the security of our countries, "our organization," would provide him $1,000 dollars a month, every month.

"OH MY GOD!!!!" Bobby shouted, at the top of his lungs, his exasperated, teary-eyed screams reverberating through the car. "OH MY GOD!!! You, you, you're CIA!!!!?? You want me to be a spy!!!! OH MY GOD!!!!!!"

Okay, hadn't seen that coming. That's because despite all of what we had been doing, and the fact that Bobby was acting in every manner as a clandestine CIA agent, he had created an elaborate coping mechanism. It was as if I had awakened someone from sleepwalking.

"I thought you were my friend!!!!" Bobby continued screaming. "You lied to me!!!! You took advantage of me!!!! OH MY GOD!!!"

"Wuh oh," I thought to myself. I'm ashamed to admit it, but at that precise moment, being human, young, and I confess, ambitious, I began selfishly calculating how this was going to make *me* look. I was also facing the real prospect that Bobby was at any moment going to bolt from the car and dash into the dark night, headed directly for the local counterintelligence service.

People are unpredictable, okay, I get it. Of course, at the moment, I was hardly relishing the joys of human nature's complexities but rather scrambling to determine how to get out of this pickle. Sparring, as we call it, is natural during a pitch. We trained and practiced how to overcome objections, since asking someone to commit espionage is not in and of itself a natural act. Concerns over security, or disappointment with the specified financial remuneration, were expected, and they required planning to overcome.

Only what I faced was Bobby's profound sense of shock and betrayal. I first had to talk him down off this ledge, the fall from which might take us both out. What a case officer says next in such circumstances will make or break the case. Words matter. Not unlike an argument with a loved one, the most constructive path is empathy and understanding, not litigation, negotiation, or defensiveness.

"Bobby," I responded soothingly, taking a page from Tom T, "you *are* what I care about in all of this, but I am so sorry for how I must have made you feel."

Bobby was still muttering to himself, but the screaming had subsided at least. "I would never have even considered offering you this opportunity if I didn't know for certain *I* could trust *you*, and this was something you and this country needed. I'm taking a huge gamble here, Bobby," I continued, "a risk I'm only willing to take *because* of our friendship, and my belief in you."

Bobby's tears had ceased, the muttering turned to attentive silence, and the fidgeting likewise decreased. "I never imagined we'd be sitting like this on that day I met you," I said in more calming, soothing tones. "I mean, I was just happy to finally meet someone while I was so far from home who shared my values, who I could trust, and was so great to hang out with. Someone willing to show a foreigner the beauty of this country and offer a view beyond the surface."

But I had to resume driving, lest I attract the interest of a passing police car. Driving now to the next place where I could park, what we refer to as hunker sites, I took every opportunity to hazard a glance back at Bobby, both to measure his reaction and to meet his eyes with sincerity and emotion.

"I know you now, Bobby, you've thankfully given me that chance, and the opportunity to see what's really important to you. You're a patriot, a man who wants the best for the world in which his children will grow. But your contributions and sacrifices are overlooked by the bad apples, for which you, your family, and other innocents will sadly pay the price."

Bobby was now nodding his head, aligning my words to what he wanted to believe, and how he wished to appear in my eyes. "But why did you lie to me?" Bobby asked with sad innocence. "Why didn't you tell me who you worked for, and what you wanted?"

I found another appropriate place to park, so I could meet his eyes. "I was trying to protect you, Bobby. It wouldn't have been fair of me to burden you with protecting my secret." He looked back at me curiously.

"Bobby, I didn't even consider the possibilities of what we could accomplish together, and just sought out your friendship, until you were generous enough to let me see your world." People don't want to think they have been targeted. And while intellectually he might have thought I was lying about the targeting, he wanted to believe otherwise. I gave him generous options to do so. The conversation continued along these lines for what was probably only a manner of minutes, but what felt like to me, and likely him, hours. At the end, Bobby forgave me, and he agreed in principle that this was a worthy pursuit. Still, he couldn't agree to undertake it. Not tonight. Not until his wife approved.

"Your wife?" I didn't see that one coming either. "What do you mean you have to ask your wife?" Bobby had spoken a fair deal about his family, but culturally he had always led me to believe that he wore the pants in the family. I had not yet been in this part of the world long enough to appreciate all the cultural nuance, particularly the dynamics among couples.

But I was getting a crash course. While men here exerted dominance and acted macho, in some cases husbands reserved some degree of palpable fear concerning their wives. Clearly, Bobby was terrified of his.

Common wisdom in the espionage world would have been to suspect Bobby's post-traumatic response was a ploy. Perhaps he wanted to buy time, either to consider approaching the counterintelligence authorities or as a means to punt. Possibly, Bobby was too afraid to say yes, but too embarrassed to tell his friend no. "Why burden her with the guilty knowledge," I tried to persuade him. "You're involving her with protecting a secret she need not know. Wasn't it better she didn't?"

Bobby insisted that he would not be able to explain this to her, and he couldn't take on the risk to their family without her support. He seemed genuine, I thought. But he served up another surprise before I could react. "You ask her, please," Bobby implored.

"What?" I shot back with wide-eyed surprise.

"She knows I have a kind, American friend that I meet," Bobby explained pleadingly, "who sends the family gifts. I just never told her about what I was giving you from the office. But she keeps it secret," he insisted reassuringly, leaning closer toward me, making his own desperate pitch. "So that others won't want the same thing, to meet you, and take advantage."

My COS Timothy, remember him? The anti-Semitic alcoholic? Well, he was neither pleased nor amused by my narrative of the preceding evening's events. Spitting as he yelled at me, Timothy's profanity-laced scolding confirmed his worst fears about my incompetence, stupidity, and unreliability. Initially, he ordered me not to make the meeting, which he expected would be an ambush, suggesting instead I lay low for a while and see how this all played out.

"The wife," Timothy observed plausibly, "is gonna be some counter-intelligence plant there to hear, maybe record your own confession, you asshole!" Not quite sober, and exclusive of the profanity-laced smackdown he delivered, his bottom line was a textbook response and not out of line. Meeting Bobby again was a risk. The business about the wife might indeed be a ploy. Even in what Timothy viewed as the unlikely event that Bobby was being truthful, just what chance did I have in convincing this foreign woman I'd never even met to allow her husband to spy for the CIA?

A smarter person would have probably acquiesced, and in today's more risk-averse operational environment I expect that's likely how it would have gone. Bobby might likewise have been thankful were I just to disappear. But in this regard, maybe I was not a smart person, and at the time, NE Division was known for its "cowboy ways." Even Timothy did not want to come across as weak by ordering a stand-down. And I was confident, certain that given the chance, I could make this work.

I belligerently insisted on going back that night to meet Bobby and his wife, as I had already agreed. Timothy, who wanted it to be my idea to stand down, based on his forceful encouragement, was stunned. "Fuckin' stubborn Jews," he said. The chair flew back as he jumped up, cursing and screaming. But that's where it stopped. He paused, looked me up and down contemptuously, and then in an eerie calm said, "Do whatever the fuck you want, but your Jew ass can rot in jail when the ambassador and I get called in! I'm gonna say you're just some stupid ass, naive kid who dreams himself a spy but doesn't have anything to do with me, and doesn't know what the fuck he is doing."

The night came and I ventured out, ready for the best, or worst, case. Good case officers always "clean" themselves of anything on their person from which a hostile service might benefit, should an ambush and arrest occur. I went over my belongings and "pocket litter" with a fine-tooth comb. I likewise warned my witting wife of the greater risk this evening. Albeit without any detail, I gave her a time after which she should call the official office's security officer and report me missing if she had not otherwise heard from me. I still believed I was right, but I allowed for the possibility of being wrong. More of my thoughts went toward the pitch I would now have to refine to persuade Bobby's wife.

Bobby and his wife, "Esmerelda," were walking along the appropriate stretch of road, within the correct window of time. Just seeing them was in and of itself immediately reassuring. We exchanged the right signals, and the nervous couple entered the back seat. I had intended for Bobby or the wife to sit up front with me, but I hadn't executed efficiently, and despite making an effort to choreograph on the spot, it was clear they both yearned for the security of sitting together, and with some distance from me.

The first hurdle was overcome. They showed. And no mob of police and soldiers appeared to drag me out of the car through the driver's window—the usual touch of an ambush. Off we went.

Exhausting the usual initial security questions, I transitioned into pleasantries and small talk with Esmerelda in an attempt to establish some degree of rapport before getting down to business. For all I knew, of course, Esmerelda could indeed have been a decoy, actually a member of the local counterintelligence service to whom he had reported my pitch, versus his real wife, just as Timothy expected.

Whatever I now said could very well be on a recording that the country's foreign minister might in time play for our ambassador, as well as for the local news, to protest America's treachery. Still, while putting into the best possible kumbaya light that the information we sought was in the context of advancing the mutual interests of two friendly countries, no spin or snake oil salesman's tale could controvert the fact I was asking Bobby to commit espionage.

And then the oddest thing happened. Esmerelda, who had been polite, respectful, and friendly, albeit reserved and clearly nervous, began taking it all in. I could see from glances into the rearview mirror that, unlike how her husband had reacted, she was processing the information calmly. Who knew how much she had been prepared for this. He must have told her something to get her out at night on a desolate road and into a strange foreigner's car. No emotional outburst, no grabbing at the door handles to flee the moving vehicle. In fact, at worst, I might say that Esmerelda had a look of surprise, perhaps even nervous anxiety. Was this a good sign, or bad? A sufficient degree of paranoia is a healthy case officer defense.

I managed to find a hunker spot where I could park, and I concluded my pitch with accolades concerning Bobby's character, love of family, and the friendship we had developed. I recapped the satisfaction it brought me that by working together, the United States government would be able to provide *them* a monthly stipend of $1,000, an amount that would grow over time, and in proportion to Bobby's contributions.

Suddenly, I heard the distinctly unique sound made when a hand slaps across someone's face. I glanced back to see Esmerelda turn to Bobby, and deliver another swift, unrestrained slap of her five perfectly extended, manicured fingers, across Bobby's now brightly red cheek. Bobby cowered and curled up, as she began in what I could best discern to be an irate tirade in their own language.

My heart sank. I believed she was thrashing Bobby for his stupidity in becoming involved with me, and the accompanying danger his family now faced. Pausing from the beating and verbal abuse being dispensed upon her husband, Esmerelda regained her composure and turned back to me. Almost reverently, she began, "Please forgive me Sir, I am so sorry for my outburst." Surprised, and momentarily relieved, I begged her indulgence another moment so that I could get back on the road, lest we were noticed. A moving target is always safer.

As I continued driving, waiting for the other shoe to drop, I invited her to continue. "Yes Sir, but I was telling my husband how stupid he is."

Okay, here it comes, I thought. But why so polite?

"Here you are," Esmerelda continued, "a good man, an important man, generous, offering him so much help to our family, and he didn't immediately say yes!" She looked back at Bobby, and smiling, threw a more playful slap his way. "My Bobby is not always the smartest, but he is a good man, and you can count on him. As for me, thank you Sir, so very much. Our family can very much use the money."

And with that, Bobby became an enduring CIA agent. He worked for several of my successors over a span of years. Timothy, of course, would take credit in relating to Headquarters his brilliant guidance and courageous risk taking that enabled our operational success. For me, it was an invaluable and fortuitously positive experience concerning people, cultures, and marriages. There was more I might have done to foreshadow my actual CIA affiliation and intentions, which would have better prepared Bobby for the pitch and more effectively predicted Bobby's shock and his need to share the news with his wife. I'd made too many assumptions and read too much into gestures that I failed to confirm.

You'll still find those in our ranks who contend an agent must always agree to keep their cooperation secret, even from their spouses. But particularly among certain cultures, they can't help themselves but to tell someone. Ideally, the good case officer can help the agent scope with whom they might, or should not, share their secret relationship. Just telling them they can't divulge this secret is not assurance they won't, and furthermore it sets you up for circumstances you are powerless to control when flying blind. It's far better to work within what an agent might do than forcing them to lie in matters influenced by their pride, manhood, or honor. Only having the insight through their honesty, even if the news is bad, can the case officer expect to effectively assess the risks and influence the outcome. Once an agent is forced to begin lying to their case officer, it's a slippery slope from which few ever return.

LOVING AND LOATHING WITHIN CIA AND FINDING COMMON GROUND WITH YOUR AGENTS

Case officers are cautioned early not to fall in love with their agents. Now, admittedly, this has on the rare occasion been literal, and CIA is not free from some degree of the salacious behaviors commonly found on daytime television dramas. One colleague gave birth to a child, not conceived with her husband as she would originally claim, but rather with a foreign agent she was handling. Discovered, the officer was eventually separated from service. Another seduced the wife of a senior foreign intelligence counterpart. Following his lover's divorce, the officer, who rose to the most senior levels of the DO, married his foreign love interest. One female case officer who had an affair with her married foreign agent helped him to defraud the US government by aiding in a car sales racket at the office where she served. Real life happens everywhere, even at the CIA.

Take the case of two senior COS's who were reprimanded for taking their CIA mistresses with them on their overseas postings, after complaints emerged from their staffs and wives. The mistresses were junior officers whose assignments their senior lovers had arranged. Not to fear, the reprimands were but mild wrist slaps. After paying penance in the penalty box of low visibility and mediocre assignments, both officers thereafter moved on to still more senior DO positions.

The seventh floor executive suite has likewise not been immune from such behaviors where the seduction of power and position has turned into seductions leveraging such power and positions. Legendary is the tale of a former DDO, the Clandestine Service chief himself, whose screams from his car in the underground executive parking lot drew the response of nearby security officers who believed him to be having a heart attack. What they found was him receiving "oral gratification" from his attractive, female, executive assistant, a woman whom I would later sit across from at morning executive staff meetings. Try as hard as I might, I could never see her without visualizing that scene. Neither could anyone else. But none of that impeded her advancement into the Senior Intelligence Service ranks, per the recommendation of, yes, the DDO.

Unfortunately, particularly in the case of these very senior officers, all of whom were men, there comes a time when they buy so deeply into their own sense of power and immunity from consequences that they indulge in such misogynistic and reprehensible behaviors that eventually go over the top. Two different associate deputy directors of operations (ADDOs), the deputy chief of the entire Clandestine Service, fell in this manner.

In one case, an ADDO was caught in the act when his lover's non-CIA spouse hired a detective to capture his wife's infidelity, evidence that was brought to the DCIA. The husband suspected his wife, but he never suspected the identity of her lover. So much for case officers always being situationally aware and looking for surveillance. The incident validated rumors concerning his ongoing affair with still another rising DO star, an ambitious climber, whose own husband was likewise aware. Both are now members of CIA's Senior Intelligence Service. The disgraced, fired ADDO was escorted out the building.

I personally happened upon the other ADDO who, curiously, was meeting a former female student of mine. The encounter was during a weekend stop at my neighborhood coffee shop. My former student, pleased to run into me, and no doubt being cultivated under the pretense of the ADDO's "mentorship," eagerly walked me over to their table. "You know 'Cam' of course, don't you?" my former student innocently asked. "Of course I do," I replied, eyeing the dirty old man contemptuously as his pasty white face turned several shades of red. Within a year, Cam would likewise find himself removed, albeit more quietly, after which he retired.

And these are but some of the cases I know firsthand. That such behaviors were many times tolerated was commonplace at the CIA for years. Cronies among the senior ranks covered for one another, while concurrently preaching morality, selflessness, and harassment-free workplaces. To the Agency's credit, and certainly under DCIA Gina Haspel and "Vicki," the DDO at the time of this writing, this was getting better. Seniority is no longer automatic protection from credible allegations, which are given fair hearings. Though, some untouchables still remain.

By and large, however, the sentiment that case officers should not fall in love with their agents is more philosophical and is meant to instill a sense of constructive detachment. A good intelligence service is constantly challenging its own assessments for bias and flawed judgment, to assure for the most accurate analysis. And a good case officer similarly questions and tests their agents, regardless the source's length of service or past achievements. Is their information still free of fabrication, embellishment, or deception? Failure to consistently assess and test the agent's motivations, reliability, and absence of hostile control can have dire consequences. It's yet one of the additional considerations when the CIA, or any intelligence service, presumes to believe handling and recruiting agents are two different skills.

The old adage that a case officer is constantly recruiting the agent is essentially true, and it's based not on hubris but cold practicality. Suggesting that anyone with a little tradecraft instruction can handle an existing agent is a dangerous take that's fraught with peril. The reality is that a case officer's skills and experience are required to assess an agent's evolving mindset over the course of time. People's lives change, so do their priorities, needs, and occasionally, even their beliefs. Reaffirming and leveraging the agent's motivations to keep them loyal, motivated, and in the fold, while likewise detecting any inconsistencies or red flags, is crucial.

A good case officer re-recruits the agent every meeting, and likewise identifies any changed behaviors or inconsistencies that might reveal a problem. Such changes might be evidence that the agent has been caught or turned, or that the reporting might be fabricated. A case officer who claims to be a good handler but lacks comfort in recruiting is simply not a good case officer, since the skills are indivisible. Likewise, a targeting officer, staff operations officer, or analyst who claims to have been trained to handle but does not possess the psychological skills that are needed to manipulate, assess, and motivate an agent, is vulnerable to missing "people clues."

Agents lie for job security or to deliberately mislead. They may lack the access they claim but need the material benefits proffered by the case officer, or they may conceal their true interest and deceive or influence their case officer so as to advance their government's or organization's interests. While some mercenary agents lie about their access in order to curry favor and maintain a reliable source of income, others do so simply to inflate their self-importance.

But many agents lie simply because their circumstances change. Our lives are dynamic and, as life transforms, so do motivations. Old problems are solved, different needs arise, and the reasons that once compelled an agent to cooperate might no longer exist. People lose jobs, get new ones, some of which might hold less access, or alternatively, more prestige and power that in turn raises the risk of compromise. The cost of taking an agent for granted ranges from unwittingly introducing misleading and false information into our system, to setting the case officer up for arrest or attack.

Double agents, of course, lie and fabricate to influence rather than inform, and they misdirect so as to protect their organization's true intentions. History is replete with fabulous schemes and capers of denial, deception, and disinformation operations. From the Trojan horse to Patton's bogus Army in World War II, throughout the Cold War and every day since, intelligence services aim to control what their adversaries think, see, and know. Need I mention the tremendously successful Russian influence and disinformation campaign of the last few years here in the United States? Having secured the assistance of former President Donald Trump in advocating, spreading, and defending their lies, Russian intelligence services scored a historically unprecedented coup.

Although an agent controlled by another service can deliberately inject disinformation into the system with a purpose in mind, there is another upside for them to do so: double agents gain valuable insights on our strengths, weaknesses, and capabilities from their work with us. In the course of running an agent, a service necessarily also exposes its gaps through the questions it asks. What we don't ask about can be as revealing as what we do. Any engagement is revealing. Agents are tasked to collect information. The questions we pose to the agent therefore offer a glimpse into our requirements, allowing insight into what we do and what we might not yet know. If we ask a question about something, it suggests we don't already know the answer. Savvy case officers can and do mitigate that danger, of course, through various methods I can't detail in these pages, but much of which is just common sense.

Agents, and our adversaries, similarly gain insights into our tradecraft. Although a good case officer mixes up the bag of tricks, there's bound to be techniques you give away. How we handle one agent might reveal others that the CIA is handling. Thus the mantra has been: one agent, one meeting site, one technical system. That's the ideal, but practicalities and expediency often make half measures rather enticing. Remember what I said earlier about integrity and avoiding shortcuts?

Bearing in mind we don't exclusively find ourselves dealing with selfless patriots who are willing to risk their lives for the sake of doing the right thing, assuring fidelity can have its challenges. Some of the institutions we must penetrate are not staffed by choirboys, and those who have secured positions of access did so through actions, sometimes brutal ones, and not by ideology alone. Getting inside such a target institution means securing the cooperation of members who wouldn't likely be found on Santa's "good" list.

Fundamentally, while it's nice when you genuinely like your asset, you're nonetheless obligated to retain some skepticism in order to objectively evaluate their veracity and how free they are from hostile control. And when you don't particularly like your agent, it's important to find in them some endearing qualities to help you relate on a personal level, even if it's a cynical degree of respect for just how terrible their malign behavior is or what they've done to get to where they are in their organization. Whether you do, or don't, hold them in great esteem doesn't matter. The case officer's foremost job is to protect them from harm, even to the degree of putting yourself at risk, and making them feel appreciated, respected, and valued by the United States.

My first such experience working with an agent whom I didn't like occurred in one of my early overseas assignments. Up until then, I had been fortunate in having genuinely liked the agents I recruited or inherited. They weren't all selfless heroes cooperating to right wrongs, battle evil, and support the great American way. But for the most part, they were people who were trying to do the best for themselves and their families under difficult circumstances. Various needs or quirks delivered them into our service, be it ego, revenge, or finances.

Another approach among intelligence agencies is reflected by the acronym MICE, which stands for Money, Ideology, Coercion-Blackmail, and Ego, as the principal levers in recruiting an agent. The concept is drawn from the Russian playbook that emphasizes negative vulnerabilities and coercion, such as *kompromat*, that is, compromising materials.

In my experience, focusing on an individual's motivations, as opposed to their vulnerabilities, makes for a more constructive approach. Whether or not the underlying motivations for an agent's cooperation are based on fears or desperate needs, the case officer is better served appearing as the benevolent benefactor, rather than the evil loan shark. Creating the illusion of the agent's commitment to a cause bigger than themselves, even when the case officer knows better, facilitates the relationship. That's not to say my agents up until this time were free of vices of one sort or another that contributed to the motivations I would leverage. For some it was drinking, philandering, embezzlement, greed, gambling, or revenge. But they all possessed various degrees of charm, warmth, and senses of humor to which I sought to appeal. And then I met "Vinnie."

When I set out to pursue Vinnie, we didn't know very much about him except for the position he held. And that was enough to pique our interest. Vinnie was a long-in-the-tooth public servant and a member of one of this country's religious minorities. You might see a pattern among targets I pursued, in that I favored those who were disenfranchised from their own countries. As an aside, this is a worrisome dynamic in the US these days, given the political weaponization of hate, particularly wielded against ethnic groups, and sadly too often at this time, by our own national leaders. Victimization, racism, and xenophobia are powerful buttons to push.

Vinnie's rank was a poor reflection of his many years in service but no surprise in a country that discriminated rather overtly against its minorities. Although on the surface, the government disingenuously claimed to be an open society and allowed minorities to seek appointments in various ministries, the reality was that such groups encountered glass ceilings. Some were tokens, and almost all were denied the opportunity to reach the highest levels, except in rare cases where political associations trumped religious backgrounds. None of our people had ever met Vinnie, so there was no scouting report offering previews of his personality to help inform an approach. His background alone, however, suggested he might have an axe to grind.

The same information that revealed Vinnie's existence and position likewise identified his particular office location and phone extension. But I couldn't just call and seek an appointment without leaving a trail. Fortunately, my official day job duties gave me a reason to be in his ministry's Headquarters on occasion. At the time, security there was lax and foreign officials were not required to have escorts except when within sensitive work spaces. Once inside the building, I was free to roam the hallways. I knew in which office Vinnie worked, and understood the ministry's work tempo. This enabled me to discern optimal windows of time in which I might find him. If I didn't run into him today, I'd just try again the next time I had a reason to visit. Keeping with the adage that it's sometimes better to be lucky than smart, I found him on the very first try.

It's great to be an American for all sorts of reasons. An American official possesses a relatively outsized degree of cachet relative to rank. Being the representative of a superpower allows for a comparatively more junior American official to be accepted by one more senior of another country. Contact with Americans is often sought after, even among some adversaries. They can brag to their bosses and colleagues about how they use their American contacts to advance their nation's agenda.

I was pretty low on the totem pole of my official day job, but I was the first American representative who had ever expressed interest in meeting Vinnie. When I showed up and introduced myself, claiming some inane yet benign research endeavor that aligned with his area of responsibility, he was more than happy to talk. Still, Vinnie had not made it as far as he did without understanding how to take care of his own exposure. He asked how I came to find him and casually inquired as to who from his ministry knew I was here. He was discreet, security conscious, interested in seeing me, and understood the risks.

Vinnie did not cut a dashing form, and while he retained some degree of elocution, his was not a rapier wit. Barely was there any evidence of charm, warmth, or substantive depth. I deliberately avoided issues of any sensitivity or controversy, hoping to get a feel for him as a person and a sense of his access. And I was doing most of the heavy lifting in terms of banter. Despite the usual ploys of, "So I'm married and here with wife and kids," my "give" was not rewarded by any demonstrable "get." Still, I persevered, and Vinnie indulged me, no doubt trying to work out in his own head the thrust of my agenda.

In this somewhat restrictive country, the natural disposition among local officials was to assume any American was CIA. It didn't hurt for Vinnie to suspect the possibility. As for me, I'd learn whether such suspicion was accompanied by a willingness to see me regardless. My goal was to get a second meeting, but one outside the building and beyond the notice of the counterintelligence service. I came up with a variety of pretexts, whether asking he provide a tutorial on his people's cultural history over a drink, or helping me buy a car on the local market—small favors that would establish a human connection. Some officers would argue that such requests risk eroding cover and creating a sense of obligation to the potential agent, but for me they were a tactic.

Vinnie didn't say no, didn't say yes, and didn't quite say maybe either. With more to be lost in pushing, I let him off the hook and suggested I'd be back. I had left sufficient clues through my unusual behavior and requests that Vinnie was positioned either to play ball and explore the possibilities or dutifully report me immediately to his security officers. I found an excuse not to offer my own phone number to him: Since I was so often away from the office, I didn't want to put him out in leaving messages. This, too, was a polite clue that I recognized the CI dangers of calling him, or him calling me. Before leaving though, I asked when were good times of the day I might catch Vinnie in the office. That much he provided, suggesting a glimmer of encouragement.

A couple of weeks passed before I found myself back in the building. As the last time, I hit a couple of offices for which I had genuine and benign official work. Leaving a cover trail would account for my having visited and should set off no flags among the ever watchful counterintelligence service watchdogs who by this time we knew through our sources had considered me a "suspect" intelligence officer. Most of the official Americans, however, were *suspect*, so I did not yet rate much attention. I could only hope that Vinnie had not officially logged my initial visit. I made my way innocently through the halls to Vinnie's office. It was as if he was expecting me, and the familiarity of our second encounter was now like that of old friends. It's funny how often that happens.

Vinnie still couldn't work up much charm, but he was a bit less wary and allowed a few conspiratorial hints at his current lot in life. While still somewhat measured, Vinnie spoke more about his background, apologizing at times in embarrassment at his relatively junior rank compared to those in service with whom he had begun, offering obliquely that I of course understood how things were in this country. While lacking in unambiguous contempt for his government, Vinnie was saying all the right things.

While practicing the age-old art of elicitation, so as to not yet expose my true agenda or cause him to be defensive, Vinnie responded by providing a number of conversational gates and public pronouncements I would log for later exploration. By that I mean Vinnie had himself raised a number of intriguing or revealing topics I could now explore directly. I didn't want to exploit too many such gates at the time, given security considerations. After all, the last thing I wanted him to do was volunteer any compromising information in his office within earshot of his colleagues or which could be captured by any internal security monitoring system. Besides the risk to him, what a lovely trap that would be in an environment that could easily have been wired for sight and sound.

I focused on the next meeting, but at an outside venue where neither he, nor I, would be recognized. Vinnie accepted my pretext (a detail I must exclude), which would serve as our cover for what we were doing together should he or I ever be confronted. I made several suggestions for places we could visit, some being shops and market areas, and other small out-of-the-way venues where we could grab a bite or drink. All of these locations had been cased. Vinnie had various excuses for why none were appropriate, and eventually he suggested that he provide me with his home phone number, which he reminded me I should not, of course, call from the office or my house. Vinnie told me to call the next evening to give him time to have a look at the place he had in mind. Opportunity or setup?

As instructed, I set off in the evening on a number of stops to be sure I was free from being followed, and found a location from which to call. Well before the advent of cellular technology, this country still did not have much in the way of public phones. There were, however, options to use public call centers, from where the many local inhabitants who lacked phones of their own could call family or friends. Alternatively, sometimes you could stop at a shop and pay the proprietor a small amount to make a local call. Both methods could generally keep you off the radar, unless the call center or shop proprietor decided, for whatever reason, to advise the authorities.

The phone rang six or seven times before Vinnie answered. Not unusual in this country, though something that drives a typical American crazy. Once we were talking, Vinnie was happy with the place he had in mind for us to meet, a local nightspot with which he asked if I was familiar. It was a pretty big town and the spot catered to locals, not foreigners, so it was understandable that I wouldn't know it. When he provided directions, I quickly realized it was on the other side of the tracks in a city that itself was largely on the wrong side of any tracks. Still, I accepted. We set a time at which we'd meet inside. I was thrilled with a sense of conquest. Vinnie was meeting me unofficially and taking a great risk in doing so. I envisioned us chatting more expansively over a meal, during which I could further our personal relationship, advance his trust, gain better insights to his access, and determine the means through which to persuade him to work secretly with the CIA.

Early indicators of what was ahead of me were evident when not a soul in my station had ever heard of this place, nor passed anywhere near its vicinity. This part of town was replete with bars, most illegal, brothels, and black market enterprises. The local housing, that which existed, consisted of, to observe generously, fixer uppers. Crime was rampant there too. My boss was a bit concerned, but supportive, as I had earned his confidence. My peers were a bit more dubious, some putting in dibs for my office possessions should I fail to return.

It was everything I could have expected, and less. Anticipating a restaurant, I arrived at a hotel of the same name. Hotel, however, is a bit overstated. Advertised as a hotel, it offered rooms for use of various durations. A filthy, rundown building on an even dirtier, rubbish-ridden street. Where in the hell was I? Certainly not in Kansas, and I was perhaps the only White man who had been anywhere near there since the Brits had conquered much of the region. I went inside to a small, dark, dingy lobby and found a lone figure at the front desk. An older fellow, with thin, greasy hair and a few days facial growth appeared and welcomed me. In broken use of the local language, I asked for the restaurant. Mixing the few words I could understand with hand signals, he pointed me toward a door that gave way to stairs. The "show," he said using a word I recognized, was downstairs in the basement. "Show?" I thought.

The music that was barely emanating from below became audible as soon as I opened the stairwell door, and it grew increasingly louder and tinny as I made my way down the barely lit flights. Another door, the only possible option, lay ahead of me. I opened it, the music now blasting, to find a darkened, smoke-filled hall of tables surrounding a stage on three sides, the strong smell of formaldehyde-treated beer in the air. On stage were women in various stages of disrobe, gyrating and dancing for their audience. They were of assorted ages and builds, though mostly on the older, thicker, and well-worn side. None were particularly attractive, nor invested in their acts, save the limited degree to which they were dressed. I tried to scan the hall for Vinnie as a host approached me. Dark as it was, I could spot Vinnie's silhouette, so I pointed in his direction to the host, who gave me entry, and I negotiated the crowded tables of men gawking at the women dancing for their pleasure.

I walked up behind Vinnie, whose eyes were likewise affixed on the entertainment. Startled, he recoiled in surprise when I tapped his shoulder. Vinnie stood, and we embraced like old friends, the pervasive smell of tobacco and alcohol from his cheeks and garments even overpowering that of the same from the establishment. He pointed me to the small, rickety wooden chair next to his. I strained to hear his voice over the music, and I struggled to keep his attention in conversation. Scanning the patrons, the clientele and atmosphere were strangely reminiscent of the *Star Wars* cantina scene, perhaps only less classy. There was no raucous shouting or slipping of currency into thongs. Thick, sweaty, and seemingly indifferent to their audience, most of the women moved slowly from one side of the stage to the other as if trudging through snow. The men simply stared, transfixed, sipping their watered down drinks. I made a mental note of the North Koreans I saw in the crowd, easily identifiable from the Kim Il-Sung lapel pins they were required to wear at the time. North Koreans tended to be in such dives, either because they were attracted to the low cost of the diversion, or because such venues were ideal for hawking the alcohol and other contraband that they smuggled for local sale via the diplomatic pouch.

"Did you bring money?" Vinnie asked. A hopeful sign, I thought. "Absolutely," I replied earnestly. His eyes moved from mine to the stage and back again. "Dollars? Did you bring dollars?"

"Some," I nodded and continued: "Is there something I can help with?" Ah-ha, I thought, here it comes. Vinnie was about to share his sad story. A child who desperately needed medical treatment he was unable to afford? Or perhaps his wife, yes, who could no longer get to her job without a car? Maybe it was payments on the house for which they could no longer keep pace, and an evil landlord ready to toss them on the street?

Vinnie looked back my way. "Which one do you want?" He yelled over the music.

"Beg your pardon?" I shouted back in confusion.

His eyes back on the stage, Vinnie clarified. "The girls," he said, pointing among the two nearest us, now looking back our way. "The short one or the tall one? Your choice, since you're paying."

As much as I sought an experience through which we might bond, this was not it. Still, I couldn't offend. "Not for me tonight, Vinnie," I excused myself humbly, "but be my guest, on me, of course, but let's first get a bite and chat a bit."

Satisfied, Vinnie called over the host and made the arrangements. Likewise playing the role of server and pimp, the host took Vinnie's order for fried chicken and whiskeys and which of the *dancers* he fancied. All, of course, my treat.

Over the food and drinks, Vinnie was at last comfortable enough to share. Spitting his food as he spoke, devouring the bones along with the fowl's flesh, Vinnie cursed his government for mistreatment. Not so much concerned with his people as himself, Vinnie in short order accounted for every slight to which he felt subjected over the course of his career. He understood what I was and what I wanted without much need for explanation.

Vinnie demanded money, and the opportunity to take vengeance. Frankly, it all was moving a bit faster than ideal. One wants time to assess the risks, gains, and realities of such an operation. If anything, I had to encourage Vinnie to indulge my need for patience. I was the right person to help him, and the United States government the appropriate partner upon whom he could count. But we needed time to do this right, and I needed his agreement to let us guide him through the process. There's no operation without vetting, and I had already earned detractors owing to a reputation for moving cases along too fast.

When our meal concluded and the conversation ended, I called over the host in order to pay. When the bill was delivered, it included the room key for Vinnie's "date." The host signaled toward the stage, Vinnie's choice paused, mistakenly gave me a smile and wink, and moved directly toward the stairs to make her way to the room. I felt sorry for the surprise that awaited her.

Over time, Vinnie and I would begin meeting under more secure circumstances. Responding to my tasking and training, he transitioned from vindictive volunteer to disciplined agent. His intelligence was consistent with his access, often verifiable, and frequently lifted directly from official documents. We were able to test him and his intelligence to the satisfaction of our standards. But it was never pleasant. The more I learned about Vinnie, the less there was to like. He was crude, obstinate, and insecure, all of which made him less receptive than desired to the strict tradecraft guidance under which we had to operate. His motivational driver was money. And so money had to be intertwined with the thresholds I outlined, which he needed to surpass to earn his salary. Our relationship amounted to an incentives-laden contract.

Vinnie was neither a nice nor a likable human being. It wasn't so much that he was a philanderer; in his country, like others in which I have served, there are different cultural and social norms. Regardless, I don't judge. Establishing an agent relationship depends on empathy and trust, and in this regard a case officer is not far removed from being a priest, rabbi, or imam.

The agent meeting is akin to a confessional, and this is where CIA case officers enjoy a tremendous advantage over their diplomatic, military, or academic peers. The intimacy of the recruitment is founded on the depth in the personal relationship between agent and case officer, which is enabled not merely through the case officer's empathy, but also the absence of judgment. That dynamic liberates the agents from pretense or shame in order to bare their souls. The case officer creates a safe space, neither approving or condemning but merely understanding. The case officer offers validation that despite whatever moral sins the agent has committed or might yet commit (apart from crimes we are obligated to report), there remains the opportunity for absolution by virtue of their clandestine cooperation.

Our goal is that agents have no reason to filter—neither their personal demons nor the sins of the father, so to speak. They can confess their desires and their sins, and find the means to atonement, salvation, or indeed, personal profit. Case officers won't tell the agent's spouses about affairs, local authorities about funds they have embezzled, or employers about their alternative lifestyles. They can entrust their personal excesses, reveal their greatest fears, confess weaknesses, and share their assorted vulnerabilities.

Vinnie was a cruel head of his own house, selfish down to the bone, and he never used the money he earned for anything but his own pleasures. His cooperation had nothing to do about striking a blow for his people, or enabling a better life for his family. It's not that Vinnie really even needed the fig leaf, but still, it helped to lead Vinnie to believe that I and the United States government saw his actions as noble, his intentions honorable. The reality was that there was little redeeming in him on which I could focus, and our relationship never rose to that of chums. It was all business, although I'd infuse rapport building to the extent he'd allow. It explained why Vinnie didn't have a friend in the world. So I figured that to Vinnie I was merely his paycheck.

Then the reality took me by surprise and taught me a lesson. I had long since turned Vinnie over to another case officer, "Steve," and subsequently moved on at the completion of my tour. Steve was an excellent officer, more experienced than me at the time, and a thoroughly decent man, deeply religious, and with strong family values. Steve subsequently ran Vinnie for a year before turning him over to yet another handler, and the experience dealing with Vinnie literally pained him. Catching up at Headquarters over lunch, we shared amusing stories about Vinnie. Steve acknowledged the personal difficulties of befriending and handling the morally challenged agent. I agreed that Vinnie was not one of the world's better people, and that he couldn't be less interested in anyone else. Steve looked at me quizzically and said, "That's not entirely the case, since he really liked *you*."

I just laughed, thinking Steve was putting me on. "Right, I was his best friend," I quipped back.

Serious for a moment, "No man, Vinnie asked about you at practically every single meeting," Steve explained. "In fact," Steve said with a laugh, "he used to write you letters which we told him we'd pass to you, all full of nice stuff about your friendship. Of course," Steve chuckled mischievously, "we took the liberty of writing your responses!"

I was surprised, but I shouldn't have been. I might not have realized, nor been willing to accept it at the time, but in Vinnie's world, I *was* his one and only friend. In me, he could share his true self without risk of judgment. I would listen, validate, and be the source of succor for his dark soul, as well as the bank through which he could finance his few pleasures. I genuinely cared about his safety and well-being, and I could always be counted upon. In me, Vinnie always had a partner. Vile as I might have found him, Vinnie believed in our friendship even if it wasn't evident. Even the most wretched creatures need to feel appreciated.

Whereas I and most case officers would find this a strength of HUMINT and value such interactions with our agents, today's CIA corporately would find not only less redeeming value in the dynamic but possibly let it compromise the value of his intelligence, its clinical corroboration aside. Data, metrics, science, and tools now hold more value than people and their secrets for far too many in today's targeter-influenced Clandestine Service.

THEY DON'T HAVE TO LIKE US... BUT THEY DO HAVE TO TRUST US

The CIA rarely uses coercion to recruit its agents. I say rarely, because to be fair, coercion can be subtle and to define it can be subjective. In some circumstances, we're not averse to employing some form of quid pro quo or ultimatum to get our foot in the door. The simple truth is that coercion is not effective. If it were, we'd probably do more of it, as many of our adversary intelligence services practice by default. It's easier. Just ask the Russians, Iranians, and Pakistanis, who prefer the simplicity of blackmail or threat, most often entrapment from a contrived and illicit sexual encounter they have caught on tape.

Coercion will never achieve the trust, insight, and control that a case requires. Those who succumb to blackmail will do the bare minimum and take the first opportunity to flee, or worse, secure revenge. In those cases, when no alternative exists and the stakes so warrant, we do play the heavy to get our foot in the door. We move swiftly, and we demonstrate genuine concern for the agent as well as prove our reliability as soon as time allows. The default is to bridge the relationship to make it one based on respect. When buying time at the outset through such rare acts of heavy-handedness, the goal is to demonstrate through deeds that our concern, reliability, and value for the agent are genuine, and that they are indeed free to go their separate way, if they so choose.

One of my more memorable cases, I'll confess, started out just this way. At a post where I was the COS, we discovered almost by accident the presence of a long sought-after al-Qa'ida operative. He was, in reality, a facilitator and not a trigger puller. Understandably, I must conceal the details. "Yousef" had been in-country for a while by the time we took notice of him or had made the connection about his affiliations. He had been on the run for some years, first managing to avoid arrest in his home country, itself a repressive police state that sought to exercise strict political control over the mosques. Yousef's association with fellow Islamic extremists had brought him to the attention of his nation's counterintelligence service. Like many, Yousef initially fled to a former Soviet state, where terrorist recruiters had invited him. Here he was vetted, indoctrinated, and trained.

From there, recognizing his particular talents, al-Qa'ida deployed him to Eastern Europe, where he provided logistical support to cells that were conducting conventional and asymmetrical warfare in the Balkans during the conflict. From reading our file on him at the time, one in which details were few and far between, Yousef was either the luckiest or the most hapless of terrorist facilitators. He had managed to escape from several countries in different parts of the world where either a group he was supporting successfully executed a terrorist operation or was discovered in the process.

It wasn't clear whether or not his ability to stay one step ahead of the law was a result of sloppiness in exposing the groups he had been supporting, or brilliance in consistently making good his own escape. Yousef was wanted in these countries, but had no US charges or Interpol warrants. Investigations into these disrupted cells consistently flagged his presence and provided links to the accused, largely in his facilitating their access to money, lodgings, and transport. There would be no smoking gun if Yousef had otherwise played an operational role, and he had managed to leapfrog ahead of discovery on each occasion.

Even CIA had only vague references to him, a physical description, his professional background preexile, and anecdotal references from various sources and detainees concerning his existence and duties. Having relocated to what he thought to be the last place any Western security service might find him, let alone look for him, Yousef thought he was safe. As it would turn out, Yousef knew everyone who was anyone in al-Qa'ida, from the foot soldiers who would kill Americans on 9/11, to its leadership.

It was only his immigration landing card and the police checks required of his work that brought Yousef to our attention. And even that was only by virtue of his somewhat unique Arabic *kunya*, since Yousef had falsified the credentials with which he secured his latest, black market passport. For reference, a kunya is an Arabic nickname, most routinely earned by a man after fathering a son. An example would be Abu Khalid, or, father of Khalid. In some cases, it's a reference to a particular passion, skill, or place of origin, as in variously: "Abu Jihad," "Abu Chemie" (as in chemical), or "Abu Ameriki." We traced Yousef's name and luckily had a photo from the local intelligence partner with which we worked.

While CIA had no photos of Yousef, the physical description, nationality, education, previous travel, and past employment were all a match. Mind you, this was just prior to 9/11, but CIA knew something evil was coming. We just were not sure of precisely what it would be, or just where and when it would happen. That Yousef was here at my post city, we surmised, meant he was supporting an operational cell. More broadly, our assessment at the time was that al-Qa'ida was planning further overseas attacks. We had been presented with a rare opportunity if Yousef was indeed whom we suspected, and if he was involved with a local cell that factored into his group's upcoming plans. Of course, his presence also suggested a local threat.

It took time and effort to develop better insights concerning who Yousef was, and just what he was doing. We ran a wide array of HUMINT and technical collection operations to develop an understanding of his activities and habits. The pattern of life that emerged revealed no smoking gun, but the additional biographic and background information further increased our confidence that Yousef was indeed the facilitator we suspected. Still, we could find little evidence linking him with a local cell or operation.

Albeit somewhat indirectly, we all came to develop a sense of Yousef as a person. And seeing him as we did on a regular basis, Yousef likewise looked like anything but a terrorist. Hardly bearing an athletic build, Yousef dressed in Western business attire, sported a fairly well groomed beard for a Salafist, and exuded a rather warm and receptive bearing. His behavior was refined, urbane, and well educated. In fact, he appeared very likable, and was in possession of a hearty laugh that rung out from his very core.

Although he regularly spouted anti-American sentiments to fellow Muslims and local Arabs, which was seasoned with particular contempt for his own country's despotic and autocratic leader, Yousef neither preached nor advocated violence. Even among his own local extremist associates, and indeed Yousef mixed with them, there was little evidence of activism or clandestine behavior. Yousef accepted charitable contributions, which we assumed were destined for both the local group he supported, as well as al-Qa'ida. But what we saw was rather incongruous from the bloodthirsty terrorist caricature we had earlier imagined. There was a softness, a humanity that didn't make sense, at least not from a typically American point of view.

Yousef was a devoted husband and loving father. And yes, so have many others who have struck without reservation in the most brutal manner against those from other races, religions, and countries. But he was also self-deprecating and disarming, mocking his own appearance or business acumen. While appearing on the surface to be a shrewd, ambitious, and somewhat aggressive businessman, the reality was that Yousef was always hatching one failed, and often naive get-rich-quick, scheme after another. One might say that he appeared to lack the killer instinct, at least in making money.

Fascinating to me personally as all of this was, our rather complex and intense operation was on borrowed time. Sensing that a major al-Qa'ida plot was somewhere in the works, Headquarters insisted I approach the local service and seek Yousef's immediate arrest. At this time, CIA Headquarters was in disruption mode. It could not determine just what al-Qa'ida was planning, or where, so it elected to apply pressure against any known or suspected nodes. If Yousef was here, he was bad, they thought, and his removal from the battlefield could serve to derail, or at least delay, whatever operation his particular cell was planning. The calculus theorized that Yousef's cell could be part of a more ambitious plan to strike multiple targets simultaneously, as was the case for al-Qa'ida's August 1998 East Africa attacks against the US embassies in both Nairobi, Kenya, and Dar es Salaam, Tanzania, that left 224 dead. Action against Yousef could throw off the grander plan, and, if nothing else, buy time.

Attempting to manage Headquarters' expectations with a dose of realism, I cautioned that there was no guarantee the local partners would arrest Yousef based on my request, given the limited evidence. We were confident that Yousef was the facilitator linked to operatives associated with other plots and attacks, but we had no indications of an active cell here, let alone a credible plot. Local cooperation was another uncertainty. The host government did not support al-Qa'ida, but they feared provoking it, given its own restless, Salafist-influenced Muslim minority. The locals might abide looking the other way while al-Qa'ida used their country as a sanctuary, to keep from becoming a target. Beyond that, the locals would not be eager to oblige resources for what, at the time, they considered a purely American problem. And finally, the locals were deeply corrupt, and Yousef had made some wealthy and politically well-connected friends.

I wanted time to reveal Yousef's true intentions, or develop enough of an understanding to inform a recruitment approach. And yes, even from my indirect assessment, I thought Yousef could be recruited. Madness, thought my Headquarters chain of command. He was a terrorist. A killer. He had to be arrested. But on what charges? Headquarters did not understand that we could not guarantee the locals would acquiesce to our request. If they did, we had no idea how long he might be held. Moreover, we had no reason to expect the locals would consider extraditing him without an Interpol warrant to one of the countries that would take him into custody, which were locations where he would likely be tortured and killed.

So began the negotiations with Headquarters. There was no room on whether or not to have the locals arrest him, but there was flexibility on the timing and mechanics. I negotiated permission to use my own special team of vetted local intelligence officers from our foreign partner to arrange the detention in a manner that allowed an opportunity for me to secure Yousef's cooperation, assuming I could convince my local counterparts.

It was hard for Headquarters to flatly refuse a COS at the time, but still, the Counterterrorist Center (CTC), which owned the case, was on edge. More than anything, CTC wanted to be proactive, or at least appear as such. They also wanted their way. And analysts and targeters had begun to increase their influence following the 1998 East Africa attacks. Far less interested in recruiting HUMINT sources to provide intelligence, they relied instead on technical collection and focused on disruption of that which was directly in front of us here and now.

In fact, CTC had become, as it would remain for years, a "tearline" machine. That is, it would pass leads to expose the presence and activities of terrorists to foreign liaison partners rather than seek to penetrate their cells, whether unilaterally or in collaboration. The idea of "outing" the bad guys was believed to be the most politically safe and expeditious means to slow terrorist operations. It's a theory to which I have never subscribed. The process delays the inevitable and makes ultimately disrupting and destroying terrorist organizations all the harder, since we pass up the few opportunities and inroads available to us.

As mentioned, the tearline is the means through which the CIA provides intelligence information to a foreign liaison partner, or a domestic US government agency, often federal, state, or local law enforcement in the homeland. It might be informational, but when shared with foreign partners, more often than not it is an official request approved under the CIA's own legal authorities based on intelligence collection. That is to say, the CIA can't ask a foreign government to do anything it is not itself legally sanctioned to do, whether it's a request that the foreign partner capture and detain the target, or take action kinetically.

As an example, al-Qa'ida senior leader Abu Muhammad al-Masri was assassinated by unknown assailants on the streets of Tehran, Iran, on August 7, 2020, the anniversary of the 1998 East Africa attacks that Abu Muhammad had reportedly masterminded. According to press accounts, the attack was ostensibly carried out by Israel at America's behest, based on US intelligence. Were that to have been the case, the CIA could not have made such a request nor passed along the intelligence if the CIA did not have the president's authorization to execute a lethal operation against Abu Muhammad.

But as part of its mantra to "find, fix, and finish" terrorist targets, CTC over-relied on taking immediate action against potential threats at the expense of collection opportunities. Too often, CIA stations became little more than messengers upon discovering the presence of a terrorist lead. Stations were routinely deprived of the opportunity to develop operations to collect against and potentially recruit targets.

Instead of considering an approach to such targets that is designed to assess their amenability to cooperation as double agents within their organizations, CTC tearlines passed the buck to foreign liaison partners just to remove them from the equation, "the finish." In a logic that likewise aligned with CIA's kinetic strategy, the default solution was disruption. Cajoling foreign partners to arrest a target, even if for a short time, would send a signal that the individual's activities, and perhaps that of the group, had been detected. The unfortunately American-centric logic was that once detected, or a key player removed (by detention or death), the plot would be abandoned or at least delayed. In many cases, however, the finish was anything but, with now-alerted targets back on the street in what resembled more of a catch and release effort among some of our more problematic or corrupt partners.

Al-Qa'ida in particular has demonstrated no reluctance to proceed with their same plots, or at least take actions against the same targets, despite their design having been exposed or their operational leaders removed. Such was the case with the World Trade Center, which al-Qa'ida targeted in 1993 and again in 2001. Convicted Pakistani national Ramzi Yousef was one of the main perpetrators of the 1993 World Trade Center bombing and the 1994 bombing of Philippine Airlines Flight 434. Along with so called 9/11 mastermind Khalid Shaykh Mohammed and al-Qa'ida strategist Mohammed Atef, the three devised the disrupted 1995 Bojinka plot to bomb multiple US airliners. That mid-1990s episode offered US intelligence its first awareness of al-Qa'ida plotting to concurrently turn multiple hijacked commercial aircraft into flying weapons, according to the 9/11 Commission Report. Our knowledge did little to deter al-Qa'ida from refining "the planes plot," as they referred to it, or changing targets on 9/11.

Directed by CTC managers coming from analytical as opposed to operational backgrounds, and who had no confidence in agent operations and mostly contempt for case officers, CYA became the Agency's priority. Most responsible for this risk-averse approach was an infamous former analyst turned targeting officer, "Alex," who will be further discussed later in the book. But remember Ian? He was the big boss at home to whom I reported, the operations chief responsible for the geographical division.

CTC was responsible for the operation, but the geographic area division owned the station.

To my eternal appreciation, even though Ian was skeptical, he went to bat for me with CTC, and in particular, Alex. Ian made a good case that gave everyone what they wanted. Yousef had to be arrested, Ian directed, but if I could turn him around immediately with a reliable means to assure our ability to vet and monitor his cooperation, I had his and CTC's approval. To be fair, Ian didn't think he was taking much risk. Given the realities, neither did Alex, who never imagined it would work. However, Alex could afford twenty-four hours to score points with Ian, for whom Alex would later work for years. Under Ian's protection, Alex later created an empire made of Teflon that guarded it from intrusive oversight, or consequences for failure.

I had to secure Yousef's cooperation immediately, and for operational security I had to keep his detention secret from even his own family. I would have to maintain a tight rein to be sure Yousef would not merely agree to my demands, which could provide him the opportunity either to flee or kill me in the process. I had a narrow timeframe for the operation, only twenty-four hours, and extremely limited resources that amounted to a handful of people, some of whom were actually local intelligence officers detailed to me from our foreign partner. Let's say that not a lot of people were betting on success, but in the end, Headquarters could trumpet having removed Yousef from whatever it was he might have been doing. And on paper, at least, they could claim to have supported the COS.

Not left with much choice, I took the narrow opportunity. Yousef was not in this country alone, but with family, one that he adored. It's harder to be on the lam with family than it is by yourself. He certainly could have ditched them before, but hadn't. And Yousef was not immature. He had not displayed any particularly rash behavior. Rather, Yousef was calculated, intelligent, and would take a risk, but not at his family's expense. Yousef was no democrat, and he wouldn't have supported al-Qa'ida had he not shared their ideology and beliefs. But I gambled that he was more invested in his own family than the group, and that he had no interest in being a martyr. His naivete in business suggested that he lacked the detachment necessary to take innocent lives with his own hand. It was all a gamble, but that's what case officers do. We solve problems and manage risk.

There were lots of moving pieces to the coming evening's operation. My local partners had to grab Yousef at a time and place where he was vulnerable and sufficiently isolated from public view. Then they had to hold Yousef at a venue at which I could make my approach. Oh yes, I had to also come up with a pitch that would secure Yousef's immediate agreement, then find a means to keep him under control long enough so that he could neither flee, warn his associates, or pose a threat to me and the team. At the time, I had all the legal approvals, authorities, and Headquarters' rather finite and perishable support.

I believed in my heart that Yousef was going to say yes. I wouldn't have undertaken the grand enterprise otherwise, knowing the consequences. I somehow felt that I knew this man and understood his hopes and fears. I did not believe Yousef was here plotting or supporting a terrorist attack. He was hiding, on the run, and trying to escape his past, but had the misfortune of landing in my backyard.

I'll necessarily limit and filter some of the operational details of how we put Yousef and myself together at the right place and time. But I can assure you it was as close to Hollywoodesque as happens in this business. Each and every one of the multiple moving pieces worked and, unusually for a high-risk intelligence operation, without a single hiccup. The team performed brilliantly, bravely, and as required. No one was hurt, or even roughed up in the process, including Yousef, and all was executed within the host nation's laws, as well as those of our own. At the time, Headquarters was unable to live-monitor any of this, but rather had to trust our station and await for even an interim report until the following day. Thank God. For his part, Ian, again to his credit, bought me the limited time, providing the backstopping and a buffer between me and Alex's rather unconvinced cadre of counterterrorist experts.

Yousef had been lawfully detained. But the local authorities had a mystique, whether credibly earned or urban legend, for making local nuisances and political dissenters vanish. These were not those goons, but rather, my people, each one vetted. My local team leader had done a nice job prepping Yousef. He was not involved with the initial detention, but came in later to conduct an interview. "Salah" was ideal for the role. Whereas we used our larger and more athletic-looking local service colleagues to execute the pickup and detention, Salah was not physically imposing. He was actually rather mild mannered and bookish in appearance. He was well educated and articulate and all but emotionless when interacting with people. What probably frightened Yousef more than anything was Salah's omission of just what might be in store. Less was more. As Yousef sat in the hot, dusty, and almost airless interview room, he was frightened to his core.

The interview room was furnished with only a small, shaky wooden table and two chairs. With one of the local team members standing watch from behind, Salah sat across from Yousef. Salah sported the plainest of reading glasses, silently reviewing a dossier. Yousef nervously tried to make conversation, offering pleasantries, obsequiously showing deference, asking questions, and pleading for any information. Salah responded with silence, not even lifting his head from the dossier to make eye contact. Finally, Salah looked up at his nervous guest and offered, "You'll be meeting Mr. David in a few moments. I recommend you tell him what he wants to know, since Mr. David gets to decide what happens to you, not me."

Yousef nodded nervously, "Of course, of course, I've done nothing wrong."

Salah then reminded Yousef that what he had just said about being innocent was quite far from the truth, given the dossier, not to mention the money he had already offered tonight to his captors to let him go.

I gave Yousef roughly another hour to be alone with his thoughts. It was the middle of a sweltering night, but I had only until daylight to make this work. Yousef's wife would understand her husband being out all night and not calling, but come sunrise, his absence would be considerably unusual, prompting her no doubt to begin a search. For the moment, we were monitoring his wife and their home, and she was blissfully asleep. It was time.

I entered the room in an expensive, well-tailored, navy blue suit, crisp white shirt, and spit-shined black shoes. And despite the hour, I was freshly shaved and wide awake. All of this, of course, was to add to the theater in making the right impression. Yousef sat nervously, wearing a crumpled, sweat-soaked white shirt and polyester black trousers, his shoes and belt having been taken from him. I took the chair across from him, making eye contact only briefly, sporting an air of annoyance at having even to be there. Opening my dossier, *his* dossier, I slowly flipped through the pages, clicking a pen on occasion, as if to highlight some interesting entry to myself, but jotting no notes as I did.

Debriefing a detainee is not entirely unlike the traditional engagement of any operational lead. Rapport and respect are crucial to advancing a relationship, not coercion, and certainly not abuse. A terrorist with blood on their hands need not be reminded how bad things are, and how much worse it could get, if they fail to cooperate. The trick is in opening their eyes, rather, to how much better the future could be if they cooperate. And to cooperate, a detainee needs, more than anything, hope, not hope-lessness, as too often is the harsher custodial approach.

Like any recruitment target, rapport and respect are merely tools to advance trust. You can't identify what matters to the operational lead such that they might be willing to betray that which they hold dearest, absent trust. Harder as it might be to earn that dynamic between detainees and their captors, it's possible, but ordinarily requires time and momentum. Sometimes weeks, more often months. I had hours.

I had to leverage Yousef's fear, but not at the expense of his manhood or his dignity. Doing so would poison whatever relationship I hoped to achieve over the long term. My objective was to provide hope as a means for him to escape his fear, but leverage the consequences such that the risk I required of him was far less a threat than the otherwise certain ends that his own imagination had by now conjured. My approach was one of seriousness rather than witty banter, and impatience so as to place the urgency in his court. Yousef had to convince *me* to take the more arduous course of working together and keeping him in place, rather than the easy road of dispatching him to another country's torturers.

I began by asking basic questions concerning Yousef's bio and background, answers for which I already knew the answers. Some of this was just to get him talking. He would lie, of course, but what he would choose to omit, fabricate, or alter would be revealing. The goal is to use that which you already know, which is itself threatening to the detainee, to compel them to tell you that which you do not know, but that they believe you already do. This sounds more complicated than it is in reality.

The greatest mistake a custodial debriefer can ever make is to confront the detainee with inaccurate information. Once having done so, the mystique of your all-knowing powers are forever gone. They will know you're bluffing and that you're willing to do so, and so they will begin to question your certainty over even the accurate accusations you make. An experienced, well-trained terrorist in captivity will often turn the tables against the less disciplined and inexperienced debriefer. When that happens, and it does, the detainee comes away with more insight as to what we do and do not know, than what we acquire from him. Al-Qa'ida even produced counterinterrogation manuals preaching these techniques, many having subsequently found their way circulated among Jihadist internet websites.

In the years following 9/11, I saw many inexperienced CIA targeters and analysts, or tough-sounding CIA paramilitary operations officers, go into the "box," as we call the interview room, and come away with nothing. Rather, outfoxed by their more disciplined, savvy, and well-prepared terrorist detainees, such CIA officers less accustomed to dealing with people, cover, and manipulation were often prone to give up more than they learned.

My goal tonight was not to get Yousef to spill it all, but to decide that cooperation was better than resistance. If there was a plot, he would not tell me tonight. I was not aiming to have him identify cell members and betray all their secrets in the coming two to three hours, but rather, and simply, to cross the Rubicon in that direction. I needed Yousef to compromise himself by providing information, the disclosure of which he knew al-Qa'ida would not approve. So I was not exactly warm, but businesslike and matter-of-fact. I took down the background and bio Yousef nervously provided, some of which was true, some not. I made no accusations nor did I interrupt or confront him when he lied.

Yousef mentioned nothing substantive, of course, of his al-Qa'ida ties or the individual operators we were aware he knew. And of course, he mentioned nothing of being wanted in his home country, let alone the others he had fled. As for what he was doing here, well, Yousef portrayed his status as that of an innocent. Despite his nerves, and the sweat pouring down his brow, Yousef sought to be warm, personable, deferential, and mild-mannered. He struggled to get through to my own humanity and earn a smile from me. There would be none, not tonight.

Lacking the time to extend this initial foray, I looked down at the dossier then met his eyes. Calling him by his true and complete name, not that which was in his passport, I matter-of-factly confirmed our knowledge that he was a wanted terrorist. I knew where he had been and with whom he had associated. As he quickly interjected that these were all misunderstandings and he could explain, I cut him off, saying it was not for me to make the legal case that his presence in these countries and relationships had amounted to terrorism. The governments of those countries believed as much, and were not necessarily bastions of justice and democracy. His accomplices were now all either dead or imprisoned in places with less than the most humane conditions. I was reminding him of his prospects were he to reject the benefits of cooperating with me.

Next, I confirmed the names and nationalities of his wife and children, bringing tears to Yousef's eyes. Again, I asked what he expected them to do upon his extradition. Would they seek to travel to that country or return to their home? I knew the answer. They could do neither. Guilt by association would likely prompt his wife's arrest were she to return home or to follow him to where he would be incarcerated. And while I asked what means of support the family would have after his extradition, I knew this answer as well. None. I did not threaten extradition, it was merely a statement of fact I wanted to put in his mind. Neither did I paint a picture of what would happen to him, or his family, if extradited. I didn't have to.

In fact, I did not have to ask Yousef to do a thing. He volunteered, as I had hoped and expected he would. "What can I do to keep you from sending me away, Mr. David," he pleaded.

I could hardly believe it. Sure, I thought it would work, but it really did. Yousef acknowledged who we thought him to be and pleaded to know what he could do to spare himself from being extradited to almost certain death. In truth, it was most unlikely we could ever convince the locals to actually extradite him, let alone hold him beyond a few days, but Yousef believed the story. My excitement overflowing, I had to keep it inside, continue to appear disinterested and incredulous, and maneuver Yousef more decidedly across the goal line of commitment.

"What is it you could do that would make it worth my while to help you, Yousef?" I shot back in return.

Yousef was wise enough not to immediately incriminate himself, but he acknowledged knowing something about people in whom I'd be interested.

"Yousef," I began with an air of mild annoyance, "the easiest thing for me to do, and the quickest win, is just to let them ship you off." I looked down again at his dossier and began to thumb through the pages. "But you're no good to me once you're in jail, and not much good to anyone once you go, well, you know where." Yousef nodded, assuring me it would be very much worth my while to let him stay.

"But it's a lot more work and complications for me keeping you here," I told Yousef.

"Mr. David, I'm not a terrorist," Yousef softly insisted, "I was in the wrong places, the wrong times, and friends took advantage of me."

I looked at him doubtfully. "Is that what you really want to tell me? Is that how you are going to convince me to trust you? To convince me to take the risk, invest my time, and go through the complications of keeping you here, rather than letting them ship you off?" I paused for effect, just looking at him. "You want my support, you need to gain my trust. I can forget about the past, if you're able to help keep innocent people from dying in the future. It's not in your interest to defend or revise what you did. Your only value to me is because of who you know and what you've done. And the fact that you're wanted in as many places as you are, can be no repeat coincidence."

Yousef maintained eye contact, worried that he was losing me. "I'm not as smart as you or your people give me credit, Mr. David. In fact, it's that I'm a stupid man, a trusting man, that I am in this mess. I just wanted to get away from all of that, all of them, and raise my family in peace. You help me do that, and I swear by Allah, I will never deceive you, and you will be glad you took a chance on me."

"Then what are you doing here, Yousef?"

"Hiding," he told me soulfully, "just hiding." He provided a few names he knew I would recognize, and suggested his ability to leverage existing relationships to provide information.

And with that, I rolled the dice. I outlined my expectations for Yousef. For one thing, he'd be staying with *my friends* for a spell, perhaps a week. Comfortable enough lodgings, but a place where we could spend a fair bit of time together reviewing what and who he knew, and how he would be of service. Doing so, he'd need to first call his family and colleagues and provide an excuse about traveling in-country so that his absence wouldn't cause concern. I warned Yousef that if he lied to me, tried to reach out to his associates, or gave me any pause whatsoever, I would not stand in the way of his extradition. At no time did I ever mention I was representing the CIA. I didn't have to.

As it turned out, Yousef was indeed not in this country to support a terrorist cell, and was in truth, at the end of his rope. He was hiding. He never thought his pursuers, or his extremist friends, would find him here at what he thought the end of the world. Yousef wanted to make money and have a "normal life," but was an atrocious business-man. Needing a job, he used his education, credentials, and familiarity with a few of his old group's local financial supporters to secure a position.

Yousef would turn out to be an exceptional agent with a near photographic memory for intricate, and actionable, details. All of which we could subsequently corroborate. Yousef provided reams of the most specific and esoteric details concerning people, habits, personalities, events, dates, and places. His information and personal insights offered us profound understanding and contributed to analysis, assessments, predictions, and targeting. Such details also were useful in confronting existing and future detainees and for anticipating plots.

When 9/11 came, Yousef was invaluable, the details of which the Agency precludes me from sharing. He could provide the backstories and connections among those we pursued. Yousef denied being aware of the 9/11 plot, but he knew some of the conspirators. Though he had not been in touch with any of them for several years, our investigation would bear out the facts. But in the months preceding the attack, neither did Yousef highlight any of the 9/11 conspirators among the al-Qa'ida members we discussed. A case officer's natural cynicism leaves me with still some lingering doubt.

When 9/11 came, Yousef was honest. He was rather proud that so small a group could inflict such damage against the great superpower. He believed God's intervention was key to 9/11's success. He never had any love for the American government, which he believed had subjugated and exploited the Muslim countries, and I never required him to make any such pretenses. And while he himself did not advocate violence, Yousef surely understood the contributions of his supporting role.

Yousef shared stories of aspirational plots that these operatives and others had discussed in his presence, and what to expect of their reaction when confronted by US forces in Afghanistan. One such report surfaced a previously unidentified threat to US infrastructure that was ultimately corroborated in other sensitive reporting. Another report saved American lives in a US military operation. Moreover, Yousef was able to travel and meet other senior level terrorist operatives from whom he secured valuable intelligence.

So effective had Yousef become that when he was detained while traveling, he used his time in custody to collect intelligence from other terrorist detainees and enhance his own credentials within the organization. He was smart enough to realize that confessing CIA sponsorship would help him neither with the local security officials nor with his fellow prisoners. He took the gamble we'd do something to get him out, and when we did, having cared for his family in the meantime, there was nothing Yousef wouldn't do for us.

In the end, Yousef worked with me because of trust, which developed over time. His faith in me, and the CIA, was not personal nor ideological. It was based on deeds and obligation. I protected him, saw to the health and welfare of his family, and was an ever-reliable friend and advocate. Yousef never grew to love America nor support our policies. And while he would have wanted no part in it, Yousef shed no tears over 9/11. Yousef merely had a problem I was able to solve that trumped ideology. He went to jail for us, suffering some abuse in the process. More unusual still for a CIA counterterrorism source, Yousef even passed a polygraph concerning his veracity and freedom from hostile control. A test, mind you, for which my colleagues at Headquarters had even developed a pool, with the smart money thought to be on his failing it.

Yousef was not my best case, but as a New Yorker who lost a childhood friend in the Twin Towers, I consider Yousef to have been perhaps my most gratifying case. Throughout, and particularly in the immediate aftermath of 9/11, his intelligence was unique and of exceptional worth. When I turned him over to another case officer and said my goodbyes, Yousef cried. As he hugged me, Yousef whispered in my ear how he was so afraid when we first met. And yet, as it turned out, he observed, I was actually, "so very soft inside." "You're a great actor, Mr. David," he told me, "and have been a great friend. Thank Allah we met."

This case might never have happened in today's more operationally risk-averse environment. Patience and conviction in HUMINT's value and the ability of our case officers to successfully ply their trade is harder than taking a potential threat off the battlefield. The difference between then and now is what today's leadership views as a risk. A risk for them is a political calculus of accountability as opposed to the operational dangers and threats to our officers, or a missed opportunity.

SEXUAL DYNAMICS

Does gender or sexual orientation impact a case officer's success? If you have to be all things to all people in order to effectively bond with a target, then you do what you have to do so as to make yourself into the persona you need to be. Unlike the Transformers of screen and cartoon, we can't reengineer ourselves superficially. Rather, case officers must do so in comportment to assume a character. As such, I have found gender or sexual orientation only relevant to the degree that case officers allow, save for the occasional practical issue where legal statutes and cultural requirements necessitate certain adjustments.

I don't see case officers in terms of gender, sexual orientation, or race. Not when it comes to espionage. Like "good police," I judge case officers by their character and talent. A good case officer, regardless of gender, sexual orientation, or race, must apply the right tools to the fundamental operational requirements. Case officers manipulate, manage risk, and solve problems. They are the utter pragmatists. They use all the circumstances and tools available to advance their operations. Local customs, rules, and norms require us to adapt. Rather than forcing square pegs into round holes, we manipulate the pegs and the playing board.

In my experience, female case officers have been every bit as effective as men, and in some cases, more so. It's not the gender, but the person. Women face additional challenges in comparison to men, as the #MeToo era has shown us. And in certain parts of the world, such difficulties are more intense due to cultural and legal differences. Many are working hard to process, address, and overcome the difficulties, but there remains a long way to go. Up until recently, for example, Saudi Arabia barred women from driving or riding alone without a male relative in a taxi or mass transit systems, which certainly presents a challenge for a case officer who depends on multiple modes of transportation. But there are options that lend themselves to creative twists in cover for meetings that exploit these same cultural biases. The predominantly male police and security members of such countries often take things for granted, place less scrutiny on a woman, or simply hesitate in challenging a female case officer—particularly one in local versus Western dress.

In religiously conservative societies, the male operational targets our female officers pursue, and the recruited agents they inherit, might never have been alone with a woman to whom they were not related, let alone an American one in Western dress. While initial engagements can be awkward, by and large the male targets and agents are curious. In some cases, the men realize they have greater operational security meeting with a woman who, in some of the more chauvinistic societies in which we operate, are less likely of being suspected an intelligence officer. Others simply welcome the opportunity to talk to a woman, especially an educated Westerner. I've just as often seen religiously conservative males open up more with women case officers than men, particularly once the false bravado and machismo is removed. In some of these societies, sons are more at ease with their mothers and sisters than their fathers, to whom they must maintain a certain image and constantly prove themselves.

That doesn't mean it's easier for women, or certain minorities, who face challenges that most White men need not overcome. I have had gay colleagues who have been unable even to live in certain countries with their same-sex partners due to the local laws. A talented African American colleague struggled at first in a country where racism was prevalent, but then leveraged the ignorance and emotions of those targets to his advantage. Still, we all have our own biases, prejudices, and lack of cultural appreciation, which colors our attitudes. It would be naive to suggest it's not a factor at all given the wide range of prejudices and cultural predispositions around the world.

During an early assignment when there was still a Soviet Union and its Warsaw Pact allies, I was trying to cultivate a female official from an Eastern European, socialist-leaning country. "Geeta" was unmarried, a few years older, and while not a runway model, certainly attractive. I met her at a diplomatic reception and invited her to lunch, claiming to be responsible for the same local political portfolio she managed, which of course, I was not. I had never before attempted to recruit a woman. At the time, male case officers tended to be rather uncomfortable pursuing female targets, and frankly, given the way of the world at the time, not many women worked in sensitive positions among the countries and organizations we targeted. But I was determined to make chase.

There were two women case officers in our station at the time. Both were far more experienced than me, and each counseled, very plainly, this was not a good idea. Neither had an issue with a male case officer's pursuit of a woman target, but, in this particular case, they felt we were headed in the wrong direction. I was incredulous when they encouraged me to break contact with Geeta before it was too late and spin her off to one of them. After all, I argued, they were pursuing male targets all the time. Why was it different for me to chase a woman?

I protested that I could handle it. I'd already recruited a fair number of agents, including hard targets, and I believed that I could succeed where my male colleagues had not. Both women continued to argue how transitioning the contact to one of them was more sensible, given the likelihood they'd have a less complicated road in developing a friendship. Of course I didn't listen. I should have. Not that the idea of pursuing a woman was ill-founded, but rather my technique sucked, and I wasn't ready. My education was about to begin.

One lunch with Geeta turned into two, and then three. We'd discuss the country, the region, and politics of the day. Of course, my intent was to get to know Geeta well enough so as to determine if she had access to information of value, and discover what motivations I might leverage to secure her cooperation. That meant getting to know her on a more personal level, including topics increasingly familiar and intimate. I wanted to know how she spent her time, if she was in a relationship, her likes, dislikes, and interests. And yes, I always picked up the check, since it was the chivalrous thing to do. I complimented what she wore, hung on her every word, and laughed at her jokes.

Geeta reciprocated in kind. So this was going great, I thought! But doesn't this sound like dating? While I made no secret of being married, and that I was the father to two rather young and precocious sons aged roughly five and three, I also attempted to infuse discretion into how we scheduled meetings so as to keep our contact from coming to the attention of her colleagues, or the decidedly anti-US local government. It was when she began inviting me to her home for drinks and late dinners, for which I regularly made excuses, that I sensed what was going on and returned to my two female colleagues for help.

"Duh, she thinks you want to fuck her, you dumbass," my colleague "Tina" bluntly offered. One of my two veteran colleagues, Tina was also my office mate. She was smart, kind, and wisecracking. Along with her husband, also a case officer, she had already served at several posts. Tina was an excellent officer, generous with her colleagues, and had a wickedly fun sense of humor. "You, my friend, are totally screwed."

"Very helpful," I replied. "But what's my next move?"

"There's still a limited window of opportunity to effect an introduction to one of the two of us," interjected "Lilly." Lilly, my other female colleague, and one of the best case officers I ever knew, took a more measured tone. Whereas Tina was the wisecracking fireball, Lilly was polished, sophisticated, and erudite. Both were around the same age with similar tenure. Likewise part of a tandem couple (the term for spouses who are both members of the Service), Lilly's husband "Marty" was actually my direct supervisor, and also an excellent officer. It was a bit risky seeking Lilly's advice, given the possibility she might tip off Marty who would subsequently take me to the woodshed for poor judgment.

"Nah, no next move, young man, you just disappear," Tina observed.

I looked at them both with confusion.

"You drop contact. No more lunches, calls, contact of any sort. And if you see her at a reception, you turn and head for the exit like you owe her money," Tina elaborated.

Lilly begged to differ. "Invite her to tea with one of your colleagues, either of us, who you ask Geeta to meet as a favor since you're all working on a similar issue."

I shook my head disapprovingly. "No," I argued, "I can still fix this. I just have to show her how she misunderstood my innocent advances, and that I'm a happily married man who just wants to be friends."

Tina dropped her face into her hands. "Innocent as in you trying to recruit her to betray her country you mean?"

"Well if you put it that way," I conceded.

"Are you crazy?" Tina went on. "She's a woman. This is going to be a blow however you do it." She shook her head. "It's just not salvageable. Trust me," Tina insisted, "you just walk away. She'll think you had cold feet, or were just an ass."

Somewhat more politely, Lilly concurred. "You're at a crossroads," she reasoned. "Even if you get past this bump, when you get around to dropping the pretense and try to convince her to spy, it'll all come back to her worst fears, thinking you led her on from the outset and used her. It's not too late to get out and keep her in play, but it has to be the next move, or it could go really bad, really soon."

Having heard them out, and given due consideration to their advice, I did absolutely nothing that either Tina or Lilly recommended. Instead, I twisted Geeta's arm to accept an invitation for lunch that weekend at my home. I wanted her to meet my wife and boys, I explained over the phone.

Geeta was thoroughly confused. She resisted, but perhaps imagined this was some bizarre way I had in mind to be able to see her without arousing my wife's suspicion. Whatever ultimately convinced her to accept, Geeta agreed, and she came to our house late the next Sunday morning.

We lived in a nice detached home in the city's suburbs. It was fairly quiet, with open fields facing our house from across the street, and well-to-do locals living at a respectable distance to our left and right. My wife knew the plan, and while she didn't work for us, she understood both the game and her role in helping to befriend my operational target. The boys were excited just to meet someone new, and had for the most part always been exceedingly polite and well behaved whenever we entertained. We also had a dog, Sandy, a female mixed breed that somewhat resembled a yellow Lab, which likewise was normally easygoing and friendly. Whether or not the moon was in a peculiar phase, or the spy gods had chosen to have their fun with my hubris, the day did not go as planned.

Geeta rang the bell while my wife remained in the kitchen preparing the meal. As I moved toward the door, my sons, and Sandy, all raced down the stairs, moving past me like the wind. Before I could bring man or beast under any measure of control, the door sprung open and Sandy leaped madly up on our terrified and unsuspecting guest. "Down Sandy!" I commanded, reaching breathlessly for the dog's collar as I caught Geeta's look of pure horror. "Bad Sandy!" I shouted, lunging for her collar, to which Sandy promptly responded by generously relieving herself at Geeta's feet. The boys howled and giggled with delight at the yellow puddle and Geeta's distraught expression. Mortified, I guided Geeta into the house, setting Sandy loose in the yard, a perverse appearance of satisfaction on the dog's face as I secured the door behind us.

Geeta removed her shoes, custom in any event, as I tried to find something to wipe them down, apologizing as I moved, and guiding her to a seat on the couch in our living room. As if the dog was not enough, Geeta, who clearly had been single and childless by choice, was next playfully mauled by my two sons who each leaped to either side of her on the couch. The boys jumped up into her arms, both competing for attention, hugging, kissing, pulling, and tugging at her hair. Geeta did her best Muhammad Ali rope-a-dope to ward off their affection as I struggled to separate her from the two boys, who I maneuvered along the couch to provide some degree of personal space.

Believing I had restored order, and calming my excited sons, I let my wife know our guest had arrived and made initial introductions to the family. Geeta's painful discomfort was apparent, but still, I struggled to convert this all into a win, despite the poor start, and I offered her a drink. Beer was her choice, though I imagine by now she was craving vodka. As I left to fetch her drink, and my wife returned to the kitchen to continue preparing the meal, the boys moved swiftly to reposition themselves on either side of her, straddling their legs over hers, and began peppering her with questions.

"What's your name? How old are you? Do you have kids? Where's your husband?" Their young mouths firing out questions at a rapid pace as I hustled myself back into the living room, her beer almost spilling from my accelerated jaunt as I sought to save her from their onslaught.

"Now boys, let Ms. Geeta have a chance to catch her breath," I implored my two sons.

"What's that?" My younger son asked, pointing to the beer.

"A grown-up drink, dear," Geeta replied, "not for little boys."

"It's beer," I told my son. "You wouldn't like it much," I soothingly tried to explain, "but I'll bring you some juice."

"I want beer, Daddy!" My son exclaimed, the older boy now likewise joining in with the chorus and giggling.

Oh where was my wife! I thought to myself, who likewise was struggling with her own crisis. What was that smell? I asked myself. I apologized to Geeta, who was clearly overwhelmed and appearing to be in no small degree of terror, and said I'd be right back. I dashed into the kitchen to find my wife fighting to contain a small oven fire. As I crossed the threshold, letting the smoke out into the living room, she tossed a lid over the pan like a Frisbee. Rather than quell the fire, the lid flew past the pot into the dishes she had just set aside, loudly breaking into a thousand pieces on the floor.

"You okay?" I asked, looking for a fire extinguisher as she made a second toss that thankfully caught and began to douse the flames. We surveyed the damage and quickly tried to salvage the meal.

"I've been better," she replied in exasperation. "But how's it going out there?"

"About the same," I confessed.

And at that moment came a piercing medley of screams. First Geeta's, and then the boys.' I turned and raced back into the living room, leaving my wife to deal with the fire, meal, and clean up. To Geeta's right, my five-year-old son held her purse in his hands, upside down, as the last contents fell to the ground, including her pricey Ray-Ban sunglasses, which of course cracked upon impact with the hard tile floor. Not to be outdone, to her left, exploiting the diversion offered by his older brother, my three-year-old grabbed Geeta's beer, took one sip, and disappointed at the foul taste, spat it back into her glass.

The brunch was now officially over. Geeta leaped up, screamed something aloud in her own language, which I don't think translated into "What a nice family," and suddenly recalled another obligation. I tried in vain to apologize, waving to dissipate the smoke that continued to fill the living room. Geeta kept walking toward her shoes, and then the front door. But it would have been far better had she waited. When she opened the door to exit, in raced Sandy, who again jumped up at her, and again managed to relieve herself at Geeta's feet. There would be no hugs goodbye, no tender farewell. That was the last I'd ever see of her.

Over the rest of my career, I applied the lessons learned and went on to successfully recruit and handle a number of excellent woman agents. I never again allowed for any confusion or misunderstanding, and drew from my women colleagues' guidance. Oh, and Sandy found a new home.

MY GAY BEST FRIEND

I was serving in yet another authoritarian Middle East country, which is how I largely spent the bulk of my adult life. Having recently arrived, I was researching possible leads. The station was low on agents and high on needs, operating in an extremely repressive counterintelligence environment where a local insurgency was gaining strength, and government stability and longevity were in question. I came across a case that predated my arrival, which had not panned out, concerning a midlevel member of the local security service. Operational files are like reading good spy stories, when properly documented.

Successful case officers have to be talented writers. Not only to bring their cases to life, but to leverage greater influence. A competent case officer will anticipate reactions from Headquarters by addressing salient points with context and planned courses of resolution. Better to document the warts yourself than to conceal them only to have Headquarters dredge them up later with helpful guidance. Doing so is not only a matter of integrity but good sense. If you highlight the issues, then you control the narrative to place the matter in appropriate context and present the best risk mitigation plan.

And this was a good spy story. A former COS had run into "Amir" through the course of brief official interactions. Despite the lack of much substantive bilateral intelligence cooperation at the time, and the local foreign government service's significant mistrust for the US government (USG) in general, the CIA in particular, there was an advantage for all in having an ongoing dialogue.

I knew the former COS fairly well, and had in fact worked under him for a short period of time. "Ken" was exceptionally smart, polished, and energetic. He was handsome, athletic, with a warm, dry wit that never offended, yet still came across as sincere. Ken was absolutely masterful with languages, and brimming with ambition. He was married and had a young son. I liked Ken, and I still do. He always treated me and others fairly, and pursued what generally seemed to be the right course of action, even if he did have a rather huge ego. But the same can be said about most case officers, myself included. Ken rose to senior Agency positions, becoming a member of the Senior Intelligence Service. Like many, Ken had his career end on a sour note owing to a power struggle with the DDO and DCIA in which he came up on the short end.

Reading over the brief file, I thought there might be an opportunity to recontact Amir and return him to the fold. Ken had managed to discreetly compel Amir to meet unofficially outside of the office without the knowledge of his superiors, allowing the opportunity to advance their relationship. In fact, the reporting indicated that Amir was motivated by the deep rapport that Ken had established. They had quickly developed a friendship, and Amir was willingly sharing sensitive information while meeting under what were essentially clandestine conditions. It was quite a coup just to get that far, as we were operating in an essentially denied operating area—the locals were closer to the Russians than the West, with pervasive police state controls and surveillance capabilities. It was all an exciting read, and I devoured Ken's reporting cables like a suspenseful page-turner.

Ken described Amir as a rather complex fellow. He was bright, thoughtful, but sensitive. Married, Amir was not close to his wife, their partnership an arranged matter like most in this country. Neither did Amir seem overly occupied with his children. He was deep, philosophical, and moody, according to Ken. He and Ken seemed to enjoy thoughtful discussions concerning life, love, religion, and politics, all in a deeply intellectual and ethereal manner. Ken was Ivy League educated, and extremely well read. Amir delighted at Ken's intellect and was stimulated by their thought-provoking conversations in a conservative country where such topics were otherwise taboo.

Over time, Amir began confiding personal thoughts and experiences, the latter, although thin and generic in detail, suggested he was gay. Being a homosexual man in this outwardly macho, Middle Eastern country would go far in explaining the inner conflicts from which Amir suffered as a person, and his fear of exposure. There were no outwardly gay men in this country, not living freely or happily, in any event. The idea that the elite praetorian guard, as the security service prided itself as being, would tolerate even a closeted gay member of the service was incomprehensible.

Ken could not be certain that Amir had directly confronted his true sexuality, or if he had consummated a homosexual experience with another man. Stories Amir related to Ken that were captured in part among the reporting cables suggested that he had flirted with the possibility of a physical experience during occasional official travels to Europe. But Amir was vague, hinting at best in his accounts, and Ken questioned whether or not Amir was able to bring himself to actually advance a dalliance beyond the point of flirtation.

Amir appeared to value sharing a secret that he could barely admit to himself, let alone anyone within his own community. In Ken, Amir had someone he felt sure would keep his confidence. Perhaps the only gift with which he knew he could reward his CIA friend was secrets. Despite Amir's provision of sensitive intelligence, he never accepted a dime in material compensation. And it was not for Ken's lack of trying.

As a case officer, you are always maneuvering to increase institutional control over your agent. We're not talking about the leverage to extort, but rather the degree of dependence the agent develops on the CIA and the United States government. And that is your objective in recruiting an agent, advancing the case to the point where the case officer can transition the loyalty and relationship founded on, or at least enabled by, friendship to one in which the agent is now tied, by choice, to the institution.

People become comfortable, and to various degrees dependent, on the extra income and validation the CIA provides. This, in time, allows them to rationalize further their cooperation with CIA the organization, not just specifically the case officer with whose friendship their journey into espionage began.

Despite Ken's best effort to package compensation in some manner to suit Amir's pride, it was a nonstarter. The cables did justice to Amir's reasoning that to take money would defile the purer motives for his cooperation with Ken. Amir was a man of principle, with great contempt toward his repressive government and deep affection for his friend Ken and the ideals he believed were associated with the United States. When it was time for Ken to move on, Amir was unwilling to accept introduction to another CIA officer. Amir was not an agent, he reaffirmed, but was working with Ken for his own reasons and on his own terms.

Ken was an excellent case officer, far more senior and experienced than I, spoke the local language like a native, and had all the polish and sophistication Amir appreciated. Mostly, these were skills and traits that I admittedly lacked. Nevertheless, I believed there was still something with which I could work. And we could surely use the intelligence that Amir's position in the service enabled him to provide.

After all, fundamentally, Amir still had motivations that could be leveraged. He was an exceedingly unhappy man, leading a secret life, frustrated in both his personal and professional worlds. In cooperating with Ken, Amir reasoned and rationalized his behavior by depicting himself as a positive instrument of change. Money didn't matter, not to Amir, nor was his unwillingness to accept money important to me. Amir, I felt confident, could be persuaded to resume cooperation based on the same needs that lead him to work with Ken, needs that had not likely changed since Ken had left. My task, then, was to find a way for Amir to accept contact, and patiently abide the time it would take to for me to replicate the same degree of trust.

Using the operational resources at hand, I was able to reconfirm Amir's home address and telephone number. While we couldn't be sure he was still in the same job, let alone the service, he was relatively junior, smart about keeping out of trouble and more likely than not where he had been when Ken left. Unlike our service or military, once someone in Amir's country was in either, it was for the duration of a career. There was not any set number of years after which one could choose to reenlist or separate, absent a medical or hardship discharge. And not many opportunities were at hand for Amir to find a regular job beyond government in this essentially socialist state. Private enterprises were beginning to appear, but almost all were parastatals or those founded by former army generals with "borrowed" state money. The economy was in dire straits, with vast unemployment, and Amir had a family. Moreover, Amir was not well suited for a life of poverty.

I'd first get in touch with Ken, who was now holding an important and senior Headquarters position. Ken had parlayed his preceding, successful COS job into what was at the time an unusual role for DO officers, which placed him in more of a policy advisory position. Ever the gentleman, though, Ken was receptive to my contact and happy to discuss this fascinating case. I asked Ken to help by drafting a letter to Amir of a personal nature in his own handwriting. The letter would not prevail upon Amir to work with CIA or even demand he meet me on a continuous basis. Rather, the letter would suggest Ken's interest in maintaining their friendship through correspondence in which he trusted me to serve as the local conduit. The rest would be up to me, should Amir accept the outreach. The letter was merely a means to get my foot in the door.

To my surprise, Ken told me the plan would never work, and he discouraged even trying. He explained that Amir was way too complex and suspicious. He would see the worst possible motives behind the outreach, Ken suggested, and would ask himself, "Why now?" Further, Ken pointed out the likelihood that Amir might see any such outreach as a test by someone in his own service masquerading as Ken's colleague. The innate paranoia so natural to intelligence officers could lead Amir to believe his contact with Ken had been somehow compromised, and that his service was using this ploy to secure additional evidence to catch him "in the act."

Ken complimented my aggressiveness and creativity, but counseled it was best to start from scratch and find another target. Easier said than done. I was not declared to the local security service and, in fact, had a significant and rather esoteric official day job. My duties would never offer me an explainable pretext to meet a member of the local security service, let alone come across someone with Amir's access. I found Ken's reluctance curious, but I assumed he was just looking out for me.

I countered that we at the station had considered all of this, gamed it out, and developed various approaches, but that it was well worth the risk. For one thing, whereas Ken spoke the local language beautifully, mine remained undeniably foreign, clearly American, and too broken in grammar and vocabulary to be that of a native speaker from Amir's own service. Moreover, I would have the bona fides of mentioning experiences that only Ken and Amir knew. Although unconvinced, Ken was really in no position to refuse. All we were asking of him was to write the letter. Ken finally acquiesced, authoring a relatively vanilla letter along the lines of what we had discussed, which arrived a few weeks later.

I couldn't wait to begin. I copied and read Ken's letter several times before sealing the envelope so as to pretend to Amir that I had not seen its contents. Ken's command of the local language in its colloquial form was a gift I would never possess. This effort to reestablish contact was essentially a tepid trial balloon from one old friend to another. Ken's letter offered vague excuses for why he had waited so long to reach out, making the case that he had waited so as to allow me, a trusted friend, to arrive. There were assurances that Ken would provide a more detailed letter catching Amir up fully once the channel had been established. There were no work-related matters raised in the letter, nor any particular demands. Ken backdated the letter to suggest I needed sufficient time on the ground before being in a position to assess and manage the risks prior to reaching out.

My first instinct was to deliver a message to his door, thereby avoiding the phone. I cased Amir's neighborhood on a few occasions to get a feel for it. He lived in an apartment that he shared with his wife and children, as best we could tell. In such countries, however, there was always a chance that parents, in-laws, and other extended family members might be around. But if I could leave a message at his door, I could likewise have been expected to leave the letter. And I needed Amir to see me in person. For that to make sense, I'd need a reason for Amir to have to meet me on the street for the letter. This left me but one option, and that was to call his home landline number. Cell phones were not yet ubiquitous. To a spy, telephones are the devil. You can never be sure who will pick up, who might be listening, and what records will remain for the duration of time, even though I would not be using a phone with which I or the USG was associated.

Without going into much detail on the tradecraft, I was able to go out and make the call. I waited for the late evening, by which time Amir would be home from the office, increasing the odds that he, as opposed to his wife or other family members, would answer. Should he not be the one to pick up, my language would give me away as a foreigner. I was, however, readied with an additional cover story for whomever might answer, as to why a foreigner was calling Amir. Fortune favored the foolish that evening, and the phone was answered by a soft-spoken, articulate, and educated male voice.

My greeting had to be sufficiently compelling to keep Amir on the phone long enough to hear me out. There was no way to know, of course, what degree of privacy he enjoyed while on the receiver even were he interested in what I had to say. And that's what came first, that I was Ken's recently arrived close friend. I asked if Amir had time and privacy to talk. Some of the early pregnant pauses did little to build confidence, but I labored through my opening lines to keep him talking while maintaining an upbeat, friendly demeanor despite the vaguely coded terms.

Amir's mischievous quips concerning my butchered pronunciations and accent reflected his sense of humor, his humanity, and sincere hope I was taken with his country and settling in. Though I struggled in the language to convey both the substance of my outreach and the friendly, nonthreatening tone I hoped to get across, I could only imagine how it sounded to him on the other end. Quips aside, I was encouraged by Amir's compassion for this obvious American's fumbling attempt to communicate. As Amir teased me for my poor vocabulary and grammar, I echoed it likewise with self-deprecation that he appreciated, soliciting sufficient forbearance to hear me out.

Convincing Amir to actually meet was more challenging. He evinced no immediate interest in the letter, much to my surprise. Rather, Amir thanked me for the gesture, but he did not want to put me out in having to deliver it. A polite no. I persevered, dancing through occasionally playful banter in bemoaning how I would be letting Ken down if I failed to at least deliver his letter, resulting in a loss of face and honor I was sure a man like Amir would not wish upon me. He laughed, thankfully, and countered that he could already appreciate I was a man sufficiently noble and secure not to waste energy on appearances. Unrelenting, I pushed, suggesting that I was hardly the man Amir was, since unlike him, I'd be unable to resist receiving a message from my long-absent friend, even if it required inconveniencing the messenger. Parables, banter, and what we might consider corny and cliché do go far in this part of the world, one of the reasons I've so long adored it.

Amir offered a soft, polite, but spontaneous laugh and at last asked what Ken had written. A start, I thought. I lied and claimed no knowledge of its contents, having only received it in a sealed envelope with a promise to serve as courier after my arrival. With that I explained why I had taken some time before I felt confident in being able to do so securely, a comment that seemed to earn his appreciation. I now sought to pass it along in the most secure manner, suggesting this would best be done by meeting in the evening. I could pick him up in a car that was not affiliated with the US government.

Ken and Amir had met this way themselves on occasion, so I knew it was something to which he might agree. Amir politely protested the meeting mechanics, but he was showing more curiosity about the letter. When he suggested I merely place the letter within another envelope and mail it to him, I countered that without either of us knowing its contents, it was in neither of our interests to risk it coming to the attention of the local censors. "And don't you want to meet me in person?" I added playfully. Grudgingly, Amir agreed, and with a bit of negotiation, accepted my arrangements.

I pushed Amir to meet as soon as possible. Allowing him time opened the possibility of cold feet, or worse still, his reporting the approach and facilitating an ambush. Amir was reasonably accommodating, and if I recall correctly, we met the following night. Besides reading about his physical description, I had seen no photos of Amir and had only a vague mental image of how he might appear. He was a professional, fortunately, so he understood my inclusion of physical signals in the meeting arrangements so as to allow him to recognize me, and vice versa.

It was a good pickup site on a quiet, rarely used street beneath an overpass that allowed him screening from onlookers at the foot of some stairs from the street above. From a fair distance as I approached, I saw him waiting, a plastic blue shopping bag in hand, our recognition signal. I slowed the car, offered a greeting that included a code word that confirmed to him it was me, to which he replied with a likewise previously determined counter. He entered my car and off we drove.

Amir was handsome, fit, sporting a well-tailored black leather jacket, dark slacks, and fashionable loafers. Outwardly, at least, he was incredibly calm. There was no anxiety in his voice nor any appearance of nerves. He neither fidgeted nor felt the need to break any uncomfortable silences. Amir made good eye contact when he spoke, but he did not stare. A capable professional counterpart, he was clearly watching as well for signs of trouble ahead on the road or trailing from behind. I went through the basic security questions, transitioning to light conversation and introductions before mentioning the letter.

Amir asked about my ability to avoid, and necessarily negotiate, any checkpoints that might arise. I had already reviewed our cover story for why we were together, should we be stopped by authorities. Amir's questions concerning my security plan helped me to establish initial credibility that I was a competent professional who knew what he was doing and, unpredictable variables aside, could see to his safety. Other than smirking on occasion at my poor pronunciation, Amir was nothing but courteous and gentlemanly, but just the same, reserved to the point of coldness.

We made small talk, the type that serves a purpose. I asked casual questions to discern his situation at the office and his home, and Amir wanted to know how long I had been in his country and what I thought about it. We were perhaps like boxers cautiously circling one another in the ring at the outset of a fight. He politely lied about my language proficiency, observing how he found my accent "cute." I expressed genuine satisfaction at finally getting to meet him, having heard much about him from Ken.

"How well do you know Ken?" Amir asked. There was an oddly pained tone in his voice that I found a bit unsettling.

"I wouldn't say we're close," I replied cautiously, "but he's a good officer and helped me prepare for the assignment."

"He is well then, Ken?" Amir asked hopefully.

"Yes," I affirmed. "He and the family are settled in now back in Washington, and he has a good assignment."

"Still responsible for my country?" Amir followed up.

"No," I answered, "something more administrative," I added obliquely, expecting Amir would be enough of a professional not to press, at least directly. "But I have the letter here, if you'd like," I said, hoping to change the subject and get it refocused on him versus Ken. Reaching into my jacket pocket and handing it over, I remarked, "I understand if you want to wait until you can read it in a safe place, or you're welcome to look at it here and I can dispose of it after, if you want."

Amir took the letter, thanked me, and worked his thumb along the flap to free its contents. "I'll read it here, if you don't mind me being quiet while I do." I invited him to please go ahead, and silence fell over the car as we moved through the lightly trafficked, late night streets. He gently removed the beige parchment from the envelope and angled the paper toward the passenger window to help illuminate it with the ambient light. A few minutes passed.

"You have read the letter?" Amir asked softly, as his eyes made their way through the contents of the handwritten, two-page note.

"No," I lied, "but Ken told me it was deliberately limited in scope, hoping to add more detail once you two began an exchange."

"So you don't know what he said to me?" Amir asked, a bit more emotion now evident in his voice as he perused the second page.

"I'm afraid I don't," I answered with uncertainty. "Is there something wrong?"

Amir lowered the pages and then again pulled the letter up to his eyes and started rereading it from the beginning, occasionally shifting from one page to the next, as if to decipher what they contained.

"The letter is cruel," Amir snapped softly, "hurtful and cruel." He turned his head to the passenger window, staring out toward the street, still holding the unfolded letter in his hand.

This was not exactly something for which I had prepared, and I was rather clueless as to what was happening. It was hardly a meltdown, as Amir maintained his composure, but his words, slow, deliberate, and tinged with what sounded like hurt, were hard to follow based on my still progressing knowledge of the language. But it was actually my weakness in his mother tongue that helped get me back into the conversation.

"Amir, I'm so sorry, but my language ability is not as good as Ken's, and I'm having trouble following what you are saying. Something clearly bothered you, I can get that much. Could you please help me understand?"

Amir initially dismissed it. "It's not important," he assured me in a rather passive-aggressive manner. "And it's no surprise," he followed, resolutely.

I pressed, nevertheless. "It's certainly something. Did I somehow offend you? Did the letter?"

Putting the onus on me compelled Amir, ever the honorable gentleman, to reassure me that was not the case. "You really wish to know?"

he asked, knowing obviously my answer but perhaps wanting to be persuaded. I answered, "Yes, please, for my sake, if you'd be so kind."

Amir sighed deeply, and then he repeated that Ken's letter had been hurtful, that it fell rather short of what he expected, and what he was due. He offered to let me read it, though I suspect Amir was clever enough to have realized I had already done so. Despite my lie, and his assuming I had read it notwithstanding, to Amir I had nevertheless missed the true meaning so obvious to him, which he wanted me to see. I found a discreet place to park for a few moments with sufficient street light with which to read. Having already read the letter, I needed only to scan it and feign understanding. But quite genuinely, I had no idea what it was that had set Amir off, and I still didn't after rereading Ken's note. I apologized to him for failing to see that to which he referred.

"It's what he says between the lines," Amir explained. "And what he doesn't say."

Amir's reaction was not what I had come to expect from a man expressing anger or offense over the actions of a presumed friend, let alone how an agent would react, even if bitter at the belief he had been used. This was hurt. Emotional, personal hurt. Amir behaved more like that expected of a jilted lover. Not drawing any conclusions, my aim was just to keep him talking. His emotion, even anger, hurt, or pain, was my best hook.

"Listen," I told him, "we better keep moving so I'm going to get the car going again to be safe." Amir was silent, his eyes panning the scene outside from his passenger window. "But I can't let you go until we talk about this some more." Amir took a quick glance my way but said nothing. With that, I very deliberately placed my hand on Amir's shoulder. For one thing, physical contact is the norm in the Middle East. For another, without knowing whether or not Amir suspected what Ken might have told me about him, or what knowledge I might have concerning his sexual orientation, I wanted to immediately demonstrate my own comfort with him and dismiss any suggestion of homophobia.

Amir didn't say much the rest of the evening. But neither did he force the engagement to end. I did most of the talking, about myself, the excitement of being in his country, and of my background. I wanted him to see me as a person, and likewise create some separation between me and Ken. Amir responded well to my energy, enthusiasm, and curiosity. In turn he asked a few questions himself. Amir eventually loosened up enough to actually make a joke or two. In all honesty, I think he found me a dork, but well intentioned and disarming.

Amir thanked me for taking the time and the risk in meeting, and wished me well on my assignment, but he seemed ready for that to be the end of it. I insisted that we needed to meet again, for my sake, really, since I felt responsible for whatever it was that had provoked his reaction. I couldn't just leave him like this, having set out to perform what I thought was a good deed. By suggesting that it was a favor to me, somewhat of a quid pro quo, Amir's sense of honor and decency kicked in. He agreed, joking that it was also a favor to his countrymen to address the horrors of my diction. Other than casually eliciting a few scant comments about where he worked, I never pressed Amir on anything sensitive that evening, nor did I ask a single direct question of an intelligence nature.

One meeting would become two, and so forth. I focused my interest on the dynamics between him and Ken. I feigned an offer to mediate, though it was merely a ruse to keep meeting, when he would at least have an opportunity to vent. I would offer whatever insights I might of a personal nature, like you would with a friend who had just suffered a breakup. And that's precisely how it felt, like I was talking to someone who had broken up with a friend of mine.

Mostly, Ken had depicted Amir brilliantly. His operational reports captured Amir's personality and demeanor, likes and dislikes, and I carefully employed Ken's "scouting report" to be what I needed in order to cultivate Amir's respect. What Ken neglected to include in his reporting was that Amir had fallen very much in love with him.

Putting the pieces together became a bit easier over the course of a few meetings. In the context of Ken's reporting, and the off-the-record comments Ken shared but failed to capture in his official documentation, Amir provided a picture that made sense. Amir never explicitly referenced his sexual interest in Ken, nor claimed directly that Ken had in turn "come on to him." Rather, Amir had an instant physical attraction to Ken that was deepened by their interactions. Ken offered Amir a nonjudgmental ear, the first he'd ever have, and at a crucial crossroads for Amir.

Sensing the torment in Amir's soul, Ken likewise provided the validation and encouragement to speak to it, albeit replete with metaphors to preserve a rather postage stamp–sized fig leaf Amir still required. Ken was decidedly handsome, kind, witty, and educated. And most important, he was a case officer who manipulated Amir's needs and fears through a thoughtfulness that raised Amir's expectations and allowed him to imagine more.

It's not that anything materialized beyond their friendship, of this I am sure, both from what I know of Ken and what I learned of Amir. And frankly, I had not witnessed their interactions to judge whether or not Ken had consciously done anything to lead Amir on. But whatever did or did not happen between the two, it was clear to me that Amir had retained hope, and Ken had done little to disabuse him of it.

I liked Amir very much. A troubled soul with a good heart, our relationship was likewise based on friendship, but without the sexual tension that existed between him and Ken. I made it clear to him that my warmth was that for a brother, a man I respected and admired. My entrée with Amir was secured by humanity, kindness, and thoughtfulness. His trust in me strengthened over time by the risks I took, which proved my willingness to keep him safe, a trust that was established at the outset because we discussed matters entirely of a personal nature to him, no strings attached.

It was an investment of time and risk. But I believed that by entering into contact with him under these circumstances I was able to immediately place myself in the "friend zone," sincerely so in a way not otherwise available to him, and that this was more valuable to Amir than anything else. Over time, I leveraged that friendship for Amir's cooperation to help me professionally. And Amir repaid my kindness by sharing just such secrets, volunteering them after I proved my interest in him was not related just to business. In the course of working together, some of the secrets were particularly good ones, earning accolades for me and the station.

Amir would be happy to hear that his reports were well received, but he cared more for how that helped me than what the CIA thought about him. Amir would never become an agent, and I never claimed to have truly recruited him. That's not to say I didn't try. What Amir did, he did on his own terms and for friendship with me. He took a brotherly pride in my success, and his ability to contribute to that, but he knew full well what it meant to be an agent. As it was, he chafed at working for his own service and in concealing his true self. He was not about to add yet another level of complex deception into his life.

One of the great benefits of this work is the people you meet. Those individuals who will serve as your tutors and facilitate a glimpse deep into their world in a way that's not readily attainable by the ordinary student, scholar, or foreign emissary. It's made possible by the fact that no one is there to judge what deep-rooted truths they offer to an outsider, because such is the nature of your clandestine contact.

When I left his country to move on to my next assignment, Amir and I enjoyed a final late evening farewell picnic in my car off the shoulder of a quiet stretch of highway well beyond the capital's outskirts. We passed, albeit vaguely, for the locals who often picnic late in the evening to get out of the heat. As he toasted our friendship and wished me the very best of good luck, Amir silently handed me a small, gift-wrapped package. At first embarrassed to open the gift in front of him, Amir insisted. A small case was inside. Flipping the top, inside I found a pair of shining officer's cuff links. In almost a whisper, Amir told me these were from his commissioning, for his dress uniform. He wanted me to have them as a remembrance.

THE CRISIS OF CONSCIENCE

There comes a point in most every case officer's career when they reach a crossroads. I've obliquely addressed one or two of my own already in these pages. We are faced with a crisis of conscience that pits the ideals that brought us into the CIA against the realities. I confess it's entirely unfair to suggest that this dilemma arises exclusively for case officers. Such a crisis looms regardless the CIA officer's occupational speciality. Irrespective of our specific job duties, those who come to the Agency choose to do so in order to make a difference. They embrace the words from John 8:32 that Director of Central Intelligence Allen Dulles insisted be etched into our main entrance lobby: "And ye shall know the truth and the truth shall make you free."

The more passionate and ideologically driven the officer, the more challenging and defining the crossroads experience. Those who see their trade as a calling will make the journey more than once, myself included. Challenging times determine whether or not you will persevere and remain, or whether you will fall on your sword and leave the service. It will also make a statement as to how you choose to define yourself and the leadership you bring, or abdicate, to the ensuing generation. After all, everyone leads, some better than most, simply by the examples they set. Will the next generation be inspired by dedication, selflessness, esprit de corps, and a commitment to the Agency's values? Or will they see narcissism and ego engendered by sycophants who prioritize their own ambitions?

To be fair, espionage is not a vocation for the faint of heart. It is a world of smoke and mirrors, where reality is shaped by perspective and perceptions, which case officers manipulate for a cause. At the outset of their careers, typically that cause is America and our nation's security. But the world has a vicious undertow that pulls at one's values and conscience. Maintaining one's values and integrity against this backdrop challenges even the most saintly among us. Doing it while swimming among a school of sharks requires a degree of ruthlessness even among the most morally chaste.

I've actively discouraged my children from following in their father's professional footsteps. Not that I don't absolutely love and respect the profession, but rather because it's a hard life, practically and spiritually. As a father, I'd rather theirs be simpler, safer, and easier. Being a case officer requires tremendous sacrifices by you and those you love. The hours and strain, both physically and emotionally, can be grueling. We miss a great deal of family time due to the sheer volume of hours put into the service, and for some, the prolonged absences. Case officers are required to spend a minimum of 50 percent of their careers abroad, and since 9/11, often on unaccompanied tours to locations where their families can't join them.

Case officers see much of the evil in mankind. We are immersed in lies and deception from our agents, adversaries, and our allies, and sadly at times, even our own colleagues. Case officers bear witness to the very worst of humans and see their horrific capacity to unleash unimaginable cruelty. Evil such as this does not see people, nor does it distinguish among men, women, children, or families. Rather it is embodied in such degrees of hate and detachment that those who practice evil can rejoice and find honor in genocide, rape, torture, and enslavement. Case officers sign on to confront such horrors in the hope of sparing our own fellow citizens from ever needing to endure them. Sadly, traits associated with such radicalization are increasingly present among Americans—those who succumb to the influence of victimization, racism, and xenophobia to participate or condone violence against their neighbors. The January 6, 2021, attack on the US Capitol should be a wake-up call for the country. Don't think that evil can't happen in America.

Such exposure to evil wears on the case officer's soul, as do the deeds we ourselves practice in order to keep evil at bay. But we cling to our beliefs that what we do is for that righteous cause. So when evil is not confined to our enemies, our crisis of conscience arises. A day comes when an officer begins questioning why they are here, and whether they can remain. It most often starts at the observation of some disturbing injustice within our own building or a moral difference with their supervisor's orders. Ideally, officers face such crossroads after realizing the satisfaction of the more noble in what we do and accomplish, the lives we save, and those of honor with whom we work, be they colleagues, allies, or agents. Absent that strong foundation, those who reach the crossroads might lack the desire and dedication to persevere, and some might themselves embrace the dark side.

For me, the crossroads came on my first field management assignment. It was my fourth consecutive overseas tour, and I was named deputy chief of station (DCOS) of a fairly high-profile, midsized Middle East platform, or at least it was at the time. At roughly ten years into service, I reached the crossroads about the same time as most. While not necessarily so dramatic for all, the ten-year mark seems itself to be a threshold. This is a career point where people often decide whether they want to stay in the Agency or if they should leave the CIA for other pursuits. In any case, this was a transition point for me. I was going from being a singleton case officer focused on my own operations to someone who was now responsible for others. As such, I would share more direct responsibility for the cases of others as well for the station's overall successes and failures.

Being a deputy is a hard job regardless of the personalities and responsibilities. It's not your show but the chief's. You're executing the chief's vision, and you can't do that well unless you appear to be fully and sincerely committed, embracing it regardless of your personal views. Your job is to provide quiet counsel to the COS, execute their vision, and defend it to others. No daylight can exist between your position and the chief's, at least not such that it's visible to the rest of the team, or heaven forbid, Headquarters.

At the time, CIA offered no formal training on how to be a deputy. In fact, there was very limited training for anything in the Directorate of Operations (DO) following graduation, particularly the art of leadership. Besides a one-week COS seminar, which is now two, and the odd short management course, the CIA did little to prepare its officers for greater responsibility or strategic thinking. It was all on-the-job training, and that's how we liked it.

Unlike the military, which prioritizes training to prepare officers and noncommissioned officers to move into more challenging and responsible positions, and which statutorily requires certain courses and particular career waypoints, the DO had nothing of the sort. In fact, DO officers beat their chests with macho pride and claimed that training was a waste, for the weak, looking down on those who pursued it. Just keep us spying in field, was the mindset. It was a terrible way to do business, which we learned the hard way on 9/11. Revisiting our training practices is but one of the positive changes post-9/11. And that change was not merely a product of the attack, but more a reflection of the cultural shift facilitated by a new generation of officers who prized and demanded training and the expansion of skills.

I had been a successful case officer, but frankly, this first time out, I was not a particularly good manager, nor was I an inspiring leader. I was supervising operations I'd rather be running myself, and not thinking corporately. Being a nonconformist had been a boon for me as a case officer, where creativity and quick thinking aided my endeavors, and when I was responsible for no one's mistakes but those of my own. But I knew nothing of navigating the minefields of the bureaucracy at Head-quarters. Worse still, I didn't think I had to: I believed being a successful manager and leader only required being a good case officer.

I would work under two different chiefs of station (COS) over the course of the assignment—two decidedly different men. And as it turned out, my case officer skills were also left wanting, since my first impression of both had been decidedly incorrect. Let's start with my first chief, "Mason." He was one of the few senior African Americans in the DO at the time, let alone NE Division. Mason had a reputation for being scary and intimidating. A Special Forces veteran of the Vietnam War, Mason had distinguished himself in the 1980s as a CIA paramilitary case officer (PMOO) operating in Central America.

Mason had what I can best describe as a presence. A powerfully built man, although not terribly tall, he possessed the strongest grip of any human whose hand I, or anyone else I know who had the experience, can recall. When you first met Mason, what immediately came to mind was how many men this guy must have killed as a warrior, probably with his bare hands. He did not warm up easily, presenting a serious demeanor, but engaging with a respectful level of decorum and propriety. I didn't think Mason took to me at first. In his eyes, I felt perceived as too young, too silly, and too soft.

In hindsight, only years later did I recognize how much patience Mason exercised with me. He could lose his temper, and Lord knows it was frightening when he did, since violence had been so integral in his professional life. Notwithstanding, a few occasions when my immaturity or mischievous conduct taxed him beyond restraint, Mason treated me fairly, and he hoped to mentor and support my growth.

As I became more open to who and what Mason was, I found him to be an extremely learned and profoundly thoughtful man. Deeply religious and family oriented, Mason's values and integrity were beyond reproach. And his sense of humor and genuine smile was worth waiting for once he was comfortable enough to relax. One was wise not to cross Mason, and particularly never to question his honor. But he believed in giving chances and in the opportunity for redemption. And to Mason, me being Jewish was not an issue, though under the circumstances I remained a closeted Hebrew to the Arabs among whom I lived and worked.

The only case I inherited at this post was an intriguing volunteer. As DCOS, I managed the officers conducting the clandestine operations but was myself declared to the local security and intelligence services with which we had official liaison. I picked up this volunteer, "Rahim," so as to allow for the possibility we might at some point need to engage the local service for assistance, and we did not want to burn an officer who was operating clandestinely.

Rahim was a fast-talking, fast-moving, always-scheming local Arab businessman. The ultimate carpet *wala*, the local term for salesman, he was in no shape or form to be a terrorist, neither physically nor in character. But Rahim was related to people who were, and he was from a rather prominent family. In fact, members of Rahim's family had risen to this terrorist organization's highest levels. Rahim came to us when he was at the end of his financial rope. Bankrupt and indebted to some rather shady characters who cared little about to whom Rahim might or might not have been related, he was unable to confess the great losses to his family so as to seek their assistance. With nowhere else to turn, Rahim thought perhaps he could make some money off what he knew about his family by approaching the CIA.

Traditionally referred to as walk-ins, given how back in the old days most such intelligence volunteers literally walked into the local American embassy in the dark of night, it is best to refer to them as volunteers. They come in all shapes and sizes, and through all manner of approach. One of the most famous was Adolf Georgievich Tolkachev, the "Billion Dollar Spy." A Soviet electronics engineer, Tolkachev provided intelligence to the CIA on radar capabilities in the early 1980s that profoundly advanced America's ability to gain the upper hand against Russian aircraft and air defenses. But according to publicized accounts, it took him over a year of leaving notes on cars with US diplomatic plates in Moscow in order to secure contact.

Given Moscow's counterintelligence (CI) environment, the CIA of course thought the approach was a provocation, a setup, or that it came from a loon. Some twenty years earlier, GRU (Soviet military intelligence) Colonel Oleg Vladimirovich Penkovsky, hero to the US for the intelligence he provided during the 1962 Cuban missile crisis, likewise struggled to secure the attention, and ultimately confidence, of the United States and United Kingdom officials with whom he attempted contact.

Volunteers can write letters, emails, make phone calls, engage over the internet, or use cutouts. Regardless of how they approach, handling volunteers is fraught with risks, but you can't pass up the chance for the next Tolkachev or Penkovsky. That said, a case officer will kiss a great many frogs before coming across a prince, and some carry risks far more lethal than warts. Intelligence services and terrorist groups regularly direct ostensible volunteers against their adversaries. The CI benefits include identifying our operatives, tradecraft, and requirements so as to surface penetrations within their own organizations, understand our gaps and vulnerabilities, and influence our understanding. For a terrorist group, there's all that and likewise the opportunity to kill or capture CIA officers, as was the outcome of the December 30, 2009, attack on CIA's Khost base, discussed previously. In Balawi's case, aka Abu Dujana, he indeed had access, but his interest and willingness to meet with the CIA was to kill, and he regrettably succeeded far beyond anything he imagined.

Given Rahim's identity and associations, and the fact we did not want him nor our contact to come to the attention of the local service, meetings were held periodically in other countries. When I first met Rahim, he really hadn't done very much for us. Most of our time to that point had been invested in vetting his true intentions to discern whether he was a legitimate volunteer or a threat. I saw a great deal of potential in him. While Rahim's insights concerning his family members were interesting, they were essentially historic and at best useful background information. That is sometimes itself a sign of a possible provocation. Limited access equals limited damage for the service directing the would-be source. Rahim could tell us about the dynamics among some of this terrorist group's most senior leaders, but because he was so far away from them he could provide no actionable intelligence concerning plans, intentions, and capabilities.

From the outset, I decided that my goal was to work with Rahim in developing a justifiable pretext for him to return more frequently to his home country. There he might actually have the means to secure current intelligence that was actionable and thus more valuable. It would certainly be the most effective way to vet him. We discussed not merely cover stories that would allow him to spend more time with family members working for the terrorist organization but also opportunities he might find to secure their interest in services that addressed the organization's needs. All of this would enable Rahim to develop far greater intelligence access.

At his core, Rahim was an entrepreneur. Albeit a bit shady, when properly backstopped and efficiently supervised, Rahim's wheeling and dealing nature, effervescent personality, and contagious good humor made him quite successful. Over the course of time, Rahim was incrementally able to increase his utility to the organization, which they profited from materially and logistically. His relatives paved the way, and during regular trips home Rahim would take meals with them or be included in their meetings. Rahim would in turn provide intelligence on specific plots and targets the group was contemplating. Some of it literally saved lives, including a senior and prominent US official who was being targeted for assassination.

Not long before Mason was ready to move on as my COS, he had a serious sit-down with me. In a rather paternal manner, Mason suggested it was time for me to turn Rahim over to another officer. Rahim was now a high-profile and important operation. Headquarters wanted to assign a new, Washington, DC–based case officer who could be dedicated to the task full time. In the most light-handed manner, Mason suggested this was best for the station, the case, and me too, since I had not been as available to fully discharge my duties as his DCOS as he might have preferred. Moreover, there was little more for me to gain personally. I had "bought low and could now sell high," having made the case into the important operation it had become, and I was being considered for an intelligence medal, based on his own recommendation.

Unfortunately, all I was taking in from the conversation was criticism for failing to perform my DCOS job to his standards. I inferred the suggestion that in trying to serve two masters I would inevitably disappoint both. That's not what Mason said, nor felt, but it's what my immature ears processed. In reality, Mason had been exceedingly patient and had allowed me great autonomy in running the operation. He never sought to micromanage nor did he interfere with scheduling even though it impacted his own requirements.

Rather than focus on what Mason was trying to tell me, or appreciate his kindhearted way, I reacted defensively and obstinately. Even though I appreciated the fact that Mason had the capacity and wherewithal to snap my neck like a chicken, I found myself arguing with him. To his credit, Mason did not order me to turn over the case, and he rebuked me far more lightly than he might have in my annual evaluation concerning how I exercised my DCOS responsibilities.

Time passed and Mason moved on. Given a gap with his successor, and the demands of my case, Headquarters initially sent a more senior officer to cover as acting COS. When this was deemed impractical, I filled in for a bit, but to the detriment of handling Rahim. So, ultimately, Headquarters expedited the new chief's arrival. When I first met "Joseph," my new COS, I thought I'd at last met someone who gets it. Yes, with Joseph, I was returned to the management by the ubiquitous old school of the White Irish Catholics who ran the DO, but he seemed different. Joseph was not much younger than Mason, but acted as if he were. He struck me as grounded and not terribly pretentious, and he always had a joke or a quip at hand. Though I was far younger and junior than Joseph, he spoke to me as if we were equals, declaring that we were partners in managing the station. Just as I had misjudged Mason, I also misjudged Joseph, but in his case, to my peril.

One of my first clues came at a dinner that Joseph and his wife hosted for me and mine not long after their arrival. Whereas Mason was fascinated by different cultures and people, and was eager to try new things, Joseph was oddly quite American-centric for an experienced NE Division case officer. In my first meal at Mason's house, we were served camel kebabs, tabouli, and hummus. Joseph and his wife served steak and baked potato, which is no sin in and of itself, but he then proceeded to speak over dinner of detesting Arab fare.

The conversation grew into a more broad discussion of race. Joseph asked about how being Jewish was a factor for me, even if no one outside of station was aware. I deflected the matter as being rather unimportant, since I was largely secular. Joseph had grown up the privileged son of a senior US military officer, which he curiously compared to my own inner city, Jewish experience. Although Joseph's upbringing, he admitted, was rather sheltered in terms of his exposure to those of different races and backgrounds, he observed that his experiences as a White American Catholic abroad allowed him to relate just the same. When I didn't seem to understand, he explained further.

"It's no different for me when I am the only White American in a Middle East grocery store or neighborhood, let's say, than for a Black man entering a predominantly White business establishment or area in America."

"You're kidding, right?" I responded, thinking, or perhaps hoping, he was only joking.

"No," Joseph continued, "I know what it feels like to have eyes upon you, contemptuously, suspiciously, disliking you merely for the color of your skin and who you are. It's the same for minorities in America, so I get what that's like."

Perhaps a more career-minded and intelligent person would have accepted that Joseph was a racist fool and politely excused himself while smiling and waving en route to the door instead of confronting him, but I was clearly not that bright.

"You must be out of your mind," I shot back instead. Not that I can claim to have been an activist on behalf of civil rights, Joseph's views were simply preposterous and offensive. "That is not even close in the slightest way," I argued. I went on to articulate a passionate indictment concerning racism in America, White privilege, and that for an intelligent and worldly man such as he to be so ignorant as to suggest an appreciation of the Black experience as he had done was testament to the depth of our problems at home. And while it certainly felt good to say those things at the time, my relationship with Joseph never recovered. The office dynamics became increasingly tense, the two of us often at odds. In retrospect, like him or not, agree with him or not, as the deputy, my job was to quietly seek to influence him behind closed doors. I had just let any such capacity die.

As punishment, Joseph ordered me to turn over Rahim as Headquarters earlier requested. I had no luxury to argue, debate, or even brood selfishly. In retrospect, Mason's rationale made sense, and I ought to have heeded his guidance at the time. Moreover, his intentions were more respectable: Mason suggested the turnover to lighten my load, which in turn would enable me to do a better job as his DCOS; Joseph's motivation was retaliation. It only became more disheartening when the Headquarters-based officer to whom the case was being reassigned turned out to be "Paul," widely known as a total disaster. His poor reputation was earned by a series of miscues and bad calls that brought more than one promising case to a premature end. Had I but agreed with Mason at the time, I would have had more leverage and time to influence the choice for who would receive the case.

Soon thereafter, I flew out to meet Paul and Rahim where the next contact was scheduled. Paul and I spent a few days together in advance, and I tried to provide him greater depth and color for the case beyond what he read in the official file. Paul was the same grade as I, but far older. He had been with the Agency many years longer, and had progressed more slowly. In part, this was because Paul was not as flexible to accept permanent field duty assignments since he was married to a State Department officer, one in fact far more senior. Her career had been quite successful and, as such, decisions concerning postings and the like were prioritized to what was best for the wife.

My worst fears were realized when it was clear that Paul had not thoroughly read the file, nor was he particularly interested in maintaining the same high-threat clandestine tradecraft I practiced, which had kept Rahim safe. Paul thought I had been overdoing it, and handling Rahim could be greatly simplified. Moreover, he wanted to push Rahim for even more sensitive information, which I suggested needed to be pursued with greater patience and care, lest he raise the group's suspicions. It's best when agents have natural access to the secrets they provide, such as coming across information in the normal course of their duties or interactions with friends and family, as was Rahim's case. When agents start asking questions for which they have no plausible reason or need to know, agents get killed.

The three of us met in a hotel room after a brief prearranged contact on the street where I had brush passed Rahim the location. A brush pass is a long-practiced clandestine exchange in which two people cross paths at a prearranged time and well-screened place during which one passes an object to the other. There are generally no greetings or discussion, as there would be in a "brief encounter." The two continue on their separate ways. I had placed a small slip of paper into Rahim's hand on which was written the hotel name and room.

Poor Rahim did not even expect to meet another officer, let alone bid me farewell, so he was a bit startled to see another figure waiting. Due to the significant attention to his reporting, I had on occasion brought a collection management officer or analytical expert to our meetings, so he wasn't entirely shocked to see someone else, though I would usually let him know in advance when we might have company. Rahim was happy to be working with a team and was ever gracious and charming with the new faces. His shock only came when I explained how Paul would be his new partner.

A gentleman always, Rahim welcomed Paul and was cordial and friendly from the outset, pledging continued cooperation. With the three of us all present, new handler, old handler, agent, I reviewed all the prior commitments Rahim and the CIA had made to one another. I did this so as to avoid any future misunderstandings about what either party owed the other. I also reviewed what Rahim had worked on, and that which he was still pursuing.

As I prepared to leave the room to allow Paul to establish himself as "the new sheriff in town," Rahim was at first composed. He stood to bid me farewell. He made an eloquent speech paying tribute to our partnership and thanking me for all I had done for him. A kind and emotional man, Rahim ultimately broke down and began to weep. We reached for one another, hugging tightly. Rahim kissed me repeatedly on each cheek, as is Arab custom, the stubble of his beard scratching at me, the moisture of his tears on my face. Rahim blessed my family, said how much he owed me, and that he would always love and cherish our time together. Within months, however, Rahim would be arrested, interrogated, and tortured.

I received word fairly promptly only because, in expectation that Rahim would provide my name and particulars under interrogation, I needed to take precautions in the event the group sought me out. I was devastated by the news, and I blamed myself for Rahim's fate. I was angry at Joseph for ordering the turnover, believing in my heart that I could have, and indeed would have, kept Rahim safe. I imagined the horrors to which Rahim must now be subjected.

The story ends relatively happily. Although he had betrayed the organization, Rahim's relatives intervened and facilitated his release. He was subsequently banished into exile. Never forgetting or abandoning its own, the CIA facilitated and financed Rahim's relocation. The only aspects of Rahim's post-detention debriefing shared with me were those directly impacting my personal security. To that end, I was advised that Rahim admitted how he had confessed most everything. Whether true or not, Rahim claimed to have kept but one secret in the course of his torture: my identity. According to Rahim, he only identified Paul.

The ugliness of how this had all transpired converged with, and only exacerbated, my ongoing tensions with Joseph. Moreover, Joseph had in parallel been messaging his own dissatisfaction with me to leadership at Headquarters, to his old boys' network. This complicated my efforts in securing a good onward assignment or the promotion for which I was then due. I only learned later that Joseph likewise vetoed the medal recommendation that Mason had submitted, and which Headquarters had endorsed, concerning the intelligence Rahim provided.

That Rahim lived made a difference. Had he been killed, my crossroads would have been still more difficult to navigate. At the end, I focused on what brought me to the CIA in the first place, which was the satisfaction that came from the contributions and influence I could only have here, and, God forgive me, the sheer joy of espionage. That had not changed, neither my motivations nor my continued ability to perform the mission I still loved. And that has been my counsel to others. Are you still realizing what brought you to the CIA? Can you do that anywhere else? Is that satisfaction still what gets you out of bed in the morning? Finally, would you miss it?

There's great heart in those new officers joining the ranks. Those with the greatest passion, whose ideals and energy survive their inevitable crisis of conscience will be the most successful agent recruiters and handlers. They will however struggle inside their own professional house. Those less bothered by the pressures of conformity and professional tradeoffs required for continued advancement in the CIA's more upward-focused, bureaucratic reality will flourish, and regrettably, set the tone. The few who can best manage both their passions and the bureaucracy while retaining their ideals and ethical standards offer hope for an Agency in need of reforms to fulfill its charter and restore its character.

FAMILIES ABROAD AND RAISING KIDS IN THE CLANDESTINE WORLD

Spying is not like in the movies. We all have lives, families, friends, and responsibilities like everyone else in this world. Only our lives must conform to the work. Moreover, it must blend such that there is no daylight between ordinary routine and espionage so that we are protected from those who hunt case officers and their agents. These demands impose on families in ways that they must embrace as the normal and without thought. Our children grow up with what to them is normal, but to most everyone else, and certainly their friends, is considered bizarre.

Raising a family while living a clandestine life and spinning a tale that is reality to your friends, family, and the world requires constant effort to lead what appears to be a normal life. Everything is harder for families living under such circumstances: mortgages, jury duty, kids' events, the PTA, family outings, and neighborhood picnics. My younger colleagues are often curious to know what it's like to raise a family while posted to various exotic locations, living a double life, and conducting the work of intelligence. What is normal? How do you raise children abroad? More-over, they're eager to know if children growing up under the rubric of their parents' espionage are, in their words, "normal." How do they differ from those raised in the cities, suburbs, and rural parts of America?

I'm also asked more personal questions about raising children under these circumstances. When did I tell them what I did? How old were they? How did they react? Did they have any desire to follow in my footsteps, and did I ever encourage them? Will their kids be better or worse off from the lifestyle to which their parents' vocations will subject them?

As with anything, there are advantages and disadvantages with this life. Truth be told, it's hard to precisely define the "American experience" that the kids are missing. Candidly, we're talking about comparing what a typical overseas life is like for a US official expatriate kid versus a kid who experiences an essentially privileged American upbringing. My five children have all done reasonably well. And if you'd ask them, they'd tell you they believe their experiences contributed to their professional success, but that there were pluses and minuses alike.

Generalities being fraught with inaccuracies and dangers, "Foreign Service kids" share some common experiences, be they children of State Department officers or those from other agencies, military service members posted abroad, spies, and other American officials. If their parents are professional members of the Foreign Service who serve abroad for extended periods beyond one or two assignments, they become accustomed to frequent moves, often among entirely different cultures, languages, and parts of the world. The need to frequently change schools requires them to constantly make new friends, adapt, and adjust to new conditions, like US military brats encounter back at home. Of course, this flies in the face of human nature, which is to pursue routine and predictability. My children have also come back to America in between these overseas tours to settle among kids who have known one another for years. Being outside of these groups made it harder for them to forge the kind of close, lifelong relationships they found among their already spoken for peers.

For some, though, and this was true for all of my own kids, the lifestyle gets into their blood, for better or worse. I found that my children all longed for the excitement of travel and ever-different new adventures and stimulus. They tended to make friends easily and found ways to get along and identify common ground with those who were different from themselves. I found my five would return to America and float among vastly different cliques in their schools. One day they might be hanging with the jocks, the next with the academic overachievers, the drama students, the nerds, and then the next day be mingling with the school's social royalty. In fact, they all seemed to grow antsy staying in any one place for too long. Some children, though, found these same conditions grueling, particularly if their first such experience occurred during middle school or high school. Exhausted by the need to constantly be "on," starting over again every two or three years, some isolated themselves from the overwhelming and constant change and yearned for the stability of living in one place, and to be among people like themselves.

Life within an official US community abroad or on a military post can be like living in a bubble. Similar to a small town where everyone knows about everybody's business, or seeks to, there's the requisite gossip and drama. Pettiness on occasion is evident among some families, as well as jealousies stemming from rival sections, units, and agencies. The smaller the post, the finer the microscope under which families and children are viewed, and on occasion, judged.

There are more opportunities to escape the bubble in big cities like Paris and London than in small or austere posts across Africa and Latin America. At a smaller post, there's little to no refuge from the rest of the official community. On the other hand, I found that the experience served to condition my children to see people beyond skin color and to prize rather than fear their differences. My kids, from the time they were born, like other Foreign Service children, were exposed to adults and children of different races, colors, languages, and outlooks. Such people entered their lives as family friends, teachers, babysitters, or distinguished and welcome guests. Children like mine grew up referring to such visitors as "aunty" and "uncle," reflecting by example the familiarity and intimacy their parents gave.

Foreign Service kids will try exotic foods from all corners of the planet, getting a taste for many. Their English will be replete with slang, colloquialisms, and foreign words from the countries in which they resided. Almost all of my children began with British sounding accents and slang learned from the still very colonially educated African and South Asian nannies and babysitters who looked after them. A few of my kids still let slip a reference to petrol, the lift, and their flats, when speaking of gasoline, elevators, and apartments.

My youngest children in particular are still likely to say "inshallah," which is Arabic for God willing, to express doubt over a dubious commitment. More often than not their sentiment is a polite Arabic-style *maybe, but not likely*; or they use the term *khalas* (Arabic for finished, or rather, "I'm so done"), when emphasizing the end of some adventure. You can only imagine the reaction of their Bronx-based Jewish grandmother when we came home to visit while on leave.

But from these experiences, many Foreign Service kids learn the foreign languages where they live, or they come away with ears ready to better absorb formal language training later in life, having been so accustomed to different accents and tongues in their formative years.

Foreign Service kids early on regularly observe or participate in complex conversations with adults from various walks of life and develop unique confidence and poise in how they present themselves. They are less intimidated, though perhaps more respectful, of those with particular rank. Not only will they have grown accustomed to meeting senior officials from the various countries in which they live, such as ambassadors, ministers, generals, and so forth, but they will have attended countless events in which they have met the likes of our own president, the secretaries of state and defense, as well as lunching with DCIAs who travel to our foreign installations.

Rather than fearing new experiences, they more often will yearn for adventure. This was recently brought home when my wife was discussing the options for a future overseas assignment with my youngest two, both going to college. She asked whether they'd prefer us in a more difficult Middle East location or one in Western Europe. To our surprise, they both encouraged the Middle East assignment, observing how Europe would be "boring."

To garner attention, as all kids desire, they learn from an early age to speak with maturity, sophistication, and earnestness, as well as with a sense of humor to merit, to their delight, the smiles and validation of their often far older audiences. This teaches them to measure their audiences, gauge what is going over and what is not, and adapt to find areas of interest to their interlocutors. They learn from the examples they see in their parents when they're entertaining. Picking up not just the basic civilities of good manners and politeness, they embrace the ideal that they're representing something more than themselves. Curious, they pursue everything there is to know about the people they meet, but they are conscious to cautiously elicit, versus interrogate, so as not to offend and in order to mask their true agendas. They learn to enjoy making a good impression and insist that guests, be they old friends, new acquaintances, and even strangers, should be made to feel well tended, comfortable, happy, and at home.

On the other hand, in some cases children will be exposed to the darker side of humanity. From the back seats of their plush, armored SUVs, they might witness truly horrendous sights: abject poverty with children, barely clothed, some even toddlers, begging for pennies around them; heavily armed soldiers brutally suppressing peaceful protestors; the squalor of tin-roofed shanty towns, their cesspools overwhelming the senses. Furthermore, they might endure the regular disappearance of their friends and acquaintances, and sometimes their families, who die from diseases both exotic and commonplace. It goes without saying that Foreign Service kids must be inoculated from all manner of illness, many uncommon or entirely unknown in developed countries. My kids' shot cards roll open like accordion files.

Moreover, whereas in today's world all parents are obligated to educate their children early on concerning the real danger of school gun violence and "stranger danger," Foreign Service kids must be drilled in that education and quite a bit more. There is no escape or shelter from the reality that as the children of Americans abroad, particularly official Americans, they are terrorist targets wherever they go.

Often, my children have been the only Americans in their classes, and they attended school at posts where Americans were unpopular with the locals. While attending school in a conservative Islamic country, my youngest daughters were subjected to taunts, bullying, and slurs, and were frequently propositioned. Even the school administrators were unsympathetic. The girls' reactions were further restrained by their understanding of the example they were required to display as the children of American officials. They put up with it, and I'd like to hope grew from the adversity, but stories they now reluctantly share reveal how deep some of the scars run.

Not all American families abroad, official or otherwise, seek to explore the local cultures in which they live or behave with the same grace and curiosity. Some try to take America with them. Instead of exposing themselves to the differences, they are content to live in compound fortresses designed to replicate a little America that they almost never leave. They and their children at times reflect the very worst traits of the ugly American by virtue of disrespectful and condescending behavior with local drivers, laborers, and staffs. It is almost as if they buy into the false image of wealth, privilege, and entitlement afforded to them by the relative differences with the local population, or the necessities required by security or incentives to attract families to such austere environments. Those children have a rude awakening when they return to American suburbia.

It's not to say these kids are immune from the dangers, risks, and behavioral issues affecting our children at home. And they also miss a great deal of that typical "American experience," unless it's replicated to some degree in whatever post their parent serves. But particularly where the American communities are smaller, the concept of prom, going to Friday night football games, pep rallies, or learning to drive will be an entirely different experience.

Still, there is a wide selection of lovely locations at which one could serve. Plush European cities, exotic Asian tourist destinations, tropical paradises, and Club Med–like sites with miles and miles of white sandy beaches. For the more austere posts, officers receive financial incentives and rest and recuperation trips for the employee and their family members to decompress during trips to such lavish tourist destinations. So while my family never lived in the more posh venues, we were able to travel to the world's seven wonders and marvelous resorts at which we could decompress and recharge. Of course my family tended to be more interested in seeing the Grand Bazaar in Istanbul, the Great Pyramids in Egypt, the Noble Sanctuary in Jerusalem, and Victoria Falls, than in basking in the sun on the Cayman Islands. Just in the blood, I suppose.

Apart from that, when you're living in the developing world, given the poverty, lack of infrastructure, prevalence of disease, and limited local health care, a case officer is going to get sick. You can't avoid it, since you are out all the time socializing to develop targets and traversing less hygiene-proficient establishments in meeting your contacts. And when you get sick, you often just have to grin and bear it. My body has hosted all manner of parasites and plagues across multiple continents. It gets so that you can reliably diagnose yourself. The mosquitoes, flies, ticks, and fleas all likewise come bearing gifts such as malaria and dengue fever.

And then there is food poisoning and salmonella. Among the cocktail and diplomatic reception circuits you attend, one of the principal topics of conversation with fellow dignitaries are your latest symptoms, stool specimens, and courses of medical treatment.

Now layer a case officer's clandestine work on top of the challenges of life itself while raising a family under clandestine circumstances abroad, particularly while in austere locations. When case officers walk out the door at night, their families can't know what they are doing or where they are going. Even witting spouses are left to worry if their partners will return safely. I don't mean to be overdramatic, because the truth is that the CIA conducts countless clandestine operational acts every day of the year, worldwide, and most proceed uneventfully. But like any police officer on the streets, or any military service member in a conflict zone, on any given day there's always risk. In the military's jargon, the CIA's operations are always "forward."

For the duration of an overseas field assignment, which on average spans three years, we can't simply turn on when we are "working" and turn off when we're not. There is no safe area, sanctuary, or "rear" in military parlance. The local counterintelligence service and whatever additional third country intelligence elements that are there to root out and neutralize CIA's operations never pause. CIA officers abroad, particularly case officers, must remain situationally aware and operationally conscious at every moment. The life they must lead requires 24/7 commitment, and attention. Everything we do has to have a reason, or fit a profile to which we need to remain conscious, inasmuch as it has an operational bearing on our security and our capacity to recruit and handle agents. That includes your errands, your family time, and all that goes with the basic components of life.

To varying degrees depending on the counterintelligence environment and the state of bilateral relations between the United States and the country in which you are serving, the local service is monitoring everything you do. They are following you around town, listening to your phone calls, hacking into your computer, and placing audio and video devices in your home. So it's not like you can call a timeout, ring them up, and say, "Hey, listen, fellas, I'm actually off tonight, so can you all take a break."

Everything you do, everyone you see, and all the people and places with which you interact feed into the profile. What you do, don't do, and how it's perceived are what shape the view held by both the local intelligence service and a hostile third country's intelligence service under whose ever-present watch you remain. The trick is to not garner their attention, and be mindful of how every moment of the day needs to be accounted for in the most innocuous manner, lest you intrigue the enemy and become subjected to their full attention. All the harder to do now in a world of ubiquitous tracking technology.

Perception is reality. Paranoid counterintelligence services, particularly those in locations where the CIA is considered foe versus friend, see the world through a prism of suspicion. It's their job. You must therefore consider not what you can logically explain away in your own mind, but rather how what you're doing could be seen through theirs, generally in the worst possible case. Their perception is always right.

Often the most innocent things we do are believed by our adversaries as serving a nefarious intent. It's ironic, but the simple act of taking your child to school, walking the dog, or going across town to buy an ingredient for dinner not otherwise available at your local grocery can be a provocation that the locals feel obligated to investigate. They are not entirely without cause, since just as we must consider everything we do to be under their scrutiny, we likewise have to manipulate our very existence to optimize our operational effectiveness. Consider the toll of having to think about that 24 hours a day, 7 days a week, 365 days a year, without losing your mind.

Case officers bear the greatest imposition, since they are the ones meeting the agents or recruiting new ones. So whether by poor judgment or dumb luck, if the local service is suspicious and focuses resources against a case officer, their professional and personal lives become exponentially harder. One of the first things new CIA officers are told upon entering duty, regardless of career occupation, is that they are the top target for every counterintelligence service. The details of their lives feed into our adversaries' analysis, and it informs their decision on who to target, and how. And it's never been harder than it is today.

We are almost never out of contact with some matter of electronic device that tracks our every move. Phones, cars, computers, Fitbits, televisions, and athletic equipment are among the most obvious devices that track us. Moreover, an ever-increasing number of cities worldwide are becoming enveloped in so-called Smart City camera surveillance systems. More and more homes incorporate smart technology too. Even if not every one of these technological devices can track your movements, they nonetheless provide data on your lifestyle and habits that feed into a pattern of life that hostile intelligence services and terrorist organizations can use to identify your routine. It provides them the predictability of where you might be at certain times and highlights instances when you are "out of pattern."

Against this backdrop, obviously the children can't know what their parents do. Consider the risks, or at least the tremendous responsibility, for them to know the identities of those with whom their parents really work, be it the other CIA officers working clandestinely, their foreign agents, or even the host and third country security officials with whom they might maintain official liaison relationships. How much a case officer tells their own mom, dad, or sibling is likewise a consideration, and I know many who maintain their clandestine facade simply so as not to stress family members with worry.

My dad passed when I was young, but I did tell my mother and older sister, though I gently advised them that if I were taken hostage to please never acknowledge my true affiliation to the press. For better or worse, neither my mother nor sister ever really understood why any nice Jewish boy would want to leave New York City and run around the world spying. Too much *mishigas*, or craziness, my mother would say in Yiddish. She never took interest in the CIA, and simply referred to what I did as "my job." When it comes to your own children, you have to balance a great many considerations. The kids' innocent disclosure to the wrong person about something Mom or Dad is doing, or where they are going, can lead to disaster.

As for me, I have five wonderful, brilliant, beautiful, and rather precocious children and have been twice married, my wife and I enjoying twenty-three years of love and partnership. Leading a double life imposes daily challenges that most people never have to consider. These comprise, but are not limited to, legal, practical, and emotional considerations. Automation and technology have made some aspects of living a fictional role easier, and some so much more difficult and complex. Let's just begin with the fundamental realization that everything about who you are, what you do, and where you do it, is a lie.

However you break it down, the face you show the world is fiction. In reality, your mask is less about lying and more about assuming a character. In fact, as a case officer, I actually lied as little as possible, since every fabrication must be backstopped to withstand scrutiny. The bigger the lie, the more backstopping is required. I'd rather spin and manipulate the truth in the course of my work to allow flexibility, not to mention ease the strain of the mental gymnastics required in remembering who you told what, and when. Gray is far easier than black or white. There are limitations, of course, such as testifying under oath in any criminal or civil matter before an American magistrate. In such cases, you have to take the judge aside, or the Agency does, to keep you from inadvertently committing perjury.

The entire issue of lying and trust was brought home to me again just recently by a number of my children on the occasion of my retirement. At some point in their lives, I had told each of my children the organization for which I really worked, accompanied by a rather generic description of my duties and responsibilities. How much I explained varied in part on where I was, what job I held at the time, and the kids' ages. You reveal yourself with children out of necessity, not to boast or for any but practical reasons. And kids likewise have different personalities. Some are more inquisitive and suspicious. As such, how much you tell them depends on what they really need to know in order to preserve the secrets they might unwittingly compromise by *not* knowing what you really do for a living.

All five of my children had similarities as well as differences in how they responded. While not precisely scientific, I believe each of the five was somewhere between twelve and fifteen years of age when I told them, and I can remember pretty well the time, place, and circumstances of how I shared with them their new burden of knowing about my secret world. And it is a burden. What child should have to lie to their friends, other parents, and teachers about what their parent does or where they might be at any given time?

It's actually asking a lot to gain your child's understanding and collaboration to explain just why Mom or Dad is not at today's softball, baseball, or football game; has to miss the evening's cheer, dance, or gymnastics meet; couldn't make the concert or award ceremony; and must reschedule the parent-teacher conference. No, they can't say that Daddy is meeting a terrorist tonight and thus is out of pocket. Or that my parent is in Iraq, Afghanistan, Pakistan, Libya, Lebanon, or Syria running around with body armor and an M4 weapons system. Your kids have a bit more to explain, and omit, when making up excuses. Is it fair for any kid aged twelve through fifteen to have to figure out how to dodge questions like, "Just where *is* your mom?"

So here you are as a parent, trying to instill all the best values in your children from the time they can walk and talk. Perhaps you're a religious family, and speak about the commandments, sins, and salvation. Think then the awkwardness of years later explaining why lying was a virtuous act under these particular circumstances. My eldest son, who was relatively young at the time, was the first of my children to learn about all this. He, along with his younger brother and sister, was evacuated from a rather dangerous post from which all families were sent home following a series of bombings and shootings that were only to worsen. I meanwhile continued on at the post, coming home to America roughly every ninety days for two-week spells. One day, while in the US on one such family visit, my son and I were taking a drive somewhere, most likely to play catch, since I remember him wearing a baseball cap and his glove was in the car. I vividly recall driving on the Fairfax County Parkway when in the most casual manner, my son, then twelve, asked if I worked for the CIA. Mind you, his question was entirely out of context from a conversation that had been, up to the moment, about the Mets' and Orioles' prospects for the coming season. I all but lost control of the car and swerved into the next lane. "What was that parental guidance again on handling such things?" I thought to myself. "Oh, that's right. Stay calm, and turn it back around."

Steering the car back finally between the white lines, and consciously trying to slow my heart rate and evoke a calm, soothing voice, I responded, "So why do you *think* I work for the CIA?"

"Well, Dad," my son explained, "before we were evacuated, all the families were confined to their homes except for us going to school during the day, or you to the office, and always with some sort of protective security."

I nodded affirmatively.

"And from our rooms at night, we could sometimes hear the explosions and see the gunfire in the city from out our windows." Indeed, at the time, there was a daily fireworks show of tracers, explosions, and fire, with the scent of sulfur and carbon rising from town, a view captured well from our strategically placed house at the top of a large hill.

"But Dad," my son continued, "it seemed like almost every night, late, after we went to bed, I also saw *you* out my window, leaving the house, with a backpack, jeans, and a dark jacket going somewhere."

Calm on the outside, my inside was saying, "Gulp." At least he didn't see my pistol, I tried to remind myself hopefully.

"And Dad, I asked my friends, and none of their fathers were going out like that at night except for some occasions when they had to do something for the office. But they always had on a suit and were picked up by our security people."

Again, listening attentively, I thought, "Gulp."

"So Dad, I figured you wouldn't be going out like that, when everyone else was staying home, and there was all that fighting going on, unless you were CIA."

My twelve-year-old son had outlined an eminently logical explanation. Intellectually, I thought twelve was way too young to require him to share the burden of protecting my story. In my heart, however, I could not continue to lie after hearing out his incredibly mature and reasonable explanation.

"Do you know what the CIA is and what they do?" I asked.

The young man provided a fairly thoughtful response that focused on the CIA having a secret role in collecting information for America. Hearing him out, I elected to confirm his suspicions, explaining that he too now had a great responsibility. We spoke for a while of it while tossing a ball back and forth. I told him how it wasn't at all like the movies, and I was certainly no James Bond. There was very little danger, I explained, and a lot of what I did was actually rather boring and routine. In fact, I told him how I genuinely did work for the government agency I officially claimed and that I truly performed those duties. At the time, being more deeply hidden, I was in fact located within my ostensible office—half the time, in any case, and that it was my "day job." The exception to all of this, I told my son, is that what I do for the CIA requires me to protect the people who help keep us safe. Were the secret of what I did revealed, those people could be identified and be placed at great risk.

My son considered it all very thoughtfully. He asked a few follow-up questions aimed mostly at whether I was ever in danger and if I liked what I did. I reassured him that it was pretty safe, and that I very much enjoyed the work due to the impact it had on keeping our family and others safe. The biggest downside, I explained, was how much time it required me to be away and the fact I couldn't share with them more about what I did. My son never revealed the secret to anyone, including his younger siblings. It wasn't much of a surprise that he would likewise go on to serve his country, a successful officer in the United States Navy.

I waited longer before telling my younger son and oldest daughter, as neither ever professed a great deal of suspicion, or even interest, in what

I did. I remember waiting until they each were around fifteen or sixteen, taking a long walk outside alone with them and sharing the family secret. Neither asked many questions and both responded similarly. They were, in fact, relieved to learn that their dad had not been a boring failure at the office for which they believed him to work.

My younger son went on to graduate from the US Naval Academy and serve as a Marine officer, serving two tours in Afghanistan. Though my sons suggested that my service had some influence on their own decision to serve their country, I took pains to deromanticize the horrors, realities, and risks of war when they told me of their plans. My oldest daughter earned a PhD in clinical psychology, working today with former and current service members and their families with the Veterans Administration. Dealing with both the physical and emotional horrors of war inflicted upon her patients, my daughter is a courageous young woman.

Of all the five children, in fact, it was really my second to youngest daughter who posed the greatest challenge. For reasons I could never quite understand, though perhaps it was after watching each of the *Spy Kids* movies one or two dozen times, the girl was convinced I was a spy, and that spying was "too cool!" She began confronting me with questions about whether or not I was a spy from practically as early as she could form words. Doubting me, because after all she was right, she'd regularly search the houses we lived in for secret compartments and doors, certain she'd find them.

I thought that keeping my home sterile of incriminating evidence from the likes of the Russians, Chinese, and so forth was hard, but keeping secrets from my daughter was harder still. Inquisitive about anything I'd do, everywhere I'd go, and anyone we'd invite over the house, my daughter always believed I was up to something, and felt entitled to ask. One could leave out no piece of paper she wouldn't look over. As could be expected, she was positively thrilled at the revelation when her time came. She felt vindicated, having come to the right conclusion, albeit for none of the right reasons. When I finally did come out from the shadows after submitting my retirement papers, it was all I could do to keep her from taking out full-page ads to proclaim the news and, more important, that she was right!

My youngest daughter, though a study in contrast with her older sister's obsession to catch her father in the act of espionage, couldn't care less about what I did and became consumed with STEM. Now an engineering student, she found all that international affairs business not her cup of tea. That said, she was blessed with near Vulcan-like hearing, prompting my wife and me to teasingly refer to her as "Mr. Spock." This likewise complicated maintaining my story a bit. Making the most of her gift, she'd often loiter just out of sight or hide in a closet or behind furniture, when her mother and I would talk, hoping to pick up some juicy tidbits concerning her sister, or herself.

Between having one daughter tossing the house for incriminating evidence and the other being a human eavesdropping device, there was really nothing the local counterintelligence services could do that was any more intrusive than what I faced 24/7 from my own children. Fortunately, by this time in my career I was largely known officially as CIA to the local governments with which I worked, and I was likewise known within the overseas, expatriate communities where we lived. This was unavoidable due to the nature of my position and duties. I had official liaison on the CIA's behalf with both the host as well as third country intelligence and security services. When I finally did come clean to my two youngest daughters, it was really to help them avoid inadvertently "outing" any of the officers I managed, but with whom I could not acknowledge professional association.

In reflecting on what it was like growing up like that, my children all largely claim to have positive experiences that helped them mature, appreciate different cultures, and get along with those from all walks of life. There were hardships to which they will confess, and many I know they still keep to themselves. But perhaps my youngest daughter offered the most candid response, reflecting back recently on how she reacted when I first told her, and the enduring consequences. She maintains today that it was said with a bit of tongue in cheek to tease me, but at the time she observed that my revelation forever changed her trust dynamic. Worse than having been deceived about Santa Claus or the Easter Bunny, my baby was shocked by how her father could have lied about who he was and what he did. Reminding me from time to time about how she'd been lied to practically her entire life, she can't help but still have trust issues. I don't doubt that the realization of how they were raised was more impactful than any of them will let on.

So spying still goes on when you have kids, as does life. The awkward moment comes now and again, which you as a parent have to explain, or for which you must perform damage control. For example, some of the posts where we served had a high counterintelligence threat. One was particularly challenging. It was in a former Soviet Republic state with a fairly pervasive physical and technical surveillance against me, as well as the family. We had to assume our home was wired for sound and video, and all of our personal electronic devices, ranging from phones to computers, had been hacked.

You get used to the fact someone may be peeking in the shower, electronically that is. Thankfully, no such images ever made it to WikiLeaks, which in my case spared the world. But life goes on. Couples have fights, sensitive family matters come up, personal finances are discussed, and kids get into trouble. It's all rather innocent information for most, but they represent exploitable vulnerabilities that a hostile counterintelligence service would seek to leverage against someone like me.

You take one of these assignments understanding that for the duration couples can't squabble, and absolutely no mention of anything work related can occur in the house. Local community or family gossip, like who's sleeping with who, and who's hitting the Malbec a bit too much, is positively off limits. Money problems? Depressed? Angry at having been passed over for promotion? Jealous of that colleague on the second floor who's getting tickets to the concert because she's sleeping with the married public affairs officer? All off limits. So what do you do?

Well, you can't talk in the car either, because it's likewise wired for sound, not to mention it's a geolocation device. There's always doing what the mobsters do, right, such as taking a walk outside? In such places, as the COS, you have an understanding with everyone, the officers as well as their non-Agency spouses, all of whom need to be witting of the severity of the counterintelligence threat. You explain the considerations and offer them the means to meet as necessary in a secure location at the office. There, they can have their privacy to do what they must: duke it out verbally, strategize personal finance or health issues, or just enjoy a cathartic vent of all the tidbits they've been dying to share but have been unable to do so in their home. It's a little weird to consider for the folks at home perhaps, and logistically challenging at times, but it's entirely normal in our lives.

For my own family, there were pluses and minuses to blanket surveillance. Like the idea of living a double life, you get used to the bizarre lifestyle and the pressures of always being under a microscope. We were rather fortunate, inasmuch as our local minders at this particular former Soviet state were not quite so brutal as the Russians can be. It's sadly common practice for the Russian FSB (the Federal Security Service, which assumed the KGB's internal security responsibilities), for example, to break into our officers' homes, poison our dogs, and even defecate on the floor. The behavior is designed to harass and sometimes, like putting sugar in our gas tanks, meant to retaliate for, say, having lost one of the CIA officers they were following. Not so with our local hosts. Their presence was annoying, but not mean-spirited. That said, their behavior would occasionally prompt questions from my youngest daughters, who were then not old enough to be told what Daddy did for a living.

"Daddy," they would ask, "why has that same car with two men been parked across the street all day?"

"Maybe they are lost or waiting for a friend," I'd say.

"Daddy, shouldn't we go help them with directions?"

"I think they might be offended to have a foreigner offer them directions in their own country, Sweetheart. I'm sure they'll be fine."

Or on another occasion when they asked their mother while en route to the stables for a riding lesson, "Mommy, look! It's those same men again in that car! Are they still lost like Daddy said? Or are they coming to ride the horsies too!"

"No Sweethearts," my wife would answer, "maybe they're just going home and live around here."

"Are they afraid of the horsies like I used to be, Mommy? They always come this way but never get out of their cars."

Now as it turns out, the local security chief at this post and I got along fairly well. The relationship wasn't quite the same for our deputy, which I'll address a little later. I'm sure the local chief wanted to keep an eye on us, and to remind me he was doing so, albeit without rubbing our faces in it. I guess it also didn't hurt that we had a huge, neurotic Doberman at the time, "Buddy," that was particularly overprotective of my daughters. Some of the local intelligence service chaps who had been by the house to deliver messages were absolutely terrified of him, and I expect the surveillance team members were too.

One day, my wife took Buddy along with the girls on a walk outside. It was a quiet street in our neighborhood, where there generally wasn't very much traffic. For whatever reason, a car approached a bit too close to them for Buddy's comfort. To my poor wife's horror and our daughter's delight, Buddy charged the car, throwing his body against it, leaving a dent in the fender. The driver, perhaps one of the local surveillants, didn't even stop to check the damage. For all I knew, even the otherwise gentlemanly locals might have tried to poison that dog, but after seeing Buddy eat his way through a plastic kennel, I doubt it would have done much good.

At another assignment where I received fairly regular surveillance attention, and where the Russians employed a carcinogenic chemical tracking agent, my sons were always amused by what they innocently thought were the quirks of how the locals drove. We'd be out going somewhere or another, when the boys, not necessarily acting discreetly, would turn fully around in the back seat of our car to watch the traffic behind. One would chirp, "Daddy, why did that car full of men go around the traffic circle twice? Are they lost? Should we help them?"

On another outing to one of the local markets, my sons noticed a team park their car while we walked among the shops. They opened their hood and pretended to be fiddling with the engine to give a reason for their presence. There were three in the team, enough members to get out on foot to pursue were the need to arise, and they were not terribly convincing under the hood, even to my young sons.

Being sweet natured, when the boys saw that the men seemed to be no closer to repairing their vehicle after we had concluded our visit, and attributing to me far more mechanical prowess than I was due credit, they insisted we render aid. I came up with whatever excuse I used at the time to fail in their Good Samaritan desires, and off we went. Of course, as we did, the boys were relieved to see the three men suddenly succeed in starting their car, slam the hood, and rapidly jump inside. No doubt coincidentally, they were even headed in the same direction as us.

On still another assignment, one evening while serving at a post that not only had a terrorist threat but also suffered from high crime, my wife and I were entertaining friends from our own embassy. Owing to exposure concerns, no one from the station was there, but we did have some guests from other local embassies and walks of life in the community. Families were generally included at events like picnics, barbecues, birthday parties, movie nights, and what not, often since they were among the few safe social activities we could have at some of these postings.

While everyone was having a great time, and I was indeed conversing with a foreign official whom I had sought to pursue operationally, my daughter, ever the social butterfly, made her way over, taking in parts of the conversation concerning the local security situation. I was of course trying to maintain and use my official job as a means to earn the target's trust. Interrupting, my young daughter piped up, "Oh, but Daddy goes out all the time at night!" Proud of mingling with the adults, my little one continued innocently, "Oh yes, Daddy goes out very late to do the food shopping so he won't miss family time, and even goes in and out from the back door so he doesn't disturb us!" The target didn't need a PhD to pick up the clues.

My wife similarly had to explain away some of our peculiar behaviors from time to time, and not merely to the children. We were living in sub-Saharan Africa and my wife was expecting. I was a bit more buried in my day job at this post, for a variety of reasons I won't elaborate, and busy in the evenings with my clandestine work. My wife was active in the local expatriate community, arranging social events, helping newcomers, and mixing with ladies from the various embassies, businesses, and non-governmental organizations, many of whom were not American.

One evening, my very pregnant wife and a few of her friends were out and about having a ladies night, and were all packed into the SUV belonging to a German woman. The roads in town were confusing, dark, with no streets markers or signs, and they found themselves lost trying to find the home of one of their comrades. It was not exactly the safest place for a car full of Western women to be, as carjackings and other violent crime were unfortunately common and occasionally lethal. I happened to be in the midst of going to an operational meeting at the time, performing my usual due diligence to ensure I was not under any form of surveillance, when I came across them stopped on a fairly desolate stretch of road.

Pulling out of a narrow side road, and concerned there might be trouble, I came up behind them where they had parked. The German driver was stunned when I tapped on her closed window, and she rolled it down in relief to greet me. I extended my hellos, of course, giving my wife a peck on the cheek, and asked if anything was amiss. The German lady confessed in her heavy accent with embarrassment at having become lost looking for their friend's house. I oriented her, and told her the best route to arrive at their destination. Confident she was okay, and that she now had her bearings, with a nod from my wife and another quick kiss farewell, I waited for them to push off before I again disappeared into the dark African night to continue on to my meeting. The German lady turned to my wife, thanking her for my assistance, and remarked in her heavily accented English, "My goodness, your husband, he is like Batman!"

All of this sounds like a huge pain, and it is, though it makes good fodder for stories later. Still, after living almost four decades around the world while wearing various masks and also raising a family, I can attest it is just something to which you become oddly accustomed. It becomes like breathing: natural, automatic. You just do it as second nature, embrace it all as real, and stop overthinking the complexities.

WHEN GOOD AGENTS DO BAD THINGS AND CALCULATING RISK VERSUS GAIN

Agents are not all built equally, and rarely, as I earlier explained, are any set of circumstances so precisely alike that there's a school-ready solution. Even the best agents occasionally go off the rails and can confront you with odd, vexing, and even risky behavior. I see it as a strength of CIA case officers, as compared to our partners among the various other US law enforcement or intelligence community agencies: Our selection, conditioning, and experience is predicated on an individual's ability to deal instantly with fluid or dynamic circumstances, and often under intense pressure. We know our parameters and make a great many decisions independently, and on the fly, to suit the evolving circumstances, often without the complete story.

Today's CIA is bigger, less intimate, and more risk-conscious politically, and its focus is more on mitigating embarrassment with the White House than the human cost of operational failures, both the cost to our agents as well as to our own officers. The reduced margin of error results in greater micromanagement and assertion of operational control from seniors far removed and long separated from the business of spying. For CIA, becoming bigger might have enhanced its ability to survive 9/11 and Iraq, but it did not make it better, particularly in the world of human operations. While leadership talks a good game of delegating increasing authority to the field, the decision makers remain the top brass, whose calculus is weighted to the decreased risk of doing nothing.

Seizing perishable but high-risk opportunities is what a spy service is in business to do. But doing it well requires trust in your people, and to enable their agility and innovation. For leaders, it also takes a willingness to protect them when things go awry despite their best efforts. Post-9/11, CIA leaders have advanced best by mastering the art of deflecting blame and using an absence of failure as a measure of success. A common characteristic among far too many of the CIA's post-9/11 leaders was the reinforced example that advancement came fastest for those who did not make mistakes, as opposed to others who gambled operationally and succeeded. The fewer risks taken, the fewer things might go wrong. And the less leaders extended themselves to offer top cover to subordinates seeking to take those risks, the less exposed they were to accountability for the failings of their charges. In other words, you can't lose if you don't play. CIA's leadership ranks had become a place reserved for conformists over cowboys, with precious room left for any in-between.

Any case officer who has been around long enough will have stories of difficult agents. And so it has been that some of my best, or most reliable, agents have occasionally drawn me into less than optimal circumstances. In most of these cases, I can look back now and see the humor. At the time, though, the circumstances did not seem very funny. I was lucky that in each case I had been allowed the autonomy to address the situation. Times are different, and it's more likely today that Headquarters would be more inclined to intervene.

While CIA leadership talks about delegating more authority to the field and simplifying the process, operational decisions increasingly require Headquarters panels and senior level approvals. This is not entirely without its place. In fairness, additional perspectives and other eyes are important. Those entirely reasonable considerations are unfortunately not the ones behind today's increased operational risk aversion.

The twist can be confusing, in that CIA has actually expanded its indulgence to place our foreign agents and CIA officers at physical risk.

But the risk of greatest concern to the CIA's post-9/11 leaders was not loss of life, but the embarrassment of having themselves or the organization lose face with the White House or a rival US intelligence community agency. The optic has become more political, with leadership concerned at how any particular operational activity might impact relations with the White House. In the Trump era, CIA leadership assiduously controlled the messaging of what came out of the building that might land in the press, or worse, on the president's television. This politicized risk aversion predated Trump, however, as post-9/11 CIA leadership agonized over any misstep that might have threatened its relative status or place at the table among USIC agencies.

I was still a relatively junior case officer when I recruited "Nasir," a veteran security service official. He was a distinguished gentleman who spoke the Queen's English. Eloquent, learned, and charming, Nasir enjoyed a long and successful career. I would have gratefully spent time with Nasir if only to revel at the colorful stories he told, which captured the region's turbulent post-colonial history.

My opportunity to enter into his life came as Nasir's career was in its twilight. He was an older man who had worked hard to rise about as high as a civil servant could within his government, absent political connections and the ruthless ambition to use them. It's not to say Nasir never indulged in the corruption from which his position enabled him to profit. Most gears within this society moved little without at least some degree of grease, whether it be securing phone service or cooking gas. But his touch was light, his community the priority, and integrity his guide.

Like some who come to the end of their career against the hard wall of mandatory retirement, Nasir grew uneasy. We had come to know of Nasir's anxiety, as well as his resentment toward those public officials who had long padded their salaries to excess. He had hoped to parlay his skills and experience in the private sector, but he lacked connections. Nasir was proud and operated with a sense of honor. Rather than challenge this perspective, it was better to leverage it.

Nasir believed he had an unwritten, moral contract of sorts with his government. He spent a lifetime working above and beyond for his countrymen without exploiting the self-serving financial opportunities his duties occasionally offered. He believed his government would look after his retirement. When he saw corrupt colleagues faring better than he, perhaps his self-righteous reputation for integrity the cause of his dilemma, the moral contract was broken. Enter me.

The conditions ripe, raw, and emotional, with an extended family depending on him, Nasir was not beyond some indulgence in what he knew intellectually was impropriety. He just needed the logical pretext and an adequate, albeit superficial fig leaf. Nasir's previous outreach to private sector enterprises was my way in. I contacted him under the guise of a businessman, using a background that suited him, which I am not at liberty to further detail. But in the jargon of espionage, it was a "false flag" approach, one that requires sufficient backstopping. For Nasir, I played the role of "Francis," or to my friends "Frank," a consultant advising clients who were considering investment in the region.

Nasir's development went well. Over the course of several meetings, we made an instant connection. Nasir was fascinating, personable, and entertaining. Professionally, I advised from the outset that my clients required anonymity, which required Nasir's willingness to accept a confidential consultancy. Doing so also required the type of tradecraft in communicating that he could not help but recognize as more exotic and complex than even a discreet business venture should need. Moreover, a security official himself whose portfolio included counterespionage, Nasir knew intellectually that what we were doing, and how we conducted our business, was hardly standard.

Thankfully, Nasir embraced the fig leaf and accepted the terms. Nasir wasn't *spying*, but rather, he was *consulting*, and by doing so he was helping his countrymen by providing a balanced appraisal of the situation on the ground, which foreign enterprises demanded before investing. In fact, Nasir believed these contributions were having genuine impact. When news of sizable foreign investment landed in the press, Nasir believed he had played a part. I never confirmed his false assumptions, but neither did I ever disabuse him of the possibility. If he believed every new major foreign investment came about in part due to his contributions, so much the better.

Conducting meetings with Nasir required no small effort and a facade that would inevitably deteriorate over time or under his close examination. Still, it was up to Nasir as to whether or not he could pretend. Over the course of our collaboration, Nasir's observations and subtle comments suggested he was becoming well aware of with whom he was actually working. Rather than force Nasir to confront the reality and risk how conscience might bear on his reaction, I slowly peeled back the onion, but only as much as needed. He never directly asked if I was a United States government official, let alone a CIA officer. He didn't want the answer.

Due to his public profile and sensitivity, and my claim to live elsewhere, we met sparingly. Nasir's intelligence was largely strategic, not as prone to the limits of an expiring shelf life as is the case with more tactical reporters. He operated at high enough levels to interact with major policy makers so he could speak to plans, intentions, and capabilities, issues that are longer in range. I'd meet him at prearranged locations, picking him up in a car that had ordinary license plates. Although we occasionally conducted the entirety of the meeting in a moving car in the wee hours of the morning, I'd occasionally bring him to a residential compound for longer debriefings.

The US was considered a political adversary and a significant counter-intelligence threat to the host country government, and as such our official community garnered extensive physical and technical surveillance coverage. It required a fair bit of gymnastics to conduct our clandestine activity, and particularly harder was meeting someone as sensitive as Nasir while in the role of an officer pretending to be a businessman with no ostensible connection to any government or official presence. Still, the residential compound we occasionally used included families from several foreign embassies, businesses, and nongovernmental organizations, so it was under some degree of observation by the host country's security service. It was a risk, one of many you take, balanced with the realities of available options.

The substantive part of the meeting on this particular night had concluded. The pickup had been uneventful, and I had spent two hours debriefing Nasir for intelligence, a rare luxury afforded by the safe house. Now it was time to drop him off. Nasir had told no one of his relationship with me, not even his wife, so he had to employ a cover story with her to account for his whereabouts that he could likewise share with colleagues, if pressed. His wife, in turn, while unwitting of the true nature of his activities, needed to be able to tell Nasir's office why he was unavailable should some crisis require them to call him at the late hour. This required a defined time window. He had to be home by a certain hour or risk suspicions.

Trouble was waiting outside the compound gate. As we slipped off the residential compound in the still of night, Nasir out of sight in the back of the car, I quickly spotted a suspiciously parked vehicle across the way. On occasion, this was where the local counterintelligence service would stage a surveillance vehicle, looking for suspicious activity associated with this Western compound. Even at the late hour, and in reality because of it, the service would position surveillance teams at various choke points throughout the city from which they could track and follow suspects of interest. The teams could communicate via radio transmissions, allowing more surveillance vehicles to trail and trade places, or to pick up targets from ahead. Most people don't realize that surveillance can just as easily be in front of you as trailing from behind.

That there was a team staged across the street from the compound was, in and of itself, not unusual. In most cases, given the late hour, they would be fast asleep. At most, one lone observer among the team would catalog those coming on and off the compound. Rather than disturb their slumber, though, the teams would not usually go through the bother of actually pursuing a departing vehicle. These were not highly paid, dedicated professionals, mind you, but disrespected street workers paid a pittance in a poor country and residing at the very bottom of the service's hierarchal totem pole. And despite all of that, I pulled on to the main thoroughfare only to observe the headlights of the staged vehicle illuminate as its engine rumbled to life.

There's a science to determining whether or not you are being followed, and this wasn't it, inasmuch as the team had immediately latched on to me in the midst of an otherwise dead night. I didn't have to be Reilly, Ace of Spies to know instantly that we were in trouble. My priority was keeping the team from identifying Nasir, whose presence in the car was obscured from their view. My options were limited.

Two ideas came to mind. As I was not associated with the car, the team would have to see me and compare their recollection to photographs of suspected intelligence officers in order to make a match. This meant that, as a first option, I could return to the compound and wait them out. Allowing time to pass, I could move Nasir off later using another car mixed in with the community's normal rush hour traffic. A second option was to give the team something to satisfy their curiosity, such as driving to a hospital or pharmacy. The problem was the possibility the team would follow our car into the hospital parking areas to identify me, and in doing so, likewise see Nasir. Stopping at a pharmacy would similarly require me to get out of the car, leaving Nasir in the car to be found, and me to be definitively identified. Going back to the compound made the most sense.

I drove for a bit, taking a somewhat circuitous route to confirm the trailing car was indeed surveillance. Hanging back a respectable distance, which they could afford to do in the absence of any meaningful traffic at the hour, the team made every turn I took. They wanted me to be comfortable, and they wanted me to believe that the distant headlights were not from the same car. I had to expect that they would be calling for backup to catch me farther ahead, and include additional teams so as to conceal their pursuit.

Surveillance is traditionally conducted by multiple vehicles, which makes it far more difficult to confirm that any particular vehicle is following you. But for the moment, the trailing team, a single car, had no such luxury and was committed to remaining discreet, just close enough not to lose me.

Certain of the situation, and the risk, I had to unfortunately advise Nasir and prepare him for what was coming. After all, at any time, one of the teams might intercept and confront us, most likely at a hastily stood-up check point. Nasir and I would have to adhere to our prearranged cover story to explain why the two of us were together. Complicating all this was the reality that Nasir knew me in a foreign alias, and I'd ultimately have to display my true name and United States government credentials.

Although I felt like a wreck on the inside, I remained calm on the outside as I began to let Nasir know our circumstances. Now was not the time to panic nor do anything to undermine Nasir's confidence in my ability to get us out of this mess. While I had every belief that Nasir would likewise maintain his composure, his sangfroid would ultimately become, dare I say, somewhat annoying. I walked him through the plan.

"So we'll just go back to the compound," I explained in a calm, docile tone, "wait them out, and move you off later in the day with a colleague, and in a different car."

Keeping low and out of the team's view of the rear window, Nasir piped up just as calmly, and politely, and after a thoughtful pause, countered in his best Queen's English, "Lovely plan, Frank, quite well played I'd say, old chap, but it won't do. You see, I rather have to be home by 0700 hours, this a.m., so as to check in with the Mrs., and make quite the important appointment I have with the superiors. Wouldn't do to miss it, you know, would raise too many questions. Be a good man, then, Frank, and just lose them. I'll be off once we're in the clear."

Not the response I was looking for, I thought to myself. "Nasir, Sir," I added respectfully, "that's a big risk. I strongly advise you let me bring you back to the house, and we'll sort it out."

"Ticktock, ticktock," Nasir said teasingly, smiling politely. "Not possible, I'm afraid. So terribly appreciate your thoughtfulness and concern, but I have full confidence you'll steer us off this nasty precipice. Right, I must be getting home then, so now, now, good man, let's be away."

Ticktock was right. We were on borrowed time. There was no guarantee I could even make it back to the compound without running into a checkpoint. And by this time, I had veered well off the beaten path of main thoroughfares, winding through less traveled residential neighborhoods I had come to know through past casing. The distant headlights in my rear view mirror remained constant, but they maintained their distance. A good sign, I thought, that they wanted to remain discreet, not realizing I was aware of their presence while they tried to determine what I was up to.

My COS was not going to like this. The conservative call, admittedly the right call, was returning to the compound, not initiating a high speed pursuit. But while in charge as the case officer, you're still operating as a team with the agent, who has to share in the planning. Nasir would not budge, despite my polite protests, and just as politely, and calmly, held firm that he had to get out of this car soon in order to make it home on time.

There were no Google Maps back then, and even GPS, though in its early stages of commercial availability, was still not a thing. I assessed our bearings and ran through what route I might take to allow some separation and distance from our pursuers, and in turn, appropriate blind spots at which Nasir could make a quick and undetected exit. Nasir, though in reasonably good health for his age, was hardly a spring chicken. Conflicted, I told Nasir we'd do it his way. I took the next street with a quick turn, and depressed the accelerator.

The trailing surveillance team was caught off guard, allowing me a decent head start, but they quickly took to chase. I accelerated along the otherwise quiet and still residential streets, my heart racing faster than the engine. The roads were narrow as I wound through the maze of small, crisscrossing streets. Cars of various makes, years, and conditions were parked haphazardly outside the old, deteriorating houses to either side. There were no street lights nor stop signs. It meant right-of-way decisions at intersections were decided not by who got there first, but who was bigger. Speeding along as we were, there was simply no way I could have managed to bring the car to a safe stop if faced with an oncoming vehicle. It was all I could do simply to avoid the parked cars and keep from running up on to the curbs as I turned from one narrow street to another.

Over the sound of my nervously beating heart, I thought Nasir was trying to get my attention. I took a glimpse in the rear view mirror to see him peering above the seat looking backward out the window. Nasir wasn't talking to me, he was critiquing the trailing surveillance.

"My God, I simply can't believe they're giving you so much distance," he muttered like a disappointed instructor. "Bloody idiots," he snapped, shaking his head. "Tisk, tisk, tisk, what sort of amateurs are these!"

For the love of God, I thought, here I am, terrified beyond words that I'm about to get my sensitive agent wrapped up, and he's calmly sitting back there evaluating surveillance's performance! I was stunned. After all, if we were to be caught, the worst of it for me, besides getting a bit roughed up, would be expulsion. For him, it was ruin and jail for the rest of his life. And that was the best case. Yet he sat behind me, completely composed, narrating the adventure as if it was a tale out of Dickens, and pointing out the team's performance failings, as if he was entirely detached from what was transpiring. Was he really that calm, or was he just crazy? Meanwhile, I was soaked with perspiration, the car tires screeching in sharp turns, pushing the poor, little old getaway car to its limits and wondering if there'd be a tomorrow.

"Right, just let him get that further distance," Nasir quipped as if sarcastically berating the failing team that was trailing behind him. "How will you bloody well know when he's made that next turn. Amateurs!" Nasir declared in muted exasperation, shaking his head judgmentally in disappointment. "It's a wonder we ever catch anyone! So much for modernizing the service and all that rubbish."

This was simply surreal. Was he actually rooting for them to catch us? I wanted to shout, "Shut the hell up!" But I said nothing, maintaining my eyes both on the hazards before me while gauging the distance of the trailing team behind.

I managed to extend the distance. Clearly, the poorly paid surveillance team members could not afford crashing, and though they raced to keep up, they lost distance on the turns. Still, by now, there would be other cars and police joining the pursuit. I was coming to a promising confluence of small, curved streets that were laid out in a most useful serpentine fashion. I gave Nasir a heads-up to get ready. He was still complaining over the pursuers' poor showing even as he pulled together his things and readied to pop open the rear car door at my command. A couple of turns in, the team out of sight, I came to a quick stop, throwing on the parking brake so as not to activate the brake and taillights.

Calmly, albeit slowly, Nasir stepped out onto the curb. In the fashion of his one-time British colonial master, Nasir paused, leaned into the front passenger window at practically a bow, extended his hand to shake, and politely wished me a pleasant evening. "Just go, for God's sake," I thought to myself, my head ready to explode. A paternal smile on his lips, Nasir smartly turned into the dark alley with which I had aligned the car. As he turned, my foot depressed the accelerator as I launched the car toward the approaching intersection, turning in the opposite direction from which Nasir was headed.

Nasir would be okay. They never found him, nor me, fortuitously, though I did not return to the compound. I ditched the car far from where I had dropped Nasir and used local transportation to make my way home. The station couldn't ever use that car again for anything operational, nor could they use the compound, but the case proceeded productively for some years to come. For his part, Nasir remained nonplussed by the event, "Never had any doubts you'd spirit me out of harm's way, old boy," he told me at the next meeting. "Delightful adventure, eh what! Made me feel like a young buck again."

My COS took it reasonably well the next morning when I outlined the evening's events. He was an old hand, senior, and fortunately for me, appreciated my mischievous ways in a fatherly manner. Satisfied that the story had a happy ending, he didn't openly question my judgment. All he would say, with a somewhat menacing smile, was, "Don't let that happen again, Peter Pan."

An agent I inherited during another Middle East tour would pose yet a different type of problem. He shared precious little in common with the gentlemanly, kindly, and erudite Nasir. "Jamal" was in hiding when he came to us, volunteering after having defected from a terrorist organization for which he had worked since a teenager. Perhaps "defection" inaccurately suggests that Jamal had a choice or was otherwise acting in the interests of a noble cause. There was nothing terribly noble about Jamal, though he did have his own sense of honor and code. Practically speaking, Jamal was a thug. His resume included theft, extortion, assault, and assassination. Officially, he had variously served his organization as a foot soldier, bodyguard, terrorist, and enforcer.

Jamal came from violent slums and refugee camps. He grew up as both victim and deliverer of violence, starting early with petty crime and working his way up. His nature and skills caught the eye of criminal and militant circles. Having begun as a foot soldier for a nationalist, anti-Israeli organization, he later aligned with a more radical, fringe, and violent organization that had long since parted ways with its more mainstream and ostensibly moderate base group. His heyday came in the 1970s, during a civil war in the country where he resided, when his reputation was forged for ruthless efficiency.

Jamal did not transition well from foot soldier, enforcer, and assassin to middle management. He was hot-tempered, even by terrorist standards. A taste for whiskey didn't help inform his judgment, patience, or decision-making. Consensus building was not exactly his thing, and neither was suffering fools. Worst of all, Jamal wouldn't tolerate disrespect, regardless of who you were. And his bar for such slights was unreasonably low.

Jamal's quick fuse, drinking, and pervasive contempt for those in his organization from whom he felt disrespected was a tinderbox waiting to explode. And it literally did. One day, Jamal's differences with coworkers turned violent, and a dispute with a superior lethal. Rather gives office politics and professional counseling a completely different meaning. Jamal was now on the run for his life when he initiated contact with the CIA. In exchange for relocating him to the relative safety of third countries in which his organization lacked a presence, Jamal would provide everything he knew about his old group, their plans, and the various personalities. In addition to his historic knowledge, Jamal agreed to help make approaches to associates who he believed could be turned. In hindsight, what were we thinking? What former associates would stick around to talk to this guy anyway? But what he knew of the group's players and their plans was genuinely valuable.

My role in handling Jamal was not terribly complex or taxing, or at least that was the expectation. Essentially, I was his babysitter, assigned to keep watch until he could move on to a more long-term location. Trying to avoid having his troubles from catching up to him, Jamal had taken refuge in the country in which I was assigned, one far too busy with internal problems of its own to worry about him. In the midst of a bloody Islamic extremist insurgency, the locals were too taxed to bother with a foreign national of a radical group with which it had no particular quarrel. The CIA was laying the groundwork to move Jamal to a safe, third country alternative where we would be able to make better use of his knowledge and contacts.

A turnover is when an agent is transferred from one case officer to another. Ideally, turnovers are "warm," that is, the current handler introduces the agent to his new case officer, as I had done with Rahim when I turned him over to Paul. Warm turnovers allow for the collective of the agent along with both the incoming and outgoing case officers to review terms such as financial remuneration, meeting arrangements, and tasking. Doing so contributes to avoiding any misunderstandings, inadvertent or otherwise, such as the agent claiming to be owed money or being accustomed to receiving greater payments. The personal touch also facilitates transition, and at least to some degree helps to transfer the rapport and personal relationship between the agent and the incumbent. "Cold" turnovers are those in which the new handler meets the agent without the former handler's introduction or participation. They can be trickier. The new officer has a physical description or photo of an agent they have never met, but finds them at a prearranged time and place. A lot can go wrong.

I inherited Jamal in a cold turnover on a dark street in the middle of the night. Given the circumstances and hurry in the manner through which Jamal came our way, he never really worked long with any particular officer. None of those who had worked with Jamal had the opportunity to develop much of a personal relationship with him, or had spent enough time in his company to better assess and evaluate him. So much of what made Jamal tick remained a mystery before our first encounter.

Like all meetings I would have with Jamal, the first was conducted in a car, and it went fairly well. Jamal was punctual, professional, and polite. Conservatively dressed in a white buttoned-down shirt worn over his polyester trousers to conceal the pistol wedged in the smart of his back, and laced up black leather shoes, he had the presence and bearing of a *heavy*. But aside from an unwillingness to engage in lighthearted banter or discuss his personal life, Jamal was cordial and respected my operational guidance. In fact, he was all business. Jamal's goal was to get out of this country as soon as possible so as to keep his old "friends" from catching up with him. And so became the crux of the issue with Jamal. He feared for his life and believed himself to be on borrowed time.

My job was to keep him patient and from doing anything reckless. Jamal had no interest in becoming friends, didn't much like Americans, and distinguished little between the CIA and Israel's Mossad. One more valuable footnote not available to me at the time was the fact that Jamal drank to excess. And believing his life at risk, Jamal was also always armed. Not quite drunk at our first meeting, there were a few physical and behavioral signs that he had imbibed. That's how he dealt with stress. The longer he had to stay here, the more stressed he would become.

At each successive meeting, Jamal was increasingly irritated by the delays and agitated over his personal security dilemma. He felt the noose tightening. Coping by drink, he showed up at our meetings in deeper states of intoxication. Jamal grew frustrated and angry, believing that the CIA's inability to effect his relocation reflected our disrespect and lack of seriousness. Going as far as to suggest that we were deliberately slow rolling his relocation, Jamal accused us of diabolically planning to drain him to the exhaustion of his usefulness, before setting him up for assassination at the hands of his old colleagues, thereby freeing ourselves of the longer-term financial obligation.

I urged Headquarters to expedite the arrangements and observed that Jamal was coming to the end of his thin and quickly fraying rope. Frightened, Jamal was not going to behave in the most rational way. Now add intoxicated, angry, and prone to violence, and one has the makings of a crisis. For their part, my Headquarters colleagues were taking the necessary steps, but they might not have been as invested. From where they sat, the sense of urgency was not as weighty. It wasn't unusual to have a disappointed or even angry asset. And what were his options, they thought? We were the only game in town to keep him safe, relocate him, and provide a rather robust financial reward for his trouble. While Headquarters judged the risk in terms of the potential Jamal might quit, I suggested that the danger could be more lethal. I was told simply, "Well that's your job, go ahead and reassure him."

I found Jamal reliably present at the correct place and time when I next went to pick him up. Unfortunately, it was all he could do in his clearly inebriated state to open the car door and stumble his way inside. The meeting only deteriorated after that. He demanded immediately to know the status of his relocation. He seemed unhinged, so I tried to settle him down. Driving, I balanced keeping an eye out for risks from the outside, like the local authorities, while taking frequent glances at Jamal to judge the risk right next to me. The more angry he became, the greater I tried to slow and soften my own words so as to hold his attention and deescalate. I really had little to offer to satisfy him. While generous, his regular salary and living expenses were not as important to him as immediately addressing his departure's logistics.

Jamal softened his tone and slowed his somewhat slurred delivery. His yelling and rants turned to deliberate and cool, albeit menacing, threats.

"David," he said to me in the name I was known to him, "I have nothing personal against you. In fact, I like you."

"Well, I like you too, Jamal, and I'm really trying to help," I responded.

"The problem, David, is not you, but your organization," Jamal continued with perfect composure, albeit with some alcohol-induced slurs. "They do not take me seriously. They are playing with me."

I interjected, without dismissing his feelings, and instead offered all manner of plausible excuses, reassuring him that he was held in the highest regard.

"No, David," he interrupted. Slowly and calmly he corrected me, "You might believe that, but they are playing us both." Pausing, Jamal looked away from me and forward, on to the street, "I need to show them I am a serious man. I will have to kill you so they understand who they are dealing with."

I tried to make light of it, suggesting he was joking. But Jamal was dead quiet and serious, arms crossed, staring forward. "Now, Jamal," I said with equal calm, "I know you are angry, and you have a right to be. I am sorry for what you're going through, but we'll work this out. Together."

Shaking his head negatively, "No, David," he finally reaffirmed, "this is not personal, I like you, but it is the only way they will understand. To show them how men should act."

I was armed myself, but I still believed that while Jamal might not be totally kidding, he was drunk, hurt, and angry. He was entirely capable of killing, his professional career having demonstrated as much. Likewise, he was prone to act out violently when frustrated and angry, and given the circumstances of how he came to us all the ingredients were there. Still, I did not expect Jamal to suddenly whip out a pistol and shoot me. He was actually looking for respect. And I dispensed that to him generously. Nevertheless, I regretted having the safety latched for the Browning 9mm Hi-Power secured in my belt holster.

"Jamal," I continued reassuringly, "hard as it is, be patient, and I'll do everything I can to keep things moving." I never challenged Jamal's threat nor made light of it with him, and focused just on his issue of concern.

"David, they are leaving me no choice," he responded, still with an eerie calm. His unwillingness to resume eye contact was the most unnerving part.

We concluded the meeting, reviewing the business at hand of security, communications, and questions I still needed him to answer, the date and time and place I'd next pick him up, and the business of paying him. All normal. All routine, as if it had not been preceded by a death threat. With that, I let Jamal out at an appropriate spot screened from public view from where he would walk until finding a taxi. Then I started to contemplate how I'd report this to Headquarters.

When I came into the station the next day and related the evening's events, my COS took it in stride. He was satisfied with my assessment that predicting what a drunk, armed, high-strung, and pissed off terrorist might do at any moment was not 100 percent dependable, but he agreed with my take that Jamal was just blowing off steam. He wouldn't shoot me. I figured Jamal might rant and rave, but he wasn't a fool, and I wasn't going to provoke him. At worst, I figured, Jamal would storm out of my car and disappear. As much as my boss was inclined to take my word and go with the odds, he was less sanguine about how our increasingly conservative Headquarters management team might react. And to be fair, my COS added, anything less than 100 percent with a guy like this is a risk, and if I didn't show up at the next meeting with a relocation plan for him in place, he might very well lose it and go off the deep end. I was willing to take the risk, and so was my chief.

My COS had accurately predicted Headquarters' breathless, hair-on-fire response, despite the backflips I'd taken in submitting a clinical account of Jamal's frustrated and inebriated reaction. So began a series of exchanges with Headquarters in which we tried to further clarify our view, offer risk mitigation strategies, and secure buy-in. The ensuing negotiations spanned almost the entirety of the gap between meetings, during which, more importantly, no progress had been made on Jamal's relocation. At best, I could offer him a window of six months before we were certain the move could be safely executed. For Jamal, six months was a lifetime, or rather, the end of his. Headquarters suggested just walking away.

We argued our point and made the case that the risk he would actually make do on his threat was quite limited, and that the gain of his continued intelligence cooperation too lucrative to pass up. He was angry, and I could deal with that. Moreover, we would take additional precautions to address the added risk. To his credit, my COS backed me fully, a risk to his very promising career. Of course, he'd still be alive! Headquarters conceded. A similar outcome would be far less likely today. To preserve having made some contribution toward whatever postmortem damage assessment that could have followed, Headquarters' concession provided one rather bizarre and nonnegotiable directive, which the censors preclude me from exposing. Suffice it to say that we all thought these folks had seen too many movies or were just desperate to disassociate themselves from the fallout should things go terribly wrong.

Headquarters' quirky directive notwithstanding, we went forward. Today, a meeting like this would have required "high-threat" protocols. That is, we would take additional measures with more steps to determine whether or not there was a threat. This protocol would include a quick reaction force of some sort. Because this event predated the cadre of security specialists upon which the CIA now depends to safeguard collectors and others in physically hostile environments, we did this on our own. It's not that we were cowboys, but we prioritized operational tradecraft and leveraged that for our safety.

Stations in hostile environments, whether the threat was physical or counterintelligence, were far smaller pre-9/11. Ironically, our stations in Western Europe and Asia were huge when I began with the CIA, though they were not the source of our most critical intelligence. They shrunk accordingly after 9/11 to be more efficient, albeit still robust, complements. The smaller the station, the more limited the footprint, making our officers a more difficult target to identify, track, counter, or attack. In hostile environments we relied on stealth over firepower. And who is more stealthy than a well-trained CIA case officer? Our modus operandi for meeting with potential counterintelligence provocations in denied environments adapted well to the requirement for meeting an individual who might pose a physical threat.

Relatively speaking, our presence in today's conflict zones is enormous, and those who would best understand the streets, the case officers, are locked away in fortified compounds. Our case officers largely don't know the cities, towns, and villages in which their agents live or operate. Those now responsible for detecting threats and assuring for safety in transit are not case officers, but the bodyguards. But the objective in espionage is staying off the radar in the first place. And low profile, such personnel are not: they rely more on firepower and armor than stealth. Bigger is not always better, and that's particularly true of an activity that prizes clandestinity.

To appease Headquarters, and so as not to brandish a pistol before my high-strung, and possibly intoxicated friend upon his entering the car, I placed my weapon in the open compartment built into the driver's side door. There was no way I could successfully locate, draw, and put the pistol into action from this location using my weak-side hand, but at least I could honestly include reference in my report to having complied with instructions, assuming I was alive to prepare said report. Unlike the Glocks we now use, the Browning 9mm Hi-Power was a beast of a pistol. Heavy, awkwardly large, and not the most reliable, I decided to leave the safety off. This, in turn, made me concerned I might accidentally discharge the weapon while recovering it from its resting place.

Despite all of this dramatic buildup, like most operational acts, the meeting proceeded safely and uneventfully. Jamal was not exactly sober, but neither was he staggeringly drunk upon entering my car. On time, professional, and respectful, it was as if the threat was never made. For all I knew at the time, he had likewise completely forgotten what he had said in the course of sleeping off that day's distilled intake. That's not to say he wasn't angry when I advised him of the estimated time still required. Jamal offered righteous frustration and disappointment, but he did not repeat his threat nor make any move to take out his anger on me. The meeting went as all others had. We shook hands and departed as friends.

That said, it was to be my last meeting with Jamal, who went to ground immediately thereafter, leading my Headquarters colleagues to freak out that he was coming for me—or others in our organization.

As it turned out, and as our station had suggested to Headquarters would be the case were they not to act more expeditiously on Jamal's request, he simply did things on his own. Jamal took the money we had been giving him over those many months, far more than he could possibly spend on his needs, and smuggled himself into Europe. This was a time when with enough money, it was doable. Upon arrival, Jamal claimed to be a refugee, and he established local residency without our help.

Once settled in Europe, Jamal walked into a US facility at this location and eventually gained access to a station officer. This European station was concerned, as suggested by Headquarters, that his approach might be to satisfy an axe to grind—and with Jamal, that was not necessarily a metaphor. They were worried even more about angering their local foreign intelligence partners on whose turf they operated, and to whom they wanted to declare the case.

Jamal was required to take a polygraph test before they'd meet him clandestinely. Among the questions was whether or not Jamal had indeed threatened me the preceding year. Jamal acknowledged so without flinching, or exhibiting any signs of deception, that he most certainly had, but knew that "David," was smart enough not to take him seriously. Jamal continued on with our organization for some time. Although he was not necessarily a noble being, his actions contributed to a satisfying degree of justice for his former colleagues.

In another tale of an agent acting out not long after a turnover, the circumstances may be different but some similarities stand out, the main one being respect. Like Jamal, "Muhammad" was a bit of a thug, but rather a more noble one. And that's largely where their similarities ended. Muhammad was a big, brutish, but good-hearted member of his government's security forces. Focused on the country's ongoing Islamic extremist insurgency, he was privy to intelligence concerning threats that might also impact US interests. Muhammad was able to provide insights concerning the threats, as well as the government's capacity to address them, that informed our understanding of the country's stability and the resulting risks to our own interests.

On the surface, you might think Muhammad was a series of contradictions. But such seemingly divergent traits are not entirely unusual, particularly given cultural considerations. Muhammad was no rocket scientist, but he came from a small village that instilled in him the old-world Arab manner of hospitality, respect, and honor. Although young, Muhammad was exceedingly polite, charming, earnest, and innately deferential to age and position. Even though he operated within a rather brutally effective unit and was somewhat of an old soul, he retained an aura of boyish innocence.

I met Muhammad through serendipity after an attempted break-in to my home. Local authorities wanted to be sure this wasn't a botched terrorist attempt. It was clearly petty crime, but it provided an excellent excuse for me to seek reassurance from the authorities—meaning a reason to meet security officials I had no other business to otherwise call on. I sought out officers from the unit who had "interviewed" the arrested suspects. Muhammad just happened to be the only member of his team still available by the time I made it to the facilities where the culprits were detained. The very idea I would see being attacked as a good opportunity should in and of itself tell you something scary about how case officers think. The thieves turned out to be petty criminals who thought they had found a European who'd have some cash lying around.

It was platonic spy love at first sight. Muhammad was a small-town boy now living in the big city who never even dreamed he would meet an American, let alone an official. He was positively flattered I'd seek him out and solicit his counsel on whether or not I was in any particular danger from these "street toughs." I bought Muhammad a cup of coffee near his office, as he operated in plain clothes except for when his unit conducted raids. We spoke for a while, and I'm sure Muhammad would have stayed for hours had I allowed.

Now that I had his interest and attention, however, the goal was to continue meeting Muhammad in a way that lowered our profile, and to use a pretext that brought him alone. I asked if he'd be willing to inspect my home for security vulnerabilities and provide advice on what I might do to better ward off home invasions. I added that since I didn't want to get him in any trouble for moonlighting, it was best not to highlight our plan to anyone else. It was certainly innocent sounding enough, and Muhammad was pleased to be making friends with an American. He readily agreed.

Over the course of months, however, I transitioned this initial gateway into a clandestine intelligence reporting relationship. I moved Muhammad to secure, prescheduled meetings on the street, and utilized an appropriately secure communications plan. Muhammad readily bought into my cover of having "special and confidential security reporting duties." Given the trust we'd developed as "friends," I explained how grateful I'd be for him to work with me as a paid, confidential consultant keeping the United States government informed on the realities of the security situation. Addressing the need for clandestinity, Muhammad was well aware of our governments' mutual tensions and mistrust. I helped him rationalize the relationship on the grounds that what he gave me wouldn't do his own country any actual harm, but they'd never otherwise part with it.

Muhammad developed into an effective agent. His cleverness and street smarts made up for a lack of formal schooling. And Muhammad lived by a code of honor. For him, it was all about respect. Where he was the warrior, he respected my expertise on operational tradecraft and substance. In turn, I respected the risks he took for his own country, as well as mine. Our trust was broadened by deeds. Muhammad appreciated the risks I took in meeting him clandestinely on dangerous streets at windows that allowed him an excuse to get away from colleagues. These were some of the worst areas in an already dangerous city, but it suited Muhammad who could fit in. He complied dutifully with requirements and never pretended to know more than he did. Over time, he loosened up, and even revealed a sense of humor. Muhammad was at his most tense awaiting me on some dark, desolate street, his hand always clutching the pistol beneath his leather jacket. Once inside my car, as we drove off, he'd begin to relax, and even banter.

I was a few months out from leaving the post and beginning to shed my case load to others. A new, young, first tour case officer, "Harold," who had recently replaced my colleague "Ryan," would take over with Muhammad. Ryan wanted to return to join his family and claimed he had not signed up for the country's deterioration, which had come within a year of his arrival. Ironically, while Ryan would later be cast into the case officer junk heap for consistently poor operational performance in agent recruitment and handling, he would be one of those resurrected post-9/11 for all the wrong reasons.

Ryan, the son of a strong-willed case officer, was educated, erudite, and exceptionally elitist and class-conscious. He would complain about how I reminded him, unfavorably, of his hotheaded dad. Rendered to Headquarters for a spell, and removed from a position of operational responsibility by NE's deputy division chief, Ryan found himself relegated to a congressional liaison role during the period of the Iraq war. His faithful parroting of the party line, which helped insulate the CIA leadership's politically biased judgments, offset his operational weaknesses in their eyes. Ryan would subsequently earn promotion into the Senior Intelligence Service ranks. Once so promoted, he was assigned to a series of senior operational commands, in which his same operational timidity and risk aversion proved lethargic and costly. Ultimately yanked back to the "pink ghetto," as it's known in the DO, where senior staff deals only with training and resources versus operational responsibilities, he eventually realized his ceiling and left.

"Harold," the new addition, struck me as a bit odd from the outset. Not that he was awkward or outwardly offensive. Rather, he simply seemed to lack the people skills or enthusiasm for the work. Funny, since he certainly appeared the part with boyish good looks, intellectual acumen, and a winning smile. There's nothing wrong with a calm exterior or laid-back style, but there seemed to be an absence of curiosity, adventure, passion, or a pulse. Harold came from a privileged, suburban background, that is to say, White and affluent. Unsurprisingly, he got along famously with Ryan, both telling tales of how, for fun, they would go bowling to see how *the other half lived*, Ryan wearing a "trucker's cap" with a false pony tail to "blend in with the riffraff."

During our initial operational act together, I was driving Harold to meet his first agent. Conversation did not come easily, leading me to think that perhaps he was nervous. When I asked in my own excited fashion whether he was nervous conducting his first operational act outside of training, Harold convincingly said, "No." Sadly, he was not lying. I had been doing this for years, and I still always had goose bumps, which indicated a healthy combination of excitement and anxiety. It was still fun to me, as it would be until my last operational act decades later. But Harold felt nothing. No thrill of the chase, joy at the caper, or passion for the work. All were traits that would likewise suit him well for the CIA's evolving image of leadership, since such behaviors minimized the likelihood Harold would take the type of risks that concern our executive ranks, among which Harold, in fact, now currently resides.

Indulge me a bit of salacious trivia concerning Harold, if only to provide more context to his character. It's true when I said that the business of recruiting assets has some parallels with dating, and this was also an area in which Harold struggled. His looks and pedigree were sufficient to get him in the door with romantic pursuits, but not to reel them in—at least not for keeps. Several romantic targets tired of Harold after seeing the lack of more "there" there, generally moving on to other case officers. Indeed, even the woman he ultimately married while coming up the ranks, destined as he was for senior positions, ran away with another, more brash, case officer colleague within a year or two of their marriage.

The plan was to turn Muhammad over to Harold, allowing me to begin my transition. When time came for the meeting, Harold and Muhammad were very quiet. This required me to do most of the talking, and to find commonalities among the two new partners for bonding.

Neither of them were very helpful. I explained to Muhammad that I would be leaving in a few months, and that for his own security I needed to move him now to another partner. Harold was new and clean, and the longer Muhammad and I met, the more likely the local counterintelligence officials might increase their attention to me, putting him at greater risk. Muhammad asked no questions, made no protests, and simply listened quietly, accepting the decision. We did the turnover meeting by the numbers, reviewing commitments, meeting mechanics, and tasking. At the end, like the minister ordaining nuptials, I bid them now "case officer and agent" and off they would go together as I made my separate way.

Harold struggled in handling Muhammad. There was nothing wrong with Harold's tradecraft. Operationally, he could execute well the clandestine mechanics and employ them appropriately in navigating the streets. The problem was that Harold could not relate to Muhammad. Their communication was abysmal, and Muhammad mistook Harold's dry and listless personality for a lack of respect. In turn, Harold would come to the office complaining of Muhammad's lack of responsiveness to tasking or initiative, which was quite unlike the agent I had known.

I offered counsel, but Harold was not interested. In his mind, the fault laid entirely with the agent, not him. Dangerously, like some weaker case officers, Harold lacked the capacity to empathize with human beings different from himself, and he didn't much appreciate the need to do so. He simply expected Muhammad to play the role of agent as if he was required to do so. Treating Muhammad like an employee who was being paid handsomely for the work, Harold saw no need to connect with his agent. He broke the cardinal rule of continuously reinforcing the recruitment by leveraging the motivations and conditions that had secured Muhammad's cooperation in the first place.

This went on until one late night I was awoken by knocking on my back door. I had a fairly large house and lived alone since the local security circumstances precluded the presence of dependents. I grabbed my pistol and moved slowly in the dark to a window from which I could see the doorway. It was Muhammad. Leaving my pistol behind, I went to the doorway and let him in. As Muhammad gave me a big bear hug, I was overwhelmed by the smell of alcohol. It was on his breath and seeped from his skin. I quickly ushered him in, trying to determine if there was any danger or risk behind Muhammad's surprise appearance. The whole point of meeting Muhammad on the street clandestinely and in turn handing him over to another officer was to precisely avoid allowing for any overt connection between us, yet here he was in my home. Still, I knew he was upset, and several sheets to the wind.

I escorted Muhammad to the living room, leaving him for a moment to fidget nervously on the couch while I brought drinks and snacks. On returning, I suggested Muhammad make himself comfortable and take off the black leather jacket he almost always paired with blue jeans and black leather loafers, fancied as the outfit of choice among the city's young men. While taking off the jacket, Muhammad also pulled the pistol from the small of his back. He cradled it on his knee. I pretended not even to notice and began engaging him in conversation, starting with pleasantries and frivolous topics to bring down the tension he had brought with him. But Muhammad was not one for small talk, and very quickly he came to the point.

"I don't like Mr. Harold," he said, bluntly. "I want to go back to working with you."

I was empathetic, but still just collecting data. "What's wrong, Muhammad, why don't you like Mr. Harold?"

"He disrespects me," Muhammad said angrily, flexing his hand over the pistol's grip. "He talks to me like I am some kind of idiot, like his servant!" Now animatedly speaking with his hands to underscore the emotion, Muhammad was unfortunately waving the loaded pistol about in the air as he gestured wildly.

"I'm sure Mr. Harold doesn't mean to do so," I said calmly, reaching nonchalantly for Muhammad's gun hand. "He's young, you know, well trained, but still learning the ropes," I said, now laying my hand over his, keeping his attention with my eyes while trying to separate him from the loaded weapon.

"I'm so sorry he might have said some things that bothered you, but I know Mr. Harold is very excited to be working with you," I lied, now easing the pistol from Muhammad's hand. "He talks all the time about how much he is learning from you," I continued, maintaining eye contact with Muhammad, who similarly reciprocated. The tension easing from his hand, Muhammad allowed me to gently grab the pistol by the barrel. "I'm sure it's just part of his learning process, and I really appreciate you giving him a chance." I eased the pistol from his hand, then swung it behind me, placing it on an end table without breaking eye contact. "I'll talk to Harold, but I'm confident this is just the natural process of you two getting better acquainted."

Muhammad was upset, offended, but there was no malice toward me nor implied threat in playing with the pistol. He was drunk, hurt, looking for understanding, and like his countrymen, had a very different perspective when it came to safe weapons handling. Still, we couldn't let Muhammad decide who his handler would be—we just wanted him to believe he was part of the team in working this out. In the end, I needed to coach up Harold a fair bit more, and we also had to sweeten the pot for Muhammad to abide the traits he found missing in his new partner. I told Muhammad that I expected him to perform as if he were still meeting me. For the honorable Muhammad, it thus was an obligation.

Fast forward roughly a year later, me long having moved on to my new assignment. My former COS let me know that Muhammad had dropped from contact. Harold, of course, believed Muhammad had self-terminated. That is to say, he quit, and without notice. I figured the more likely truth was that he couldn't bear to indulge Harold any further without putting a bullet between his eyes. So, while disappointed, I didn't think much of it. We both turned out to be wrong.

Muhammad reinitiated contact some months later with Harold's successor using the existing communications plan. When he was finally met,

Muhammad showed up while in recovery from life-threatening wounds sustained during a raid against a terrorist camp. Although Muhammad miraculously lived, he was without a means of contact during his extended convalescence. Largely disabled, he was granted early retirement from his security position and lost access, requiring our parting of ways. Muhammad was given a handsome separation bonus, and he bid farewell to Harold's successor, asking that I be given a message from him of thanks and friendship for our time together. There was no message for Harold.

A LIFESTYLE NOT FOR THE SQUEAMISH OR FAINT OF HEART

It would not be fair of me to claim that a CIA case officer's life is better or worse than what most people experience. But absent a universally acceptable definition of "normal," if there is such a thing, I feel on safe ground to say that the experiences and requirements of spying overseas make our lives at least "different." I was living at one of the rather austere posts I've already described when I took terribly ill the day I was scheduled to meet an important agent. It wasn't food poisoning, I self-diagnosed, but a parasite of some sort that had caught up with me. At the time, we had the good fortune of receiving a visit from one of our own CIA doctors. Physicians, psychologists, medics, nurses, and other health care personnel working in the field for the CIA are gifts from heaven, and they are incredibly well suited for the particularities of our requirements. They join from a desire for mission and adventure. I have rarely experienced stateside the bedside manner and attention to care provided by CIA medical professionals—all of it done under often challenging conditions.

Now this particular doctor was similarly talented, warm, and engaging. But he had adopted an approach not unlike that perhaps of a professional sports team's physician. I suppose it was appropriate under the circumstances, seeing that his responsibility was getting us back on the field for the next play as opposed to prioritizing our long-term health. I explained the situation in the clinic room. There was little science required to determine that I was most likely suffering from dysentery, and the specimen I provided—yet one of the other joys of life in the service— would likely confirm that within twenty-four hours. Only I didn't have twenty-four hours, just six before I'd be launching for my meeting. Dispensing therefore with the standard medical questions, and sitting in a wheeled executive chair as I sat on the examination table, the doctor instead focused on my meeting to determine the most appropriate course of treatment.

"You meeting in a car or on foot?" he asked, looking over my medical file and jotting notes.

"I'm taking a car, dumping it, then walking to the meeting," I replied.

He nodded thoughtfully. "So a walking meeting then?" He jotted down more notes.

"Yes," I said with a nod.

"Walking and talking then?" He wanted to nail it down.

"Right, walking and talking."

"About how long do you think you'll be walking and talking, and over what distance?" he asked.

"Probably not more than twenty minutes," I replied.

"But you have a variant, right? So if he doesn't show, how long do you have to be out there before you walk through the site again?"

"Two hours," I told the doctor.

"Okay, so let me see if I have this right." He looked down at his notes. "Driving to a car dump site, then walking to your meeting location, and on your feet talking for about twenty minutes. No bathrooms available, well," he chuckled, "other than the street. And the chance you need to be out an extra two hours if he's late."

"That's right," I confirmed.

With that, the doctor spun around in his chair, wheeling himself over to his bag. He pulled out a couple of unlabeled medicine bottles, dispensing a cocktail of pills and tossing them into a plastic baggie.

"Okay, so here's what you do." He pulled out the tablets and arranged them before me. "Take these two now, drink all the water you can stand, then make sure you use the facilities before you get on the road. Then take these other two pills, but don't drink anything else. Two hours later, take the same two pills."

"And that's going to get me better?" I innocently asked.

The doctor broke out into a chuckle before regaining his composure. "Oh hell no. These pills will keep you buttoned up, water tight, and free from fever and pain until your meeting is over. But then," he paused and shook his head, "you're going to be pretty miserable for a week, so start taking these." He handed me a separate bottle, this one in a proper pill dispenser on which he wrote my name and dosage instructions.

Let's just say the doctor did his job and I met my agent. On the other hand, for the ensuing week I was incapacitated, worshipping from my knees the porcelain god in my bathroom to which I literally had to drag my diseased body. We were all pretty certain that some of the remedies our doctors were able to dispense while abroad were not likely even legal in the United States.

On top of disease, there's occasionally physical risk. As I'm sure I've made clear by now, no one would ever confuse me with Liam Hemsworth, Matt Damon, or Jason Statham. CIA has legitimate war heroes operating daily in dangerous combat conditions. These are mostly, but not entirely, our PMOOs and security specialists. I am not among this proud group, although I have served extensively in war zones and high-risk locations. When I've been armed, it was for the purpose of "getting off the X" and defending my colleagues and agents. I'm more a con artist than a warrior, armed with street smarts and wit.

But like many of my colleagues, I have found myself in circumstances for which I had not planned, aimed, or could even imagine, dealing with risks for which I had not signed up. One of the threats was indirect fire (IDF), blasts from rockets and mortars. I served at such posts before we sufficiently hardened our living areas to withstand such attacks. Even the real warriors concede that if IDF gets you, it's just God's plan. If you're hit by a random rocket or mortar while going about your day, your number was up. Where I've been, IDF most often came in the early morning or late evening hours. At one such post, I have to confess, given my work hours, the attacks most often arrived in the midst of a sound sleep. I'd briefly wake as the concussions shook my tin quarters. Having already lost hearing in one of my ears, I usually returned to slumber, having mistaken the vibrations as coming from approaching helicopters. My "pod" was aligned with their landing path. It was only when the accountability checks commenced that I realized it was a rocket or mortar attack. Rambo I was not.

My closest call, at least while conscious, occurred at the assignment mentioned previously while serving as chief of base in what might be called a conflict zone. It was in reality a platform in a high-risk terrorist location where a small number of us were the hunters targeting al-Qa'ida not long after 9/11. We had a small footprint, extensive operational autonomy from excellent leadership at station and Headquarters, and a decent enough relationship with our local foreign partners. Our team foiled plots and located targets who would ultimately be brought to justice. The city was considered one of the most dangerous places in the world, not just for US officials and foreigners, but likewise for the indigenous and ethnically divided local population.

While operating freely on the streets, given our small visible footprint and the use of good tradecraft, our risk was manageable. Once on the street beyond the range of our official facility, we were able to blend and melt into the local color. Our destiny was controlled through an ability to detect and avoid threats and by finding our prey before they could find us. But few days passed without an attack of one sort or another. Al-Qa'ida and its partners, namely Islamic extremists organizations, angry at the country's cooperation with the US, mounted bloody attacks against the government, including assassination attempts against the head of state. More routine was the ethnic strife of one group against another and the ensuing retaliation.

I am embarrassed to admit that one became rather tone deaf to it, desensitized almost, since much of it could be avoided. More frightening was that which you could not control. Our official facility was the target of several attacks during my tour, the most memorable being a huge car bomb staged along our perimeter wall aligned just parallel to our offices. The explosive content placed in this particular van was so heavy that the vehicle's chassis bottomed out along the street as it was being staged.

Thankfully, whoever ultimately assembled this particular Vehicle-Borne Improvised Explosive Device (VBIED), had failed to mix the chemicals properly. It didn't detonate. There were sufficient explosives in it to have collapsed our office at the time, killing everyone inside. Ours was a temporary location with weak prefabricated structures that would not have withstood the concussion. We have long since relocated to more secure and defensible facilities.

There was what you might consider a bizarre level of shock felt throughout my team after the failed VBIED attack. Surprising, you might think, given the environment and our clear appreciation for the threat. But when you're living in such a place, life becomes somewhat routine, including all the precautions you take mechanically and, in time, automatically. Even if your actions don't reflect complacency (you continue to go through the quite appropriate motions), you stop considering the reality.

While your tradecraft thankfully does not become complacent, because you're a professional, your emotions do. It happens in a way that I imagine is simply a coping mechanism. Officers working for me who valiantly went out on the city's dangerous streets night after night without hesitation were visibly shaken by the failed attack. They were most shaken from the experience of having to remain inside the facility helplessly waiting for the VBIED to explode, or be disarmed, as sirens blasted and red strobe lights flashed.

It wasn't until years later that I realized how these events affected us all. I returned to America from such deployments unconsciously agitated and on edge. I had a particularly short fuse, and I tended to be far more defensive. I recall driving quite aggressively upon returning home from one such deployment with several near road rage incidents over the first few weeks. After all, in my work environments, one was always bracing for an attack, an ambush, a car bomb, or a kidnapping attempt. So you drove aggressively to detect and counter such threats. Adjusting to suburban commuting did not come easily.

Even with family and friends, I would become short and irritable, and often over the most trivial matters. Daily work frustrations were especially ripe for such behaviors, far too quickly escalating into confrontations with superiors or colleagues who didn't immediately share my point of view. I didn't recognize any of this at the time for what it was, and I fell victim to the mindset that I was too strong to need help. Doing otherwise struck me as being weak. Our leadership was likewise remiss, allowing officers to return immediately to their duties at home upon concluding such assignments, a practice we have since changed.

For me, like my teammates, the greatest fear came in the absence of control at our facilities where we work and live. Our efforts to harden defenses came mostly by blocking traffic to enhance our position in its standoff from the street. The goal was to keep would-be car and truck bombs at a distance sufficient to mitigate the damage from a blast. But unable to penetrate our perimeters, terrorists would simply build bigger bombs. Ours and some of the nearby official government buildings continued to be targeted. When a suspicious vehicle was detected, alarms would begin sounding and we would make our way to fortified shelters.

The waiting was the worst part. All you can do is stand among your friends, powerless to do anything, just hoping it will be another false alarm. You waited. Mostly it would be a false alarm. But on several occasions, it was the real thing. Even deep within the fortified shelter, you'd feel the concussion before you'd hear the sound. Though the devices lacked enough force from a distance to do our facility much harm, the explosives tore into those who were in their destructive paths, mostly innocent locals who just happened to be there. Although we emerged physically unscathed, many of us felt guilty by the loss of life around us.

My still worst experience came in my final days there, ironically, on the heels of a rather spectacular operational success the team had been working for months to achieve. Collaborating with our local foreign partners and acting on intelligence we had been collecting through well-placed agents and complex operations, we located a terrorist leader who, at the time, was our number one target. He was a senior planner close to al-Qa'ida's leadership who knew the most important secrets we sought at the time, including the whereabouts of Osama bin Laden.

It was a spectacular capture. But in full disclosure, the target never shared what he knew about Osama bin Laden, at least not during our brief opportunity to talk with him. He was never placed in CIA custody and our limited contact always included a minder from the local foreign partner service. He had too much inside information concerning the questionable fidelity of our own local foreign partner, whose government refused to hand him over. Success alone came from depriving al-Qa'ida of this target's contributions. It was only some years later CIA learned that this man knew the locations for both bin Laden and Zawahiri at the time of his detention, and the identities of their caretakers. Whether or not he shared these secrets with our local hosts, I can't say. But I do know they released him a few years after the Abbottabad raid that killed Osama bin Laden, and allowed him to disappear across the border into Iran.

My team had been up for days in the final stages of the operation that resulted in the senior planner's capture by the local foreign partners, with our assistance. Serendipitously, the operation also netted the capture of a particularly brutal, notorious Sunni extremist who had conducted a series of attacks against Shi'a mosques that had left scores of locals dead. The two targets were collocated. Frankly, our local partners, believing themselves to be cooperating against al-Qa'ida under some degree of political coercion, were far more happy to reap the political rewards of capturing the terrorist who had been targeting the Shi'a community.

I lived quite some distance from our official facility and housing area. It was a deliberate choice that allowed my residence to survive as an offsite should our office be destroyed, put under siege, or otherwise inaccessible. I was equipped to live, work, communicate, and defend myself. In reality, I confess, my home was probably safer than where my colleagues lived. The terrorists didn't know where I lived, or that there was even an American residing amid this cluster of posh homes owned by local generals. My best defense was stealth. The neighborhood was not a walled enclave, but it was well patrolled and manned by soldiers under orders not to allow any damage to their generals' important financial investments. Still, there was a commute, and it was always on my travel to and from the office that I was most vulnerable to attack. By contrast, my colleagues lived where they worked.

I normally took the appropriate precautions to detect and avoid any threat. I varied my routes and times of departure and arrival, used different cars, and remained unpredictable. These actions made it harder for terrorists to case and target me without it coming to my attention. There were several different routes to work, and all inevitably had choke points of one sort or another, which in most cases consisted of a bridge or overpass across a body of water. I used them all at varying times of day, but I generally avoided one in particular that featured a wide thoroughfare and more modern bridge. It was the most obvious and direct route, which is why I never took it. Except for this particular morning.

Like so many such stories, mine begins with the recollection of it being a beautiful day. But indeed it was. I'd had my first solid sleep in forever, was celebrating a tremendous victory over evil, and was days away from returning home to my family, safe and sound. There was a cloudless blue sky, with warm but not oppressively hot morning temperatures. I was still groggy from lack of sleep, like the sensation of being hung over, but emotionally I felt good. I decided, what the hell, I'd take the direct route with the usually flowing stream of morning traffic, it being just past the worst of rush hour, sometime after 9:00 a.m. The odds of anything happening today, and at this hour, were just too long. Besides, I was anxious to see my team and get an update on our operation.

The ride was uneventful up until I approached the wide bridge, which would bring me to the more congested downtown area where our facility was located. There was almost no traffic in front of me, but to my rear, a military convoy of jeeps was approaching from the distance. I knew it was best to keep ahead of them, since such convoys usually included pickets that might block traffic to expedite whatever VIP was in its midst. A last traffic light before the bridge was thankfully green, and as I began the incline, I noticed what looked like a school bus to my left on the side street parallel to the bridge's ascent. Honestly, it stood out, but I didn't really give it much notice. I reached the crest of the bridge, and as I descended, all hell rang out. I heard explosions and automatic rifle fire, and I did as trained: speed away as fast as my car would take me.

Behind me, explosives placed on the bridge span's divider, which I had passed but seconds ago, had detonated. They had been timed to take out the lead vehicle in the military convoy that had been trailing me, which happened to be the provincial military general traveling to his office. I was thankfully unrecognized or simply not worth targeting ahead of their intended prey. On the school bus, a line of shooters had jumped up from cover, extended their AK-47 assault rifles from the windows, and unleashed a hail of fire.

I did not stick around to see any of this, mind you. But this same group targeting the general turned out to be the very same group that had unsuccessfully attacked our facility with the large VBIED that failed to detonate. The general turned out to be one very lucky man. Several members of his personal security team to his front and rear were killed, as well as his driver. It was the general's aide-de-camp who grabbed the wheel, depressed the accelerator, and steered his boss beyond the line of fire and to safety.

When I made it to the facility moments later, I found it was already on lockdown due to the close proximity of the attack. I was at once both terrified and exhilarated as I learned the details. I just as excitedly related the news to my COS, who was located in the country's capital city. He, understandably, was less exhilarated as I shared the story of my near miss. Practical and smart, and sensing the increasing concern for risk being exhibited by Headquarters, the COS cautioned me in preparing my official report. Rather than write how I missed the ambush by a matter of a minute or so, my COS recommended that in the interest of keeping my base open, I perhaps observe having passed through the vicinity of the ambush site "earlier that morning." In the interest of the mission, I agreed.

With that as background, you might better appreciate why I never encouraged my children to take after me. On the contrary, I did all that I could to discourage them. It's a hard life, and I didn't really choose this work. It was the CIA that came looking for me. My kids had more options. For me, the CIA was a natural fit, my calling. It's not that my children wouldn't necessarily be good at it, but parents want better, safer lives for their children. Spies are no different.

LOST FRIENDS AND COMRADES

C IA's Memorial Wall is a sacred shrine to those of us who have served, as well as to the friends and families of the fallen. It is located in the main entrance of CIA Headquarters in Langley, Virginia. Most of us rarely pass by it, accessing the building instead from one of the more convenient entries from the sprawling parking lots. Although CIA was founded in 1947, the wall was not established until 1974, at which time there were 31 stars etched in tribute to those lost over our initial twenty-seven years. As of September 2020, following the most recent dedication ceremony, there were 137. This includes a number with whom I trained, served, or led, and among them, dear friends.

We accept risk due to the nature of the work. CIA officers are placed in difficult places around the world, often with dangerous jobs. I lost one dear friend with whom I entered on duty to terrorist gunfire on the shuttle bus she took to work, a young mother of two lovely little girls. An administrative support officer, I had actually introduced her to the man she married, one of our Marine security guards. The 2009 Khost suicide bombing accounted for CIA losses exceeding even those from the April 1983 Beirut embassy attack. A jailbreak in Afghanistan resulted in CIA's first casualty of the conflict, with more to follow, including three lost on my watch in support of counterterrorist operations within my area of responsibility. Yet those just account for colleagues who perished while operating against the very targets they were combatting, and where the dangers were more recognizable. But as I've explained, CIA officers are always forward, operating where the targets are located. Just being there, they endure lethal risks beyond those brought on by their targets.

A bright, charming young officer who worked for me on his first tour died in a traffic accident on a Middle East overpass, a victim of the dangers of living in a wealthy Gulf kingdom where locals drive with reckless abandon, are immune from prosecution, and often are under the influence. A young woman, and mother, with whom I served in South Asia, succumbed to encephalitis while serving at a subsequent post. The local doctors at her European location were unable to diagnose her symptoms until it was too late, never considering that they might stem from a mosquito bite at her previous assignment. A classmate and one of the few women with whom I graduated the Farm contracted HIV while serving in the Caribbean, dying in an era when we lacked effective treatment, and when the US government remained reluctant to even care about the disease. Another classmate died from a cancer he incurred during exposure to radioactive materials in the course of his work. And one young female officer died when her flight was commandeered by hijackers and crashed into the sea after running out of fuel. Although witnesses report she was seen helping others escape the sinking aircraft, she never managed to get out herself and drowned. She had been on vacation from the austere African post at which she served.

And far more foreign agents have given their lives than have CIA officers, with the barest of recognition. There's but the smallest, least noticeable memorial to their sacrifice at CIA Headquarters. In fact, one is hard-pressed to catch the sculpture that's inlayed along the Headquarters lobby wall beyond the entry turnstiles and rather out of the way. The inscription reads: "In honor of those who made the ultimate sacrifice in the silent struggle for freedom." CIA's website offers how the sculpture "is representative of a global matrix of people working together, like the threads that make up fabric. The laurel, a symbol of commemoration, is knotted because the knot is a symbol of unity, solidarity, and trust." Given that agents are the CIA's lifeblood, the memorial is disappointingly small and overlooked. Moreover, the inscription is rather ironic in the current anti-immigrant and xenophobic political climate, despite the recent change in the White House.

For me, perhaps the most enduring scar was suffered while I was in a former Soviet state. Although I had long worked the Russian and East European target in previous postings, this was my first time living behind the one-time Iron Curtain. It's different. The atmosphere, I must confess, was beyond even that of some of the more repressive Middle Eastern countries in which I had dwelled, or the high counterintelligence and counterterrorist posts in which I had operated.

The nature of such surveillance states, like those of the autocratic countries in which we must operate, goes beyond the notion of a police state. Not just the rules and restrictions, it is a state of mind. It is so deeply imbued within the population as to become part of the culture. The fear of informers even among your family members and closest friends is fully engrained into the atmosphere and is a way of life. While chasing Russian, Chinese, North Korean, Iranian, and other hard targets over the years, I began to appreciate how such environments permeated the art, music, and literature of a culture. It certainly explains the fatalism, suspicion, and darkness of such places.

The embassy was in the process of moving. A new capital had been built far into the country's rather inhospitable interior. The government pressured reluctant foreign diplomatic missions to abandon the rather charming, urban, and developed commercial capital for the new Potemkin village on the Siberian steppes. The long-tenured, wily head of state took the lesson from the region's now deposed strong men to relocate his palace and national leadership to this rather inaccessible and sparsely populated custom-made city. The distance between the two cities was not inordinately long, but arduous if traveled overland due to the limited roads and lack of infrastructure. Much of what the embassy moved went by air, except for some of the heavier and more sensitive items.

The embassy had largely relocated, but the station still had to be split between the two locations. The time was approaching, however, for the final move, during which I was required to be at CIA Headquarters for important meetings. I left my team to complete the move, which required a vehicle caravan carrying the final load of station property. Joining the caravan would be our support officer, "Bonnie." A young and relatively junior officer not long removed from training, Bonnie was the embodiment of "can do." Taking to heart the mantra of CIA's support cadre that theirs is not to say no, but to find a way to yes, Bonnie was quick on her feet and a born problem solver. Her love for the service, our mission, and the adventure of these more exotic parts of the world was chaste, sincere, and entirely absent the cynicism of those of us who had too often been down these bumpy roads. Bonnie was everyone's friend, as had been the case from the time she was a trainee.

It had been a relatively mild autumn that year in the United States and my hotel offered a generous view of the surrounding hills. It was replete with colorful trees, the foliage resplendent in yellows and reds. I went to sleep that evening feeling good about how the trip was going and relieved that my team, including Bonnie, would have all the logistics settled by the time I returned home. The ring of the hotel phone disturbed my peaceful slumber in a way that takes one a moment to recognize whether or not you're actually still sleeping and just where you are. A bit disoriented, I grabbed the receiver without turning on the night table light and heard the familiar click of a connecting international call before my wife began to speak. I immediately worried something had happened to one of the children. Her voice was strained, the words coming slowly.

"There's been an accident," she said softly, "and it's really bad."

"Oh my God," I recalled replying, still groggy, "is everyone all right?"

"We lost Bonnie," she said.

It took me a moment, I confess, stunned at the news, not yet processing the weight of her words. "What do you mean?" I asked, hoping perhaps for some revision of the outcome.

"Bonnie was in a car accident on the way here." My wife, her heart heavy, paused for a moment, before again saying, "and she was killed."

CIA censored the details of the accident from this book, though the accident came at the fault of a reckless local driver and not Bonnie. Further censored were details of the CIA's cold and impersonal management of the tragedy and its fallout. Bonnie's death significantly impacted others at the station, including an officer who bravely risked death in trying to save her. The events themselves are not classified, but revealing in what the Agency prioritized, and how the episode poisoned the relationship between my station and its Central Eurasia Division (CE Division) leadership team, and does not cast CIA in the best light.

Not long after that fateful day, the division chief who had selected me moved on, replaced by his deputy, "Sam." Unlike his predecessor, Sam did not take kindly to those from the CIA's other operational divisions, as was the case for me coming from NE Division. Sam focused on metrics and listened to only those in his inner circle. I didn't really have a relationship with him, so when I lobbied for my people who were emotionally impacted by the tragedy, he would have none of it. Against the advice from Agency medical experts, his first step was to remove "Will," the officer who had been struggling with misguided guilt over Bonnie's death. Will was not keeping up the reporting metrics that Sam insisted on from his field officers. I had lobbied and succeeded in securing the former chief's approval to keep Will on at post, but Sam saw things differently. Sam did what was best for Sam.

Will's decline impacted metrics that Sam needed to make a mark for himself. Moreover, Will's successor, not due until the following summer, had become available. Indeed, the designated successor, "Sebastian," had lobbied intensely to come out early. Sebastian, as I would later learn, was trying to redeem himself, having received an official reprimand during his previous tour for mishandling operational funds. Ironic as it may be, case officers, as manipulative as they are, become easily swayed by flattery, particularly the adoration of sycophants, as they grow more senior. Certainly this had worked for Sebastian with Sam, despite Sebastian's checkered past.

Ultimately, my relationship with Sam grew toxic and he relieved me just a few months prior to my scheduled rotation—to make sure it was on the record. I wasn't without fault. My emotions remained high over Bonnie's death, for which I felt responsible having agreed to her inclusion in the convoy. Sam's lack of compassion and interest in his people's well-being likewise left me contemptuous. The mere questioning of authority had become akin to insubordination in the post-9/11 Agency, so my failure to salute smartly and shower Sam with praise was to him on par with mutiny.

When I acted contrary to his mandate on a fast-moving and sensitive operation, Sam had his opportunity to relieve me. A friend working for the deputy director of operations (DDO) at the time told me the overall Clandestine Service chief to whom Sam reported had no emotion over the issue or had a similar inclination. But appropriately, he deferred to Sam who claimed "loss of confidence" in my leadership. I confess that had I adjudicated the circumstances less emotionally, I could have managed the operational decision without antagonizing Sam. But I was not thinking as maturely as I needed to.

Ironically, Sebastian, whom Sam elevated after my departure, would likewise struggle. Having directed his energies into ingratiating himself with Sam and the CE Division leadership team, Sebastian worked less to win over the local foreign partners and concurrently pursued leads with less scrupulous tradecraft than was required under my watch. Sebastian was not gifted with sound operational judgment nor particularly good interpersonal instincts. He wanted to impress Sam in securing a quick recruitment of a new reporting source while likewise showing strength by "putting the locals in their place."

Sebastian invested his energies in reestablishing contact with a former target who had been dropped owing to suspicion that he might have been under the local service's control. A dangle, we call them, a target who the local counterintelligence service might run against us or otherwise "turn" in pursuit of a double agent operation. For context, a dangle is controlled from the outset, placed "serendipitously" in the path of a suspect intelligence officer. A target who is turned is one in which the individual with whom we began contact and development was either caught and "doubled" against us, or who reported the contact to his superiors and agreed, voluntarily or otherwise, to cooperate with the service.

When Sebastian raised the target, I counseled caution, given that my assessment largely supported the previous conclusions. After initial meetings, Sebastian failed to secure any intelligence to suggest the target was providing compromising material. That is, information to which we expected the source would have access but was unlikely to be shared by the local service given its sensitivity. While this is not an absolute indicator of hostile control, since some services trade secrets in order to establish their double agent's bona fides, it's a start. On the other hand, the absence of sensitive intelligence despite a source's promise to deliver is a bad sign. I counseled Sebastian to slow the pace and focus on testing before exposing our agenda or, moreover, pitching him. Under pressure from Sebastian's front office supporters, I was not at liberty to turn it off.

Sebastian would likewise antagonize our local foreign partners. His engagement was laced with a demanding and often condescending manner that offended our proud and somewhat prickly hosts. Making matters worse, shortly before I was relieved, a friend from home privately shared news that Sebastian had established a direct channel to Sam and his leadership to serve as their eyes. Sebastian did not depict me in a favorable light, let us say, which fit the narrative he knew Sam already believed.

Meanwhile on the ground, Sebastian had suspiciously become subject to signs of discontent by the local foreign partners, details for which have likewise been censored. But suffice it to say that the harassment Sebastian, and only Sebastian, received was not subtle, and its timing was not coincidental to Sebastian's push with his recruitment target. It was all rather curious, since his harassment followed a successful joint terrorist disruption against a high-profile capital city landmark for which the local service felt had been protected thanks to CIA. So significant was this success that the local service chief awarded me the highest civilian medal his government could award a foreigner.

Our local foreign partners were sending a signal, I cautioned Sebastian and Headquarters. It was obvious they wanted to avoid a dustup that would derail cooperation, which the local service chief valued. Just disliking Sebastian didn't account for the rather obvious harassment of him, again, details I can't share, but without doubt the local service's doing. There was more to this, I reasoned. Cooperation with the US was hardly a popular concept so close to Moscow's shadow, so the local government proceeded cautiously and labored to keep engagement low-key. Revelation of US misbehavior might force their hand.

Neither Sebastian nor Sam would heed the warnings. Upon my departure, with Sam and his leadership's endorsement, rather than take a step back to assess what was going on, efforts to develop, recruit, and clandestinely meet the target accelerated. Sebastian and Sam triumphantly touted the new recruitment, coming after my departure, validating their decision to dispatch me. In the meantime, I went off into exile to assume an instructor position at the Farm, a job I was lucky to secure given Sam's effort to paint me as a bad influence on junior officers.

Not long thereafter, circumstances took a rather ugly turn. It was a setup. Indeed, as both the file and my read of the situation suggested, the target had been under the local service's control from the beginning. Waiting until after I had departed, a team of the service's counterintelligence directorate ambushed a clandestine meeting. Dragging Sebastian from behind the wheel of his car with great zeal and enthusiasm, roughing him up somewhat in the process, the team literally disrobed him on the street in the middle of a cold night. Sebastian was shortly thereafter released, after a night of taunting, and expelled. Relations between the CIA and the local partners remained toxic for years.

Sam would soon after retire from the service, and Sebastian's career continued to spiral downward. As for me, the assignment to the Farm turned out to be the tonic I needed. In addition to recharging my batteries by mentoring enthusiastic trainees, it was an excellent off-ramp to a slower pace that I took advantage of by spending more time with the family. It's a beautiful location, and perhaps the safest kids' paradise in the world, and it continues to stand out among my family's happiest postings. On the downside, while I would ultimately overcome the black mark, it took some time in "the penalty box" before I would again be entrusted with executive management assignments.

Another stark difference in today's CIA from that of the past is what constitutes a career-ending mistake. Before 9/11, such transgressions were those of integrity violations and loss of life. Fabricating intelligence and agents, of course, and irresponsibility with money, were the fastest tickets to unemployment. However, loss of life due to poor judgment was not always career ending, because one's fate was more dependent on protectors in the proverbial royal court. But it's far worse today, where those who survived the penalty box include officers whose operational decisions have not only cost lives and required memorandums of reprimand, but whose infractions included egregious examples of sexual harassment, toxic work environments, and abject operational failures. Their saving grace? Fealty.

HARD TARGETS: "RENDER UNTO CAESAR THE THINGS THAT ARE CAESAR'S AND UNTO GOD THE THINGS THAT ARE GOD'S"

E spionage is a very personal business. And yet, it is also terribly cold. The nature of the risks requires the case officer to maintain a degree of detachment. Your agents are not your friends. They can't be, because you need to impartially make the right decisions that impact their safety, and yours. Just as surgeons don't operate on their own family and military officers must send the young men and women charged to their care on missions from which they might never return, case officers task their agents with undertakings that are not always in their best personal interests, but rather, America's.

The biggest difference, of course, is there's no pretense for the surgeon or military officer. The separation between personal and professional is statutory and open. In order for case officers to exercise the leverage necessary to suborn their targets to a life of espionage and all the risks it entails, they must become the agent's best and most important friend. That does not happen without the sincerity required to overcome the slick, used car salesman persona depicted too often in spy literature and movies. And getting there comes at a price.

Case officers are chameleons, as they must be to establish such profound connections with so diverse a variety of targets. Recruiting the hardest targets comes at a cost, a personal cost. It requires giving up a piece of your soul each time. I'm not talking about recruiting those agents who volunteer to spy for reasons noble or otherwise, having already come to the decision themselves. Nor am I talking about mercenaries and opportunists merely waiting for the means to secure the unrealized fortunes or revenge they believe themselves due. Rather, I am thinking of those prospective agents with essentially good, albeit flawed hearts, who need to be coaxed and set on their journey.

I have found that despite the pervasive flaws that exist in people, which case officers naturally manipulate, they mostly want to do good, down deep, or at least be judged as such. It's easier recruiting those with no such moral compass than those whose navigation is a more complex and contradictory mesh of right and wrong. It's similarly more challenging to recruit those who follow the path of least resistance to mere survival, given the inherent risks in espionage over the status quo. Such prospective agents must be led to believe that their personal risks are for a greater purpose, a noble cause, and require a great deal more personal investment. The case officer seeds and cultivates the idea in their hearts of betraying their country, group, people, or even family for whatever greater good, personal need, or score to settle, albeit wrapped in the cloak of honor and code as opposed to treachery. This is the emotional journey the case officer and agent must take together.

To be empathetic and credible in order to relate to the target and overcome their own defenses, the case officer must project conviction and sincerity. They need to appear real, human, and made of the same flesh and blood. That's necessary in creating the conditions that disarm the target to allow the penetrating depth of knowledge and ensuing control that the case officer requires to constantly assess and guide the prospective agent.

Not all my colleagues believe this. Some unfortunately see their targets as "less than," or they are fundamentally insecure in their own resolve. In my experience, however, doing the job well, particularly with the more complicated and reserved targets, requires a case officer's willingness to reveal to some degree their own vulnerabilities and truths. It's a fine balance to project a character who is entirely trustworthy, strong, and reliable, while appearing likewise human.

You can't fake it. Targets see through the transparency of insincerity under which some case officers believe they can hide, particularly those who have survived in the most oppressive police states. Exhilarating as the thrill of the chase, and as profoundly satisfying to the case officer's super competitive nature as the conquest, it's emotionally draining and physically exhausting to disarm and overcome the defenses of the most difficult targets.

At the end of this path, and after all the case officer has done, you're reminded that the agents don't belong to you. You might have been the one who collected their souls, but they are owned by the CIA. Intellectually, you realize this is as it must be. No case officer is irreplaceable. The intelligence your agents provide serves the country. A recruitment is therefore not really a recruitment until the agent makes the emotional transition from working for their friend, the case officer, to working for the CIA, and whomever it chooses to assume the case handling.

A transition is required of both parties, since the case officer likewise accepts the need to step away for a successor and not look back. Ongoing contact can only bring more risk to the agent and undermine the institutional control the organization must achieve through a union in which agents accept that what they are doing is bigger than themselves.

Nowhere is this mentality and reality more at work than when it comes to the recruitment and handling of "hard targets." For a CIA case officer, this means an individual from a country hostile to the United States who lives in a police or surveillance state. Hard targets reside in countries where the counterintelligence obstacles to meeting, cultivating, and clandestinely handling a spy are enormous. It's when Big Brother is everywhere, where no officials are beyond suspicion and your agent's dearest companion or family member could be an informer. No agent is harder to recruit, and no operational success is more sought after as the ultimate badge of honor. If the proportion of DO officers who do most of the recruiting is 20 percent, then those who account for the recruited hard targets, as opposed to those agents who volunteer and find us, would be but a fraction of that.

The reality is that recruiting such agents can often be a matter of luck: bumping into the right person, under the ideal circumstances, and where the chemistry between case officer and target just clicks. In recruitment operations, success is aligned with opportunity and time on target. That confluence is often facilitated by attending the right event at the right moment. It is said in most pursuits that you make your own luck. In espionage, I believe success is about seeing the opportunity when it comes, and then making the best choices to seize it. My career was blessed with a great deal of luck, but I capitalized on it by a hunger and drive to let no opportunity pass. As a friend of mine used to tease, I did indeed "smell the blood" when opportunity presented itself, and then sunk my teeth into it like a dog with a bone.

I met "Nick" at a multilateral forum in the austere capital to which we both found ourselves assigned. As it turned out, we were both doing the same thing: trolling. Nick was from one of America's Communist adversaries. An intelligence officer like me, Nick had used his day job credentials to join his countrymen who were attending a large gathering for what would be yet another of the routine diplomatic, cultural, and technical events that we case officers cruised on the lookout for targets.

Working the crowd at such events can be a surreal experience, especially for the case officer. Most people are moving about, socializing, chit-chatting, networking, or carrying out legitimate official business. Some come for the free booze or food, others simply to escape the boredom of their daily routine. Many are there to show the flag and represent their country, with no particular agenda. For them, it's just another official function that quickly fades into the back of their consciousness.

Spies, however, come with a purpose. They're seeking out prey. Like sharks and lions, they make their way deliberately through the crowd. Coming upon small circles, they insert themselves long enough to survey the herd; they take a sniff of the shy loner in the back of the room; or they put themselves in the background as a speaker holds court and prattles on. Perhaps with a drink in their hand as a prop to help them blend in, unlike most in the crowd they'll eat little and stay constantly on the move.

Hunters that they are, spies are not there to have fun. It can get very old, very quickly, but it's a ritual that a case officer repeats over the years. Good case officers never stop seeking out new sources. But spies aren't looking for just anyone. They don't have time for such frivolity. The hunt is narrowed to finding a particular lead they have already researched, or a target of opportunity who has the right access to address specific intelligence requirements. These are sources who can fill collection gaps that the intelligence community identified, which in turn can only be obtained through clandestine collection. Secrets.

Nick and I lived in a big, dirty, crowded and often violent city, but one that was not the epicenter for insurgency or terrorism where I would often find myself. In fact, I was there with family, my young children enjoying the adventures of the country's rural beauty, wildlife, and history. Nick was there alone, his wife and young son staying behind, a vestige of the "hostage taking" policy his autocratic country maintained over officials by denying their children the opportunity to accompany parents abroad. The intent was to deter bad behavior such as betrayal or defection.

The locals were not quite our friends nor were they truly enemies. But the country's semblance of neutrality was more superficial than genuine given its close relationship with most of America's adversaries. As such, the local counterintelligence service kept a close eye on us. My day job offered a degree of protection from the intense scrutiny the locals could apply when it suited them. Just being an official American made one a suspect here and liable to become the flavor of the month when one might find themselves accompanied by any number of surveillants probing for nefarious behavior. Of course, that just made the spying all the more fun, and obtaining the stolen secrets all the more satisfying. Spies are not entirely unlike thieves, but those who like to steal from under the noses of their adversaries, like cat burglars who relish the thrill, coming and going without notice or detection.

Given the local politics, Nick enjoyed somewhat of a home field advantage. He had greater freedom of movement than I had and was less likely to be given attention around town by the local counterintelligence service. He and I were both seasoned but relatively junior when we spotted one another from a distance, working the crowd.

We eyed one another at times over the course of the evening but avoided contact. It's all part of the dance. The case officer acts like the lion stalking its prey concealed by the crowd rather than the high grass. You don't throw yourself recklessly at potential targets without a plan, and even an approach divined on the fly benefits from the opportunity to observe. How does he carry himself? Is she wearing a particular garment or accessory that tells me something? Are they sullen or jovial in conversation? What's the language being spoken, the accent? Are they a wallflower or dominating conversations? With whom are they speaking? Is that alcohol or a soft drink in their hand?

Nick would correctly make me out for an American, and I could only suspect his nationality by virtue of appearance and accent, but I knew he would regardless be among the "criteria country targets" CIA pursued, a tier one geopolitical priority. As it would turn out, we likewise both presumed the other to be an intelligence officer just from the observed behaviors at the event. Still, we were each looking for easier prey, and going up against a rival intelligence officer was generally a more challenging match unless you had received tips through other collection that suggested their potential.

All I would later find out about Nick in the station's local files was his name on his government's diplomatic list. We had otherwise never previously heard of him, nor could we yet confirm Nick's intelligence affiliation. That assessment was, for the moment, entirely based on my own instinct. Still, there was something even more intriguing about Nick in a country where the CIA's modest station was vastly outnumbered by intelligence officers from rival and adversary states. He must have thought likewise. As the evening wore on, we both became less concerned with appearing not to notice one another, and the odd wink as we crossed paths turned into a shy smile an hour later, and ultimately, a handshake to introduce ourselves to one another at the end of a long night of hunting.

Success for a case officer is about judgment, and a big part of that is about how you manage time. There are always more targets to chase and agents to handle than hours in a day or days in a week. That's why you only pursue agents you need, since handling an unproductive case requires the same tradecraft and bears the same risks as a solid reporter. Given the demanding tradecraft requirements to discreetly develop and ultimately clandestinely handle your agents, you have to know when to walk away from a lead that's unlikely to go anywhere, and when to keep at it because you just know there's something there. I was fortunate throughout my career, being able to quickly surmise whether a target had potential. Hard target or not, with Nick, I knew instantly in my gut he could be had.

Nick emoted sentiment and warmth in what at first almost appeared to be an aura of innocence. He spoke like a poet, with eloquent turn of phrase and frequent use of metaphors and literary references. Though some of it was a test, a means to probe my own intellect, depth of knowledge, and interests, it was nevertheless odd for a case officer to be so forward and oddly revealing of their passions and character. But it was less innocence than an expression of desire to be in a completely different world than the one in which he found himself. For whatever reason, Nick allowed me a quick but sufficiently enduring glimpse inside that first evening to inform my assessment.

We didn't speak long that first night. Neither of us wanted to highlight our interest in the other to whomever might have been watching, though as it would turn out, for different reasons. Likewise neither of us aggressively sought out further contact or exchanged personal phone numbers, a move that would risk security and come across as too aggressive. Switchboards at both our official establishments were monitored, in Nick's case by his own security personnel, as well as the local counterintelligence service, with which his organization enjoyed close ties. We did exchange cards, though, allowing us each to task our respective Headquarters for a records search, if we so elected, which would have been standard practice.

Nick might have been junior in rank, but he had a pedigree. Meeting him in person gave me reason to send a trace request to the sensitive CIA office that oversaw operations against Nick's country. A former CIA agent had included a passing reference concerning Nick that had more to do with his father, a powerful government official who had developed influence through years spent in his country's armed forces. Many officials in Nick's country secured their "in" through relatives and patronage, despite the government's Communist propaganda concerning the equality of the masses. CIA Headquarters was immediately interested. Although Nick might not have ready access to the crown jewels, his network would facilitate a steady rise. The hunt was on.

I couldn't just ring Nick up at the office without exposing our contact, so I continued to troll venues where I expected he might show up. A few weeks later my luck paid off when I spotted him at another official event. Nick and I abandoned pretense and approached one another as soon our eyes met. It was perhaps less than a platonic version of when Tony and Maria find one another in *West Side Story*, but still, it was as if there were no one else in the large reception hall. And it's a funny thing when you meet someone the second time in such circles at these events. It can be like two old friends reuniting. We greeted each other as if we had known one another for a lifetime.

Nick and I each went through the ritualistic stages of elicitation that case officers practice to gather bio, background, and assessment. Conversations in this particularly difficult country related to health and the last gastrointestinal ailment from which one had just recovered. When it came up that I was here with young children, Nick was intrigued, immediately expressing concern about how I managed to protect them from the assorted parasites, pests, and pestilence that abounded.

Though he betrayed nothing about his influential father and little more regarding his family, there was undisguised sadness in Nick's voice as he talked about his own son. And there was my hook. So yes, while it is an overstatement to suggest case officers pimp out their families, our spouses and children can indeed be integral to getting our foot in the door on occasion, and we're not shy about doing so.

Bringing the conversation to an end, I suggested how Nick might enjoy a family movie night at my home some time. If he missed the sound of screaming children watching *Teenage Mutant Ninja Turtles*, I was sure my kids would love torturing him. Not pushing, I largely left it at that, but I made sure to let him know where I lived. It demonstrated discretion. And if there was one common trait among those from countries like Nick's who worked with us, it was their understandable need to vet those in whom they would entrust their lives. So pushing too hard, too soon, tends to backfire. A low-key approach, on the other hand, that features subtlety and reliability is another matter. Yes, those traits go a long way. And Nick did likewise in response to my offer, which he neither accepted nor rejected, instead making excuses about his schedule but agreeing to consider it. We again parted ways.

A few days later, I carefully made my way to his house in the evening hours. Bear in mind that case officers don't just "go out." No, every move, particularly one involving an operational act, especially in a high-threat counterintelligence environment, must be planned; and every place you expect to do something clandestine must be cased. As advertised, it appeared he lived alone. It was a small place, one car in the driveway. After putting in the required operational effort to confirm I could pass by his house undetected, I dropped a postcard in his mailbox. Unsigned, it simply said: "Ninja Turtles movie night this Saturday at 7PM."

This in itself was a fairly aggressive step that might have backfired in all sorts of ways. It clearly flagged me for an intelligence officer, since what innocent US official would go through such efforts? That I had passed by his house and left a message, albeit innocuous and unsigned, could have scared him off. Alternatively, as required, Nick should have immediately reported it to his superiors. This would have in turn allowed them to choose from a suite of options that ranged from complaining of harassment to our chief of mission, identifying me for scrutiny by their local host government intelligence partners, setting me up for a pitch by initially dangling Nick as a double agent, or just having a bunch of goons beat the living crap out of me. All of these options were on his government's menu.

So, yes, none of this comes without risk. And apart from the more consequential outcomes, the behavior itself can be like dating in high school, or perhaps even middle school. In this case, the postcard was the grown-up version of a note passed in class with boxes to be checked as to whether or not your object of desire likes you.

My wife and I prepared a modest meal of hot dogs and fixings for the kids and readied for our movie night, hoping he'd show up. And, yes, as the hour neared 7 p.m., I was as nervous as a boy with a crush on a girl from whom he expected a call, pacing anxiously around the house, waiting for a knock on the door. I even checked the peephole from time to time! Don't judge me. I decided there'd be a greater vantage point upstairs, and it felt less demeaning to be glued to the upstairs window than explain to my small kids why Daddy was staring out the peephole. By 7:15, I came downstairs. He wasn't coming. Movie night began. Fifteen minutes later, there was a knock at the door.

Nick might have been American, dressed in blue jeans, sneakers, and a short sleeve button-down shirt. Initially nervous, it took maybe five seconds for my two young sons to spot their latest victim. Jumping on their new friend, they grabbed him by the hands and dragged him to the TV room. Nick melted in their presence. He loved every minute of it. I barely was able to get in a word to ask what he wanted to drink before the boys had him sprawled on the floor playing with their trucks, toy airplanes, and of course, Teenage Mutant Ninja action figures, as the movie roared in the background. I already knew every word of the dialogue by heart, having seen it at least a dozen times.

And so it went like this for months. Nick would come every two or three weeks for movie night, spend an hour or two lying on the ground playing with the boys, and the rest of the night drinking and talking with me. Nick was a melancholy and complicated figure. He occasionally brought the most tragic movies from his own country for me to watch. Absent subtitles, he would translate himself, occasionally breaking down into tears as he explained the dramatic scenes. There was always a Romeo and Juliet sort of love story with bickering families. The boy would die heroically albeit tragically in battle, days before scheduled to leave the front, and the girl, living on a farm, would succumb to some horrific disease just shortly after receiving the news. In the end, the two tragic figures would be granted eternal togetherness, buried next to one another by their grieving and now unified families. Nick didn't require me to love the films, but he was taken by my willingness to give them a try and discuss them with sincere interest afterward. Like romance, espionage is as much about the gestures and considerations, placing the needs of the agent first, or at least leading them to believe as much.

Nick's life was dominated by an overbearing, disapproving father whom he constantly disappointed. He loved his country, its history, and people, but he hated his country's political system, which was one of greed, corruption, and injustice represented by his own father. When he agreed to spy, Nick did so initially out of loyalty to me, and also contempt for his father. But just getting the target to yes does not a recruitment make. In fact it is often just getting to the agent's agreement when the real work in a recruitment begins.

To protect my new agent, I had to get him to stop coming to the house. Nick was an intelligence officer, a case officer in fact, so he needed little training in clandestinity, just rather, motivation to be diligent. He knew precisely what he was getting himself into, but the reality of acceptance was nevertheless emotionally taxing.

This was actually all somewhat like the five stages of grief, which occasionally occur when recruiting someone who, like Nick, has made a life and death decision to accept the recruitment pitch.

Nick first denied to himself that he was doing anything wrong. He was a free man, he insisted, knowing that was certainly not the case in his country. Such denial made getting him to take the required steps to assure his security harder for him to embrace. People who aren't doing anything wrong need not lie about it, or run around in the middle of the night having clandestine meetings with "the enemy."

Next came the tests of our friendship. Anger. Was this a setup from the outset? He and I were both spies, so he knew the answer, but he didn't need to be slapped in the face with it. Rather, he needed an excuse, a romantic one more appropriately, befitting of his dark and dramatic nature. My pitch was wrapped in nationalistic fanfare about his doing right by his country's people and their history against a brutal and illegitimate regime that had perverted all that was good about their culture and contributions. He had an opportunity to take back control of his life, serve his nation, and strike a blow of defiance and retribution against his father. But, he countered, what had he done? For that matter, what had his good friend done to him? Would I allow him to quit? A true friend would, he insisted. I of course affirmed his freedom to walk away at any time. And he "quit" several times, always coming back.

Then came the negotiation. Nick began bargaining with himself, really, and then in turn me, on how to conduct this relationship. He was looking for a way to be half in, but half out, so that he could with his own good conscience deny he was doing anything wrong. But it was pretty clear that passing state secrets to the enemy would not easily be rationalized or explained away, especially in a closed society.

Depression was tough, especially with Nick, being rather somber and fatalistic on a good day. Hours would be spent convincing him that a tragic end was in fact not inevitable. There were risks, but nothing good came without them. Appealing to his fundamental motivations always, I reminded Nick that what he was doing would free him from the torment of serving a system he so despised, and make a difference that might be realized by his son, and his grandson to follow.

Acceptance came at last. Though with the risks and consequences so high, and considering the changes we all experience in life as our circumstances and environments change, a good case officer is always re-recruiting their agent at each and every meeting. Have their motivations changed? Any second thoughts? New risks? Have they been caught? You don't take your loved ones for granted, and neither do you your agents, who can change their minds or worse, turn on you, for any number of reasons. You must always remain attentive. Nick was ready, fully bought in, and had come to take direction that was intended to protect him well.

It takes a great deal of work to ready an agent to return to his home country where the risks of compromise are higher and the tradecraft more demanding. Part of that process meant I had to let him go. I brought Nick into this dicey new adventure, but to prove he was working for the CIA and would accept direction from the institution, rather than doing his friend a favor, I was directed to turn him over to a colleague.

That was a hard conversation, and one I could not confidently predict would end well. I had already taken him away from the family atmosphere of my home as demanded by the need for clandestine contact, and now I would be passing him off to a stranger. It was an emotional night, but I appealed to his soulful nature of right and wrong, and he agreed. For me, it was hard, but I remembered who and what I was, and I found the detachment necessary to do the job. Nick did not belong to me. He belonged to the CIA.

Turning Nick over to "Robin," who I respected professionally and considered a friend, made it easier for me. And Robin did a good job of establishing his own level of rapport with Nick, though it was a completely different dynamic. In a way, that helped for the demanding requirements Nick would face in readying him for what would be a triple life, since he already lived under cover as an intelligence officer, and had now added to that operating clandestinely as a CIA agent.

Time moved along and I was now at another post. I had lost track of Nick's circumstances since the reality is that the rules of compartmentalization and "need to know" preclude you from "checking up" on old agents—especially sensitive ones being run in denied areas. I knew from Robin that Nick had made the leap, and he was now inside, back in his own country. Robin and I had run into one another in the halls of CIA Headquarters, both traveling back briefly for business. Robin was kind, telling me Nick spoke constantly about me. But mostly he talked about my sons, whom he missed as if his own. But even Robin knew nothing more than that.

It was toward the end of my next tour the news hit. There had been a series of arrests. My heart sank. Was he compromised? Tortured? Dead? CIA was keeping the news tight internally, and various theories abounded about a mole or some other means of compromise. When I was next back in Washington, I went to the handling desk for answers, even though I knew what to expect.

CIA took pains to censor much of what was behind that which went wrong, so I am limited in regard to providing greater detail. The reality that I can share, however, is that CIA relies on the practice of standing behind "sources and methods" to deflect responsibility for its mistakes. From public accounts we have all read of in the press, this process is best reflected by the fact that no CIA officers were held accountable for 9/11, Iraq, "enhanced interrogations," renditions gone awry, the Khost bombing that killed seven of my colleagues, or our failure to identify the rise of the Islamic State before it spread across two countries and wreaked havoc in Europe.

It is understandable that the CIA makes no public comment when adversaries claim to have arrested our agents. Doing so can further endanger the agents. What follows is an internal damage assessment that seeks to determine the cause of the compromise, the risk to other operations, the extent of our losses, and lessons learned to protect and facilitate current and future activities. What such assessments lack is accountability. Rarely do conclusions ever point a finger at who was responsible. Even when an assessment diplomatically ascribes the contributing causes to the handling officers, the tradecraft, or the chain of command, it's the exception to see consequences.

I have been part of these investigations and written such damage assessments, which is sometimes tasked to an operationally seasoned senior operations officer. And with such firsthand knowledge, I can't ever recall over the course of my career seeing any Senior Intelligence Service

(SIS) officer suffer professional consequences for the loss of an agent, or even a network of agents, due to tradecraft and judgment errors by them or the officers in their command. But if there are no consequences when CIA staff officers lose their lives due to negligence within their chain of command, as was the case in Khost, I suppose it would be unlikely to expect any accountability when agents die.

Perhaps because the CIA leadership is able to insulate itself by virtue of the secret world in which it lives, and does well to appease the political leaders to whom they report, they evade the accountability required, say, of US military leaders. While the US military is not itself without sin when it comes to accountability, it at least accepts more of it than the Agency. Agency leadership warns of the debilitating effect on workforce moral were CIA leaders and officers to suffer consequences for such errors. But when the Marine barracks in Beirut was attacked by a Hizballah suicide bomber in 1983 leaving 241 service members dead, the heretofore promising career of its commanding officer, Marine Colonel Timothy Geraghty, essentially came to an end, although he had previously been on the fast track for general. And several promising naval careers ended after a series of collisions between Navy destroyers and commercial shipping in the last several years, regardless the degree of the captain's direct responsibility. At the end of the day, they were in charge, and accounted for the mishaps accordingly.

For the CIA, even the agent handlers who are directly responsible for a lethal mistake tend to get off lightly—perhaps some time in the penalty box, an official glass ceiling for further promotions, or limitations on future responsibilities. But more often than not, the responsible senior bosses, as well as those agent handlers with solid godfather networks, seem to escape unscathed, some going on to make the same mistakes again.

In this case, as among too many others I have seen where good agents go to the wall, the CIA's approach was to circle the wagons, minimize access to what went wrong, and protect careers, particularly SIS careers. If you think about it, the enemy already knows what we did wrong since they arrested our agents, so just what are we protecting? And adversaries like

Russia, China, and Iran tend to share their lessons learned among each other and with their allies when they've duped us or otherwise enjoyed a counterintelligence success. So from whom then are we hiding this?

Ironically, this reality runs against the very ethos of integrity to which all CIA officers must embrace given both the responsibility and the trust with which we operate. It also runs counter to our training. Good case officers must always be skeptical, questioning and challenging their assumptions and assessment. They need to be the first to highlight the warts in any case so as to allow for different possibilities and to address any potential threats. But CIA's leadership has time and again sided with self-preservation at the expense of the organization's future, and the lives of those for whom they are responsible.

For CIA, it's less about further risking modus operandi and more about the embarrassment of once again being had. And in my experience, when CIA is had, it's generally the result of our own hubris or our reliance on shortcuts and quick fixes to complex tradecraft challenges.

HUMINT operations are risky. We can't prevent the CIA and its people from taking well-considered risks. Even doing our best, we will make mistakes, and we will, on occasion, get caught. And you can't do it well without being aggressive, seizing opportunities, and pushing the envelope. But when things do go wrong, and there's fault to be assigned owing to incompetence, ambition, and disregard of the rules, we are doomed, as Santayana wrote, to repeat these failures. And repeat them we surely have. Compartmentalizing lessons learned from our own and making the same mistakes repeatedly is a betrayal of our oath, our agents, and their handlers.

Still, I was determined to learn Nick's fate, and what caused it. The "back room" that managed the sensitive internal operations for this country was off-limits except to those cleared with a need to know. I made it as far as the branch chief, "Ralph," a misanthropic soul who appeared not to have seen the light of day beyond his backroom cave for years. Close-cropped hair, horn-rimmed glasses, and pairing short sleeve button-down shirts with narrow ties from a time long passed, Ralph had probably not served in the field since the days of Khrushchev and Mao. He was an old-school, denied area handler who was more comfortable with "sticks and bricks" through which to pass and receive information.

In fact, Ralph had never recruited an agent himself and had limited experience even meeting them in person. To him, agents were not people. They were just the cryptonyms for which they were known. And for more protection, even Nick's crypt had been changed, making it a struggle to even identify about whom I was inquiring. But it didn't matter, as Ralph didn't care. He promptly dismissed me from the secure spaces, saying, "Nick is no longer any of your concern." For grins, he called my boss to complain about my "unprofessional behavior."

I'm not a terribly religious person, but I have a fundamental belief in mankind. My nature is to be optimistic, ever hopeful, but always skeptical, as any good spy must be. You have to question almost everything and plan for the worst case. Moreover, in espionage, you can't afford to accept anything at face value that can't be tested and explained. The risks for failing to do otherwise are too great, and people can and do change as life around them does. But that doesn't preclude an intervention by "the spy gods."

Back overseas, I received a big yellow envelope one morning with my personal mail that included a thick collection of what had been forwarded from my stateside home address. We rented out our house back in America while overseas and the forwarding mail service only endures so long. From time to time, the tenants would mail a batch. I went through what appeared mostly advertisements and credit card offers when I came upon a postcard. It was unsigned, postmarked from Nick's country, and read simply in broken English, "Mutant Ninja Turtles Live. Miss you all. Lots of love."

When I brought the postcard to the back room's attention this time, I got a little more information from the woman who had now inherited the branch chief's job. Nick had stopped communicating prior to word of the arrests or other telling events I am not at liberty to describe. When he failed to respond to recontact efforts, the back room assumed that he had been imprisoned and was eventually executed along with others mentioned in the press surrounding the arrests. Quite some time later, through renewed insight, they determined that Nick remained a viable case, having been saved by "self-terminating" at the time he did. They made another effort at recontact, but again, to no avail.

Based on the timing of when he mailed the postcard, Nick had quit just before the net would fall on other cases. Nick was worried enough about me to send word that he was okay. I might have let go of Nick, but he hadn't done the same with me, and it seemed he forgave me for necessarily disappearing myself.

The branch chief was kind, in fact flattering to me, about how I had brought Nick aboard in the first place. She asked me if I would be prepared to help them on the day Nick might show up in another overseas posting. I wanted to tell her as the last branch had told me, "Nick is no longer any of your concern." But I knew it wasn't necessary. Nick had left a job he hated and the triple life it forced him to live.

If he showed up again overseas, it wouldn't likely be for his government. I'd like to believe Nick was living his dreams, the life he imagined without the pressure from his father. Regardless if it's true or not, and perhaps it's a coping mechanism to address my own guilt for the life I pushed him to lead as my mission required, this is how I still see him today.

HUMANITY IN ALL

What truly distinguished the CIA I joined from that which it has become is the abandonment of its core values as an espionage service. An appreciation for Humanity, spelled with a big H to emphasize that a spy service is at its core about people. It's about those we recruit as foreign agents, the case officers who engage them, the subject matter and technical experts who enable the activity, and the support teams who fuel it. CIA is a spy service. The quirks, failings, and beauty of people represent the humanity we need to appreciate and leverage, even when the behaviors of those we pursue are, to our standards, inhumane. Understanding does not equate to condoning, a concept that's difficult for the Agency's increasingly influential targeting, paramilitary, and analytical elements. But the further CIA distances itself from the core values of being an elite spy service, the less unique value it will offer, and the less operational success it will yield.

There are moments in the work that seem normal, even routine, but that you realize later are not typical for the average human. I've seen the best and the worst the world can offer. Experiences I could not possibly relate to relatives or friends with whom I grew up, whose lives were so different. Would they even care? At times your actual life is so surreal in the context of those still living in the world from which you came, it reinforces both the privilege and curse of being a CIA case officer.

I recall a fortunately timed mission that took me to East Berlin as the Wall began to fall, a true watershed moment in history. I had the privilege of a front row seat to watch the very symbol of our enemy's repression crumble and collapse beneath its own weight. I've also stood on the bridge of an aircraft carrier in the midst of combat operations facilitated by CIA intelligence, stolen code books, and military manuals. I've sat with al-Qa'ida terrorists my teams had brought to justice. I adventured on African safaris, laid eyes on Mount Everest, Victoria Falls, the pyramids, the Taj Mahal, the Grand Bazaar, and so many of the greatest sights from around the world. I've been lucky for the opportunity.

But I've also witnessed the brutality of heavily armed security forces set loose on crowds of protestors armed only with their voices shouting for change. I've seen men and women bound, gagged, and tortured, some put to death by their terrorist captors. Many never made a sound or protest as their throats were slit or their bodies were riddled with bullets. I've seen too many bury their spouses, children, and infants, owing to the ravages of war, disease, and dehumanization by adversaries and oppressors. I've sat with our most unrepentant enemies as they quite casually narrated tales of torture and brutality, and without even the appearance of a downshift, shared photos of a child's birthday party, a new grandson, or a gift they bought their wife on their anniversary. I've dined with a charming, cosmopolitan, and glib chief of a brutal intelligence service with whom I negotiated as he nonchalantly shared frustration over his inability to compel captured terrorists to talk, despite beating them into unconsciousness with his own hands.

Still, you were reminded that despite how awful these people could be, they were still people. One provided me a tutorial on bird watching, from another a lesson on cinematography, a third offered best practices for keeping a flower garden, and one instructed me on how best to mix watercolors. Many loved the same music or art as I did, while some introduced me to literature, poetry, paintings, and sculpture that I would not otherwise have ever considered. They were all at once human and inhuman, but terribly real and entirely authentic. That they could so compartmentalize themselves from what they did, and how they did it, escaped logic or reasoning. But this was a reality of the landscape in which I long dwelled. The beauty and opulence, the natural wonders, all served with a complementary portion of inhumanity, hatred, brutality, and venality. Perhaps one could not exist without the other. Perhaps this marriage of good and evil, happy and sad, at times less balanced in some worlds than in others, was by necessary design.

It prompts the realization that yours is not a "normal" life. The experiences change you, for good as much as bad, or so I hope to believe. But change you it does, and I am often amazed at colleagues who still can separate themselves and their experiences so as to "return home again." Some do it better than others, reclaiming their past after decades of espionage. But I found the return to be less a revisionist departure from the reality and more a brief escape. In any event, case officers are nonetheless quite adept at compartmentalizing, and making the conscious detachment from obstacles that would otherwise complicate their mission. How else could one direct those for whom we are responsible into harm's way?

Successful recruiters tend to embrace a similar set of guiding principles to navigate the good, bad, and ugly in which they are immersed. We may be predators, committing ourselves to finding and leveraging the motivations and weaknesses of those upon whom we prey, but we need to believe we are doing it for the right reasons, staying true not only to our laws but also to our American values. Case officers need to have confidence that our institutions and leadership keep faith with us, and that we'll not be left behind on the battlefield, figuratively or literally.

And finally, successful case officers usually have a deep love for mankind, if not people themselves. Case officers see the very worst among people, their ugliness, venality, and brutality, but sometimes they witness the very best, as people make sacrifices and act selflessly for a cause or comrade. It accounts for our contradictory state of hope and cynicism. It's a condition that brings to mind a quote by Dostoyevsky who said, "The more I love humanity in general the less I love man in particular," or Einstein who said, "I love humanity, but I hate humans."

There is humanity in all people. You need not condone to understand and empathize with those from different walks and backgrounds. But without understanding and empathy, you will lack the critical tools you need for relating to or engaging others, particularly our enemies. It doesn't excuse their behaviors or deeds, but it humanizes them so that you can recognize and in turn leverage what guides their actions.

Case officers must get beyond the facades and caricatures. What people reveal while in custody, or through a drone's full motion video, is not the same as watching them rolling on the ground playing with their children, or your own. Even those who are quite appropriately seen as monsters cry over lost children, siblings, and parents; suffer from broken hearts; and muse the vexing, philosophical questions about life. You can't begin to predict what people, nations, or groups will do based on your own perspectives and experiences.

I recruited my share of agents with blood on their hands, American blood included. Likewise, I debriefed those with whom we finally caught up while they were in custody. In truth, few regretted taking up arms against the West. Indeed, this included even those who would eventually cooperate against their own. They believed in what they did to rationalize their brutality to others, and the consequences that befell them, their families, friends, and communities. Among those who do cooperate, most must rationalize it by delegitimizing their leadership who, they say, led them astray by corrupting the cause.

A senior al-Qa'ida leader whom one of my teams brought to justice had himself inherited responsibility for the children of several of his brothers, uncles, and nephews, all of whom had been killed or captured in pursuit of their extremist cause. "Omar" had sat it out for a while, running a business and assuming responsibility for his extended family. Finally, the bench depleted, senior leadership called upon Omar to step into his family members' shoes. Unfortunately for us, he was particularly good at it. Omar facilitated multiple lethal operations, while providing exceptional administrative support to protect al-Qa'ida's top leaders. Omar was a personable, soft-spoken man with a quick, engaging wit. He was a father to several children himself. He took his personal responsibilities as seriously as he did his work, and he invested great effort in seeing to the health and welfare of the extended family for whose well-being he became responsible.

Omar was not easy to catch. He practiced good security and knew how to play his enemies off one another, having at an earlier time evaded custody by claiming to our local intelligence service partners that he would serve them as an informer. The day after his capture, I remember conducting his first debriefing. Omar did not fit the mental picture we had all formed of this sinister terrorist mastermind. He looked small, vulnerable, and frightened, resembling more a simple bazaar shop owner than my mortal enemy.

I began with pleasantries and basic conversation, trying to establish some degree of rapport to encourage him to talk about anything. We spoke about our backgrounds and families, and Omar betrayed deep affection and longing for his. Like captive terrorists almost always do, Omar minimized his role in the organization, portraying himself as a victim of circumstances and suggesting he had no shared affinity for their violent goals or any knowledge of their plans, intentions, or whereabouts.

Likewise, as they almost always do, Omar claimed he was being truthful and would assist us to the best of his capabilities, but lacked the knowledge we sought. Omar acknowledged *who* he was, but not *what* he was, insisting only to be a simple gofer and puppet, unwitting even as to the true identity or location of those from whom he received direction.

I focused on his family, spending more of our time together getting to know about his children and those under his care, including the wives of those brothers and uncles killed or detained. I asked what would happen to them all now that he, too, was in custody. His ethnic group was part of a community unwelcome and suspect across several borders. The reality was that many would become refugees, subject to various degrees of persecution and hardship. With him going to jail, where would they get the support they needed? Who would see they were fed, housed, educated, and taken care of when ill? Omar raised his hands into his face and began to weep. When he looked up, coming to grips again after his short loss of composure, Omar calmly observed that he had no choice. This, he said, was their nature, his fate, theirs, and God's will.

In my day, one of the first things new NE Division case officers were taught, or reminded, was that to understand the Middle East one had to appreciate the old fable of the frog and the scorpion. The story is that of a scorpion who comes to the banks of the Nile River. Seeking a way across, he spots a frog floating blissfully on the calm, deep waters. The scorpion asks the frog to carry him across. The frog eyes the stranger and scoffs that he most certainly could not comply. The scorpion asks why this might be. The frog replies, as if obvious to all, that he is afraid of being stung.

The scorpion laughs and reasons that were he to do so, both would sink and the scorpion, who could not even float let alone swim, would drown and likewise perish. The scorpion argues that there was simply no logic or cause for him to sting his only means of safe transport across the river. The frog pauses, considers the scorpion's logic, and agrees. The frog is casually making his way across the river with the scorpion calmly upon his back when midway through the scorpion suddenly strikes. As they both begin to sink, their mutual ends now certain and near, the frog asks, "But why, why did you sting me? We shall both die!" The scorpion responds resolutely, calmly, in his final words: "It is but my nature. I am, after all, a scorpion."

WHEN CASE OFFICERS GROW UP

As you move up in the DO, you receive increasing responsibility for programs and people that limit your opportunities to continue working cases and operating on the street. While the DO has experimented at times in developing "expert tracks" for officers to advance without being managers, it's particularly rare for case officers. Targeting officers align well with a particular geographic area of expertise, one in which they've demonstrated substantive mastery, such as Russia, China, or Iran, for example.

It's more complicated for a case officer. One can't claim "recruiting" as an expertise, since all are expected to do so, regardless of the reality that only a fraction of the cadre is particularly masterful at the art. And case officers tend to have outsized egos, leading them to seek a COS or other leadership positions that have authority and prestige. And even a case officer who overcomes the deliberately imposed hurdles in securing "expert status" in a geographic or functional area must still demonstrate a corporate comportment. It's a trait that bodes poorly for divas, regardless of their talent and track record. Finally, promotions to Secret Intelligence Service (SIS) ranks as "expert" are limited, only a fraction of the slots reserved for "executive managers."

The unpleasant truth is that promotion to the senior ranks remains political. Ascensions are driven by networks, and determined by favorability among current SIS officers, the DDO, and the DCIA, who must all sign off. This was where the expert option paid off for "Chad." A targeting officer and former analyst, Chad was in a senior operational management position in what was then the Counterterrorism Center. Reviled by subordinates and peers but adored by the targeting officer and former analyst department chief for whom he worked, as well as the mercurial overall center chief with whom he had obsequiously won favor, Chad was still being passed over at the yearly SIS panels.

The department and center chief maneuvered to make Chad an "expert," which ultimately facilitated his promotion, only to move him right back again into a senior management position, against both the letter and spirit of the system. Once promoted, it was not like they could take it back. Chad is now a front office operational manager in one of the CIA's geographic mission centers. He oversees complex and sensitive operations and supervises station chiefs even though he himself lacks case officer certification or experience.

Most case officers remain player coaches, to some degree, even upon assuming field management positions. There is the old-school tradition that once a case officer, always a case officer, and regardless of grade and position, you're never above handling agents. I always found it disappointing when colleagues would even have to be reminded of this, but not all of them enjoy the operational work. There are those happy to leave the "unpleasant" street work behind, believing themselves "spymasters," versus "master spies," so as to enjoy the greater prestige from engaging other USG agencies and foreign counterparts.

I never let go of the operational and street aspect of my profession despite serving in senior positions. Never did I stop spotting, assessing, developing, recruiting, and handling foreign agents. It was too much fun, and practically speaking, kept me operationally grounded. It was "Andy," a senior officer I worked for at times over the course of my career, who gave me the nickname "Peter Pan." Andy was one of those old-school Irish Catholic NE officers who ran the DO in my early days. He wasn't entirely wrong about me. Case officer work suited my somewhat impish and mischievous inclinations.

Andy, like other seniors, would tell me to enjoy the case officer's life while I could. He was right. All case officers have to grow up. Even me. And without realizing it, I fashioned how I adapted to the increasingly more strategic responsibilities I'd shoulder using Andy's example. His management style, however, doesn't translate well to current times. Passionate about the mission and the people for whom he was responsible, Andy could be eviscerating you at one moment, and thirty minutes later telling you a joke. It would be as if the earlier dustup was long forgotten or had never occurred. I've known other managers like that, and I never much appreciated the approach. It's a lot easier for the eviscerator to get over the episode than the victim.

Still, there was a lot to like about Andy. He didn't hold grudges, nor did he realize his ambitions on the backs of others. Andy was a live-and-let-live kind of guy, a gentleman and a scholar. So long as you did nothing to attack him, then any differences of opinion, approaches, or backgrounds were never threats to him. He was also a gifted Arabist and a rather bureaucratically progressive thinker for his day. Andy's early assignments were served among NE Division's more austere and exotic locations.

Andy's passion and quick temper notwithstanding, he always impressed me with his ability to simplify complicated issues and develop innovative solutions that he could dispassionately argue. Andy could make his points and counterpoints regardless of any emotional escalation by his counterpart. Even when a debate's decorum began to break down, Andy maintained a calm composure and focused on the logic and merits. This was not the Andy whom I could easily anger owing to my latest "Peter Pan" transgression, but rather, corporate Andy, businesslike Andy, the

Andy at the helm of a station, task force, or component, the Andy working across organizational and agency lines to champion his perspective in a manner that did not rob others of their value. Andy always kept his eye on the ball. He was focused, professional, and determined.

Andy was a key player at the best of times in negotiations among Arab and Israeli stakeholders during the 1990s. The best of times, I say, because there were consistent, reliable communications in an atmosphere of shared risks and tangible opportunities that he helped to create. Not that such talks didn't frequently break down into heated emotional exchanges that threatened success, but there was at least a will to make progress that, along with Andy's impressive arbitration skills, kept participants returning to the negotiating table. What he lacked in effusiveness and warmth, he made up for in being genuine and thoroughly reliable. When Andy made a commitment, you could bank on it.

Following 9/11, the buzzword was *transparency*. It was all about collaboration and consensus building to make sure all the various USIC agencies had the information and insight they required to do their jobs. The quickest way to tank another officer's career these days is to accuse one of not working corporately with counterparts in other organizations. As a principle, learned perhaps the hard way from 9/11, this makes absolute sense. But intelligence does not lend itself well to black and white. It's, at best, opaque. It takes the judgment of the originating agency to determine how much insight to provide, and when, so as to support rather than undermine the efforts of other organizations, and similarly protect your operations so that they can continue to produce vital intelligence.

The CIA is rather transparent with other USIC agencies. Access to the raw intelligence reporting CIA disseminates from HUMINT assets is generously provided throughout the community, as is likewise the case with CIA's finished intelligence products. There are degrees of sensitivity, but at least some element in every USIC agency, albeit reserved at times to that agency's principal and immediate staff, will see virtually every raw and finished intelligence report. What they do not see, and that for which consumers continue to clamor, is the operational reporting regarding the sources and methods. That said, in the spirit of transparency and collaboration, CIA senior officers have some degree of discretion in providing the insight necessary concerning operational particulars when required to secure the confidence, trust, and cooperation of another agency.

The assignment of increasing numbers of fully cleared officers from other USIC agencies into CIA centers has also helped. I had the privilege of working with, and in fact counted among my own staff, those detailed or assigned from the FBI, DoD, Treasury, ATF, NSA, NGA, and State, just to name a few. Those detailees and assignees were well "inside the tent," and they were invaluable in facilitating engagement, communication, and understanding. They had access to sensitive operational details and could vouch for CIA's word, even when unable to share the particulars, so as to overcome apprehensions and misunderstandings from their own home agencies.

In my final CIA assignment, I was responsible for counterterrorism operations and intelligence issues across South and Southwest Asia, including the conflict zones. My turf traversed borders with friends, rivals, and outright enemies alike, not all with whom we were even on speaking terms. Issues included preemptive operations to disrupt terrorist threats both in and emanating from the region, locating US hostages, supporting war fighters on the ground, covert action, and contributing to peace process negotiations.

After President Trump's August 2017 declaration of his South Asia strategy, there was a great deal of focus and anxiety on the part of the multitude of stakeholders, both within the USIC and among our foreign intelligence partners. One of my favorite station chiefs, an excellent officer and leader, coined the phrase, "win faster," appropriately foreseeing the limited window we had to effect what the president would appreciate as progress.

Liaison cooperation with our foreign partners varied, as you would expect, depending on the broader bilateral relationships and mutual interdependence. Still, it meant being respectful and not overbearing with allies, and remaining similarly proper, but nevertheless candid, with those among whom degrees of enmity and distrust existed. Cooperation with the latter came almost entirely on a transactional basis, or when there were significant and credible consequences. The ever-present questions in such engagements with the more mercurial partners were (1) Do we have something tangible to exchange for their assistance? or alternatively (2) How hard can we push before realizing diminishing returns, and can we back up our pressure with concrete and meaningful consequences?

Within the USIC, I appreciated the strong collaboration between the CIA and our DoD counterparts within my area of responsibilities. CIA and DoD all had people serving in harm's way and operating in overlapping space, so coordination and deconfliction was paramount for safety, and likewise for not undermining the other's mission. The CIA would have been hard-pressed to operate without the infrastructure, security, medical resources, and firepower DoD provided. In turn, DoD profited from CIA's intelligence and operations that secured their platforms from threat, and that vectored their resources against the most critical targets.

During my tenure, the overall commander of the special operations efforts rotated, and the two with whom I worked were equally generous and supportive. For my part, I provided insight and transparency to secure their confidence that the CIA would withhold nothing that might impact the safety of their troops. Likewise, whenever I needed to request a change in one of their activities that might threaten a sensitive, ongoing operation or agent, all I needed to do was make a phone call.

Such equity proved key while we patiently worked an operation focused on a high-value al-Qa'ida leader. Our collection provided us the ability to know, in an increasingly predictable manner, the leader's whereabouts. Perhaps more critical was the intelligence we could develop on his plans and activities, as well as that of his operational associates. There were a great many moving pieces to this operation, significant resources invested, and the employment of sensitive sources. It had taken years to develop this access through patience, perseverance, and the courage of our agents and their handlers. Equally important was the top cover up the chain of command, and their buy-in and support to keep going, since results were anything but immediate. Given the sensitivity, it was a highly compartmentalized operation into which even few CIA officers were read.

I had just arrived at the office, showing up as I did around 6 a.m. in order to come up to speed on the preceding evening's events, the day's operational and intelligence reporting, and upcoming activities that would merit briefing at the chief's daily 9 a.m. meeting at the Counter-terrorism Mission Center. This, in turn, would enable my boss to brief the DDO and DCIA on developments, accomplishments, and problems that merited their attention, or might otherwise catch them off guard if raised by the White House, NSC, Congress, or a senior from another USIC agency.

Waiting as I arrived was one of my senior officers. The look on his face gave me pause and suggested that I might have a long day ahead. The officer explained how through our DoD liaison elements, we had just come to learn of a US Special Forces operation that would be carried out deep into enemy-held territory. Their objective, unfortunately, was within spitting distance of the location from which our own sensitive targets resided and from where our collection was coming. If DoD struck as planned, at a minimum, our targets would go underground. We had spent years developing access to reacquire them, and just like that they would be gone. Moreover, given the justifiably heightened paranoia among our foes, it was just as possible the targets would grow suspicious of our sources and might even suspect their culpability in leading DoD to the area, which was so remote as to have been generally safe from DoD or allied military operations for some time.

At first glance, I thought my officer's evident despair was unwarranted. After all, I was confident in my relationship with the DoD commander in charge of the operation. Well, I was until asking about the identity of *their* target. As it turned out, the DoD target was likewise a terrorist high-value target (HVT). This particular fellow was somewhat a lesser priority for CIA at the time. This was largely because his was an associated group, not al-Qa'ida core, and more important, CIA had a fairly reliable means of collection against him to which DoD had insight.

The reality was that DoD's target was the leader of a group that also had American blood on its hands and thus was an NSC priority. DoD was using CIA collection to vector their efforts, though our own assessment offered low confidence he was at the specific location DoD believed, at least at this particular time. That this HVT remained at large for as long as he had was more a matter of timing. We could find him often enough, but the resources to take action always seemed unavailable when confidence was high that we could pinpoint him. Given his high priority for DoD, their success would be a significant achievement so their threshold for action was somewhat lower than our own. The operation would launch within hours.

The DoD detailee in my unit coordinated a time for a secure call to his commander. Given the prize, I frankly thought the odds were roughly fifty-fifty that I could convince the commander to stand down the operation. As always, and despite the busy ops tempo and its demands, the commander made himself immediately available. I began with the usual pleasantries and a quick catching up, but given the circumstances, I could not afford to delay or beat around the bush. Promptly, I explained the purpose of my call as being related to his impending operation. The commander listened attentively as he acknowledged the many moving pieces involved and his target's importance. Cutting to the chase, I said my call was to seek his agreement to stand down the operation, owing to its potential impact on a sensitive target against whom we were collecting in the same area.

I was fully prepared to go into detail when the commander simply replied, "Of course." Really? I thought. Like from the movie *Jerry Maguire*, I had him at hello? But that's all he needed. My word that his operation could impact something of great significance to CIA was all he had to hear. In fact, he said as much. The commander reminded me how he trusted my word, and that if I told him that his unit's activity could threaten a greater prize to US national interests, that was good enough for him. Granted, it took years to get to the point where that was all it required for the CIA to secure DoD's willingness to stand down an activity, and vice versa.

Despite his confidence, I nevertheless gave the commander a somewhat sterilized, executive level understanding of our operation's significance, the amount of time it had taken to get to this point, and the consequences were the targets to go to ground. Moreover, I assured him that we could continue to help prosecute his own target. I had just recently directed additional resources to focus on the commander's target in any event, as there were indications this HVT was planning an offensive against US targets in the coming months. If the commander would be willing to defer, I'd make his target our next priority. Being a gentleman, the commander chuckled warmly, not requiring any quid pro quo. But he was still pleased with my assurance. Our operation succeeded. The targets felt safe enough, long enough, for us to maintain persistent collection, expand access, and enable our goals, all while protecting our sources. As for the commander's target, he, along with that target's next two senior deputies, would all be dead within the coming six months.

WHEN THE PARTY ENDS

A spy should know when it's time to hang it up, but few of us do. Some stick around for the adrenaline. It's not everywhere you can steal Russian secrets, thwart terrorist operations, and break the law overseas in the name of God and country. Many stick around for that one, last great assignment, or they stay because of the unswerving belief that if they were to wait a bit longer, they'd finally be recognized with that big promotion. A few convince themselves that the place would be lost without them, and some are lifers who are unable to walk away or have nowhere else really to go. Many of the most senior stay for the power. Private industry will pay better, but those who have reigned as directorate, component, and station chiefs will never even approximate in private industry the fear and awe they receive from sycophants seeking favor in the CIA.

Thirty-four-plus years is a long time. And maybe my excuse for sticking around as long as I did is a cocktail of the above. Even when contemplating what the end might look like some years ago, my ideal was that when it was time to hang it up, I'd not look back. I had a great career, notwithstanding some bumps here and there, and I didn't want to be the old guy hanging on to past glory, nor did I want to be beholden still to the organization once finally free of it. I also didn't want to be like the boxer who doesn't know when to get out of the ring. I have colleagues in their late sixties and early seventies still running around the conflict zones with body armor and weapons. It pays well, but that's not what I wanted to be doing at that stage in life. Not to mention that I felt fortunate for having survived such environments and didn't want to push my luck.

The pity, perhaps like an NFL quarterback, is that a good spy gets better with age. Espionage is an experiential vocation. But like NFL quarterbacks, with perhaps the exceptions of Tom Brady and Drew Brees, the body begins to give way even as the mind sharpens. Like reading defenses on the football field, the greater the number of circumstances and situations to which a case officer is exposed, the more effectively they read and react to unfolding situations.

Physically, at least, I would tell you, spying is a young person's game. Too many miles to walk, people to see, adversaries to outwit, and energy to expend. And for me, even as I held commands and more senior positions, I relished carving out at least some time to be on the street, work cases, recruit agents, and be the one stealing the secrets. The physical wear of that part of the business, however, regardless of the rush it still gave me, was just something I realized I lacked the hunger and energy to do while remaining at the top of my game.

Unlike law enforcement, particularly the FBI and Secret Service, CIA officers do not necessarily take as good of care of their colleagues in securing them post-Agency work. For one thing, we do not have the domestic contacts, which retired law enforcement types have, to support a pipeline. Although who would know better how to counter so-called insider threats than a case officer whose career concerned directing such plots against our foes? Law enforcement retirees tend to secure the lion's share of senior security, intelligence consultancy, and advisory positions in the private sector. The idea of "sending a thief to catch a thief" makes sense to us, but it holds less practical appeal to the private sector. In some cities, networks of former law enforcement types have a virtual monopoly over such positions, and they do not take kindly to CIA interlopers intruding on their turf.

DoD also has an excellent network, one deliberately designed and implemented to facilitate veterans, officers, and enlisted alike in transitioning to private sector and commercial careers. They take good care of their own and appropriately enjoy massive appeal from a public thankful for their service. Too many Americans unfortunately continue to believe that CIA officers spend their time killing people and spying on their own fellow citizens.

The "afterlife" for case officers reflects the consequences of their careers. Having spent a lifetime living in the shadows, we lack the freedom to tap into public sentiment like the military does. Moreover, those same restrictions concerning exposure of your past life's work challenge how effectively you can identify your skills and experience or translate your certifications to the private sector. I've often received feedback from prospective employers concerning my CIA-approved résumé ranging from intrigue to palpable confusion. What I can share provides little detail and substance to reflect that which I can truly offer. It's a decided disadvantage when our résumés are juxtaposed with the more robust and transparent versions of our law enforcement and DoD comrades, not to mention those who have focused on security and intelligence issues in the academic and commercial sectors.

Another unfortunate reality is that among CIA officers there are cliques, generally those that perpetuate the networks one had while inside the service, and these too are hierarchal. Moreover, DO officers in particular, I regret to say, are also a rather vindictive lot. They remember slights, real and perceived, and will go out of their way to settle old scores. The SIS ranks tend to facilitate only others of their own kind.

Below SIS, there's a bit more cooperation among retirees. Most of these individuals tend to return to the USIC, often right back to the CIA as independent contractors to serve as instructors, or as contractors to fill the many open desk officer and targeting positions. There are also a large number of private companies that provide various forms of intelligence training to DoD elements and other USIC agencies. Of course, one could write, lecture, and consult, but again limited by reputation and restrictions concerning how much one can divulge.

It's a pity really that confidentiality considerations prevent the creation of a *People* magazine, *Us Weekly*, or *TMZ* program for the Agency. Perhaps ironic, but the very same people hired to protect our nation's most guarded national secrets are absolutely the biggest gossips. Whether it's who's sleeping with whom, who just lost their assignment over sexual harassment allegations, and who's leapfrogging the competition for promotions and lucrative assignments thanks to a patron or lover, CIA officers absolutely adore talking trash about their colleagues. More ironic still, for those whose day jobs demand reliable, vetted, and well-sourced intelligence, when it comes to gossip, they'll eagerly believe and pass on the most poorly sourced rumors. In fact, the more salacious, the better.

ALEX AND THE TARGETERS

rom all that I drafted and submitted to CIA for prepublication approval, the censors' greatest sensitivity concentrated on one chapter that tells the story of "Alex," a senior targeting officer whose career began as an analyst. Not that any of the material was classified, but the story touched a nerve, particularly among the DO's most powerful—those who long protected Alex, and those who recognized how this senior targeting officer's tale would reflect on the organization. I've rewritten it so as to balance acceptance of CIA's redactions with how the anecdote highlights best this book's illustration of the Clandestine Service's cultural, functional, and ethical changes.

Long a member of CIA's Senior Intelligence Service, you might recall Alex from my earlier story about Yousef. Alex was left with no road for advancement in the Directorate of Intelligence after alienating analytical colleagues, owing to poor and often biased tradecraft complemented by a pugilistic style. Instead, Alex sought refuge in the DO. Alex did this well before the post-9/11 mass exodus of analysts applying their skills as targeting officers.

Targeting officers are not case officers, and as such, are not hired for their people skills. And while today's targeting cadre is provided a core foundation in operations, and spend the majority of their careers in Headquarters, they are more analyst than operations officer. Deep in substance, they are skilled to direct the hunt for elusive targets based on all sources of intelligence, variously HUMINT from agents on the ground, foreign liaison partners, and technical collection. As such, it has become more routine that targeting officers exert significant influence when it comes to aligning resources and prioritizing. However, their recommendations concerning who should be pursued, by what means, and when, result in second- and third-order consequences, at times, for the very sources and methods used to secure the actionable intelligence that enabled whatever operation that would follow.

CIA has an amazing stable of targeting officers, but the profession is vulnerable to the same risks any analyst faces. That is, some fall in love with their own theories and become rather self-righteous in defending positions, regardless of evidence to the contrary. Others become so singularly focused on the target of their manhunt as to lose the bigger picture in terms of other operational equities and future consequences. And more dangerously, some have theories that the less scrupulous and talented will validate to themselves and others by cherry-picking intelligence that aligns with their conclusions and negates any suggested drawbacks.

In the DO, Alex secured favor in a hybrid occupation that would in time become defined as a targeting officer. Success came from an impressive command for substance. Alex likewise possessed an uncanny ability to *work* senior DO leaders, blending a head for details with seductive charisma. Traits that had failed Alex as an analyst were in fact prized by the DO. The facts were nuanced to fit the theories and preordained solutions preferred by Alex's DO superiors. Telling DO seniors what they wanted to hear and offering a deep level of detail with which they could justify their decisions upward made Alex a DO star. Moreover, the DO seniors having aligned themselves with Alex's theories, flawed that many would in fact turn out to be, would soon make their star untouchable from peer criticism and neutralize rivals. They would sink or swim together.

Alex rose ever higher in the DO, remaining in the same mission center for over two decades. Such was Alex's fame that Alex was the subject of media exposures and books regarding a reckless disregard for facts and, in some cases, human rights considerations. Buried deepest was Alex's role concerning pre-9/11 operational details denied to the FBI and other USIC agencies concerning the suspects being tracked by Alex's unit. Alex did not trust the other USIC agencies and was outspoken in frequent criticisms of their being "weak and unreliable." In reality, Alex didn't want other agencies to get the credit. But Alex was protected at the time of the investigation, as were the other responsible senior officers, since it would have likewise caused damage for the CIA executives who had empowered and deferred to them.

Over the years following 9/11, Alex overcame various bumps resulting from changes in leadership, outliving rivals and detractors to survive, and indeed prosper, including the occasional CIA director less hypnotized by Alex's act. A number would later acknowledge regrets at not having fired Alex when they could. One of the more courageous executives who had sought to remove Alex found himself relieved over a political falling out with the seventh floor before having had the opportunity.

Alex was given responsibility for one of our most important and sensitive endeavors, and was empowered with authority over both the field and Headquarters operations, managing the complex program. From the outset, Alex insisted that the foremost requirement was greater urgency, introducing a timeline that was impractical and reckless. The goal was worthy enough, but the scorched-earth process was a big risk.

Successful intelligence operations take time to mature. Just as Rome wasn't built in a day, new sources must be identified through exhaustive research, engaged with creative and often risky operational ploys, cultivated and ultimately recruited, and tested, all in a clandestine process. There is an ever-present tension in balancing aggressiveness with security. Lives are at stake. Not just the agents and collectors, but those of our countrymen whose protection will be enhanced by the continuity of intelligence these sources can provide.

With no operational training or source handling experience, Alex demanded that the team further push their agents to conduct activities that their handlers and field managers resisted as too aggressive. "Stop worrying about burning agents," Alex demanded of the team, and to those foreign partners on whose source operations we likewise relied. "Tell them to get in line or else" became the new marching orders.

Alex was presented with counterarguments, even by those handpicked from past association who Alex believed would reliably carry out orders, regardless of their personal differences. Alex was nonplussed, referred to the field officers as *weak*, favoring the term *dumbasses*, and adding a broad sampling of profanity to emphasize the point of who was in charge. The career DO officers were astonished, but powerless. "Act as if there is no tomorrow," Alex ordered. "Push them harder, and take action on their intelligence as soon as it becomes available." Even dismissing the moral and ethical obligations for recklessly endangering the sources, Alex failed to share the team's concern that with these agents would also go their collection, leaving us blind to our adversaries' plans. Dissenters were reassigned or otherwise gagged.

The reality in this case, more recently, was that the Trump White House directed CIA to address a specific requirement according to a self-imposed timeline to support a political agenda. The president wanted a "win" in time for the 2018 midterm elections. Two years later, even as Alex's goal remains unrealized, many of the collection operations Alex risked to meet that timeline were burned. Several of our most critical foreign partners redirected their efforts or otherwise pulled back from earlier cooperation in order to protect their own equities. Good agents are now dead or on the run. And targets we had hoped would lead us to the ultimate prize were removed from the battlefield to show progress and reflect metrics. We are in fact further behind now than when Alex took over. But Alex remains in charge, untouchable for the moment, protected still by those who would themselves be taken down were truth and accountability to prevail.

MODERNIZATION'S CONTINUING COSTS

B y the time John Brennan took over in March 2013, the CIA was already well along into its post-9/11 institutional decline. Brennan's detour to his CIA appointment was spent as the country's first assistant to the president for homeland security and terrorism (APHST), as he was believed at the time to be tainted for nomination to DCIA owing to his earlier support for CIA's rendition and enhanced interrogation programs. Brennan was a career analyst, although he served once as COS in the Middle East, with debatable prowess and results.

Brennan left CIA under a cloud the first time around, details about which I'll necessarily leave to others. Those circumstances, however, and his preceding experience as a station chief left him with a chip on his shoulder and an axe to grind. Over the course of President Obama's first term, Brennan foreshadowed his future intentions toward the Agency. The DO braced for the worst when he moved into the seventh floor executive suite. DO officers realized that Brennan would take the opportunity to settle old scores.

Brennan made clear his intention to change the CIA from a spy service to an intelligence agency. The difference extends beyond semantics. From the outset, DCIA Brennan declared, to the shock and horror of not merely DO officers, that the business of the CIA was no longer to steal secrets. It was not merely a misconstrued soundbite from his NPR interview in which it was captured, but a genuine reflection of his direction, one he would routinely repeat with the workforce. Brennan's emphasis was that

CIA employees should consider themselves first and foremost intelligence officers rather than identifying with their particular directorate or career service. It was part of a calculated approach for turning an espionage service into a bureaucracy and eroding the DO.

Were Brennan earnest in his intent to engender greater pride in the organization, I would have cheered the sentiment. As a former Marine, I had been disappointed that the CIA did not enjoy the same sense of pride and elitism. Every Marine can recite at length details of the Corps' birthday and legend. And we can sing the hymn, toasting together at our infamous yearly celebrations. Few Agency officers can tell you when the CIA was born, name the first director, or likewise narrate any of its daring tales, no few of which are well documented for public account; yes, including some of the better ones.

Brennan could have more aptly sought the truism Marines share, regardless their career specialty, that "all Marines were riflemen" and take pride in the title, Marine. But all Marines are in fact trained as riflemen, from the snipers to the cooks. However, CIA officers are trained to various requirements as related to their particular specialties, be they case officers, analysts, support, or technical officers. But then again, so are members of the other US military branches. Not everyone in the Air Force is a pilot, but they seem justifiably a pretty proud bunch. So that we are all CIA officers and, as such, part of an elite spy service protecting the nation, I could have certainly and happily embraced.

Instead, Brennan proclaimed the need to "modernize" the Agency, facilitating the policy-focused and bureaucratic role he sought for it. Rather than serve in the shadows to enable its apolitical and clandestine functions, Brennan sought to secure the CIA a more prominent and public seat at the table with the likes of State, Defense, and an increasingly influential Department of Treasury. In practice, this meant diminishing the DO's role and particularly the influence of case officers in running the operational divisions.

I spent a fair bit of time sitting in briefings delivered to DCIA Brennan, occasionally providing them myself. He struck me like the man bullied as a child who sought revenge later in life once he became a prosperous adult. During briefings, he came across as sullen, caustic, and condescending, making no pretense regarding his personal sentiments concerning the senior officers who sat around him. You knew where you stood, at least. Brennan was quick to use profanity and not shy about threatening careers. He made analytical arguments to contradict the points with which he disagreed, despite lacking the facts, maintaining an air that he was the smartest person in the room at all times.

Brennan's ultimate trump card to whatever compelling argument with which he disagreed was his oft-referenced special relationship to President Obama. When facts no longer supported his case, and frequently he was the lone voice of dissent among other USIC principals, Brennan made it clear he was representing the president's views. It was as if to suggest that no one else knew the president better, not even the other cabinet secretaries. It was ironic to the workforce that, at times, consensus among the USIC principals endorsed a course of action recommended by the CIA careerists in which its own director was the single dissenting voice.

I will give him credit for carrying his organization's mail to such meetings, which enabled the consideration of dissenting points. Only, he was the lone dissenter, and it reflected a dysfunctional system that did little to help the CIA's credibility, not to mention workforce cohesion. Rather than embrace the talking points his experts would spend hours perfecting to support, Brennan's delivery of his agency's findings would let our written work speak for itself, only to punch holes in the conclusions, leaning again on his "special relationship" with the president in offering the "correct" position.

Some historians might suggest this was reminiscent of US Secretary of State Henry Stimson's shortsighted 1929 decision to shutter the State Department's Cipher Bureau. It seems that Stimson thought this type of surveillance unethical, prompting him to remark, "Gentlemen do not read each others' mail." Indeed, Brennan's preference was to rely on foreign partners as opposed to having CIA directly assume the risks in running aggressive, unilateral, clandestine operations. But Brennan's actions were less derived from Stimson's genuine sense of propriety and naivete, misdirected as it might have been. Rather, Brennan chose some rather questionable and ethically dubious operational endeavors of his own. Surprisingly for an analyst, some had been pursued without the due diligence that might have better informed understanding of the ensuing exposure to extensive political, security, and operational risks. Such was the case with CIA's adventure, or perhaps misadventure, concerning Syria.

Brennan placed faith in his own personal relationships and his ability to operate as a problem solver through direct engagement with senior intelligence and security service counterparts and political figures in the Middle East. In practice, and in direction, this was Brennan's vision for the CIA's future, versus the traditional focus on clandestine intelligence collection. Brennan wanted to be the key himself. Covert action was still a preferred tool, but not unilaterally, rather, by enabling allies and proxies in whom he mistakenly believed.

Neglecting his own analytical upbringing and tradecraft, Brennan's vision was fundamentally flawed from the outset by the gross overestimation of his own personal gravitas, the influence of his chosen counterparts, and the historic and political realities on the ground. This was illustrated best through his bromance with Saudi Arabian interior minister Prince Mohammed bin Nayef (MbN). Not that MbN wasn't a committed partner and possessed good intentions, by American standards anyway, but that he likewise carried significant political baggage, not to mention personal demons.

Brennan dismissed and controlled reporting concerning MbN so as not to lower the minister's stature in the eyes of the White House and Washington policy community. Rather, having backed that horse, Brennan could not allow negative or even critical reporting that questioned the Saudi prince's reliability to advance Washington's aims. Unfortunately for Brennan, the US, and the Syrian people, palace intrigue enabled by MbN's personal and political baggage undermined his performance and in turn his authority. But Brennan was all in with MbN, to the extent that he diminished the influence and gravitas of his station chiefs. Brennan intervened repeatedly, directly, and unilaterally in engaging MbN and other senior counterparts around the world. Station chiefs were forced to play catch-up.

If a service chief can regularly and directly lobby the DCIA for his or her agenda, why bother dealing with the COS? It would be the same were a foreign minister to cut out an American ambassador from dealings with the US president. Complicating things further, stations often had to turn to their local counterparts following a Brennan call or visit in order to fully understand to what the DCIA had committed them. Rather than being part of the planning from the beginning, stations were required to keep up, occasionally relying on their clandestine sources just to find out what their own leadership had in mind, rather than what the local government was planning.

In the case of Saudi Arabia, history shows that by disregarding the warnings and limiting reporting concerning Saudi internal issues and MbN's vulnerabilities, the CIA failed to foresee the rise of Saudi's current crown prince and de facto leader, Prince Mohammed bin Salman (MbS). As a result, the CIA made no effort to cultivate its own relationship with MbS, or even make the effort to leave him with a favorable impression. Such a channel was available when then deputy Crown Prince Mohammed was also his father's minister of defense in a war with Yemen that depended on US material and intelligence support. And knowing how unabashedly CIA favored MbN, don't you think MbS bore that in mind in subsequent engagements? Once again, here was a case where the raw reporting offered the clues, but analysts, or in this case the CIA director himself, spun the reporting to align to personal interests and views.

A good case officer will be the first to agree that balance in all things is worthy, and that the CIA's clandestine operations should be the collection of last resort if safer means are available. Brennan's reorganization, personnel decisions, control over what the CIA disseminated, and risk aversion solidified cultural changes and those to the organization's power dynamic. This accelerated the downward slide of the Agency's place as the premier HUMINT agency. Aversion to HUMINT, as reflected in his abhorrence to "stealing secrets" or dealing with less savory agents, drew resources away from collection, and further diminished HUMINT's value to analysts and targeters.

Putting teeth behind his directives, Brennan pushed out senior DO officers who resisted modernization, the first casualty having been the deputy director for operations, or DDO, who functioned as chief of CIA's Clandestine Service. Although this particular DDO was not a fan of mine, I credit him in refusing to surrender the DO's culture, legacy, and ethos for his own professional fortunes. As a quick aside, when this particular officer was initially appointed DDO over Ian, whose temperament and many skeletons impeded his own advancement, I recall Ian having had a tremendous fit, subsequently sulking at being passed over, and ultimately remarking, "Fine, so clearly the position's prerequisites were being fat, dumb, and ugly." Seniority does not always equate to maturity and class.

Today, the DDO might be the titular head of the Clandestine Service, but it is no longer the chief of its operations. Modernization changed the chain of command. Whereas division chiefs reported to, and derived their authority from, the DDO, today's assistant directors for CIA who run the mission centers report directly to the DCIA. They antagonize the DDO at their own risk, of course, but while stripped of much of the position's direct operational command, that office still maintains control over resources, personnel assignments, promotions, and tradecraft. Moreover, the DDO can raise objections to the DCIA over particular operational initiatives, maintains an approving authority in the chain of command concerning covert action activities, and can therefore be a spoiler if the assistant directors do not render to the DDO the appropriate pound of flesh. But it's the DCIA, not the DDO, who appoints the assistant directors, and makes or breaks their careers.

On the surface, modernization required the fusion of the operational and analytic elements that variously worked geographic and functional issues. Having on many occasions worked in or with the CIA's Counter-terrorism Center (CTC), the idea of this fusion was not that to which I ever took issue. CTC was a model of success in proving the fusion concept, though it took time, and its leadership was not always willing to be transparent and collaborative, even with other CIA stakeholders, let alone the USIC.

Brennan took this a step further and assigned career analysts to over-see operational centers. Moreover, he selected analysts who shared his vision, since not all did. Those operations officers he installed into com-mand positions were often subordinate to career analysts. Such officers were either all too willing to compromise their beliefs for ambition, or hoped to quietly ride out the storm. But in the process, the CIA walked away from HUMINT operations that Brennan considered too politically sensitive, embarrassing, or simply unseemly, some particularly important and productive operations at that. This ended collection that was saving lives, the damage from which the CIA continues to suffer.

STRATEGY, TACTICS, TOOLS, AND BLOODLUST

The US Intelligence Community preaches sustained pressure as its stra-tegic counterterrorism mantra, a euphemism for a kinetic-dependent approach against terrorist leadership. CIA's Counterterrorism Mission Center branded the catchphrase "Preempt, Defeat, Disrupt," etching those words on the lanyards once issued to its cadre. Every presidential adminis-tration since 9/11 focused on preemptive strikes against terrorists in their foreign sanctuaries before they could attack the US homeland, and this is still the case today. The intent is to disrupt planning and capabilities by forcing terrorists to spend more time on survival and less on operations while we concurrently remove their most important leaders and operatives from the battlefield. Depriving groups of key talent results in less experienced and capable operatives moving up who theoretically pose less of a threat and would be easier to neutralize. Complementing the offensive strategy was an overall hardening of America's defenses around key infrastructure and potential terrorist targets.

There is ample evidence regarding this strategy's effectiveness. For one thing, as far as we know, neither al-Qa'ida nor any other foreign-based terrorist organization has planned, directed, and executed a major successful attack on the US homeland, at least nothing approaching 9/11's scale. But there is also evidence to reflect its failings. Neither the US nor other Western countries escaped attacks entirely, owing largely to ever-adapting terrorist tactics with which we ourselves have been slow and limited in countering. And while this strategy accounts for high numbers of terrorists removed, there seems to be an endless succession of those assuming their places. The numbers in fact are expanding. The world has not necessarily become a safer place, as we realized during a series of brutal ISIS attacks beginning in Paris, some fourteen years after 9/11.

There is no arguing that America became very good at locating and removing terrorists in the ungoverned sanctuaries of far off lands, particularly in South Asia, the Middle East, and Africa. Dead terrorists indeed often take their plans, contacts, and means of communications with them to the grave, given their focus on security in countering the credible effectiveness of Western intelligence services. But it's arguable that the capability became the strategy, and brought with it diminishing returns.

"Pat," the CIA chief for one particularly all-important capability, has managed the program since practically its inception. A technical specialist versus operational officer by training or background, Pat became a passionate advocate for the capability, one for which Pat's own blood, sweat, tears, and innovation were undisputedly critical. But Pat's oversized role in determining when, where, and how often it was best used lacked any understanding of its strategic operational and political consequences on the ground, and the damage it often caused.

Though a DO officer, Pat was neither trained in operations or analysis nor had any credible experience with intelligence reporting. A technical officer with an engineer's mentality, Pat looked purely at metrics and machinery, success measured tactically but not strategically. Over the years, Pat created an enormous and generously funded empire, along with a cult of personality. Those working in Pat's department loved or hated their chief. Pat was not one for delegating authority and so chose favorites, generally those sharing the same outlook.

With this dynamic came an immunity from accountability that Pat used to bulldoze over CIA elements focused on collection and analysis. But to Pat, metrics didn't lie. Neither did the gripping video presentations known around the community as "pred porn." Pat successfully advocated the hammer's use in a Whac-A-Mole application to degrade enemy capabilities. This "find, fix, finish" approach would become the counterterrorism default for CIA leadership and the White House. By doing so, CIA traded away the preservation and pursuit of upstream operational leads and international collaboration to irrevocably destroy such groups. As a result, we rolled the problem downhill like a snowball. New terrorist recruits signed up to take revenge, autonomous al-Qa'ida franchises appeared around the globe, ISIS's growth was neglected until it reigned over a vast caliphate and could conduct complex terrorist operations across Europe, and fewer international partners could politically risk the damage at home from cooperating with the US.

Ironically, Pat was on a glide path toward removal while late into DCIA Brennan's reign. Two successive Counterterrorism Center chiefs realized Pat had become too inflexible and an increasing mission liability. The risks were exacerbated when Pat further encroached on the independent targeting and analytical teams that assessed the program's impact and merit. Pat's teams began to replicate their own analytical teams, which spun and cherry-picked intelligence to make their case of the capability's use for each occasion, and validated their own successes. Pat's team was grading its own homework and blurring the conditions it needed for striking a given target.

More vexing still for Pat's superiors, their program manager began openly attacking the DCIA's interest in limiting and thereafter reducing the capability's use as "treason." Sheltered from such knowledge, Brennan would actually stand in the way of Pat's removal. Brennan feared Pat could do further political damage to him on Capitol Hill, where the officer had become almost a folk legend on both sides of the aisle. Indeed, sitting among the supporting CIA team during one of Pat's congressional meetings, senators from both sides of the aisle lavished Pat with praise for making America safer, a rather questionable conclusion based on the realities.

But the most poignant vignette occurred during President Trump's first visit to CIA Headquarters after his 2016 election victory. The president spent most of his time on Pat's floor where the capability was briefed and he was shown videos depicting the program's "greatest hits." Trump was transfixed. Pat relished Trump's satisfaction and declared, "I'll kill anyone you tell me to, Mr. President." President Trump was delighted.

There certainly remain vast areas of ungoverned space across the likes of Afghanistan, Pakistan, Syria, and parts of Africa, in which transnational groups such as al-Qa'ida and its affiliates, and ISIS, can thrive. The CIA's capability remains an important tool in America's counterterrorism toolbox and should not be altogether abandoned. But in response to the pressure, terrorist adversaries have adjusted. Working within their limitations, terrorist groups have adopted the guidance of deceased, American-born al-Qa'ida preacher Anwar al-Awlaki to invest foremost in propaganda and influence to incite localized "do-it-yourself" attacks rather than grand, centrally directed and resourced 9/11-scale operations. Ironically, our terrorist foes have adopted a more fiscally viable long-term plan while we debate an all or nothing kinetic approach.

While awaiting the opportunity to reconstitute from within their sanctuaries, come the day American pressure decreases, terrorist guidance and example inspires lone wolves who are less vulnerable to discovery because they are absent the centralized command, interdependency, or communications. More disconcerting still, such lone wolves and threats come increasingly from among White supremacist and ultranationalist groups replicating the models al-Qa'ida and ISIS have championed while pursuing domestic terrorism.

This is not purely a CIA issue, but the strategy, much of it developed and sold with success to the White House by the Agency, is ultimately a political choice that existentially altered the spy service's character. American leaders took what appeared to be the easier and less politically charged path, too often at the expense of more pressing challenges.

My personal experience likewise lends to the certainty that absent our ability to change the strategic conditions, terrorists will adapt to purely kinetic tactics. But the argument should not be all kinetic, or no kinetic, or about discarding the preemption concept. Rather, we require a truly "whole of government" model that employs a balanced approach that emphasizes soft power, reconstruction, governance, training, and messaging that complements surgically employed kinetic tools, but delivered under covert Title 50 authorities, or by the US military.

The 9/11 Commission Report is not a perfect document, but it offers much for discussion and consideration. For one thing, it addresses the critical need to recognize the battlefield as extending beyond the kinetic realm: the need to "Engage the Struggle of Ideas," acknowledging that "The United States is heavily engaged in the Muslim world and will be for many years to come." Panel members were alarmed to find how support for the United States plummeted among those in Islamic countries so quickly after 9/11, writing: "By 2003, polls showed that the bottom has fallen out of support for America in most of the Muslim world. Negative views of the U.S. among Muslims, which had been largely limited to countries in the Middle East, have spread. . . . Many of these views are at best uninformed about the United States and, at worst, informed by cartoonish stereotypes, the coarse expression of a fashionable 'Occidentalism' among intellectuals who caricature U.S. values and policies. Local newspapers and the few influential satellite broadcasters—like al Jazeera—often reinforce the jihadist theme that portrays the United States as anti-Muslim." The report further recognized the compounding impact of harsh economic conditions that jihadists so effectively exploited, acknowledging, "In short, the United States has to help defeat an ideology, not just a group of people, and we must do so under difficult circumstances."

The report recommended, "The U.S. government must define what the message is, what it stands for. We should offer an example of moral leadership in the world, committed to treat people humanely, abide by the rule of law, and be generous and caring to our neighbors.... That vision of the future should stress life over death: individual, educational, and economic opportunity. This vision includes widespread political participation and contempt for indiscriminate violence. It includes respect for the rule of law, openness in discussing differences, and tolerance for opposing points of view." Juxtapose this against how the very communities we seek to influence with our values perceived President Trump's social media comments. Perfect fodder for use by terrorist recruiters and propagandists.

The incoming Biden administration has demonstrated an intent to reexamine the US counterterrorist strategy with an eye on achieving a greater balance between hard and soft power and a more holistic use of America's tools. That balance should not eliminate the use of preemptive, kinetic strikes as executed by the CIA when necessary in the absence of alternatives, and when the threat demands.

It's appropriate for the US to find a more sustainable counterterrorism strategy that efficiently achieves its goals without disproportionately expending finite resources. Terrorism has not gone away, nor will it anytime soon. If anything, the threat has become more complex and interwoven with great power competition, even as violent, domestic extremism from White supremacists and ultranationalists threatens us at home. Rather than entirely abandon counterterrorism—our preemptive strategy and the use of kinetic tools—the US needs balance between hard and soft power and the cooperation of foreign partners in sharing the responsibility.

Referred to as "capacity building" in policy circles, the US will need to enable, inform, train, and often arm our foreign partners, asking them to take the lead where the threat lies within their own borders. The foreign partners act as force multipliers enabled by US intelligence and military elements, as the US did rather successfully with the coalition to defeat the Islamic State in Iraq and Syria.

That said, it's not so simple. Money, matériel, training, and intelligence are currency when working with foreign partners. "Capacity building," though far less costly in blood and treasure than sending Americans abroad into combat, can be conflated with "nation building" or foreign aid—issues fraught with domestic political liabilities. Some opponents might charge that such cooperation requires the US to get in bed with despots. Or, that the US is doling out largesse better used at home.

Ultimately, the US needs a broader strategy that addresses the conditions from which extremism rises. The CIA has the tools to inform this strategy through effective intelligence collection and analysis. Killing all of the potential sources rather than trying to cultivate some, as has been the default, will fall short of achieving that mission. Drones should still fly, since in reality, their primary intelligence mission is not killing, but rather collecting information as intelligence, surveillance, and reconnaissance platforms.

The 9/11 Commission Report also observed: "The United States must do more to communicate its message. Reflecting on Bin Ladin's success in reaching Muslim audiences, Richard Holbrooke wondered, 'How can a man in a cave outcommunicate the world's leading communications society?'" The panel members' recommendation: "Just as we did in the Cold War, we need to defend our ideals abroad vigorously. America does stand up for its values. The United States defended, and still defends, Muslims against tyrants and criminals in Somalia, Bosnia, Kosovo, Afghanistan, and Iraq. If the United States does not act aggressively to define itself in the Islamic world, the extremists will gladly do the job for us."

So why don't we do a better job of using covert action for messaging and influence? Americans have certainly been on the receiving end of

Russian denial and deception campaigns over recent years in which Moscow sought to influence our political views and create wedges within our society through aggressive disinformation. It's a technique as old as espionage itself, one in which you seek to increase your own security by negating versus overpowering your adversary's threat. Addition through subtraction, that is precisely what the Russians have tried to do in weakening the US by distracting it internally, causing divisions, and influencing opinions.

Official public diplomacy can and should be complemented by focused covert messaging. Perhaps "winning the hearts and minds" of those who perceive the US as an enemy is too grand of a goal. But if it's true that politics is always local, we can certainly effect campaigns that appeal to the practical needs, interests, and consequences among the places and stratum of the global community from which these threats arise.

The simple truth behind why we're not doing more of this is that the covert influence field fails to attract our best and brightest. For the CIA, winning the hearts and minds is not nearly as glamorous as it was during the Cold War, stealing secrets, or removing terrorists from the battlefield. And bureaucratically, it's hard to measure its impact, such as those people you dissuade from an alternatively violent path. Compare that to the hard kinetic numbers, not to mention the sexy strike videos.

In turn, securing money, people, and top cover to invest such resources is a risk for CIA seniors. Far easier to make an argument for funds and staff that procures and supports the gadgets and hardware that provide a clear body count. In the end, programs concerning ideas and influence make for great rhetoric and talking points, but the proof is in the hard numbers. It's ironic that such psychological operations were fundamental in the CIA's OSS roots, and remained a key element of our military's order of battle psychological operations. Our investment in these arts receded and ultimately disappeared following the end of the Cold War inasmuch as defeating Communism had been its principal focus.

Another recommendation of the 9/11 Commission Report: "Where Muslim governments, even those who are friends, do not respect these principles, the United States must stand for a better future. One of the lessons of the long Cold War was that short-term gains in cooperating with the most repressive and brutal governments were too often outweighed by long-term setbacks for America's stature and interests." Consider this in the context of the Trump White House's position on Saudi Arabia's assassination of foreign dissidents such as Jamal Khashoggi.

The 9/11 Commission Report recognized that "terrorism is not caused by poverty. Indeed, many terrorists come from relatively well-off families. Yet when people lose hope, when societies break down, when countries fragment, the breeding grounds for terrorism are created. Backward economic policies and repressive political regimes slip into societies that are without hope, where ambition and passions have no constructive outlet." As such, it recommended, "A comprehensive U.S. strategy to counter terrorism should include economic policies that encourage development, more open societies, and opportunities for people to improve the lives of their families and to enhance prospects for their children's future."

An Intelligence War requires America's use of all means of national power in a consistent but proportionately resourced long game, namely soft, kinetic, legal, diplomatic, and covert, to name but a few. You can't win a counterterrorism fight via attrition, but neither can you close your eyes and wish away the dangers. Synergy is required to align messaging and influence campaigns with a broader strategy. Though a negatively charged word under the Trump administration, soft power is necessary to rebuild what we lay to waste as we pursue our enemies.

The Biden White House has, to its credit, demonstrated an interest in the greater use of diplomacy and multilateral collaboration. But will it also invest the required financial resources and foreign assistance that Americans might balk at?

A counterterrorism Marshall Plan of sorts is needed so that the ruins we leave behind on the battlefield do not merely give rise to new generations of terrorists. It's not quick, and it's not cheap, but it leverages our advantages against terrorist organizations over the long term. Our long-term investments on the Korean Peninsula and NATO are good models.

Our kinetic tactics likewise require adjustment if our aim is to destroy these groups. The question isn't if we should undertake kinetic operations, but when, particularly should leaving a terrorist target on the battlefield offer a means to further intelligence collection or land a bigger fish. But doing so comes with political risk. In the current atmosphere, neither CIA nor DoD will incur the risk of allowing targets to remain on the battlefield in order to maintain collection and work upstream. The danger of leaving these targets in place is political, as it leaves leaders accountable for any ensuing terrorist operations that the group might undertake, or so goes the fear.

Pat's approach to such issues has been one of prioritizing industrial efficiency that often dismisses relevant intelligence or political considerations in the name of technical efficiency. Once having found a target in the capability's crosshairs, Pat becomes anxious to move on. Pat didn't want the platforms used to keep an eye on the target indefinitely. Pat's argument is always to take action and move to the next target. Whac-A-Mole is therefore a volume-oriented approach. One less operative on the battlefield: metrics.

The CIA's hammer is a valuable tool, but one that should be used sparingly, to strategic effect, and in the absence of alternatives. Its overuse has diminishing returns, increasing the rolls of those eager to take arms against Americans rather than diminishing them. Moreover, its abuse as a default taints the service and degrades its critical role in safeguarding America's security as a spy service. CIA should be assigned missions that no other USG element can accomplish, not just because we happen to be better or faster at our jobs, as the 9/11 Commission Report observed.

CIA's robust capability has come at a price to its focus, ethos, and culture. And with it, more practically, its effectiveness as a spy service. I regret to say that, while sexy and appealing, the capability's technical success, impressive metrics, and astonishing videos inflamed the bloodlust of some among those empowered to unleash its fury—a tool that is, by law and policy, a weapon of last resort. In turn, its abuse as a strategy, as opposed to a tool, has diverted the CIA from the mission of stealing our adversaries' secrets and divining and disrupting the threats they pose. And today, our enemies are not limited to terrorists or even nation states.

America's counterterrorism strategy should heed Frederick the Great's warning: "He who defends everything, defends nothing." In that regard, the US has overinvested its limited resources in counterterrorism at the expense of other critical requirements. The COVID-19 pandemic is just one example, as is that from climate change and domestic terrorism, not to mention the rise of threats from our traditional adversaries: Russia, China, North Korea, and Iran. Even as we look to implement appropriate corrections, we found during the Trump years how the USIC was being realigned from counterterrorism disproportionately against illegal immigration and counternarcotics. Targets that suited the Trump administration's political interests, but not what posed the greatest threat. Today, we must likewise add the urgent threat of domestic terrorism to this list.

TRANSITIONING INTO THE FUTURE

May you live in interesting times," a Confucian quote, is meant really as a curse. But all times are interesting when it comes to world events, and there is no shortage of job security for intelligence services at the forefront of the ever-present international crisis. No day passes without some crisis somewhere. Whether the challenges are geopolitical, military, or economic, the reality is that the world in which we live is a fiercely competitive and often dangerous place. The isolationism that placed America in such jeopardy leading up to World War II has unfortunately resurfaced as a panacea for our country's challenges. As a major power and international stakeholder on all matters, if not the most powerful and influential country in the world, there is no escape for the United States from the world's dangers. Choosing to ignore these dangers only invites those threats to come knocking, quite literally, on our door.

At its best, the CIA operates in the shadows to protect America from the host of prevailing threats we face every single day. There are always terrorists contemplating how to attack us, as are the Russians, Chinese, Iranians, and North Koreans. Such conventional state foes ready their kinetic weapons, while they likewise actively attack us with cyber means and disinformation campaigns that are aimed to weaken, distract, and undermine our system and values. It's just how the world works, which is why we have, and will always need, a secret, civilian, overseas intelligence service.

Whatever your thoughts regarding the morality of spying, I did it to the highest ethical standards, and for a virtuous cause, just as the Agency preaches, though perhaps does not consistently practice. That's not to say the CIA is without its faults, as certainly is illustrated in these pages. Nor should the CIA be above scrutiny. The beauty of our country's laws and character is that we are, as Lincoln said of our country in his address at Gettysburg, "a government of the people, by the people, for the people."

CIA officers should be proud of who they work for and what they do, and they should be entitled to a sense of elitism and esprit de corps. The Agency is not, as some detractors suggest, and some concerned Americans without insight fear, a rogue organization of miscreants. Rather, it's composed of your neighbors, people who respect both the letter and spirit of the authorities and laws that guide their work, people who risk their lives to serve you. Along with their families, they incur sacrifices and hardships of the tallest order, all for the satisfaction of protecting our homeland.

I had grown to believe that the CIA was healing, becoming a better place now than it was in my final years. The toxic political climate of the Trump years, though, reversed the gains I had begun to see. Other reforms remained slow, or were turned back given the disproportionate influence of the predominantly White, male officers among the senior ranks who abused their positions and power to incur sexual favors or discriminate. Some notable offenders remain in positions of authority. A number of them have sought to reinvent themselves.

One example is a former seventh floor DO executive named "Bernard," notable for his exceptional capacity to tack with the political winds to advance his professional fortunes. Infamous for his dalliances, he ironically became an outspoken defender of a harassment-free workplace. While at the forefront enforcing modernization from his seventh floor perch during Brennan's tenure, he likewise became its greatest critic upon the DCIA's departure in a revisionist accounting worthy of a literary award, were it not for the poor writing.

Unfortunate, since Bernard was a capable officer and considerate leader in his day. He evinced operational acumen and no small degree of daring under difficult conditions and was a loyal advocate for subordinates. Like Ian, Bernard was another casualty to success and outsized ego. I don't dismiss the possibility that it's an inherent vulnerability in the psychological profile of case officers. But once having climbed the ladder, Bernard moved to settle scores with rivals, deflect accountability for his own transgressions, and reward sycophants—all while presenting himself to the workforce as a bold innovator and intellectual.

In reality, Bernard championed a number of costly and ineffective concepts that were appropriately slow rolled, ignored, and thereafter abandoned upon his departure from the seventh floor suite. Besides his continuing sexual escapades and impractical initiatives, Bernard might be best known to junior officers for his long and rambling messages to the workforce—pages of rambling, stream-of-consciousness prose replete with errors in syntax, grammar, and spelling. Practically no one read them, skipping to the end in order to see the latest personnel announcements.

Despite the trappings of full transparency in personnel decisions, promotions, assignments, awards, and medals, the hard truth is that favoritism and the settling of old scores remains pervasive in the Agency. The CIA's modern, high-tech rebranding now seen in streaming ads to attract new recruits and repair its image is the makeup applied to a system that continues to recycle senior officers such as Ian, Bernard, Pat, and Alex, leaders who are guilty of running their commands like personal empires and cults of personality. Like these four, there are others in leadership who are just as difficult to remove given their political followings and their knowledge of where the bodies are buried, literally and figuratively in their case.

I was hopeful after having finally witnessed the advancement of a female CIA operations officer to the role of DCIA, and that of another into the role of operations chief (DDO). However, I found DCIA Gina Haspel and DDO "Vicki" both to be disappointments. Both struck me as officers who in the past had good intentions. They both certainly had the ability to recognize the issues expressed in these pages. I had enough interaction with DCIA Haspel to know she is smart, substantive, and mindful of the true nature of the CIA's mission and likewise wary of pretenders and opportunists. Aside from lacking a personal past with, and as such tangible influence over, President Trump, Haspel was the most qualified DCIA in my professional lifetime since William Casey, who had served as an OSS operative in World War II.

It's not that no one around her failed to encourage Ms. Haspel to seize the moment. I know for a fact that some did. Her answer to them, unfortunately, was an acknowledgment of the CIA's existing problems and the required antidote, but the refrain that "it was not the time." To borrow an oft-used sentiment, if not now, then when? If not her, then who? Ms. Haspel's pretext for inaction was the need to secure even greater autonomy, presumably from then President Trump, and the time to further galvanize her ability to take on the existing Agency powers. Despite solidifying her position internally with a loyal ally leading the DO, and appeasing President Trump throughout her tenure despite the ills he wreaked on the country's security and the workforce for which she was responsible, she never acted. The resulting loss of hope for a generation of officers expecting better of the CIA's first woman director, and the first career DO officer in the seat since the early 1970s, drove still other disillusioned senior operations officers to head for the door, myself included.

Unfortunately, Ms. Haspel had never been known for standing up to authority or dissenting over matters of conscience, though she had no such problem speaking caustically with subordinates. A good soldier, she always did as told, which was clear in her predisposition to align CIA priorities and resources with Trump's political interests versus with what her own experts recommend. Her willingness to be the president's cheerleader while indulging his maligning of the Agency's integrity was bad enough.

DCIA Haspel's obsequious compromises were not merely disappointing but dangerous for US national security. I was not surprised by media reports alleging her obstruction and interference with finished intelligence on Russian election meddling and malign behavior. That Haspel would make it harder for CIA analysts to produce assessments that diverged from Trump's narrative concerning his relationship with Vladimir Putin was consistent with my experience at her prioritizing the personal interests of her superiors over mission. Nor was I surprised at her willingness to permit the Trump White House to insert retired Army brigadier general and Trump campaign advisor Bert Mizusawa into the chief operating officer's (COO) suite. In a betrayal of the workforce, Mizusawa was positioned to use his access to the vast holdings of personnel, security, psychological profiles, and medical files to identify perceived "deep staters" in the CIA. Had Trump won in 2020, I expect CIA would have suffered a loyalty-inspired purge exceeding that of Turner's infamous 1977 Halloween Massacre.

Neither were DCIA Haspel and DDO Vicki immune from suffering some of the same faults as their predecessors in preferring their own camp followers and subscribing to hallway perceptions about others for whom they lacked firsthand knowledge. DCIA Haspel and Vicki failed to rid the Agency of its worse elements, with Ian, Bernard, Alex, and Pat being at the top of an unfortunately rather long list. Neither the DCIA nor Vicki was willing to address the old corporate, cultural impediments at the CIA, break down the walls of the old boys' club, or root out the systemic racism in the organization. If anything, they merely added the status quo to their own old girls' club of sycophants.

Vicki was a Haspel favorite and long-time personal friend who, like Gina, lacked extensive street credibility with the DO workforce. Vicki served for a time as Haspel's acting deputy director (DDCIA), with word trickling down that the DCIA hoped to make it a permanent appointment. Instead, perhaps concerned with optics for Trump, who would likely not appreciate having women as both the DCIA and DDCIA, Vicki was formally appointed DDO, a lesser position. In the end, as DDO, Vicki was cautious about making enemies, having strived throughout her career to avoid controversy and get along with everyone. It's easier to be everyone's friend and avoid mistakes when you don't make decisions. On the bright side, Vicki was less abrasive to brief than was Gina. In the DCIA's case, I believe she fell victim to hubris, believing the compromises to preserve her position were in the service's best interests. But the only interest it served was hers, in that it kept her in the job of DCIA.

Today, and tomorrow, we need CIA more than ever to be our first, last, and sometimes only line of defense against the myriad threats to our way of life. The Agency has its bad apples, and its failures are sensational, and often costly. Such failures frequently do not come from within a vacuum but rather are the consequence of dubious White House direction and the ambition, hubris, and closed-mindedness of the CIA's own leadership. Truth be told, CIA has some of the most talented, dedicated, and brilliant patriots any generation has ever boasted. Success in thwarting the threats from terrorists and powerful rivals alike, and global scourges such as pandemics and climate change, depends on making the right choices at the right time, decisions that depend on insight. And such insight takes time, requires no small degree of risk and patience, and at the end of the day, is driven by HUMINT collected from foreign agents, something no organization in the world does better than the CIA.

As I hope these pages illustrate, espionage even at its best is neither easy nor risk-free. Those who conduct it must be held accountable and face consequences, but the CIA must also be allowed to fail. Even the best planned operations do sometimes. It's the human nature of HUMINT and the confluence of circumstances and conditions that create risks we can't always control. The CIA workforce should be protected from risk aversion, particularly the political sort, and receive support for its ability to assume and manage well-considered risks. That takes knowing that one won't be hung out to dry as a scapegoat should things not go as planned. It's a lot easier to speak truth to power when the system is trusted to protect those who do.

While congressional oversight might be a pain, and goodness knows I rarely found my own appearances on the Hill much fun, it's healthy for the CIA and necessary for the country. But oversight needs credibility to secure the trust of the American people, as well as the Agency's. The CIA needs the public's buy-in that what it does in secret for an open society is lawful and in their interests. Some matters must remain secret for the public's welfare, but the people need the confidence that such clandestine activity is vetted by the nation's elected representatives based on national security requirements and the law, not partisan politics. Given how toxic the political climate has been, such trust among the CIA, the Hill, and the public might take both time and deeds to restore. The process, however, need not be confrontational. When it works right, and I've seen it happen, senators and congressional members behind their committee's closed doors show the capacity to meet their responsibility as the CIA meets theirs, in a politically neutral and cooperative fashion aimed to strengthen, not weaken, what the CIA does for the country.

The CIA similarly benefits from a strong, independent Office of the Inspector General (OIG). One that has the respect and standing to assure us that the CIA is operating by the right standards, and when the CIA is not, creates an environment for those with stories to tell to feel safe to come forward. It should be staffed by intelligence professionals who have walked in the shoes of those they review. Inspections and investigations should focus on righting wrongs, when they arise, and making the organization better at its job, not settling old scores.

However, if deserved, there should be consequences for responsible individuals when things go terribly wrong—failures caused by negligence, incompetence, ambition, or closed-mindedness to the truth.

The CIA will also have to embrace its ability to adjust to the dynamic security threats facing the nation and innovate tailored strategies and tactics. The greatest day-to-day threats to our security of late have been as much if not more derived from global pandemics, climate change, domestic terrorism, and social injustice as they have from the designs of foreign powers and external transnational organizations. COVID-19 is not likely to be the last pandemic we will face in our lifetimes. And climate change is like a ticking time bomb given its direct impact on water, energy, agriculture, food supplies, and land erosion that some countries might see the need to address with militaristic versus economic or diplomatic solutions.

While China is indeed rising as a threat to our global influence and the security of our East Asian allies, requiring more of our country's attention and resources, we must see it in context. China's own prosperity requires a reasonably healthy America, economically at least. Admittedly an oversimplification, China needs perpetual growth to counter the internal thirst for political freedoms. The country is simply too huge for its Communist government to ever put down a mass, civil revolt, a lesson learned from the past.

Russia, Iran, and North Korea fare best when the US is in universal political, economic, and social decline, and will only do more to damage us internally. China is more of an adversary and competitor than an enemy, though likewise eager to match, exceed, or weaken our own military strength and international influence.

On its present course, given its divergent aspirations, ideology, and need to settle history's humiliations, China will not become America's friend. But we ignore China at our peril should its leaders ever believe their generally conservative risk calculus has changed in the face of

American weakness. Still, there is room to work with China's challenges using strategies informed by good intelligence collection.

Some pundits warn of a Chinese-Russian alliance against the US, but a history of violence between the two countries and a shared border of over two thousand miles, complicated by a multiplicity of other international borders, stand in the way of a genuine, lasting Chinese-Russian alliance. At their core, in my own experience, I have found that Chinese and Russians believe the other is a far greater threat and less trustworthy than the Americans, who are also much farther away.

The blinding speed with which technology accelerates also extends both threats and opportunities around which we need to wrap our thoughts and creative energies. Operational tradecraft in how we meet and clandestinely communicate with agents needs to evolve with these times. Doing so requires a freedom to let go of old customs, leverage the tools that likewise threaten us, and develop new techniques—new thoughts about cover, and a more flexible posture on the diverse mix of talents and backgrounds the workforce needs.

Human characteristics that enable the recruiting of agents have not changed. We still need to treat prospective agents as people, and that means getting our own people up close in order to do the recruiting. With cameras and biometrics being ubiquitous, and given the capacity of artificial intelligence to manipulate such data, not to mention all that is readily available online, HUMINT requires a quantitative leap forward in its modus operandi. These challenges are not insurmountable, but now is not the time for the status quo, to be conventional or conservative. Innovation requires trust, resources, and risks, and the freedom to try new things, not all of which will pay off, at least not immediately.

The CIA has ample opportunities and means to improve. But it starts with looking inward, and holding the CIA's leadership more accountable for successes and failures. For a civilian spy service to be effective, it must operate in the most objective, brutally honest, and apolitical fashion. Its fidelity to these ideals were undermined post-9/11 by problematic internal leadership, and more recently worsened by President Trump's obstructionism and political weaponization of the intelligence community. The repairs for such damage will need to proceed concurrently with the reforms required to restore the Agency's charter, values, and integrity of which this book is largely consumed.

The tradecraft innovations required means challenging our beliefs and existing practices with provocative new approaches not restrained by the egos of the CIA's ruling elite, who since 9/11 only entertained ideas that aligned with their own. It's time for many such senior officers to move on as the CIA concurrently addresses how better to recruit, develop, and nurture talent. The CIA will have to step back and strategically focus itself in order to align resources and capabilities with its mission based on the hierarchy of threats America faces, and not political rhetoric or partisan pandering.

DCIA William Burns and Deputy Director David Cohen inherit an organization once again at the crossroads. The CIA is, however, composed of the best, brightest, and most dedicated American patriots. In his confirmation hearings, DCIA Burns's testimony offered hope that he would focus on a more inclusive and diverse CIA that the agency's workforce, and the country, can trust. But these new CIA leaders will have to earn back such trust with actions, not merely words, and not all of them are likely to please everyone inside the Agency, on the Hill, in the White House, or among the American people.

Mr. Burns and Cohen will need to embrace diversity and inclusion proactively. Smart choices for leadership and command positions at home and abroad will need to expunge the failed, recycled, conformist, and politically risk conscious personalities who hitched their wagons to powerful patrons. Burns and Cohen will need to cut through the resistant bureaucracy, and its smoke and mirrors, in order to identify and advance officers based on merit and integrity rather than politics, cronyism, and systemic racism.

The CIA needs to look beyond its traditional recruitment approaches. As an organization willing to go to any climate or place to access and recruit its targets, it certainly has the wherewithal to go beyond the suburbs and top twenty-five to fifty American universities to find the best and brightest. Case officers, for example, need to know about life, people, managing risk, and thinking on their feet. Such lessons are better acquired coming up the hard way and overcoming adversity in difficult urban or rural circumstances, and not by a Stanford degree or an entitled upbringing.

Perhaps most important of all, I hope too that the Agency's new leaders share the vision of the CIA as the elite spy service it was intended to be, relieved of politically partisan restraints. Agile, innovative, crafty, able to punch well above its own weight, a small band of shadow warriors dedicated first and foremost to the American people, for whom no challenge is insurmountable, and whose integrity is beyond reproach. To likewise heed the 9/11 Commission Report's judgment that the intelligence community's greatest failure then had been "a lack of imagination." And in so doing, champion the words etched in the CIA's main lobby, "And ye shall know the truth and the truth shall make you free."

ACKNOWLEDGMENTS

I dedicated this book to my wife and five children who have supported me through good times and bad over the long course of my career. Their lives were certainly not always their own, impacted by where I was assigned, what I was doing, and the occasional dustups in which I found myself. No one was impacted more than my wife by these choices. She nevertheless allowed me to prioritize my career over her own, taking a back seat at times, and finding herself collateral damage when our family suffered the consequences of my bad choices. She has been a true partner, is the love of my life, and my best friend.

The childhoods to which my children were all subjected were anything but conventional. Giving up much of the traditional experiences most American kids have, while they might have been gifted exposure to diverse cultures, the opportunity to travel to exotic locations, and a closer view of the world's history, they were likewise exposed to war, terrorism, racism, disease, famine, and poverty. At times required to travel internationally on their own or find themselves evacuated from perilous locations, they all at times were forced to shoulder more responsibilities than kids should from the earliest ages. Whether because of or inspired by this, all have become incredibly decent human beings who fill me with pride beyond any other accomplishment I could ever imagine. Compassionate, dedicated to service, and quick to put the needs of others over their own, they are my best legacy.

Through it all, my children were kind enough to make me feel cool after coming to learn what I did and never faulted me for their hardships. My daughter Jenny was probably the biggest cheerleader among them for this book. She was a constant source of encouragement and validation in setting my thoughts and experiences to paper, and believing others would be interested in what I had to share.

I have to thank Sam Nicholson, who was willing to give my initial efforts an early look, and who encouraged me to believe I had a story to tell. And to former CIA spokesperson Bill Harlow, who provided me guidance and encouragement, not to mention all-so-important proposal instructions, in pursuing a literary agent.

And there would be no book without that literary agent, Howard Yoon, who likewise took a chance. Howard gave me tough love early on about what the manuscript required to make it into more than just a story that *some* might read. His feedback and direction was precisely what I needed to take it to the higher level that answered the audience's question, "Why should I care?," so that more than *some* would read. Howard connected me with the publisher that would ultimately be the best fit, Hachette, whose team indeed looked at the work as more than just a book, and rather as an important contribution to a critical conversation about the CIA and US national security.

And to the team at Hachette who made my book so much better. My editor Brant Rumble, who was a source of constant energy and support. He too believed in me and the book from the start. Brant taught me a great deal about this art form. His questions, comments, guidance, and suggestions led me always to the right form of words and organization, without ever feeling my voice was compromised, or my story changed. Brant let me tell this very personal and cathartic tale in my own words, and my own style. He removed obstacles for me and made the publishing process so much easier than I feared it might be.

Of course I expect the price for Brant's generosity was paid by Mike van Mantgem, my magnificent copy editor. Mike no doubt aged considerably as he toiled through my oft employed use of spyspeak in making the manuscript understandable. He challenged me to clarify and flesh out thoughts over episodes and matters that I took for granted but that required better wording or additional detail and context, and all within the parameters that the CIA allowed. Mike's ardent application of the *Chicago Manual of Style* and standards for clarity was worthy of the best CIA collection management officer!

To all of those past and present who have represented the best of the CIA and America. My colleagues who risked their lives and sacrificed normalcy, comfort, and time with family and friends to serve as America's shadow warriors.

And finally, to the foreign agents on whom the CIA depended to keep America safe. For many, living in constant danger without a safety net. And for some who paid the ultimate price for a country in which, during these toxic times, they as foreigners might never have been welcomed. Unlike the case officers in whose hands they trusted their lives, they lacked the ultimate escape hatch to go home. Home was where their danger existed.

INDEX

Note: Names of people within quotation marks are fictitious names to protect identity.